The West and the World

A History of Civilization

The West and the World

A History of Civilization

FROM 1400 TO THE PRESENT

KEVIN REILLY

 **Markus Wiener Publishers**
Princeton

To Pearl

Third printing, 2009.
Updated and enlarged edition, 2002.

Copyright © 1989 and 2002 by Kevin Reilly.

For information write to:
Markus Wiener Publishers
231 Nassau Street, Princeton, NJ 08542
www.markuswiener.com

Cover illustration: Maria Madonna Davidoff

Library of Congress Cataloging-in-Publication Data

Reilly, Kevin.
The West and the world: a history of civilization
from 1400 to the present/Kevin Reilly
Includes bibliographical references and index
ISBN-13: 978-1-55876-153-7 (alk. paper)
ISBN-10: 1-55876-153-5 (alk. paper)
1. Civilization, Western.   2. Civilization—History.
I. Title.
[CB245.R44   1997]
909'.09821—dc21   96-37674   CIP

Markus Wiener Publishers books are printed
in the United States of America on acid-free paper,
and meet the guidelines for permanence and durability
of the committee on production guidelines for
book longevity of the Council on Library Resources.

❄❄ Contents ❄❄

❄❄ PART I
A Unified World: 1500–1800 1

PART III
A Divided World: 1914–1945 267

PART IV
The Nuclear World:
1945–Present 325

✖ Topical Outlines ✖

In Six Units

In Three Units

✄ Preface ✄

I would argue that all approaches to teaching modern world history are based on some contemporary (and often unstated) sense of relevance. Textbooks that attempt an overview of all peoples with the equanimity of the gods reflect a liberal United Nations vision of the world, presenting an even-handed neutrality that reads like a UN resolution. Another increasingly popular model in the last decade, in which world history is presented as the story of encounters and interconnections, fits our age of free trade, marketing entrepreneurs, mass tourism, and global communications. No history is without agendas, recognized or not. Having said that, it would be disingenuous of me to ignore the personal, political, and at times passionate, tone of these essays. Some will consider them controversial or opinionated, others, perhaps, even wrong-headed. In the process, students will learn not only what they think but also how to think about perspectives apart from their own.

I focus on the problems that concern our society—individual identity, racism, political morality, economics, ecology, nationalism, and globalization. An explanation of how these problems evolved and how others have experienced them in the past can aid our attempts to solve them. In turn, thinking historically about each of these problems strengthens our historical muscles and improves our ability to think historically about other problems. Our separate histories of each problem will lead to the most useful and inclusive history of the modern world.

The revised edition contains three new chapters on world history from 1945 to the present and a complete update of bibliographical suggestions. With the indulgence of all my friends in the World History Association, my colleagues and students over the years at Raritan, Rutgers, and Princeton, my own teachers in and outside the classroom, I refer the reader to the acknowledgments section of the earlier editions published by HarperCollins. To my friend and new publisher, Markus Wiener, his book designer, Cheryl Mirkin, his editors, Susan R. Lorand and Regina Tan, artist Maria Madonna Davidoff, who generated the painting for the cover illustration, and Simon Finger, who prepared the index, thank you. Finally, thanks to Aaron M. Wiener, Noah J. Wiener, and Yuriy A. Prilutskiy for their meticulous craftmanship of the charts and illustrations.

I dedicate this book to my wife Pearl who transformed many of my grains of sand from irritants into lucid prose.

New York, July 10, 2002

❧ Note on Chinese Spelling ❧

Two different systems are in use in the world today for the spelling of Chinese words with Roman letters. One is the Wade-Giles system, developed by missionaries and used by almost all Western scholars until fairly recently. The other is the pinyin system, used by the scholars and government of the People's Republic of China. The pinyin system is probably the most accurate, at least once one gets used to pronouncing "Q" as "Ch," and "X" as "Sh." It is also becoming the standard. The problem with using only the pinyin system is that most English library books and references are Wade-Giles transliterations.

The solution adopted here is to use the pinyin system but to add the Wade-Giles equivalent in brackets (e.g., Song [Sung]) the first time the word is used. Thus, in most cases, the first use of a Chinese term will contain the version that is most accurate for pronunciation and future recognition, followed by a bracketed version that is most useful for library research.

There are only a couple of exceptions to this procedure. The Wade-Giles equivalent will not be added when it is the same as the pinyin or when the only difference is an apostrophe or hyphen (e.g., Tang, T'ang or fenshui, feng-shui). Furthermore, in some cases, the first mention of the word will be only in the pinyin or Wade-Giles format. This is in the case of an author's spelling of his or her own name and in the quotation of original sources or translations. Sources that are translated in Wade-Giles are presented in the original format with pinyin equivalents indicated in the citation note. This is to avoid changing the intent of the original author or translator and to allow the quote to read smoothly.

Saltcellar. Nigeria, Bini-Portuguese. Late 15th to mid-16th century. Ivory. H. 7-1/8".
The Metropolitan Museum of Art, Louis V. Bell and Rogers Fund

I

A Unified World

1500–1800

Japanese view of the Portuguese in Asia. Detail from screen attributed to Kano Domi (1593–1600)

Preview of the Period
1500–1800

The world became unified after 1500. Educated people knew the world was round before Columbus established that fact, but the European colonization of the Americas that began with Columbus in 1492 created a single global ecosystem. Soon there were no foods, ideas, or germs that could not be shared.

There had been occasional contacts between the hemispheres after the Bering Sea land bridge was flooded by melting glaciers around ten thousand years ago. But the most systematic settlements, those of the Vikings, were limited and infrequent and may have been curtailed by increased glaciation between 1350 and 1450. Not until the voyages of Christopher Columbus did the Western and Eastern hemispheres become permanently part of the same world. Why Columbus? we might ask. Or, more specifically, why did Europeans unite the hemispheres? The Chinese were capable of a transpacific voyage in the fourteenth century, having sailed as far in the other direction as East Africa, but they saw no reason to.

Christopher Columbus (1451–1506) was an unlikely person to inaugurate this new age. He set out to find a western route to Asia. When he reached the Bahamas on October 12, 1492, he thought he was on an island near Japan. Until his death, he remained convinced that he had found a westerly route to the Spice Islands of the Indies (modern Indonesia). That is why he called the Native Americans "Indians."

The Portuguese after Prince Henry (the Navigator, 1394–1460) were smarter. They rejected Columbus's proposal for a westerly voyage to Asia because they knew he underestimated the distance. They proceeded to show that an easterly voyage was quicker. In 1487 Bartholomeu Dias rounded Africa. In 1497 Vasco da Gama left Lisbon; he arrived in India the following year. He returned with spices

3

worth sixty times the cost of the voyage. In 1513 the Portuguese sailed into the Chinese port of Canton. From Indian,
Chinese, Japanese, and Indonesian ports in between, the
Portuguese successfully challenged the Arabs and Vene-
tians for control of the Spice Islands trade.

The Spanish stumbled upon a different prize. Columbus
was at first dismayed not to find the fabled cities of China
and Japan described by Marco Polo. Nor did he find the
pepper, nutmeg, cinnamon, and other spices that the Spanish crown expected to pay for the voyage. In this new
world he had wandered into an entirely different ecosystem. "I saw neither sheep nor goats," he wrote home. "All
the trees were as different from ours as day from night."

There were also no horses, cattle, or Old World draft
animals for farming. There were no chickens, geese, or pigs
for food. There were no wheatfields or grapevines, and thus
no bread and wine for the Mass. Without bread, wine, and
olive trees, how was a Spaniard or an Italian to live? The
deficit was rapidly balanced. Without natural predators, the
European plants and animals that Columbus brought on his

*Christopher Columbus (1451–1506) arriving in America (From Theodore de Bry,
Collectiones peregrinationum in Indiam, Frankfurt/M 1599–1634)*

second voyage reproduced unchecked. Entire islands of sheep, goats, and cattle were soon reported. Throughout the Americas European animals replaced human beings.

Eventually Europeans discovered that not everything in the world had grown in the European Garden of Eden. In the New World they discovered an abundance of plants and animals that they had never seen. Tomatoes, potatoes, corn, beans, squash, pumpkins, peanuts, avocados, chilies, and pineapples were all new to the European taste. They discovered the mysterious properties of tobacco and rubber. They marveled at jaguars, iguanas, catfish, rattlesnakes, toucans, condors, electric eels, stingrays, piranhas, cougars, hummingbirds, anteaters, sloths, monkeys with tails, vampire bats, llamas, and guinea pigs. And they learned to hunt buffalo and domesticate turkeys and ducks. The New World vegetables were brought back as specimens and became staples of Old World cuisine. Who can imagine Ireland without potatoes, Italy without tomatoes, West Africa without peanuts, or India without chilies?

The Eastern and Western hemispheres eventually became a unified biological and microbiological realm. But initially the cost was enormous. The pre-conquest Native Americans, a population of twelve to eighty million, were almost wiped out by European diseases, like smallpox, against which they had no immunity. (Europeans probably received syphilis in return, but with less devastating results.) Native Americans were replaced not only by horses, sheep, and goats, but also by Africans and Europeans. Far more Africans than Europeans made the Atlantic crossing, but since slaves generally do not reproduce to the same extent as free people, by 1800 there were about ten million Native Americans, ten million Europeans, and four million Africans in the New World.

The Pacific also became part of the single global ecological realm between 1500 and 1800. Europe, North Africa, and Asia had been part of a common zone of communication and trade since the second century. Muslims and steppe nomads had, in different ways, increased the levels of interdependence for the next thousand years. By 1400 Muslim travelers, Indian traders, Christian missionaries, Chinese officials, and the merchants of Venice were aware of their participation in a single global civilization. After 1500 European ships began to appear regularly in the

Indian and Pacific oceans. By 1800 Australia and the islands of the Pacific had become part of the single world organized by Europeans, often with the same devastating consequences for the indigenous inhabitants.

European Rise, Renaissance, and Reformation. The "rise of the West" is one of the most important historical developments of the last five hundred years. How did it occur? Europe did not control the seas until after 1700 or Asian territory beyond some port cities until after 1800, as a result of the industrial revolution.

The success of European expansion on the high seas owed much to specific improvements in naval technology. These included the Portuguese caravels that combined Arab triangular sails for tight control and the square sails that were effective for travel in the open seas of the Atlantic ocean. Ocean sailing also was facilitated by the mariner's compass. But European control of the seas depended as much on the superior European cannon (after 1500), as well as on the willingness to use it. Under princes like Henry, Europe developed a range of aids—sailing schools, merchant adventurer companies, joint stock companies— that were the expression of a much larger economic, social, cultural, and political revolution.

One of the most important reasons for Western economic and political expansion was the rise in Europe between 1400 and 1650 of a vigorous series of independent nation-states with competing economies, religions, and ambitions. The dynamism of the West can be seen in its pluralism. Territorial states were created that were larger than cities, smaller than empires, and independent of churches or ruling orthodoxies, yet each was relatively homogeneous in ethnicity, language, and culture. Western Europe benefited from the absence of a single, universal, theocratic, or imperial unity and from the relatively minor destruction by the Mongol invasions of the thirteenth and fourteenth centuries. New city-states, and then nation-states, could be created by new monarchs with territories and armies suited to the new technology of cannon and gunpowder, in competition with each other for the bullion, resources, and markets of entire continents thrown at Europe's feet.

This was a competition between powerful, often long

reigning monarchs: in Spain, Ferdinand and Isabella (1479–1504), and later the Hapsburg family under Charles I (who was also Holy Roman Emperor as Charles V, 1506–1556) and Philip 11 (1556–1598); in England, Henry VIII (1509–1547) and his daughter, Elizabeth 1 (1558–1603); in France, Francis I (1515–1547) and the Bourbon dynasty, begun by Henry IV (1589-1610), made legendary by Louis XIV (1643–1715), and ruined by Louis XVI (1774–1792).

The political transformation of Europe was driven by a new urban "middle class" of merchants. It was aided by a rebirth (or renaissance) of classical Greek and Roman thought and a religious reexamination of the relationship of God and humanity, church and state, in the Protestant Reformation and Catholic response. The Renaissance (c. 1350–1550) and the Reformation (c. 1500–1650) over-heated the political conflicts between particular principalities, city-states, and monarchs, and intensified the philosophical debates or religious commitments of particular rulers, eventually determining the identities of entire nations. The Renaissance and Reformation were important for providing the cultural pluralism (though few sought it) that prevented the creation of a single empire or orthodoxy (which many wanted). An understanding of the importance of this political and cultural pluralism can be gained by comparing the states of Europe in this period with the more orthodox and stable empires of Eurasia.

Muslim Empires: Ottoman, Safavid, and Mughal. Three Islamic empires dominated the center of South Asia between 1500 and 1800. They were the Ottoman (1453–1918), centered at Istanbul; the Safavid (1501–1722), in Persia (Iran); and the Mughal (1526–1739), in India. All three descended from Turkic and Mongol nomads of the Eurasian steppe. Their initial source of strength was as militarized tribal confederacies, but they each created empires of great wealth and power and in governing suffered from the instability of their origins. Traditions of succession by combat and the readiness of rival chieftains to go to war led rulers to depend on personally loyal forces recruited from captured slaves.

The Ottomans were Turks whose movement into present day Turkey was stimulated by the Mongol pressure of the thirteenth and fourteenth centuries. They became an

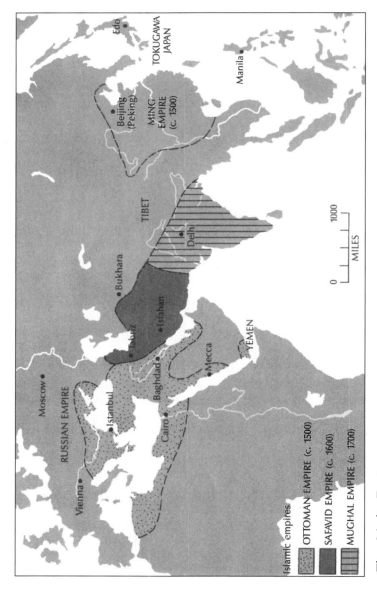

Three Muslim Empires

agricultural people but retained their warrior traditions and fervent Islamic faith. In the 1390s they captured Greece, Bulgaria, and Serbia. Young Christian subjects were taken from these Byzantine lands as slaves, converted to Islam, and trained as an elite corps of army officers, known as Janissaries. With the help of such dedicated soldiers and a huge cannon built by a Hungarian engineer, Sultan Mehmet II (the Conqueror) captured the city of Constan-tinople in 1453, effectively ending the Byzantine Empire. In the next few years the Ottomans conquered the Arab successor states of the Abbasid caliphate: Syria, Iraq, much of Saudi Arabia (including Mecca and Medina), the area around the Black Sea, and North Africa, including Egypt by 1517. They almost united the prior Byzantine and Arab empires, except for Spain and Morocco in the West and Persia in the East. Militarily, they remained a threat to Christian Europe until almost 1700: they threatened Vienna in 1683, but were defeated by the Austrians at Zenta in 1697. Under Suleiman (the Magnificent, r. 1520–1566) the Ottoman navy was strengthened as well. Despite its defeat by the Spanish at Lepanto in 1571, it was able to protect Ottoman shipping in the Eastern Mediterranean.

The Ottoman society was a relatively tolerant one. When the Jews were expelled from Spain in 1492, they were welcomed in Muslim Turkey as valuable additions to a mercantile class that also included Greeks and Arabs. But it was the lack of an Ottoman middle class that left the old-est commercial economy in the world unprepared for the new dynamism of Europe's market economy.

Ottoman society was faced with a threat from Persia as well. In 1499 a fanatical Shi'a sect, led by a young boy named Ismail Safavi, won a series of startling military vic-tories. In 1500 his troops took the city of Tabriz, and Ismail Safavi was declared shah. By 1506 he had conquered the entire Iranian plateau. In 1508 he ruled Baghdad and most of Iraq. In 1510 he extended his power over the Uzbeks of Transoxiana in the east, sending the straw-stuffed body of the Uzbek ruler to the Ottoman court as a warning.

Ismail's remarkable military successes depended on the fervor of a militant sect of Islam, Twelver Shi'ism, especial-ly its sense of persecution by Sunni Muslims (including both the Ottomans and Uzbeks). It also depended on his Turkoman warriors. However, their loss of Iraq and

Western Iran to the Ottomans in 1514 and their domination of domestic affairs under Ismail's successor, Tahmasp
(r. 1524–1576), encouraged the new shah to develop troops
more loyal to him. These were, like the Ottoman Janissaries and Arab mamluks, young Christian prisoners (mainly taken in military campaigns in the Caucasus Mountains), who were called *ghulams*. These "slaves of the royal
household" were converted to Islam and Persianized.

The *ghulams* became the heart of the standing army created by Shah Abbas (the Great, r. 1588–1629). Supplied
with muskets and artillery, previously disdained by Ismail,
and supported by Turkoman troops who were organized by
districts rather than by tribes, this army was able to regain
Iraq from the Ottomans. Shah Abbas was also successful in
ending Portuguese control of the Persian coast and beginning his own trade and diplomatic relations with France
and England.

The most lasting achievement of Shah Abbas was the
capital he built at Isfahan, a city of wide avenues, mosques
of azure blue tiles, more pools than Paradise, and so many
trees (according to a French visitor) it seemed like a forest.
Isfahan was also to serve as a sanctuary for Indian kings
whose ancestors came from Persia.

The Mughal Empire of India was founded by Babur
(r. 1483–1530), a Persianized descendant of Turks and
Mongols, including Timur and Chinggis [Genghis] Khan.
However, it was his grandson, Akbar (r. 1556–1605), who
secured the boundaries of the empire and gave it its distinctive stamp. He did so with an army of 140,000 troops
and a domestic policy that recognized the religious diversity of India. A Muslim who was probably most influenced by
the Sufis, he was a student of all religions, gathering together orthodox Muslim *ulema* (scholars), Sufis, Hindus,
Zoroastrians, Jews, Jain and Buddhist monks, and Christian
Jesuits from the Portuguese port of Goa for an exchange of
views. He also married an Indian Rajput princess and appointed Hindus to important offices. He abolished the special tax (*jizya*) on non-Muslims and outlawed the killing of
cows, sacred to Hindus.

Akbar's son, Jahangir (r. 1605–1627), and his grandson,
Shah Jahan (r. 1628–1657), continued Akbar's policy of
religious toleration, despite their cultivation of a more
Persian culture and more sumptuous court at Agra and then

The Taj Mahal, Agra, India, built (1630–1648) by Shah Jahan as a mausoleum for himself and his favorite wife, Mumtaz Mahal.

Delhi in 1648. The India of Shah Jahan was a scene of incredible beauty and luxury, and of considerable human suffering. The Taj Mahal, a tomb for the shah's favorite wife who died giving birth to their fifteenth child, is still one of the most beautiful buildings in the world. The shah's palace at Delhi had marble walls inlaid with precious stones, and ceilings of gold. The famous Peacock Throne of gold, studded with diamonds, emeralds, and rubies, cost ten million rupees. The cost of much of this was born by heavy taxation of the peasantry. Then, when hundreds of thousands were starving in a famine, the shah provided only five thousand rupees a week to feed the people.

Shah Jahan was imprisoned by his second son, Aurangzeb (r. 1658–1707). Aurangzeb reduced taxation, but he also ended three generations of religious tolerance. Hindu temples were closed, non-Muslims were taxed heavily, government employees had to convert to Islam. As a result, Hindu resistance mounted. A new Hindu state was created in the south. In the northwest, the Sikhs, who had developed a new religion that combined elements of Hinduism (rituals and reincarnation, but not caste) and Islam (monotheism and a militant brotherhood), also established an independent state. With internal conflict on the rise, eighteenth-century India was no match for the increasing pressure of the British.

The Chinese Empire: Ming and Qing. The Ming dynasty (1368–1644), founded by the leader of a popular rebellion against the Mongols, and the Qing [Ch'ing] dynasty (1644–1911), established by foreign invaders from Manchuria (the Manchus), were actually quite similar. This is because the institution of the emperor, the bureaucracy, and Confucian culture were accepted by rebels and nobility, farmers and merchants, Chinese and "barbarians." A certain rhythm was expected. Dynasty founders were expected to vigorously chase out the remnants of the old dynasty and extend the frontiers of the empire, and so they did. No emperor was expected to tamper with a system that had worked for over a thousand years.

China did change between 1500 and 1800, even if not according to dynastic rhythms. Thanks to intensive agriculture and the introduction of new crops from America like corn, sweet potatoes, and peanuts, population tripled despite the lack of increase between 1600 and 1700. The cultivation of uplands and North China (where population had declined from thirty-two million to eleven million during the Mongol invasions) was vastly expanded. Agricultural cash crops like silk and cotton were such successful exports that sections of the Yangtze Valley in southern China imported food in order to grow them.

Between 1500 and 1800 China experienced what some historians have called a second commercial revolution (the first having occurred between 1100 and 1300). While neither of these commercial revolutions led to an industrial revolution, they did create a highly urban, specialized, and prosperous Chinese economy.

After 1500, more than ever before, political power was concentrated in the person of the emperor. Fortunately, the Qing dynasty had some very effective rulers. Kangxi [K'ang Hsi] (r. 1662–1722) and his grandson Qianlong [Ch'ien Lung] (r. 1736–1799) dominated the period of greatest prosperity. Kangxi came to the throne at the age of seven, and at the age of fifteen personally commanded an army that suppressed a rebellion of dependent states in the south,

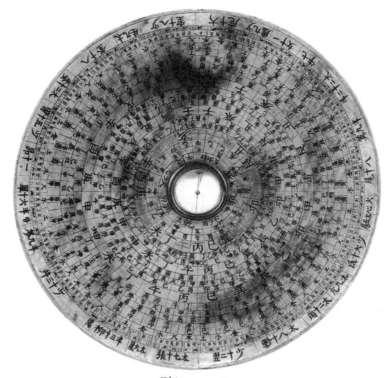

Chinese compass

adding control of Taiwan in 1683. He was vigorous, curi-
ous, and able. He fathered fifty children by thirty consorts,
read voraciously, and studied Western science with Jesuit
court astronomers. He traveled throughout the country,
opened four ports to foreign trade, and improved the river
dikes and canals. Always a Manchu, he loved to hunt in his
summer palace beyond the Great Wall. He also was attentive to the rise of Russia under his contemporary, Czar Peter
the Great (r. 1682–1725), and negotiated a treaty with the
czar that allowed Russian caravans to visit Peking but
excluded Russians from Manchuria.

Qianlong was very much like his grandfather: energetic,
hardworking, wise, and proud. He too was an avid reader of
the classics. Like his grandfather, Qianlong undertook the
collection and copying of all Chinese books (at least those

*Chinese Emperor Kangxi, 19th-century portrait. (Anony-
mous. Portrait of the Emperor K'ang Hsi [r. 1662–1722]. The
Metropolitan Museum of Art, Rogers Fund, 1942.)*

that were not anti-Manchu). The resulting *Complete Library of the Four Treasures* put fifteen thousand copyists to
work for fifteen years. His confidence and sense of superiority (in declining trade with England, he said, conde-
scendingly, "there is nothing we need") wore thin toward
the end of his reign. Corruption at court and a weakening
economy prompted peasant revolts, one of which—the
White Lotus Rebellion of 1798—was difficult to crush.

Palace intrigue and a heavily burdened peasantry became commonplace in the nineteenth century, making the pressure of the Europeans more damaging.

Japan: The Warring States and Tokugawa. The period beginning with the Warring States (1467–1600) and ending with the Tokugawa (1600–1868) was institutionally quite different from the period of the Ming and Qing dynasties in China. The Warring States and Tokugawa periods also were quite different from each other. The first was an age of constant warfare between the armies of feudal lords, very much like the feudal age in Europe. The second was an age of pacification, prosperity, and state building, also like the seventeenth century in Europe (but with far less bloodshed).

The Warring States period began with hundreds of states, each supplying armies of thousands. Castles dotted the countryside. By the middle of the period there were dozens of large regional states with armies of tens of thousands. By the end of the sixteenth century, only a few states, with armies of hundreds of thousands, fought for control of Japan. These masses of soldiers, with spears that could pierce medieval armor and (after about 1550) Portuguese muskets, no longer fought out of loyalty and in exchange for land. They were vassals, and they were called by the dignified name samurai, but they were paid in rice instead of fiefs.

Victory came to Toyotomi Hideyoshi (1536–1598) in 1590, but after his death war broke out again. Finally in 1600 Tokugawa Ieyasu (1542–1616) defeated the last feudal armies and made Japanese unification permanent. The Tokugawa period is, of course, named after him.

The Tokugawa age saw, among other things, a remarkable reversal of the years of internal war. The attempt to establish peace started with Hideyoshi. In 1588 he ordered a "sword hunt" to gather all weapons that might be used in a rebellion or renewal of civil war. In one county, for which records remain, over thirty-four hundred swords and daggers were retrieved from as many households. Hideyoshi was interested in eliminating peasant weapons, not those of the samurai, who numbered about 150,000 in two invasions of Korea. But when the invasions failed and Ming China weakened, Japan turned inward.

In 1597 Hideyoshi banned Christianity, whose adherents had grown in number from about 130,000 in 1579 to about 300,000 (constituting a higher percentage of the Japanese population than Christians do today). The reasons for Christianity's success lay with the Jesuit missionaries sent by the Portuguese and the similarities between Christianity and Pure Land Buddhism, which the Japanese favored. They recognized the Christian God in the Buddha of Shingon, the Christian heaven in the paradise of Amida, and the Virgin Mary in the female bodhisattva of mercy, Kannon. Those who chanted the holy name Amida understood the meaning of the evangelist Paul in his letter to the Romans (10:13) that "whosoever shall call upon the name of the Lord shall be saved."

The efforts of Hideyoshi and Tokugawa to silence any competing sources of authority led to a general turn inward. During the 1630s the policy of eliminating Christianity was combined with a more general policy of isolating foreigners. Foreign trade was limited to the Dutch and Chinese at the port of Nagasaki, and no Japanese were allowed to travel abroad. (The travel policy was reversed in 1854, the year after the first visit by Admiral Matthew Perry of the U.S. Navy).

The Tokugawa also gained strength by undermining the nobility. Just as Louis XIV of France undercut the independence of the French nobility by constructing his palace at Versailles and inviting them to live there, Tokugawa built an enormous palace at Edo (Tokyo) and demanded that the families of the nobility live there. This "hostage system" also required the nobles themselves to live there one year out of every two.

The process of state building requires more than capturing the foreigners and nobles, however. The Tokugawa age also established a prosperous national economy and the rule of law. The Tokugawa economy benefited from the establishment of peace. The introduction of new crops, seeds, fertilizers, and techniques, which had been shelved during the period of the Warring States, doubled agricultural production and, in consequence, doubled the population between 1600 and 1700. Prosperity also depended on political stability. "Law is the basis of the social order," an edict entitled Military Households declared in 1615: "Reason may be violated in the name of the law, but law may not be violated in the name of reason." A popular story called "The Forty-seven Ronin" also taught that law could not be violated in the name of traditional virtues, such as loyalty. The story was based on an actual event in 1701, when 47 *ronin* (samurai who lost their master) avenged their master's death by killing the man they held responsible. The law demanded their execution. The storytellers and generations of listeners and readers admired the loyalty of the *ronin* to their master, but were forced to agree that the law must be supreme.

Even more than China, Tokugawa Japan was transformed by neo-Confucianism. The movement gave a practical, scientific, and humanistic cast to Tokugawa culture that earlier Pure Land Buddhism lacked. Tokugawa was a secular culture. The woodcuts of Utamaro (1753–1806) and the Kabuki theater plays of Chikamatsu (1653–1724) display as much attention to natural detail as to poignant feelings.

Like China, Japan weakened on the eve of the most insistent Western penetration. But while China was weakened by a rapidly increasing population that could not be adequately fed and employed, Japan suffered from population decline. Famines and plagues in the eighteenth century, which struck especially hard in the new cities, kept Japanese population constant from about 1720 to 1850. If Admiral Perry's ship had come in 1700 instead of 1853, the Japanese would have been far less eager to learn the ways of the West. But with the preparation of economic decline, political stagnation, and practical neo-Confucianism, they were ready to learn. In fifty years, when China was the doormat of Europe, Japan defeated the youngest European nation, the Russian Empire.

The Russian Empire. In 1240 the Mongols conquered Viking Russia and depopulated the cities, especially Kiev, the center of politics. Opposition to the Mongols developed north and west of Kiev in the city of Moscow. In 1380 Grand Duke Dmitri of Moscow defeated the Mongols, but was unable to drive them out permanently. It was left to Ivan III (the Great, r. 1462–1505) to free a large part of European Russia (the Ural Mountains in the east to the borders of Poland in the west) from Mongol overlordship by 1480.

Ivan IV (the Terrible, r. 1533–1584) continued the transformation of the principality of Moscow into a state. This transformation depended on the maintenance of a large army and a working arrangement with the two most important social groups, the boyars (or landed aristocracy) and the Orthodox clergy. The boyars were given control over the peasants, who became increasingly tied to the land after 1500, and an opportunity to expand their holdings as the territory of Russia expanded. This arrangement ensured the loyalty of the boyars to the czar (Caesar). As a result, Russia retained peasant serfdom (until 1861) and an oppressive aristocracy joined to an absolute monarch (until 1917), far longer than any other European country.

The arrangement between the czar and the Orthodox church was more complicated. The czars wanted political control of the church, and they usually got it. In return, the church kept its land. The czars sometimes used their political power to reform the church and found themselves dangerously in conflict with the so-called Old Believers (Orthodox Fundamentalists). But the Orthodox faith offered much. It enshrined the czar, united the people, and stimulated the faithful to a holy mission as the "third Rome" in the steps of the Byzantine Empire.

Ivan the Terrible turned in his last years from an accomplished administrator and dedicated reformer to a cruel, perhaps paranoid, despot. Broken by the death of his first wife in 1560, he suspected everyone of disloyalty, had many boyars killed, and even executed his own son. Without a clear heir to the throne, Russia underwent a period of civil war known as the Time of Troubles (1584–1613). From this emerged the founder of the Romanov dynasty, a seventeen year-old boy named Mikhail Romanov (r. 1613–1654). The Romanovs would govern Russia until the Revolution of 1917. Elected and controlled by the boyars, Mikhail and his immediate successors, Alexis I (r. 1654–1676) and Theodore III (r. 1676–1682), entrusted much of the government to them. One result was increased peasant unrest, notably in the revolt led by Stenka Razin in 1670–1671.

A renewed attempt to control the boyars and the church came from Alexis' son, Peter (the Great, r. 1682–1725). Peter created a centralized European-style state with a modern army and a new capital overlooking Europe named Saint Petersburg. Like his father, Peter was fascinated by

Western culture. In 1697 the barely disguised six-foot-eight-inch emperor traveled throughout Europe, meeting the rich and famous along with the poor and unknown. Particularly interested in mechanics and engineering, he even spent some time working as a ship's carpenter in Holland. He returned to Russia with a mission. In short order, Peter westernized the army, developed the economy, supplanted the boyars with an enhanced state bureaucracy, and established state control of the church. As a symbol of his policies, he personally cut the long Mongol-style sleeves of boyar clothing. He issued an edict requiring the nobility also to shave their beards. There was considerable opposition to Peter's efforts at westernization, secularization, and development. Cossacks (free peasants) and Old Believers were particularly hostile to the changes, and, like the English Puritans and pioneers in America, they sought freedom by establishing new communities in remote areas. Some were beyond the Urals in Siberia, to the northern Baltic; others were in the southern Caucasus. The arm of the state was long, but its grip was weak. When Peter's representatives arrived in a Volga town in 1700 to shave, uniform, and mobilize Cossacks for the war with Sweden, the Cossacks swarmed into the city at night and massacred the officials. Heads without beards were cut off and mutilated. Those who survived went into hiding until their beards grew back.

Peter's reforms were muted rather than defeated. His state-run ironworks in the Ural Mountains produced more iron for Russia in the middle of the nineteenth century than did any other country in Europe. While Russia never developed an independent merchant class, the state played an important role in continued development. Russia remained a European state, while at the same time expanding into southern and eastern Asia. The central power of the state remained strong, despite periodic rebellions by peasants and religious fundamentalists.

For most of the seventy years after Peter's death in 1725, Russia was ruled by women. The popular saying was that "grain does not grow because the feminine sex is ruling." Peasant rebellions (well over fifty between 1762 and 1769 alone) promised a return of "the true czar," though never the end of czardom. The largest of these revolts was led by Emelyan Pugachev between 1773 and 1775. It was brutally suppressed by one of the truest czars of the eighteenth century, Catherine (the Great, r. 1762–1796).

Catherine, a German princess schooled in the European Enlightenment, professed interest in parliamentary reforms but ruled without debate. She was forced to favor the nobility above the bureaucracy, but she pursued an aggressive foreign policy. She annexed the Crimea (taken from the Ottoman Empire and offering a warm-water port in the Black Sea) and much of Poland, which was divided with Austria and Prussia. In 1796 Catherine ruled over the largest land empire in the world: it stretched from the Baltic and Black Seas in the west to the Bering Sea, including Alaska, in the east.

African States and Stateless Societies. Africa was not one but many states, some quite large and powerful, and others limited to a single city. Some African peoples also lived in stateless societies, governed by clan and village elders.

The Ottoman Empire controlled North Africa from Egypt to Algiers. Morocco, in Northwest Africa, was ruled by an independent Islamic Sharifian dynasty from 1553 to 1912. Islamic influence extended across all of North Africa just beyond the southern boundary of the Sahara Desert and along the east coast as far south as Great Zimbabwe.

Some of the largest African states were situated in the Western Sudan, in the band just south of the Central Sahara. The largest of these was the Songhai Empire, centered on the city of Timbuktu. Conquered by Mansa Musa of Mali in 1325, Songhai regained independence in 1375 and flourished under Sonni Ali (r. 1464–1492) and Muhammad al-Turi (r. 1493–1528). Many Muslim scholars came to the cities of Gao, Timbuktu, and Jenne. In 1591 Songhai was overrun by the Sa'did dynasty of Morocco, which had sought control of the gold trade. Sudanic power passed further east to the Hausa states around Kano, and Kanem and Borno around Lake Chad. A Muslim state of Kanem-Bornu had existed in the eleventh century. It was revived by Idris Alawama (r. 1575–1610) with the aid of Turkish military instructors and firearms. Its role in Central Sahara trade was taken over by the Hausa states further west, especially in the nineteenth century, when they formed the Hausa-Fulani sultanate of Sokoto. Further east in the sixteenth century was the Funj sultanate on the Nile and the Christian Abyssinian state in Ethiopia.

Denser populations, but smaller states, existed side by side, south of the Western Sudan in the savanna and tropical coastline (especially the area of modern Nigeria). The largest of these were the Yoruba Oyo states of the seventeenth century and the Ashanti states of the eighteenth century. Much smaller was the Yoruba state of Benin (c. 1100–1897), which was known for its beautiful bronze statues. The cities of Benin and the independent city-states of the nearby Ibo also were commercially active.

There were states in eastern and southern Africa as well. The largest were the Lunda (sixteenth and seventeenth centuries) and Luba (fifteenth to eighteenth centuries) of modern Angola and Zambia. On the east coast there were many independent city-states—Mombasa, Pemba, Kilwa, Zanzibar, and Malindi, among others—that traded with Muslims, Indians, and later the Portuguese. There are also impressive stone ruins of a Great Zimbabwe Empire inland (in modern Zimbabwe).

The lives of many Africans between 1500 and 1800 had little to do with great states (or with Europeans, for that matter). Most Africans lived among their people without recourse to kings, officials, or foreigners. Farmers enjoyed greater control over their land and produce than did most peasants of Europe and Asia. The elaborate interrelationships of family and clan provided support in time of need. Traditional religion unified art and life, individuality and community, myth and meaning.

✖ 1 ✖
Self
and
Society

Individuality
and Modernity

It is often said that individuality is a characteristic of modern society, a trait that distinguishes us from our ancestors. We will examine some of the evidence for this idea. Individuality is also sometimes said to be a European or Western trait, given free reign in Europe and North America but suppressed in other cultures of the world. We will evaluate this idea as well. Finally, it is sometimes argued that a particularly Western individualism produced modernity. We will explore what this means and weigh some of the evidence.

What does it mean to be an individual? Is individuality something we learn? Are people today more individualistic than people used to be? Are we becoming more individualized or more alike? These are some of the questions we will explore in this chapter. Whatever you decide about some of these questions, you should think of individuality more historically so as to better understand yourself.

MEDIEVAL SOCIAL SALVATION AND
MODERN SPECIALIZATION

In the sixth century, the Christian theologian Boethius defined "individual" as "something which cannot be divided at all." When we say that someone is a real individual, we mean that he or she is different, unusual, or separate from the rest of us. In the Middle Ages, "individual" meant "inseparable"—almost the exact opposite of what it means today. An individual in the Middle Ages was someone who was representative or typical of, or inseparable from, his or her group. The individual was the person who was the best example of the class, family, trade, nation, or general group that was being described.

The society of the Middle Ages was organized into stable, unchanging classes—called "castes" or "estates" because a person was virtually unable to work his or her way out of one class and into another. Consequently, a man might think of himself first as a member of a particular estate or occupation. He was not primarily John Jones. His main identity was as a priest or bishop in the church's estate, or as a duke or baron in the nobility's estate, or as a farmer or baker in the "third estate." Personal names were used to indicate membership in a large group. The members of a noble family would be known by their titles: the prince, the count, or the baron of such and such. A family of metalworkers would come to be known as Smith or Goldsmith. Barrel makers were called coopers. A particular barrel maker might be known as Gary the Cooper.

Since identities in the Middle Ages derived from the groups in which individuals were born and died, their hopes and ambitions focused on the group, not on themselves. They wanted things for their village, church, friends, and relatives, not for themselves. People felt a great number of responsibilities to others, responsibilities we have forgotten, and they enjoyed a greater sense of belonging and security than we do.

In Europe, the modern individual emerged as this secure, stable, estate society of the Middle Ages disintegrated. There were many causes of the breakdown of ordered, estate society. One of the most important causes was the rise of a middle-class population of merchants and traders who found estate society too confining for their individual talents and ambitions. These early capitalists gradually made money and wealth as important as birth and family, and they turned the largely public land of the Middle Ages into modern private property.

Finally, in the 1700s and 1800s, these new middle-class capitalists began an industrial revolution that continues today to make people's jobs and life-styles more and more specialized or individualized. While people in the Middle Ages belonged to only three estates and worked in only ten or twenty occupations, modern industrial society has created hundreds of thousands of different ways of working, living, relaxing, and thinking. The variety of lives in industrial society has given us a variety of experiences. Each person today has unique experiences that separate him or her from neighbors and allow the development of individuality.

Modern individuality is, then, at least partly the result of the fantastic degree of specialization in industrial society. But some aspects of that specialization were more influential than others in developing our privacy and individuality. Two kinds of specialization—so crucial that they are often taken for granted—are the room and the printed book.

THE ROOM AND THE BOOK:
ORIGINS OF MODERN INDIVIDUALITY

There were no specialized rooms (except for kings) before the last couple of hundred years. In Europe around 1700, both the large town houses of the wealthy and the cabins of the poor contained no special bedrooms, dining rooms, offices, or living rooms. The very rich (as well as the poor) used collapsible beds in each room for sleeping and collapsible tables for eating. Lawyers, bankers, and judges entertained their friends, ate, conducted business, and slept in the same rooms (and often at the same time). Visitors, children, and servants frequently slept together in the same rooms, often in the same beds. The toilets of those who could afford indoor plumbing were also located in one of these all-purpose rooms. (The unusually modest would sit behind a special hand-held mask.) Each room led directly into another. Hallways and closed doors were extremely rare in 1700.

Privacy was clearly impossible in this kind of society. Without special rooms and private rooms, no one could ever be alone for very long. The houses of the rich and well-born were crowded with servants, priests, employees, clerks, shopkeepers, doctors, debtors, widows, children, and friends. Swarms of visitors were forever coming and going, staying the night or a few months. Hired teachers constantly complained that they could not teach the master's children because the traffic was too heavy, the rooms were too crowded, and there were too many distractions. Because of these conditions, some of the wealthy even took the chance of sending their sons away to college, even though everyone knew that colleges were places of vice, moral decay, riots, and violence.

Even a king had little privacy. In 1682, King Louis XIV of France brought his entire court to live with him in his new palace at Versailles in order to keep an eye on them. In return, they were given the privilege of watching his every move. Each day some twenty or thirty of these nobles would receive the special honor of assisting the king at his toilet or participating in the daily ritual of the king's waking and retiring. When the queen gave birth to a child, everyone crowded around to watch and partake in the royal event. Even our most private event, the wedding night, was a public occasion three hundred years ago. The friends and relatives of the bride and groom would barge in on the couple after they had gone to bed, and they all would drink, dance, and joke most of the night.

Since there was no privacy, there could be very little private identity. All of life was public partly because there was very little private space. Before the 1700s almost everyone lacked the room and rooms to develop private lives and private identities. The "inventions" of the bedroom and the bathroom and the office in the 1700s were significant events in the development of the individual.

However, empty rooms do not alone make individuals; nor do rooms that are full of what everyone else's room contains. Instead, individuality depends on private experience, especially private learning experience. This was made possible after 1500 by the printed book, a source of knowledge and experience that could be (in fact, had to be) read and digested in private.

Before the printing press came to Europe, around 1450, all written knowledge in Europe (literature, philosophy, science) was handwritten. Since copying was such an arduous task, there were very few copies of anything available. As a result, people read very little, or if they acquired something interesting, it was read aloud to others. Most people knew essentially the same things. They read the same limited material, and they read it as a group. Few people had any specialized knowledge.

The invention of printing eventually put books into the hands of almost everyone, and it vastly increased the number of titles that could be "copied." Reading aloud became a waste of time when people (at least among the upper and middle classes) could read for themselves. Private reading was faster than public reading, but it also led to personal interpretations, which were not continually checked with the interpretations of a group. As a result, people's ideas no longer developed along exactly the same lines or at the same pace. Books also permitted people to become specialists in certain subjects. Since a single person could no longer know everything that was written, different people learned different things. People became more specialized in their knowledge and more individualistic in their experiences.

THE ITALIAN RENAISSANCE

We can date the origins of the modern Western idea of individuality from the Italian Renaissance. The Italian city-states between 1400 and 1600 made individual achievement almost a religion. The great historian of the Italian Renaissance Jacob Burckhardt has written:

> An acute and practiced eye might be able to trace, step by step, the increase in the number of complete men during the fifteenth century. . . . When this impulse to the highest individual development was combined with a powerful and varied nature that had mastered all the elements of the culture of the age, then there arose the "universal man"—*l'Uomo universale*.[1]

As an example of this universal man, Burckhardt mentions the life of Leon Battista Alberti (1404–1472). Alberti was a great artist and architect, but he is equally well-known for his literary works, which included important studies of art theory, four volumes on domestic life in Florence called *On the Family*, novels, plays, and other pieces in Latin and Italian. He studied everything from law, mathematics, physics, and music to the skills of the shoemaker. He became an adept horseman and gymnast, saying that in three things he desired to appear faultless to others: walking, riding, and speaking.

Then there was Leonardo. Leonardo da Vinci (1452–1519) described himself to the duke of Milan in 1482 as a military architect, hydraulic engineer, and demolition expert, as well as a painter, sculptor, and architect. While he is best remembered for his paintings (two of which, *The Last Supper* and the *Mona Lisa*, are prob-

Michelangelo's David (1501–1504): a biblical theme transformed into a celebration of man.

ably the most famous in art history), his notebooks are full of drawings of flying machines, tanks, submarines, exploding shells, and rapid-firing artillery that were not invented for another four hundred years.

In Renaissance Italy even a Leonardo could have a rival. Michelangelo Buonarroti (1475–1564), who dismissed Leonardo as an incompetent craftsworker, was less of a scientist but a better sculptor and architect. His sculpture *David*, his dome for Saint Peter's Cathedral, and his paintings on the ceiling of the Sistine Chapel at Saint Peter's are among the world's greatest treasures.

Artists like Leonardo and Michelangelo contributed to modern ideas of individuality not only in the universality of their interests and talents but also in the new social position they gained for the artist. Medieval artists were considered to be craftsmen. They were members of guilds, often working in groups of masters and apprentices. It became common practice after 1400 for a single artist to sign a painting, but the patron who commissioned the painting usually paid for the paints and chose the subject. (A contract signed by the painter Ghirlandaio in 1485 even specified the price of the colors he could use.)

Increasingly after 1500 the artist became more independent. In a contract dated 1498 Michelangelo bought the paints. In the enormous commission from Pope Julius II to paint the 10,000 square feet of the Sistine Chapel ceiling (1508–1512), Michelangelo insisted on doing most of the work himself, giving his assistants only incidental work, despite the crippling toll on his back. A contract in 1531 between

Michelangelo and a collector left it to the artist to determine not only the subject matter but also whether the work would be a painting or a piece of sculpture. The number of patrons in Renaissance cities and the relative ease with which painters could move from one court or city to another increased the artist's independence from the guilds.

From these beginnings the Renaissance fashioned the modern ideas of genius and celebrity. In the cult of genius, the personality of the artist replaced the work of art. Drawings and incomplete works were saved and studied for what they revealed of the artist, the artist's style, and the artistic process. Biographies of artists became the vogue. The personality of the artist was studied for fatal flaws that were supposed to accompany genius. Giorgio Vasari (1511–1574), himself an accomplished artist and something of a universal man, published his *Lives of the Most Eminent Painters, Sculptors and Architects from Cimabue until Our Own Time* in Florence in 1550, inaugurating the study of artists and art history. In it Vasari praised the genius of Leonardo in terms that might only be compared to religious devotion:

> The greatest gifts are often seen, in the course of nature, rained by celestial influences on human creatures; and sometimes, in supernatural fashion, beauty, grace, and talent are united beyond measure in one single person, in a manner that to whatever such a one turns his attention, his every action is so divine, that, surpassing all other men, it makes itself clearly known as a thing bestowed by God (as it is), and not acquired by human art. That was seen by all mankind in Leonardo da Vinci, in whom, besides a beauty of body never sufficiently extolled, there was an infinite grace in all his actions; and so great was his genius, and such its growth, that to whatever difficulties he turned his mind, he solved them with ease.[2]

Vasari here creates not only an idea of the perfect person, but also the derogatory idea of the perfectionist:

> It is clear that Leonardo, through his comprehension of art, began many things and never finished one of them, since it seemed to him that the hand was not able to attain to the perfection of art in carrying out the things which he imagined; for the reason that he conceived in idea difficulties so subtle and so marvelous, that they could never be expressed by the hands, be they ever so excellent.[3]

Vasari described his favored Michelangelo in similar terms: "The judgment of the man was so great that he was never content with anything that he did."[4] This became a commonplace of the European idea of genius after Vasari. Perfect artists could not tolerate imperfections. Therefore, the greater the genius the greater the failure to complete or satisfy. The modern idea that genius is neurotic begins here.

Much the same can be said of the origins of the modern idea of fame and celebrity. It was the Italian humanist Francesco Petrarch (1304–1374) who said that he would rather have fame after death than during his life. But he also said he was pleased that he was known through his writings by the emperor of Byzantium as well as by Emperor Charles I. Even during his lifetime he was taken by the citizens of his native city, Arezzo, to the house where he was born and told that the city had declared that no changes could be made in it. This was an honor, Burckhardt remarks, that was previously reserved for saints. Now the birthplaces and graves of poets were similarly revered.

HUMANISM AND INDIVIDUALISM

Petrarch has often been called the father of humanism. His lifelong celebration of the life of ancient Rome suggests some of the contours of humanism. Humanists championed the study of human achievement in both Christian and pagan cultures. Their study of the ancients led them to Plato, where they found an optimistic view of human potential that they attempted to meld with Christianity. This new Christian vision of humanity was perhaps best expressed by Pico della Mirandola (1463–1494) in his *Oration on the Dignity of Man*. Pico imagined God as the Great Architect of the universe, who, after completing his creation of all higher and lower forms, turned to his greatest creation—man. The other creations all had their appointed places, and God said the following to Adam:

> You, who are confined by no limits, shall determine yourself your own nature, in accordance with your own free will, in whose hand I have placed you. I have set you at the center of the world, so that from there you may more easily survey whatever is in the world. I have made you neither heavenly nor earthly, neither mortal nor immortal, so that, more freely and more honorably the molder and maker of yourself, you may fashion yourself in whatever form you shall prefer.[5]

To celebrate humankind's capacities, Pico shows, is not necessarily to deny the powers of God. But the vision of a God who wanted humans to mold their own humanity, to shape their own destinies, to make and remake themselves could be explosive. The Catholic humanist Lorenzo Valla (1406–1457), for instance, used the rudimentary skills of humanistic historical scholarship to show that the Donation of Constantine, purportedly a fourth-century document that gave the emperor Constantine's lands to the Roman church, clearly was a later forgery, since it inadvertently used words that were not current until much later. His expose of the church's claim, as well as his defense of predestination over free will, gave solace to later Protestants. Indeed, the humanists' reliance on human reason and analysis often led to conclusions that undermined the established consensus of church and clergy. It is not surprising then that many humanists were among the first supporters of Martin Luther.

THE PROTESTANT REFORMATION

Did the Protestant Reformation contribute to an increased sense of individuality in European thought? In many ways it did. Protestants insisted that the Bible was a more direct source of God's will than the laws of the church and that every individual could understand God's word by reading the Bible. Martin Luther (1483–1546) spent many years of his life translating the Bible into German so that every German could read it. Luther's argument that a Christian was justified by faith alone, rather than by "good works," such as sacraments, seemed to make individuals the final arbiters of their own salvation. To Luther, the activities of popes, bishops, and church councils seemed more like administration than religion. The church had become so compromised and materialistic, it could no longer satisfy either the cravings of the heart or the demands of the intellect.

For Luther, the matter came to a head in 1517 over the issue of indulgences. The selling of indulgences by the church seemed to him the worst kind of compromise with worldly needs. In order to finance the rebuilding of Saint Peter's in Rome, the pope had authorized the selling of "letters of indulgence," which were said to release the souls of loved ones from purgatory. The selling of these indulgences in Germany caused Luther to post ninety-five theses on the church door at Wittenburg in order to engage the papal forces in debate. "Any truly repentant Christian has a right to full remission of penalty and guilt, even without indulgence letters," Luther wrote. The pope could not release from purgatory someone who was not repentant. Repentance was an internal matter, a matter between the individual and God.

> They preach only human doctrines who say that as soon as the money clinks into the money chest, the soul flies out of purgatory. It is certain that when money clinks in the money chest, greed and avarice can be increased; but when the church intercedes, the result is in the hands of God alone.[6]

While indulgences might seem a particularly obvious interference of the church in matters best left to God, they were but the tip of the iceberg for Luther. If the pope could not release souls from purgatory when the soul was not truly repentant, could a priest forgive the sins of one who confessed without remorse?

> When our Lord and Master Jesus Christ said, "Repent", he willed the entire life of believers to be one of repentance. This word cannot be understood as referring to the sacrament of penance, that is, confession and satisfaction, as administered by the clergy.[7]

Martin Luther (1483–1546) commends the simplicity of the reformed sacrament (left) while consigning the Roman rite to hell.

Indeed, just as the sacrament of penance is an unwarranted intrusion, so also are the other sacraments, Luther reasoned. Except for baptism, the sacraments seemed to be administrative inventions of the governing church.

Baptism became an extremely important issue for another group of early Protestants, the Anabaptists. Baptism signified conversion to a new life, a life in Christ, a life of Grace, a life as a Christian. The Catholic church had baptized all children as a matter of course. This was a convenient administrative decision: it implied that everyone would be Christian and governed by the church. It was also an assertion of community membership rather than individual choice.

The Anabaptists, and many Protestants after them, thought that baptism ought to signify individual conversion rather than group membership. Therefore, they insisted that only adults be baptized. In that way, it would be an individual choice, a result of a personal decision or experience, not an automatic event.

Anabaptists, who referred to themselves more simply as the Brethren, preached complete religious freedom based on a literal reading of the Bible. They chose to live together in independent communities, electing their own priests and separating themselves as much as possible from the state and society.

For Luther and established Protestant leaders, the Anabaptists were extremists, but in many ways they just took the individualism of the Protestant Reformation to its logical conclusion. When the former Catholic town of Munster in Germany became an Anabaptist stronghold, Catholic and Protestant armies joined forces to suppress them. Nevertheless, they survived in independent sects in Europe and in the Mennonites and Hutterites of North America.

The Protestant Reformation meant individual responsibility to the Swiss citizens of Geneva who voted in 1536 to adopt the new creed. Their deliverance from the Roman church, however, provided an ambiguous freedom. John Calvin (1509–1564) taught a harsh doctrine of predestination and converted to Protestantism in 1534, and the city of Geneva accepted his constitution and administration as God's law. Those who missed church services received a light fine. Those guilty of fornication were heavily fined and sentenced to sixty days of bread and water. Before long, the body of offenses in Geneva included insulting remarks about Calvin as well.

The root of Calvin's theology was a belief in predestination—that is, a belief that God had predetermined some souls to be saved and others to be damned, and there was nothing the church, priests, or even prayers could do about it. On the surface, such a belief might seem to cripple individual initiative. In fact, it often did the opposite. Like many of the other ideas of Protestantism, the idea that everything was predetermined eliminated the power of all institutions between the individual and God. The Protestant individual was alone, naked before God, without intermediaries or second chances. Perhaps the terror of that condition was enough to convince many Protestants that they were indeed members of God's chosen, the "elect."

The Protestants of Geneva and elsewhere often displayed an unusual personal confidence, a sense of certainty and righteousness that might suggest to the modern psychologist a way of conquering the naked terror of impotence before an almighty God. Max Weber observed in his classic *The Protestant Ethic and the Spirit of Capitalism* (1904) that there seemed to be a connection between the sobriety, discipline, and certainty of these early Protestants and the businesslike accumulation of wealth in early capitalism. Their self-denial would explain one part of their business success; their self-confidence, another.

EUROPE AND CHINA

Perhaps we now can ask the series of questions first posed by Max Weber. How unique was European individualism? Was there a comparable development elsewhere in the world? Was there, for instance, a Chinese equivalent of the Protestant ethic or the Protestant sense of individualism?

But before we try to answer these questions, one additional point must be made. These questions are European, or Western, questions.

There is a measure of cultural arrogance in asking if Chinese culture has the particular trait—individualism—that we have found important in Western history. The question inevitably evaluates Chinese culture on Western terms.

Let us try to imagine the equivalent Chinese question of the West. Filial piety, or devotion to one's parents, is an important Chinese value. How might we feel if Chinese historians attempted to figure out if Europeans or Americans ever developed filial piety? Implicitly, we would know, the question would be why the West did not develop filial piety. Europeans or Americans would probably want to say, "Admittedly, filial piety has never been an important value in Western culture. But there have been other values. Why don't you ask about them?"

We are going to try to avoid the twin pitfalls of cultural arrogance and mindless relativism. As products of Western culture, we are going to ask about the problems and concerns of Western culture. We are going to ask about individualism, not filial piety. But we must be careful not to ask why other people have not done what we have done, and we must be careful not to assume that our traits were better than those of another culture or that another culture never developed them, or rejected them.

With that in mind, let us jump in with the most Eurocentric of Weber's questions. Was there a Chinese equivalent of Protestant individualism? The best answer, which may be surprising, is probably yes.

We must recognize that the context of Chinese thought was very different from that of European thought. China was a single centralized empire the size of all of Europe. There was less intellectual or cultural variety than in the world of European states and city-states. In China, there was a single orthodox school, Confucianism, and a single official class of intellectuals, the scholar-officials, who ran the civil service. The elaborate system of civil service examinations tested applicants on their knowledge of Confucianism to determine if, and at what level, they would serve in the imperial bureaucracy. Thus, the structure in which Chinese intellectuals operated was very different from that of Europe. A European equivalent of China would be one in which all intellectual and political jobs were under the Roman Catholic church.

It is often said that the intellectual innovation of European culture was nourished by the tensions between Athens and Jerusalem—that is, between its classical and Judeo-Christian roots. European thought grew in debates between science and faith, reason and revelation. Christianity grew stronger as it was forced to answer the claims of Greek philosophy. In the confrontation of the two traditions, European thought became more secularized, subtle, and varied.

The situation in China was actually similar. While there was a Confucian orthodoxy, there was also an opposing tradition that the Confucians had to confront: Buddhism, imported from India at about the same time as Rome imported Christianity. By the sixteenth century, Chinese Buddhism was on the defensive, but it still provided a significant learning opportunity for Confucians who were dissatisfied for various reasons. These new Confucian, or neo-Confucian, thinkers were dissatisfied with the power of the emperor, with what they perceived as the abandonment of true Confucian values by a monolithic state, and with the self-perpetuation of that state through civil service exams that rewarded memorization and conformity rather than thoughtfulness and humanity. In short, the neo-Confucians looked at the emperor and the imperial bureaucracy with the same moral impatience displayed by Luther, the early Protestants, and many Catholic reformers toward the Papacy in the same period. And just as the Christian reformers used some of the critical skills of the humanists and attempted a return to "original" Christianity, the neo-Confucians borrowed some of the moral zeal and mystical revelation of the Buddhists.

NEO-CONFUCIANISM AND THE INDIVIDUAL

Buddhism and Confucianism held very different attitudes toward the individual. We might call the attitude of Buddhism a "personal" or "private" individualism, and that of Confucianism a "social" or "public" kind of individualism.[8] Buddhist individualism was the personal withdrawal of the hermit or recluse. While this withdrawal freed the Buddhist from society, it had no effect on other individuals. In that sense it might be characterized as negative. Confucian individualism was more positive in the sense that it attempted to establish some positive role for the individual in society. It was public and social as it sought a place for the self in relation to others. "The humane man," Confucius said, "if he seeks to establish himself, will help to establish others."

The problem is that this Confucian concern for the individual in a reciprocal, supportive social structure withered under the despotism of the Ming dynasty (1368–1644). By the time of the sixteenth century official Confucianism seemed to many to be an excuse for obedience and conformity. Those Confucians who felt the emperor and bureaucracy had betrayed the meaning of Confucianism and stifled individuality turned, ironically, to the Buddhists. These were called neo-Confucians, after a previous attempt in the Song dynasty to integrate Buddhism and Confucianism. They were also called the Wang Yangming school after the most renowned neo-Confucian of the sixteenth century and perhaps the most influential Chinese thinker in the early modern period, Wang Yangming (1472–1529).

WANG YANGMING

It would be too neat to call Wang Yangming the Martin Luther of China. But in his desire to reform, the impact of his following, and his effect on the individual, he was very similar to the father of the Protestant Reformation. Confucians were not generally religious, but Wang Yangming sought out the spiritual sense of self that was taught by the Buddhists, especially the more mystical Zen Buddhists, in meditation. Isolated as an official in a remote province, where there was no one he could talk to, Wang practiced meditation ("quiet sitting" in Chinese).

Then late one night as he was pondering what a sage would do in such circumstances, he suddenly had a "great enlightenment." In it was revealed to him the real meaning of "the investigation of things and the extension of knowledge," which earlier had eluded him as he tried to apprehend the principle of things through contemplation of the bamboo in his father's garden. Transported by his discovery, he called out exultantly and his feet danced for joy. His companions, awakened from sleep, were amazed at his behavior. Thus he first learned, it is said, "that the way to sagehood lies within one's own nature."[9]

"Ming thought," according to the modern scholar William Theodore de Bary, "originates in an experience of the self." We might say the same about Protestantism. Even the results of a Buddhist type of "enlightenment" can be very similar to those of a Protestant conversion. Another leading Ming thinker, Chen Xian Zhang [Ch'en Hsien-chang], experienced an enlightenment that gave him a sense of unlimited power in dealing with the world and an unshakable confidence. We are not too far here from what Weber described as the Protestant experience of the elect.

The vocabulary differed. While Luther spoke of immortal souls, Wang said all people had their own "innate knowledge." While Luther insisted on a "priesthood of all believers," Wang popularized the idea that "sagehood" exists not in the sage but in oneself. Their purposes differed as well. Given the importance of the civil service, schools, and exams in China and the church in Europe, it should not be surprising that while Luther was a reformer of religion, Wang preached reform of education.

"Study must be for one's own sake," Wang said. "Memorization and recitation" hindered education, as did the "chasing after success and profit."[10] His *Instructions for Practical Living* was full of dialogues with his students that showed how they learned for themselves. In one, a student complimented Wang, saying one could not go any further. Wang replied that the student should try for a half-year and then for a year. The student's education was too important to stop with the teacher's authority. No authority, not even that of Confucius, should be accepted in place of one's "innate knowledge." Through discussion, activity, and self-criticism, he said, we develop ourselves.

Wang Yangming had enormous influence in Ming China. His emphasis on personal, interior knowledge might have hindered the development of physical science in China. In his own work, Wang sometimes denied the reality of a world outside the mind, as did Bishop Berkeley (1685–1763) in England. It was a position that questioned the possibility of objective scientific study. But Wang Yangming stimulated many neo-Confucians to explore the meaning of the self. Among his followers, the most radical was the "left," or radical Tai-zhou [T'ai-chou] school founded by his student, Wang Gen (1483–1540).

WANG GEN AND THE TAI-ZHOU MOVEMENT

If Wang Yangming was a kind of Luther of China, Wang Gen and the Tai-zhou movement were the Anabaptists, or radical dissenters. Like the German peasants who revolted in 1525 in the name of Luther's idea of Christian freedom, the Tai-zhou school was the beginning of a mass movement based on neo-Confucian individualism.

Wang Gen was not a scholar-official. He was a self-educated salt dealer. By the time he met Wang Yangming, at the age of thirty-eight, he had experienced his own enlightenment in which he felt united with all things, the source of the universe itself. Without credentials or formal education, he put on the robes of the scholar, built a cart like that used by Confucius, and traveled to the courts of princes, teaching that sagehood resided in the common man. It was a strange combination of personal power and humility that Wang Gen taught, again reminiscent of the polar tensions in the Protestant ethic. One should always look for the cause of one's problems in oneself, he said with humility. The aim of all study, however, was that "Heaven and earth and all things should be dependent on the self, rather than the self dependent on Heaven and earth and all things."[11] Anything else was "the way of the concubine," he added.

The mass appeal of the Tai-zhou school was not entirely different from the mass appeal of Protestantism. Wang Gen's town of Tai-zhou was in an area that, like Germany and England, was experiencing rapid economic change in the sixteenth century. It was the center of the salt trade for the dynamic and prosperous Lower Yangtze Valley. It was a world, Gui Youguang [Kuei Yu-kuang] (1506–1571) observed, where "the status distinctions among scholars, peasants, and merchants [had] become blurred.[12] The following of the Tai-zhou school cut across class lines. It included scholar-officials, some of whom held the *jin-shi* [*chin-shih*], the highest civil service degree. It also brought together uneducated commoners. "One of these uneducated commoners," according to de Bary,

> the potter Han Chen, after his "conversion" and a period of study with Wang Ken's brother, took up the mission of spreading the new gospel among ordinary folk, and developed a large following among peasants, artisans, and merchants. After the fall harvest he would gather the people together for lectures and discussion. When he had finished in one town he moved on to another. A regular feature of these gatherings was group singing: "With some chanting and others responding, their voices resounded like waves over the countryside." The atmosphere of a religious revival prevailed, and Han Chen personally exemplified a kind of religious dedication to the cause. When at these meetings the talk turned toward partisan politics and personalities, he would ask, "With life so short, how can you spend time gossiping?" And when the discussion became too pedantically involved with the niceties of classical scholarship, he would ask if those so engaged thought they were on a scholarly lecture platform.[13]

PROTESTANT AND CONFUCIAN INDIVIDUALISM

The mixing of classes into new communities, the mixture of serious discussion and old-time festival, these were elements of the meetings of Protestants as well. From the German peasants' revolt and the Anabaptists' occupation of the German town of Munster in 1534–1535, to the parliamentary debates of Cromwell's New Model Army in the 1640s and the American "Great Awakening" and revivals of the seventeenth and eighteenth centuries, Protestantism created new personal identities in new communities through lecture, discussion, gossip, and song.

But, of course, there was no Protestant Reformation in China. The Confucian Reformation, if we can call neo-Confucianism that, took many different forms, as we might expect in a country the size of China. Wang Yangming and Wang Gen taught only two of many forms of neo-Confucianism. And in opposition to reform stood bureaucratic neo-Confucian gentlemen content with their position and jealous of their privileges. There were eunuchs who guarded the royal harem and protected the emperor from any disturbing news of the world beyond the palace. There were Buddhist monks and Daoist sages and people who found the greatest security in unquestioned obedience to authority or the ways of the past. In the Ming dynasty these other groups were more numerous and more powerful, and that is one of the reasons that the Ming dynasty crumbled in the seventeenth century, even before the Manchu invasion replaced the last Ming emperor in 1644.

To understand why the initial stirrings of an individualistic revolution did not take hold in China we must look at political and economic developments. Protestantism was successful in Europe because of a system of independent states that gave the new creed protection to develop. Individualism was nurtured not only by Protestantism but also by the development of a capitalist industrial economy. These political and economic developments are the subjects of later chapters.

FOR FURTHER READING

There are two very good studies of the individual in medieval Europe. Colin Morris documents *The Discovery of the Individual, 1050–1200* in European culture during that period. Walter Ullmann examines the legal and political emergence of the individual over a broader period in *The Individual and Society in the Middle Ages*.

On the role of printing and book publishing on individuality, the most suggestive starting point is the work of Marshall McLuhan, especially *The Gutenberg Galaxy*. Lucien Febvre's *The Book* is a rich history of early European book production, though it does not focus on the broader issue of individuality.

The classic statement on individuality in the Italian Renaissance is in Jacob Burckhardt's *The Civilization of the Renaissance in Italy*. A challenging theoretical study is provided in *Individual and the Cosmos in Renaissance Philosophy* by Ernst Cassirer. Among general histories of the Renaissance, *Power and Imagination: City-States in Renaissance Italy* by Lauro Martines is particularly good. On humanism see

Herschel Baker's *The Image Of Man: A Study of the Idea of Human Dignity in Classical Antiquity, the Middle Ages, and the Renaissance* and Eugenio Garin's *Italian Humanism: Philosophy and Civil Life in the Renaissance*. For northern European humanism see Thomas More's *Utopia*, the introduction to Erasmus edited by John C. Olin called *Christian Humanism and the Reformation*, and *The Praise of Folly* by Erasmus.

For a good introduction to the Protestant Reformation, see Roland H. Bainton's *The Reformation of the Sixteenth Century* or Owen Chadwick's *The Reformation*. On Weber's thesis see *The Protestant Ethic and the Spirit of Capitalism* by Max Weber or *Protestantism and Capitalism: The Weber Thesis and Its Critics*, edited by R. W. Green.

There are a number of other approaches to the texture of individuality in Europe in the sixteenth century that we have not followed here. One might, for instance, learn about the meaning of individuality for peasants as well as intellectuals by viewing the film *The Return of Martin Guerre* and reading Natalie Zemon Davis's book of the same title, or by reading Carlo Ginzburg's *The Cheese and the Worms*.

The comparison with China was begun by Max Weber. See his *Religion of China*. William Theodore de Bary's essay "Individualism and Humanitarianism in Late Ming Thought" in his collection *Self and Society in Ming Thought* has been enormously valuable in reformulating the issue. The other essays in that volume and de Bary's *The Unfolding of Neo-Confucianism* also are very useful. More recent is De Bary's *Learning for One's Self: Essays on the Individual in Neo-Confucian Thought*. These studies span the period from the twelfth through the seventeenth century and include discussions of the Neo-Confucians in this chapter.

For China, too, there are other approaches to understand the meaning of individuality. Jonathan D. Spence has provided two fascinating windows on seventeenth-century Chinese individuality, for instance. *Emperor of China* reveals the interior world of the Emperor Kangxi. His *The Death of Woman Wang* graphically depicts the limitations on individual growth, especially among women and the poor in seventeenth-century China. For the social background, see Ping-ti Ho's *The Ladder of Success in Imperial China: Aspects of Social Mobility, 1368–1911*.

For India, Mattison Mines' *Public Faces, Private Voices: Governments and Individuality in South India* is an anthropological study of the meaning of individuality in the modern Tamil culture of urban Madras in south India. On Japan, Eiko Ikegami explores the historical meaning of individuality in Japanese "honor culture" in *The Taming of the Samurai: Honorific Individualism and the Making of Modern Japan*.

NOTES

1. Jacob Burckhardt, *The Civilization of the Renaissance in Italy* (New York: New American Library, 1960), pp. 124–125.
2. Giorgio Vasari, *Lives of the Most Eminent Painters, Sculptors and Architects*, vol. 4, p. 89, trans. Gaston C. DeVere (London: Medici Society, 1959).

3. *Ibid.*, p. 92.

4. *Ibid.*, vol. 9, p. 83.

5. Giovanni Pico della Mirandola, "Oration on the Dignity of Man," adapted from translation of Mary Martin McLaughlin in *The Portable Renaissance Reader* (New York: Viking Press, 1953), p. 478.

6. Helmut T. Lehmann and Jaroslav Pelikan, eds., *Luther's Works*, vol. 31 (Philadelphia: Fortress Press, 1957), pp. 25, 28.

7. *Ibid.*

8. This distinction and much of the following argument follows William Theodore de Bary, "Individualism and Humanitarianism in Late Ming Thought," in his *Self and Society in Ming Thought* (New York: Columbia University Press, 1970), pp. 145f.

9. de Bary, introduction to *Self and Society in Ming Thought*, p. 13.

10. de Bary, "Individualism and Humanitarianism," *op. cit.*, p. 152.

11. *Ibid.*, pp. 166–167.

12. *Ibid.*, p. 173. Quoting Ping-ti Ho, *The Ladder of Success in Imperial China: Aspects of Social Mobility, 1368–1911* (New York: Da Capo Press, Inc. 1962), p. 73.

13. *Ibid.*, p. 174. The pinyin equivalent for Han Chen is Han Zhen, and Wang Ken is Wang Gen.

❧ 2 ❧

Race
and
Racism

Color
and Slavery

What is the state of racial relations in the United States today?

A recent national poll by the *New York Times* (1999) reveals some interesting cross-currents. Most Americans, black and white, think racial relations have improved in the last ten years.

But "even as the rawest forms of bigotry have receded they have often been replaced by remoteness and distrust in places of work, learning, and worship."[1] An example: 85 percent of whites said that they did not care if they lived in a neighborhood which was predominantly white or black, but two-thirds of the whites said that they thought that most whites prefer to live in white areas. More tellingly, 85 percent of whites said they actually live in an area with few black neighbors, the same percentage that claimed no preference.

From the perspective of the last fifty years, the era of integration, civil rights, equal opportunity, and affirmative action has had a marked impact. "When I first started practicing law [in 1949]," Jack Greenberg, retiring Director of the NAACP Legal Defense and Educational Fund reminisced, "if I saw a black at an airport there was no question I knew who he was. It seemed there were only 25 blacks in the country who ever flew on commercial airplanes."[2] Today, African-Americans preside over major U.S. corporations, serve in government up to the level of Secretary of State, are among the most popular and well compensated celebrities and entertainers, and the role models of young athletes, artists, educators, and entrepreneurs, black and white.

Yet inequalities persist. In recent years, African-American median household income was $25,351, 60% of the median white income of $42,439. An even greater gap divided the net wealth of black and white families in the United States. The median black household had a net worth of just $7,400 compared to $61,000 in median wealth for whites. If the value of one's home is excluded from the equation, median black financial wealth fell to $200, compared to $18,000 for whites.[3] In 1999, though blacks were only 13 percent of the U.S. population, they were half of all prison inmates. In 2000, one out of three young black men was either locked up, on probation, or on parole. African-American life expectancy is 70.2 years, compared to an average of 76.5 years for all population groups. The difference in life expectancy is even more striking among African-American men, who have a life expectancy of only 66.1 years, compared to the national average of 73.6 years for all men.

A professor in Philadelphia has studied "black English vernacular," the words and sentences of blacks in segregated Philadelphia neighborhoods. He found that, despite the uniform sound of television actors and announcers, black English had been diverging from "standard English." At the same time, he found, the patterns of speech of white Philadelphians were also diverging from standard English, so that it became increasingly difficult for whites and blacks to talk to one another. A situation spawned by neighborhood segregation is making inter-racial communication increasingly difficult.

"The more we study and analyze," the researcher, Dr. William Labov, said, the more it appears that blacks and whites are "developing their own grammar." The result is not only the splitting of America into two societies, but also the creation of enormous obstacles when black students learn to read.[4]

Is the United States being split more and more into two societies, one black, one white? Are neighborhoods and schools becoming more segregated? Do blacks and whites communicate less? Are they increasingly speaking different languages?

Any understanding of the future of whites and blacks in America must begin with an understanding of the past. This chapter will explore what is possibly the most important period of that past—from the formative stage of first contact through the period of slavery.

WHAT IS RACE?

Race is actually a much more difficult term then you might at first think. We use the word "race" to mean someone's physical appearance. Unlike religion, class, or economic status, race is supposed to refer to what a person looks like physically, without their clothes. But what physical differences does "race" refer to? Clearly race has nothing to do with the physical differences between men and women, or between fat and skinny people.

Race is supposed to have something to do with skin color (pigmentation). It does, and it doesn't. European colonialists a hundred years ago had a difficult time figuring out if the dark skinned Africans were the same "race" as the dark skinned people of southern India or the aboriginal people of Australia because they had decided there was a "black race" and a "white race." They were only looking at skin color. Since then scientists have become much more sophisticated about physically classifying the various peoples of the world. They recognize that people have different genes, blood types, hair, and facial features as well as different pigmentations.

But scientists no longer use the word "race." In general, they don't find it useful. They speak of "breeding populations" or different groups of people who have continued to interbreed for long periods of time. The problem, they realized, is that on the outskirts of every "breeding population," people are interbreeding with other "breeding populations." Further, populations move, individually and in groups, large and small. The old idea that there are "pure races" and then "mixed races" doesn't hold. The old idea of "race" has been replaced with a much more dynamic notion of many, many breeding populations that are continually shifting, changing, and mutating. Call them "races" if you like, but it won't help you any.

WHAT IS RACIAL PREJUDICE?

If "race" has no clear meaning, how can we speak of "racial prejudice?" Well, obviously, there are many people in the world who think race does have clear meaning. Some, by no means all, of those people are prejudiced against people whom they see to be members of "x" race. The fact that there is no clearly defined "x" race does not affect their prejudice. The problem is that we do not always understand who they mean by the "x"s.

This is even more complex because people often confuse membership in a breeding population with membership in a religion, nationality or ethnic group, with speakers of a particular language, or with people who display characteristics that might have much more to do with "culture" or learning than with their "nature," biology, or genes. Indeed, it is that confusion that makes people prejudiced. No one is prejudiced against people with type "O" blood. That's too abstract, too irrelevant. It is human behavior that concerns people. Racial prejudice is prejudice against the "x"s who are presumed to behave in some distasteful way.

WHAT IS RACISM?

The word "racism" is a short form for racial prejudice or racial discrimination, often both. Usually attitudes and actions go together. Racism involves a series of assumptions that most scientists would agree are inaccurate. These assumptions might be

briefly summarized as the following: (1) there are different races, clearly distin-
guishable from one another; (2) people of different races think or behave differently; (3) some races (almost always "theirs") are "inferior" to others in the way
they think or behave; (4) those inferiors can't change: it's in the blood, genes,
"race." What makes racism insidious is this assumption that one's behavior is
innate: nothing can be done about it. This confusion of nature and culture con-
demns all of the members of the presumed race forever. If it's in the genes, nothing
can be done. Education, legislation, persuasion: all are useless.

IS RACISM UNIVERSAL OR RECENT?

Have all people been "racist" in one way or another? Have all people assumed that
their way of doing things was naturally, inevitably superior to that of other people?
Anthropologists who have studied the enormous variety of human experience do
not agree on the answer to this question. One anthropologist, Claude Levi-Strauss,
argues that all people have believed themselves superior. In fact, he says, it was
common for preliterate peoples to imagine themselves as the only real human
beings, calling themselves "the men" and others "the ghosts."

The myths of tribal and traditional societies have sometimes denied a common
human origin. Eskimos, for instance, tell a story about the Great Being creating a
colorless people called "white men" before getting the ingredients right for the perfect *in-nu*, the ancestors of the Eskimos. A similar North American legend recounts
how the Great Spirit had to create man three times. The first time the creation was
not baked long enough and came out white. The second time the oven was too hot,
and man came out burnt black. Finally, the Great Spirit created the perfect golden
human being. Myths like this, according to Levi-Strauss, suggest that racism is virtually universal.

A different view is offered by another anthropologist, Michel Leiris:

> The first point which emerges from any examination of the data of
> ethnography and history is that race prejudice is not universal and is of
> recent origin. Many of the societies investigated by anthropologists do
> indeed display group pride, but while the group regards itself as privi-
> leged compared with other groups, it makes no "racist" claims and, for
> instance, is not above entering into temporary alliances with other
> groups or providing itself with women from them.[5]

Any generalization about primitive, tribal, or traditional societies is difficult, if
not impossible.[6] What we can do briefly is look at some of the ancient societies we
know for evidence of racism. If we turn to the ancient Mediterranean world, where
there was a considerable amount of contact with lighter-skinned people in the
North and darker people to the South, racism is difficult to find.[7]

Black people, especially, were viewed favorably by the ancient Egyptians,

Hebrews, Greeks, and Romans. The Africans from Nubia and Ethiopia were frequently praised for their beauty, fighting ability, and civilization. Moses married a Kushite woman (from Nubia), and "the anger of the Lord was roused" against those who objected.[8] For the Nubian was to live with the Egyptian, Babylonian, Philistine, and Tyrian, and Zion was to "be called a mother in whom men of every race are born."[9]

The ancient Egyptians also both praised and condemned the people of Kush. But even those Kushites who were their enemies were not racially stereotyped by the Egyptians. Some Kushites fought in Egyptian legions, married Egyptian women, and helped shape a racially diverse society.

From the time that the Greek poet Homer spoke of the "blameless Ethiopians" the attitude of the Greco-Roman world toward Africans and Asians was tolerant and respectful. The ancient Greeks called some of their neighbors "barbarians," but this meant only that they could not speak Greek. Greeks accepted foreigners who seemed to be cultured, which is to say, foreigners who learned Greek language and customs. When the Greek troops under Alexander the Great conquered Persia and India, ten thousand Greek soldiers married Hindu Indian women, and Alexander himself married two Persian princesses. Since Alexander and his soldiers imagined that they brought the benefits of Greek culture and civilization, they knew that their sons and daughters would be raised like other Greeks. They had no fear of producing offspring less than human or of corrupting a Greek "race" or "blood." They were concerned about culture, not biology, and they did not assume that culture had anything to do with biology.

In relation to blacks, a recent study concludes as follows:

> It is important to emphasize that the overall, but especially more detailed Greco-Roman, view of blacks was highly positive. Initial, favorable impressions were not altered, in spite of later accounts of wild tribes in the far south and even after encounters with blacks had become more frequent. There was clear-cut respect among Mediterranean peoples for Ethiopians, and their way of life. And, above all, the ancients did not stereotype all blacks as primitives defective in religion and culture.[10]

THE COLOR OF SLAVES

In the Roman Empire, Roman slaves came from captured peoples of Africa, Asia, and Europe. Since slaves could not be identified as a single physical type, the Romans did not develop racist ideas about slavery. But in periods when the Romans enslaved a particular ethnic group in large numbers, they did tend to stereotype that group as slaves. Thus, after the Romans conquered and enslaved many of the light-skinned Scythians from Thrace—north of Greece—they thought of Thracians as slaves. Then a Roman actor would wear a red wig to play a slave because Thracians had red hair. Similarly, the Thracian name Rufus came to be regarded as a typical slave's name. Thracians were even depicted as lazy, called "boy," and considered inferior.

Ethnic stereotypes changed as the Romans drew their slaves from different ethnic groups. With the Roman conquest of Gaul (France) and Britain in the first century B.C.E., the Roman stereotype of slaves more closely resembled the light-skinned, blond Gauls and Britains.

After the collapse of Roman power, one of the main sources of slaves for the Byzantine Empire and the emerging European states was the Caucasus Mountains, an area the size of California between the Black Sea and the Caspian Sea south of modern Russia.

Caucasia was a prime source of slaves throughout the Middle Ages because it remained politically fragmented and highly populated. It also was an easy area in which to play one ethnic group against another and was easily accessible from the Black Sea; thus the Caucasians, who ironically came to define "whiteness" after 1800, were the stereotypic slaves of the Middle Ages. "Chastity is unknown and theft is rampant among them," wrote one eleventh-century observer. "Coarse is their nature and coarse is their speech. . . . He only works under the threat of the cane or the stress of fear. When you find him lazy—it is simply because he delights in laziness and not because he does not feel equal to work. You must then take to the cane, chastise him and make him do what you want."[11]

In the later Middle Ages, European slaves were taken increasingly from areas north and west of the Caucasus. The Slavic peoples of the Balkans and Southern Russia were pressed into slavery by Italian traders, while the Slavs of Central Europe fell victims to the German expansion eastward. Ever since, the word "Slav" has been synonymous with "slave" in European languages.

Where then did the identification of slavery with black Africans arise? It probably originated in the Muslim world of the Middle East and North Africa. The Koran is free of color prejudice, even of Arab ethnocentrism, seeing the racial differences of mankind as a divine miracle. But despite the Muslim idea of brotherhood and the writings of the Prophet, the logic of Islamic expansion meant that slaves had increasingly to be drawn from the periphery of the Muslim world. Islamic law held that no freeborn Muslim could be sold into slavery. Nor could a Jew or Christian who remained under the protection of the Muslim peace, the Dar al-Islam. Thus, slaves had to be taken from captives outside the expanding borders of the Muslim world. In the early history of Islamic expansion that area included Europe, and Muslims first made no distinction between European and African slaves. However, as European armies became better able to defend their territories, the supply of European slaves diminished. Increasingly after the tenth century, Muslim slaves were drawn from the more politically fragmented areas of tropical Africa.

The strong centralized states of Sudanic Africa were usually converted to Islam, rather than conquered militarily, but that conversion put the Muslims within the reach of the stateless, more vulnerable black peoples further south.

As the proportion of black slaves increased in the Islamic world, slavery became increasingly identified with blackness. As early as the ninth century, the traditional Arabic word for slaves—*abid*—was being limited to black slaves. White slaves were called mamluks. Soon *abid* was used to refer to blacks whether slave or free. While there were examples of important blacks in Muslim society (a ruler of Egypt in the tenth century, for instance), blacks increasingly found themselves at the bottom of the social pyramid and the butt of racist generalizations. By the fourteenth century even the great historian of Islam, Ibn Khaldun, could write that "the only people who accept slavery are the Negroes, owing to their low degree of humanity and their proximity to the animal stage."[12]

And like the Thracians, the Caucasians, the Slavs, and so many before them, blacks were described in Muslim accounts of the thirteenth and fourteenth centuries as lazy, lecherous, dishonest, thieving, lying, careless, stupid, and "the most stinking of mankind in the armpits and sweat."[13]

Fourteenth-century Europeans still knew slaves as "Slavs," but a series of developments—especially sugar production and ocean navigation—introduced them to African slaveholding and the racist justifications that had already been developed.

SUGAR, SAILS, AND SLAVES

Sugar cultivation originated on the Bengal coast of India. It reached Egypt by the tenth century, and the Europeans discovered it in Syria during the First Crusade. Both Christian and Muslim planters spread the cultivation and refining of sugar throughout the Mediterranean from 1300 to 1500, and in about 1520 the Portuguese began production in Brazil.

Two factors made sugar a key stimulant to slavery. It was an extremely labor intensive crop, requiring vast numbers of unskilled laborers. And it became enormously popular. "What used to be a medicine is nowadays eaten as a food," one observer remarked in 1572. Virtually unknown beyond the pharmacy shelves in 1400, the new "food" became the main product of the slave plantations of the New World. By 1800 Parisians were consuming ten pounds per person per year.[14]

The European sailing vessel was as important as the sugar plantation in the rise of African slavery. Indeed, without sailing ships that were able to negotiate the rough seas of the Atlantic, there would have been no New World slave plantations. The Portuguese, under Prince Henry (the Navigator, 1394–1460), were in the ideal position to combine the heavy construction and square sails of Northern European sailing ships with the maneuverability of the smaller lateen—triangular sail—craft, which had become common in calmer Mediterranean waters since the Arabs had brought them from the Sea of Oman. By using triangular sails, Portuguese caravels could sail against the wind along the coast of Africa, while square sails allowed them to make use of favorable winds. Portugal was especially well placed to secure its own supply of African slaves. The Mediterranean trade was increasingly controlled by the Italian city of Genoa in the early fifteenth century. Genoa was an aggressively commercial and egalitarian city that excluded nobles from public office but sold thousands of Christian slaves to the Muslims of Egypt and Syria along with anything else that would turn a profit. As the Ottoman Empire secured control of the sources of Christian slaves in the Black Sea area and the Balkans (and finally Constantinople in 1453), Europeans were forced to turn to African slaves for their households and Mediterranean sugar plantations. In the early 1400s, most of the slaves on the island of Crete were Greek. By the end of the century, most were African.

Portugal was able to benefit from the closing of the Eastern Mediterranean source of Christian slaves and to gain its own foothold along the Atlantic. Encouraged by a papal order to conquer and enslave the infidels, pagans, and unbelievers, King Dom João I (r. 1385–1433) and his son Prince Henry forced the Muslims out of Portugal a century before the Spanish forced the Muslims from Spain. In 1415 Henry conquered the city of Ceuta in Morocco, on the North Africa coast. In 1420 the Portuguese occupied Madeira for wheat, and then sugar, cultivation. The Azores were integrated into the Portuguese Atlantic trading area in 1430.

Henry's goal in Africa was to convert the Muslims and obtain the gold of the Sudan. But it was a short step from conquering Muslims in Morocco to taking captives on the Mauritanian coast. In 1441 one of the prince's household knights led a landing party on a nighttime assault on coastal villages south of the Sahara and brought the captives to the prince. Henry "reflected with great pleasure upon the salvation of those souls that before were lost."[15] But his response to the enslavement of Africans may not have been typical.

On an August morning in 1444 the first cargo of West African slaves arrived at the Portuguese port of Lagos aboard a caravel. The Portuguese historian Zurara was there.

> What heart could be so hard not to be pierced with pity to see that company? For some kept their heads low and their faces bathed in tears, others stood groaning in sadness; others buried their faces in the palms of their hands and threw themselves on the ground. Though we could not understand the words of their language, the sound of it measured their grief. Then to increase their sufferings came the captors to divide their captives into fifths; to part fathers from sons, husbands from wives, brothers from brothers. . . . And what a difficult task! As soon as sons were parted from fathers they rushed over to join them; the mothers clasped their children in their arms, threw themselves on the ground, caring little for the beatings they received, if only they might not be torn from their children.[16]

Zurara evidently was not the only onlooker to be repelled by the sight. He suggests that the townspeople of Lagos and other spectators were so overcome that they intervened to prevent the distribution of slaves. As a consequence, some were freed. Women were adopted by Portuguese families. Men were taught trades and skills. Some men as well as women married Portuguese after accepting Christianity.[17]

Not all Europeans were as "color-blind" as these Portuguese on the dock at Lagos in 1444. Indeed, not all Portuguese were. In Christian Europe as a whole, and possibly in northern Europe more particularly, a traditional religious symbolism of whiteness and blackness had become more significant in the centuries before the Portuguese overseas expansion.

THE PROBLEM OF WHITENESS

Christians thought of sin as the blackening of a white soul. They thought of God, virtue, purity, and redemption in terms of radiating light or whiteness. Angels and the holy were bathed in white light. Even the Middle Eastern Jesus was gradually whitened until he became a fair-skinned, blond, blue-eyed European in the paintings of the Middle Ages. In striking contrast, the devil was dressed in black; he was the "Prince of Darkness."

According to the *Oxford English Dictionary*, by the end of the fifteenth century the meaning of "black" had clearly negative implications:

> Deeply stained with dirt; soiled, dirty. . . . Having dark or deadly purposes, malignant; pertaining to or involving death, deadly; baneful, disastrous, sinister. . . . Foul, iniquitous, atrocious, horrible, wicked. . . . Indicating disgrace, censure, liability to punishment.[18]

Whiteness may have become more of a problem for northern Europeans than it was for southern Europeans. Not only were the northerners more fearful of the powers of darkness they believed to be taking over the world, they also were physically whiter and blonder. Whiteness became a mark of beauty for those whose skins were particularly pale. Queen Elizabeth, the Protestant daughter of Henry VIII, was celebrated by the English for the lily-whiteness of her skin:

> Her cheek, her chin, her neck, her nose,
> This was a lily, that was a rose;
> Her hande so white as whales bone,
> Her finger tipt with Cassidone;
> Her bosom, sleek as Paris plaster
> Held up two bowles of Alabaster.[19]

DIRTY WORDS AND WHITE LIES

The problem of whiteness was examined indirectly by the great poet of Elizabeth's England, William Shakespeare. *Othello*, one of Shakespeare's greatest plays, gives us a clear indication of the Elizabethan Christian responses to whiteness and blackness. The play, which was probably written in 1604—the year after Elizabeth's death—is based on an earlier Italian story of a black African general's marriage to a fair-skinned Venetian. Shakespeare contributes so much to the original story, though, that we can consider it his own.

Othello is the black Moor or Muslim. Shakespeare pictures him as especially noble, generous, and loving. Desdemona, his wife, is completely devoted to him. They love each other selflessly and without suspicion. But their love is corrupted by the racism of those around them. For example, the Venetian gentlemen, including Desdemona's father, continually refer to Othello as the "lusty Moor" or the "lascivious Moor." Desdemona's father was dead set against her marriage to the "damned" Moor, whose "sooty bosom" must, he feels, have won his "fair" daughter's heart by "foul charms." Othello is "damned" because he's black; even his name suggests he has come out of hell. His black skin must be only the exterior of a "sooty bosom" inside. It seems unnatural to the father that a daughter as fair or white as Desdemona could be attracted to someone as black as Othello. Therefore, Othello must have used "foul charms" (we would say "black magic") to trick her. All of the elements of white racism are there.

The real force of a racism that identifies black skin with dirt, sex, and sin is displayed in the play by one of Othello's white assistants, Iago. Iago was passed up for a promotion. Perhaps that is why he suspects that Othello has seduced his wife: "I hate the Moor; / And it is thought abroad, that 'twixt my sheets / He has done my office." Iago is able to save himself from being poisoned by the absurd suspicion only by infecting others. He proceeds to attack Desdemona, whom he says he loves, in order to get at Othello, whom he has come to hate. He resolves to "turn her virtue into pitch"—in short, to "blacken" her image in the eyes of Othello.

Othello is himself so indoctrinated by the racist color scheme of his adopted culture that he easily believes that his loving wife would accept a white lover. Manipulated by Iago to suspect his wife, even Othello can see her sin only in racist terms: "Her name, that was as fresh, / As Dian's visage, is now begrim'd and black / As mine own face."

Finally, the noble Moor is driven to kill the loving wife that he calls "the fair devil."

It is white racism that really kills Desdemona. Iago uses "dirty" words, spoken from "dark shadows." But the noble Moor is the instrument, the victim, and the accused. After he "puts out the light" of his life, he is condemned by Desdemona's servant: "O! the more angel she, / And you the blacker devil. . . . / She was too fond of her most filthy bargain. . . . / O gull! O dolt! As ignorant as dirt!"

Shakespeare's play is not racist, but it exposes the racial attitudes of Elizabethan society by playing upon the symbols for white and black. Othello was part of a long tradition in English theater that used the Moor to portray sexuality, evil, and the devil.[20]

NEGRO Y BLANCO

It is interesting to compare the image of blacks in the plays of Elizabethan England and in those of Spain and Portugal, where there also was a literary renaissance in the sixteenth century.

The great Spanish dramatist Lope de Vega wrote dozens of plays that dealt with various aspects of Spanish life. One of his plays that offers us an insight into the Spanish understanding of race is *El Negro del Mejor Amor*.[21]

The play is also the story of a Moor, a black North African Muslim, who visits Italy. Antiobo, the black prince, is the son of Duliman, king of Algeria, and the beautiful black Sofonisba. Antiobo, raised a Muslim, worries his father because he displays an unusual concern for his father's Christian captives. To test his son, Duliman sends Antiobo on a fleet of Algerian warships to join the Turks in an attack on the Christian island of Sardinia. When the fleet arrives, Antiobo's true faith asserts itself and he joins the Sardinian Christians to defeat the combined Muslim forces he was supposed to lead. Victorious in the Christian cause, Antiobo spends the rest of his life a hero among the Sardinians. The play concludes after Antiobo's death, with another Turkish assault on Sardinia. This time the body of Antiobo rises from the grave to save the island for Christianity again.

The differences between *Othello* and *El Negro del Mejor Amor* are striking. Antiobo is a Christian hero—not despite the fact he's black, but despite the fact he was raised as a Muslim. Religion, not race, is the important issue that Lope's play depends upon for its emotive power and meaning. Antiobo was part of a long tradition in Mediterranean literature that depicted the "good black," the Christian Ethiopian, who fought alongside the Christians against the Muslims.[22]

Spanish Christians, who included converted Moors, acknowledged the Ethiopian Christian church as older than their own. Piety and legitimacy were often "black" for the Spanish. Don Juan Manuel (1282–1349) told the story in *El Conde Lucanor* of a king who was duped by three men who pretended to weave a garment so fine that only a legitimate son could see it. As the king rode through the streets naked, all of his fawning subjects complimented him on his "beautiful robe." Only a lowly black stable boy stepped forward to tell the king he had no clothes.

THE RED AND THE BLACK

"In Spain it is a kind of title of nobility not to descend from Jews or Moors. In America, the skin, more or less white, is what dictates the class that an individual occupies in society." So wrote Alexander von Humboldt of his visit to the Americas around 1800. While this was generally true, at least of Spanish America by 1800, racial distinctions developed gradually in America.

While the Spanish conquistadores brought some of their African as well as European slaves with them in their campaign of conquest of the Americas, the social position of these slaves was established by tradition. Native Americans had no defined place in the European social system.

The very first European response to the Amerindians was Columbus's enslavement of some as specimens of scientific curiosity and a present for Ferdinand and Isabella. The first response of the conquistadores was to ally with some and to capture and kill many more of the Native Americans in the course of their conquest. As a result of war, and especially disease, it is likely that 70–90 percent of the Native American population was wiped out in the first century of European penetration, from 1492 to 1600.[25] Any European toleration of racial differences must be put in that context.

The toleration deserves notice, however, if only because it contrasts markedly with what came later. In 1503 the governor of Santo Domingo was instructed by the Spanish crown to see to it that some Spanish Christians were married to Native Americans. While this order might have been a limited experiment, it was also a reflection of the crown's overriding concern for Christian marriages. At the same time white female slaves were sent to Santo Domingo. By 1514, 171 of 689 Spaniards in Santo Domingo were married, 64 to Indian women.[26]

The half-Spanish, half-Indian "mestizos" of the early colonial period often found themselves at the top of the social hierarchy. If they constituted a new aristocracy, it may have been, in part, because of the social background of later Spanish immigrants. Miguel de Cervantes described Spanish America in 1613 as follows: "The refuge and haven of all the poor devils of Spain, the sanctuary of the bankrupt, the safeguard of murderers, the way out for gamblers, the promised land for ladies of easy virtue, and a lure and disillusionment for the many, and a personal remedy for the few."[27]

Indians were protected from the more exploitative colonists by the crown and the church in the sixteenth century. Bartolome de Las Casas and other Spanish theologians even argued, before a change of heart in the 1520s, that Africans ought to be enslaved so that Indians could be protected. On 9 June 1537, Pope Paul III declared that Indians were true men and not beasts and, thus, should not be reduced to slavery. But while Spanish kings, including Charles I and Philip II, eliminated slavery among the Indians of Mexico and the Andes out of a concern for their own souls as well as those of the natives, King João III and other Portuguese monarchs contented themselves with guidelines. Instructions of 1548, for instance, declared that the purpose of the Portuguese in colonizing Brazil was the conversion of the natives and that this could best be achieved by protecting them and preventing slavery, but that slave licenses could be issued in times of need, and captives of "just wars" on hostile tribes could be enslaved.[28] By 1574 the notion of "just war" was broad enough to include almost any slave raiding, and even when the Spanish king Philip II took the Portuguese crown in 1580 the laws remained the same.

Indian slavery in the Americas was to prove short-lived, however. Of the three forces of European conquest—church, crown, and colonists—only the colonists benefited from Indian slavery. The church thrived on free souls, the crown on sub-jects. A continent of slaves would benefit the landowners. A continent of free souls could be shepherded by the church and governed by the crown.

The initial grants of land and power to the conquistadores had the effect of set-ting up a new feudal class in competition with the crown. Initially Hernan Cortes (1485–1547), the conqueror of Mexico, received a grant, called an *encomienda*, of twenty-two towns in Mexico that gave him control over 115,000 people. By 1600 the Spanish crown was able to replace the encomienda system with one of crown administration and labor control, called the *repartimiento*.[29] The royal repartimien-to did not turn out to be less brutal than the feudal servitude of the *encomienda*. The Indians' masters merely changed from local colonists to the distant monarchy as administered by local colonists. While Indians lived in villages rather than planta-tions, their lives were dominated increasingly by the local hacienda and labor mar-ket.

Nevertheless, it might seem odd that the church and crown discouraged Indian slavery while encouraging African slavery. But on reflection, the reason for this dis-parity is apparent. Neither the church nor the crown could control or influence Africans in Africa. Aside from occasional explorers, European forces did not pene-trate the coast of Africa until the late nineteenth century. Prior to that, Africans could be exploited, mobilized, or converted only after they were taken to the New World as slaves.

THE BURDEN OF SLAVERY

Sometimes the exception proves the rule. Listen to the master of a slave ship, Captain Thomas Phillips, in 1694. The good captain complained of the developing racism of his fellow English, and found it odd that Africans were despised simply because they were black. The good slaver said that he could not imagine why they should be despised for their color, "being what they cannot help, and the effect of the climate it has pleased God to appoint them. I can't think there is any intrinsic value in one color more than another, nor that white is better than black; only we think it so because we are so, and are prone to judge favorable in our own case, as well as the blacks, who, in odium of the color, say the devil is white, and so paint him."[30]

Statements like that could not have been made by many slave ship captains, nor by many other people who profited directly from the capture, sale, or use of African slaves. The fact that this captain could be so open suggests that there could be good men operating cruelly in a brutal system. But the fact that his statement was unusu-al also shows that most people were molded by the system, however noble their feelings initially were. It was not possible for many slavers to maintain such views very long and still go about their business. It was almost inevitable that a society that made slavery a way of life would normally think in racist terms, at least when all those slaves were black. Certainly Europeans were better able to tolerate their

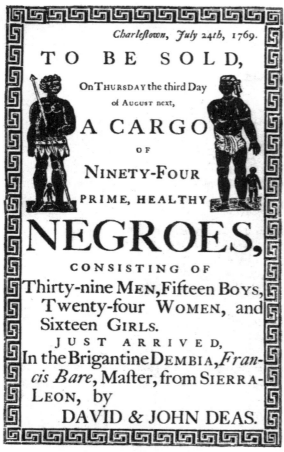

Charleſtown, *July* 24th, 1769.

TO BE SOLD,

On THURSDAY the third Day
of AUGUST next,

A CARGO

OF

NINETY-FOUR

PRIME, HEALTHY

NEGROES,

CONSISTING OF

Thirty-nine MEN, Fifteen BOYS,
Twenty-four WOMEN, and
Sixteen GIRLS.

JUST ARRIVED,

In the Brigantine DEMBIA, *Francis Bare*, Maſter, from SIERRA-LEON, by

DAVID & JOHN DEAS.

Most of the eleven and a half to fourteen million slaves came, like these, from West Africa. (American Antiquarian Society)

brutal exploitation of Africans by imagining that these Africans were an inferior race or, better still, not even human. In this sense, slavery encouraged European racism. C. R. Boxer has observed, "One race cannot systematically enslave members of another on a large scale for over three centuries without acquiring a conscious or unconscious feeling of racial superiority."[31]

Slavery was not a single system, however, not even on the plantations and mines of the Americas.

It developed at different times and at different paces—earlier and, in general, more quickly in Latin America than British America. It also developed in the context of different European social systems. Latin American slavery from 1500 to 1800 developed in a traditional society where feudal law, ideas, and habits were still important. Spaniards were born into a particular estate or caste and accepted that. Virtually no one believed in equality. They took the Church, the sacraments, and salvation very seriously. Members of the nobility really cared about their honor. Soldiers were motivated by fear and plunder. Religious fanaticism was considered virtuous. Life was a trial, usually brutal and bloody, offering only rare moments of passion. English society, on the other hand, was becoming increasingly capitalist and middle-class between 1600 and 1800. The English paid more attention to money and profit. Society was more fluid, less fixed. Science was beginning to take the place of religion, and the idea of equality was beginning to replace that of caste.

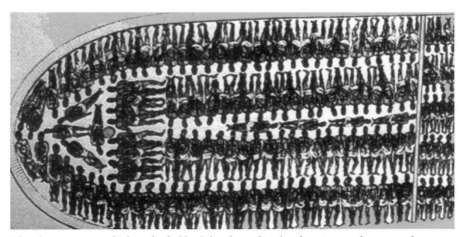

The slaves were packed in the hold of the slave ship for the two- to three-month voyage from Africa "in two rows, one above the other like books on a shelf." (Abstract of Evidence on ... Slave Trade, 1792)

This is not to say that English society was opposed to slavery. Some Englishmen were. Others were defensive about their involvement in slavery, or aggressive about pursuing their own profits. English slavery was neither more humane (out of a greater sense of equality) nor more brutal (out of a freer profit motive) than Spanish slavery. Some English societies could be among the worst in the Americas. Jamaica certainly was.

> This was a society in which clergymen were "the most finished debauchers" in the land; in which the institution of marriage was officially condemned among both masters and slaves; in which the family was unthinkable to the vast majority of the population and promiscuity the norm; in which education was seen as an absolute waste of time and teachers shunned like the plague; in which the legal system was quite deliberately a travesty of anything that could be called justice; and in which all forms of refinements, or art, or folkways, were either absent or in a state of total disintegration.[32]

Perhaps Jamaica represented one side of capitalism. Absentee landlords organized the entire island into plantations for the single purpose of producing sugar and making them rich. Perhaps the other side of capitalism was represented by the colonies that became the northern United States and Canada—legislating against slavery, preferring free or wage labor. In between, areas like the southern United States blunted both the exploitation and equalitarianism of emerging capitalism in

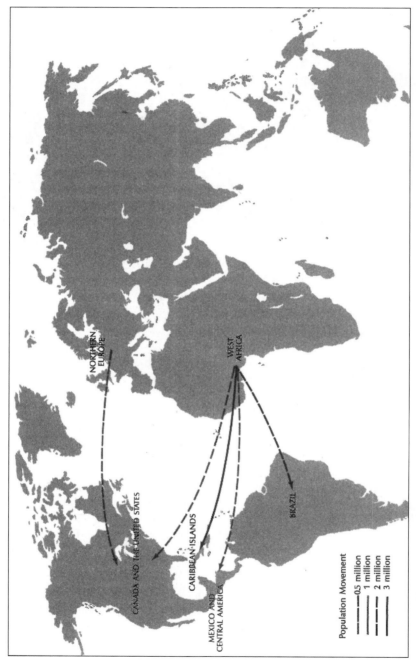

Major world migrations, 1700-1810. The slave trade was one of the great migrations of world history. Far more Africans than Europeans came to the Americas before 1810.

creating plantations "at home."

In general, the slave systems of the Latin America may have been harder on the slaves than those of British North America. Since the Iberians imported more slaves and continued the slave trade longer, the lives of slaves were often cheaper. The slaves of the southern United States were among the few to reproduce themselves; they were often able to maintain families; and to a certain degree they shared in the higher standard of living of the United States by 1800. Two qualifications must be kept in mind, however. The first is that slavery was always coercive and demoralizing. If there were fewer slave revolts in the United States than in the Caribbean and South America, it was because greater white power in the United States made revolt suicidal.

The second qualification, more important for the purpose of this chapter, is that the worst slave systems might not have been the most racist. While there is clearly a correlation between slavery and racism in general, there may not be a correlation between the brutality of the slave system and the highest degrees of racism. In short, it is possible that Latin American slavery was worse than British, but that British racism was worse than Latin American. We will look at two indicators for this judgment—manumission, the act of freeing slaves, and miscegenation, racial interbreeding, in both Latin and British societies in order to evaluate this possibility.

BRITISH VERSUS LATIN AMERICAN SLAVERY: RACISM AND MANUMISSION

Let us take a look at some of the evidence. For one thing, it seems pretty clear that bondage was a more permanent condition for the slave in the United States and British Caribbean islands than it was in Latin America. A much higher proportion of slaves in the Spanish and Portuguese colonies were given their freedom than in the British colonies. This attitude toward giving the slave freedom—manumission—is very important because it shows that the white colonizers need not view the Africans as permanently and incurably inferior.

In Brazil, settled by the Portuguese, and in Spanish America the law did not declare that a slave was necessarily a slave for his whole life or that his children were necessarily slaves—as was legally the case in the United States after the 1660s.

In Latin America there were a number of ways that slaves might attain freedom. They might purchase it by hiring themselves out on Sundays or one of the 85 holidays on the Catholic calendar. In Cuba or Mexico they had the right to have their purchase price declared, and could pay it in gradual installments. This became a widespread custom, especially in Cuba. A slave who was worth $600 could purchase freedom in 24 installments of $25 each. Each installment purchased one twenty-fourth of freedom, and the first payment allowed the slave to move from the master's house. Though the cost may have been considerably higher than the price of passage from Africa, slaves who were able to work for their freedom were not dif-

The caption of this eighteenth-century engraving reads: "An Englishman from Barbados sells his mistress." In the English colonies taking a black mistress was one thing, freeing her something else entirely.

ferent in principle from the white debtors of Europe who were forced to work as servants for a stated period.

The relationship between master and slave was almost contractual, based on a legal agreement—usually unwritten though not entered freely—between two parties. There were at least some cases of slaves paying everything but the last installment in order to avoid complete freedom and the taxes and military service that went along with it.

There were other ways for a Latin American slave to be freed. Thousands of slaves in Venezuela and Colombia were freed by Simon Bolivar when they enlisted in the army for the wars of independence. Similarly, many of the slaves who joined the armies of Brazil and Argentina were freed. Cuba periodically issued a degree that automatically freed slaves who escaped to its shores and embraced Christianity.

In most Latin American societies a slave who was unjustly punished could be freed by the judge. A Brazilian slave who had ten children could demand freedom legally. Other legal routes to freedom included denunciation of a brutal master, purchase by an African brotherhood, providing information in a criminal case, or discovering an especially large diamond or gold vein in the mines. The existence of *quilombos*—colonies of runaways—also offered the possibility of illegal escape from the slave system.

The legal roads to manumission, however, were probably not as important as the social approval that custom and the church gave to the act of freeing a slave. Even the culture of the slave owners held that manumission was a noble and generous act, a good thing to do. Happy occasions—the birth of a son, the marriage of a daughter, religious and national holidays, and family celebrations—were considered opportunities to ceremonially free one or a number of slaves in Latin America. It was considered appropriate and commendable for a slave child to be freed at baptism with the payment of a small fee ($25 in Cuba), and many slaves chose a godfather for their children with this hope in mind. While there were objections to manumission on everything from security to morality grounds (it encouraged theft and prostitution, some said), in general Latin Americans were far more favorably disposed to manumission than North Americans.

In the British colonies manumission was frequently viewed with alarm. Most of the British islands placed heavy taxes (often more than the value of the slave) on those slave owners who attempted it. In all cases a slave could not be freed without the owner's consent, and sometimes the consent of others was also required. In most of the British colonies (including the United States) a black or dark-skinned person of African descent was automatically assumed to be a slave. In some cases the slave was allowed to prove that he had been freed whereas he was presumed free in Latin American courts, and had to be proved a slave. Laws in Georgia, Mississippi, and South Carolina did not even allow the slave to establish a claim to freedom. According to the South Carolina law of 1740 "all negroes . . . mulattoes, or mestizos, who are or shall hereafter be in the province, and all their issue and offspring, born or to be born, shall be and they are hereby declared to be and remain forever hereafter absolute slaves." Thus, when William Sanders, recently freed in Virginia, returned to South Carolina in 1756, he was arrested. "For evidence of his being a freeman," the warden of the workhouse wrote in the *South Carolina Gazette*,

> he produces a pass, signed David Stuard, August County, Va., August the 18th, 1755, for William Sanders, a freeman, to pass and repass, which is indorsed by several other magistrates in North Carolina which name of William Sanders he now assumes, and pretends he is the same identical person, and a freeman. But as there is great reason to suppose he is a slave, and escaped from some person in Virginia or thereabouts, any person that can claim their property in him within six months, may have him upon payment of charges to the warden of the workhouse.[33]

One wonders what proof would have been sufficient. Even those few freed slaves in the United States were often forced back into slavery. Virginia required a freed slave to leave the state in a year or be sold "for the benefit of the Literary Fund." In many states of the southern United States, a freed slave could be sold back into slavery for the failure to pay a debt or a fine. The laws of the British West Indies and of the United States offered no hope for the slave to purchase his or her freedom, and these laws assumed that slavery was perpetual. The only hope was manumission by the slave's owner, and though this occasionally occurred there were too many obstacles for it ever to become a widespread practice.

In the slave states of the United States by 1860 only about 6 percent of the black population was free. If we include the equal number of free African-Americans who lived in the northern states, only 10 percent of the black population was free. In startling comparison, at the time of Brazilian emancipation in 1888, about 75 percent of the black population was already free. This was largely the result of different attitudes toward manumission.

These different attitudes toward manumission are significant in two ways. They show that South Americans were more willing to allow black people freedom and independence, and also that South American societies became so populated with free blacks that it was impossible to identify the cultural condition of slavery with the biological condition of black skin. Spanish and Portuguese settlers often spoke of slavery as an unfortunate condition to which anyone might fall prey. They saw slavery as the mark of social, not racial, inferiority. They were able to distinguish between a person's color and culture. In that sense, Iberian slavery was the result of less racist attitudes, and it created a society where racism was less pronounced.

Again, we are speaking only of racism, not the brutality of slavery. It is quite possible that South American societies treated their slaves more brutally than North American societies did. The Iberian willingness to manumit slaves only tells us about their attitudes toward black people; it says nothing about their treatment of the slaves who were not freed. Some historians have argued, for instance, that the Spanish and Portuguese slaveholders frequently freed the sick and elderly slaves

The white head of a large Brazilian household typically presided over a racially mixed retinue of wives, children, dependents, and slaves in an extended family.

because they had become too expensive to keep. North American slaveholders were rarely that cruel—or that willing to have a free African population in their midst.

The popularity of manumission in Latin American slave society may not always have been a tribute to their kindness. Since the slave trade continued well into the nineteenth century in Latin America, slaves were considerably cheaper than in the United States, which suspended the slave trade in 1808. That meant that Latin American slave owners could afford to work their slaves to death, buy more, and still free some of them. Even if that occurred, however, Latin American slavery still created a less racist society.

Let us return to the evidence. Perhaps the most striking feature for northern visitors to Latin American slave society was that black people were found everywhere. One English visitor to Brazil in the middle of the nineteenth century expressed his surprise this way:

> I have passed black ladies in silks and jewelry, with male slaves in livery behind them. Today one rode past in her carriage, accompanied by a liveried footman and a coachman. Several have white husbands. The

first doctor of the city is a colored man; so is the President of the Province.[34]

Another visitor said that the African-Brazilian

> seemed to be the most intelligent person he met because every occupation, skilled and unskilled, was in the Negroes' hands. Even in Buenos Aires theirs was the hand that built the best churches. They were the field hands, and in many places the miners; they were the cooks, laundresses, the mammies, the concubines of the whites, the nurses about the houses, the coachmen, and the laborers on the wharves. But they were also the skilled artisans who built the houses, carved the saints in the churches, constructed the carriages, forged the beautiful ironwork one sees in Brazil, and played in the orchestras.[35]

Free Brazilians of African descent achieved positions of considerable prestige, and were recognized in their time and by the Brazilian history books since. Two of the leading political figures of the seventeenth century were mulattoes. João Fernandes Vieira (d. 1681) was a guerilla leader, military commander of a mulatto regiment that defeated the Dutch, and a provincial governor. Antonio Viera (1608–1697) was one of the Portuguese Empire's most gifted scholars and preachers, a Jesuit advisor to King João IV, and persuasive spokesmen for human rights. Brazilian mulattoes also included the country's first portrait painter (Manuel da Cunha, 1737–1809), the leading architect and sculptor (Antonio Francisco Lisboa, c. 1735–1814), and a number of important Brazilian writers, composers, and musicians. Such men were exceptions, especially in politics. One is reminded of the visitor who was told that wealth rather than color was the basis for political office. "But isn't the governor a mulatto?"[36] the visitor asked. "He was; but he isn't anymore," was the reply. "How can a governor be a mulatto?" But Brazilian culture was a richer blend of the African and Portuguese than was Brazilian politics. Brazilian religion, music, and dance retained distinct ties to Africa. Brazilian literature, as well, has always been written by descendants of Africa and Portugal, and many of the most heroic and human of Brazilian heroes and heroines in fiction and history are African.

The *United States Magazine and Democratic Review* in 1844 recognized the gap between the treatment of Africans in the United States and Latin America. In Mexico "and in Central America, and in the vast regions still further south," the *Review* observed, "the negro is already a freeman—socially as well as politically, the equal of the white. Nine-tenths of the population there is made up of the colored races; the Generals, the Congressmen, the Presidents are men of mixed blood."[37]

Many North Americans recognized that their own prejudices against black people were greater in the United States than south of the border. Some like George Bancroft echoed the above quoted sentiments of the Review by arguing that the

Simon Bolivar (1783–1830) comes to the aid of a wounded black soldier in the Latin American struggle for independence.

acquisition of Texas would allow black people "to pass to social and political equality in the central regions of America, where the prejudices of race do not exist."

It was not true in 1844 that all South American blacks were free; some were still slaves. And it would be an exaggeration to say that no racial prejudice existed in the Iberian colonies: almost no whites were enslaved, and it was much more difficult for an African or Indian to become prosperous and accepted. With that qualification, however, the contrast holds. South American society was much more open for the descendants of Africans. Freedom was easier to attain, and it meant more once it was won. Prejudice was less, as was the discrimination in neighborhoods, schools, hotels, and public accommodations that became such a hallmark of racial experience in the United States. The lynch law and anti-Negro riots that became such a standard feature of the history of the United States in the nineteenth and twentieth centuries were absent from South American experience. In Latin American struggles for independence, blacks—free and slave—were recruited without prejudice. White dockworkers in Brazil worked for the abolition of slavery by refusing to work on slave ships at the same time that North American white workers rioted against Lincoln's draft law by attacking black families instead of Southern troops.

BRITISH VERSUS LATIN AMERICAN SLAVERY: RACISM AND MISCEGENATION

Why the difference? What accounts for the virulence of British, North American racism compared with the relatively mild prejudice in Latin America? The answers are many, and they have been hotly debated. We have already suggested a few. Perhaps the simple fact that British and other northern Europeans were so white skinned compared to the more olive-skinned Spanish and Portuguese was a factor. The patterns of settlement were also different. The Spanish and Portuguese conquerors came to the New World without their wives. Many, in fact, were not married. From the earliest years of the settlement they developed a permissive attitude toward interracial sex—miscegenation. The British settlers of North America, on the other hand, generally came with their wives and families. British wives were also often independent enough to insist that their slave-owning husbands keep their racial affairs private. Even when Iberian women came to the Americas to raise families, they came from a European culture where men and male values—machismo—were more clearly dominant. Iberian men in the Americas flaunted their black mistresses, recognized their black children, and often moved all of their families into the same large patriarchal home. While most states in the United States passed stiff laws against interracial sex, forcing men to be discreet, Latin American societies openly encouraged miscegenation as a proof of male potency and a way of life.

Miscegenation, like manumission, may have been popular in Latin America for less than noble reasons. But both practices created a population and a set of values

Racial Assimilation of Former British
and Iberian Colonies[1]

Current percentage black and mixed

British		
Bahamas	80	10
Barbados	75	17
Belize	46	30
Guyana	42	7
Jamaica	90	10
Trinidad and Tobago	43	17
United States	11	0[2]
Iberian		
Brazil	11	26+[3]
Costa Rica	3	40
Colombia	4	74
Cuba	12	15
Dominican Republic	12	60
Honduras	2	88
Mexico	1	70
Nicaragua	9	69
Panama	13	70

[1] Selected from warm Atlantic area with most
African slaves.
[2] U.S. defines mixed as black.
[3] Brazil adds 62 percent "mixed and white."

The "Bronzing" of the Americas. The Mexican ideal of the "bronzing" of the New World population is much closer to reality in those countries that were colonized by the Iberians (Spanish and Portuguese) than in those countries colonized by the British. What are some reasons for this?

A respected British business

which made race almost meaningless. How could one talk of "pure" races or even of race when the vast majority of the population was neither black nor white, but shades of olive and brown? How could one speak of the natural abilities or inabilities of the Negro when they were neither slave nor free, but both, and when they were planters, writers, masons, and bureaucrats?

By at least the nineteenth century, the majority of African-Americans in most countries south of the United States were neither black nor slaves. It became impossible to make generalizations even about the Negro. That was the very least that a racist had to be able to do. In the United States before the Civil War "Negro" meant slave. Neither the northern nor southern states wanted a population of free Africans. Southerners saw free blacks as deadly threats to the slave system: they believed that freed slaves incited slave rebellions, and the mere existence of prosperous or free blacks challenged the official racist doctrine that Africans were inherently inferior. Again, the Brazilian situation offers an interesting contrast. Brazilians not only used free blacks to capture runaway slaves, but Brazilian slave holders never developed the official North American doctrine of inherent African inferiority. Free blacks were banned from northern territories in the United States as well as from the southern slave states. Even the northern abolitionists who worked for the end of slavery often sought the disappearance of Negroes as well. They toyed with schemes to resettle the freed slaves in Africa, or like George Bancroft, they sought black emigration to Mexico or South America. The United States, North and South, was largely a society of two groups: black slaves and free whites. The North American hostility to miscegenation and manumission kept the descendants of Africans as black or visible as possible, and blacks were assumed to be slaves. This insistence on a two-caste society was so strong that even today North Americans classify any light-skinned person with a touch of African ancestry as a Negro. Even today in the United States people must be white or black and they are white only if their ancestry is all white. Blacks include, in common language and official census reports, not only "pure" Africans but anyone who is not "pure" white.

South American whites never insisted that there were only two races (excluding Indians); they did not relegate all people of mixed ancestry to the status of "the other" as if they were mongrel dogs. North Americans persisted in the belief (despite the evidence of their eyes) that there were only two racial types: pure whites and the others. South Americans recognized that there were many, and they encouraged the miscegenation which created many different racial categories between lily white and jet black.

Brazil, again, offers an interesting contrast to our way of thinking of race. In Brazil people are *pretos* (blacks) or *preto retino* (dark black) or *cabra* (dark) or *cabo verde* (dark with straight hair) or *escuro* (less dark) or *mulato escuro* (rich brown) or *mulato claro* (light brown) or *pardo* (lighter still) or *sarara* (light skinned with kinky hair) or *moreno* (light skin and straight hair) or *branco da Bahia* (native whites with slight African ancestry) or brunet whites or blond whites.

Spanish Americans think in equally rich racial terms. To the extent that Spanish Americans think of *negro* at all (or Portuguese of *nego*) it means black. No Latin American would think of calling an *escuro* or *pardo* a *negro*; *escuros* and *pardos* are obviously lighter.

This complex racial vocabulary south of the Rio Grande shows that Latin Americans are not color blind. Instead, they see much greater racial variety than North Americans do. Actually, their extreme sensitivity to racial differences

Racial stereotypes from anti-abolitionist cartoons

enables them to be less racist than the North American black versus white vision permits. White racism still exists in Mexico and Latin America, but many frankly recognize that most people are "mixed," and they find value in continuing the mixing. The Mexicans express this goal by calling themselves proudly "a bronze nation." They enthusiastically proclaim the destiny of Mexico to be the miscegenation of Africans, Europeans, and Indians—the "bronzing" of all peoples. Try to imagine the "bronze nation" as a cultural idea in the United States, despite all the talk of melting pots. Latin Americans have broken down racial barriers through miscegenation. Partly because they came as soldiers or conquerors without families, but also partly because they took so many Africans as slaves, they almost inevitably established societies which paid scant attention to race. It was never possible for people, the majority of whom considered themselves shades of brown, to work up fears of being overwhelmed by Africans. All but one of the slave states of the United States ended the slave trade before the federal prohibition in 1808. Brazilians continued the slave trade until 1851. By that time over half the Brazilians were black or brown. In the United States never more than 19 percent of the population was classified as Negro, and the percentage declined steadily from that high point of 1790. Brazilians may have been more committed to slavery, but the whites of the United States were more committed to racial separation.

FOR FURTHER READING

For general histories of slavery see William D. Phillips's *Slavery from Roman Times to the Early Transatlantic Trade* and David Brion Davis's *The Problem of Slavery in Western Culture* as well as his *Slavery and Human Progress*. M.I. Finley's *Slavery in Classical Antiquity* is a good introduction and his *Ancient Slavery and Modern Ideology* is a demanding analysis. Frank M. Snowden, Jr., challenges many accepted ideas with his *Before Color Prejudice: The Ancient View of Blacks*.

On the Atlantic slave trade, Robin Blackburn's *The Making of New World Slavery* is a big global survey. Hugh Thomas's *The Slave Trade* is a big book full of colorful characters, mainly European. There is a brief overview and a useful collection of documents in David Northrup's *The Atlantic Slave Trade*. Philip Curtin's *The Rise and Fall of the Plantation Complex* is an interesting overview. The African background is well presented in John Thornton's *Africa and the Africans in the Making of the Atlantic World, 1400–1680*. Sydney Mintz's *Sweetness and Power* places the history of slavery in the context of the history of sugar.

On Latin American slavery the best introduction is Herbert S. Klein, *African Slavery in Latin America and the Caribbean*. For the history of racism in Latin America, see Marvin Harris's *Patterns of Race in the Americas* and *The Idea of Race in Latin America*, edited by Richard Graham. For Portugal or Brazil one should begin with C.R. Boxer's thin *Race Relations in the Portuguese Colonial Empire, 1415–1825*, but then add A. J. R. Russell-Wood's *The Black Man in Slavery and Freedom in Colonial Brazil*. Other valuable current interpretations are *A Social History of Black Slaves and Freedmen in Portugal, 1441-1555* by A.C. de C. M. Saunders and *Red Gold: The Conquest of the Brazilian Indians* by John Hemming. The older works of Lewis Hanke, Boxer, and Gilberto Freyre are still worth reading, as is Carl N. Degler's *Neither Black nor White*. For Spanish America specifically *The African Experience in Spanish America: 1502 to the Present Day* by Leslie B. Rout, Jr., is good.

On North American slavery and racism a good place to start might be the brief study of the origins of slavery in the British Caribbean and North America: Betty Wood's *The Origins of American Slavery*. Eric Williams's *Capitalism and Slavery* sets slavery (especially in the Caribbean) in a larger context. Winthrop D. Jordan's *The White Man's Burden: Historical Origins of Racism in the United States* (or his larger *White Over Black*) argue against the economic interpretation of Williams and others. Eugene D. Genovese's *Roll, Jordan, Roll* and his *The World the Slaveholders Made* are models of Marxist scholarship. The extremes of interpretation are Stanley Elkin's *Slavery* (as concentration camp) and Robert Fogel and Stanley Engerman's *Time on the Cross* (as reformatory). Herbert Gutman's *Slavery and the Numbers Game: A Critique of Time on the Cross* and his *The Black Family in Slavery and Freedom* criticize both optimistic and pessimistic extremes as does John Blassingame's *The Slave Community*. Other valuable titles are David Cohen and Jack Greene, eds., *Neither Slave nor Free*, John Hope Franklin's *From Slavery to Freedom*, and Peter Woods's *Black Majority*. Mark M. Smith provides a useful introduction for students on the debate about the economic profitability of slavery: *Debating Slavery: Economy and Society in the Antebellum American South*.

NOTES

1. Kevin Sack with Janet Elder, "The *New York Times* Poll on Race: Optimistic Outlook But Enduring Racial Division," Appendix to *How Race is Lived in America* (New York: Times Books, 2001), p. 365.
2. David Margolick, "Ex-Director of NAACP Legal Fund Reflects on State of Civil Rights," *New York Times*, July 5, 1984, p. A9.
3. Years of last available statistics are 1998 for income and 1995 for wealth.
4. *The New York Times*, March 15, 1985, p. A14.
5. Michel Leiris, "Race and Culture," in UNESCO, *Race and Science* (New York: Columbia University Press, 1951), p. 214.
6. Orlando Patterson, in *Slavery and Social Death: A Comparative Study* (Cambridge: Harvard University Press, 1982), surveys fifty-five slave-owning societies (many of which are tribal and traditional) and finds some to be racist.
7. Frank M. Snowden, Jr., *Before Color Prejudice: The Ancient View of Blacks* (Cambridge: Harvard University Press, 1983).
8. *Numbers* 12:1–15, quoted in Snowden, p. 44.
9. *Psalms* 87:4–5, quoted in Snowden, p. 45.
10. Snowden, pp. 58–59.
11. Ibn Botlan, "Introduction to the Art of Making Good Purchases of Slaves," as quoted in William McKee Evans, "From the Land of Canaan to the Land of Guinea: The Strange Odyssey of the 'Sons of Ham,'" *American Historical Review* 85:1 (1980), p. 24.
12. Ibn Khaldun, *An Arab Philosophy of History: Selections from the Prolegomena of Ibn Khaldun of Tunis (1332–1406)*, trans. Charles Issawi (London, 1955), p. 98. Quoted in William McKee Evans, *op. cit*, p. 32.
13. William McKee Evans, *op. cit.*, p. 32.
14. Fernand Braudel, *The Structure of Everyday Life*, trans. Sian Reynolds (New York: Harper & Row, 1981), p. 224.
15. A.J.R. Russell-Wood, "Iberian Expansion and the Issue of Black Slavery: Changing Portuguese Attitudes, 1440–1770," *American Historical Review* 83: 1 (1978), p. 28.
16. Zurara, *Chronique de Guinee*. Adapted from the English translation of Beazley and Prestage, *Chronicle of the Discovery and Conquest of Guinea*, vol. 1, ch. 25. Quoted in A.J.R. Russell-Wood, "Iberian Expansion and the Issue of Black Slavery," p. 30.
17. Russell-Wood, *op. cit.*
18. Winthrop Jordan, *White Over Black* (Baltimore: Penguin Books, 1968), p. 7.
19. [George Puttenham?], *Partheniades*, quoted in Winthrop Jordan, *op. cit.*, p. 8.
20. Elliot H. Tokson, *The Popular Image of the Black Man in English Drama, 1530–1688* (Boston: G.K. Hall & Co., 1982), p. ix. Earlier quote is from p. 136.
21. The following discussion of the play is derived from Howard M. Jason, "The Negro in Spanish Literature to the end of the Siglo do Oro," in Miriam de

Casta, *Blacks in Hispanic Literature: Critical Essays* (Port Washington, N.Y.: Kennikat Press, 1977), pp. 33–34.

22. See, for instance, Henri Baudet, *Paradise on Earth: Some Thoughts on European Images of Non-European Man* (New Haven: Yale University Press, 1965).

23. Sylvia Wynter, "The Eye of the Other: Images of the Black in Spanish Literature," in Miriam de Casta, *op. cit.*, pp. 14–15.

24. On this issue see Francis Jennings, *The Invasion of America: Indians, Colonialism, and the Cant of Conquest* (Chapel Hill: University of North Carolina Press, 1975), pp. 16–31, and John Hemming, *Red Gold: The Conquest of the Brazilian Indians, 1500–1760* (Cambridge: Harvard University Press, 1978), pp. 487–492.

25. Magnus Mörner, *Race Mixture in the History of Latin America* (New York: Little Brown, 1967).

26. *Ibid.*

27. Opening lines of "Celoso extremeno" (1613). Quoted in C. R. Boxer, *Race Relations in the Portuguese Colonial Empire 1415–1825* (Oxford: Clarendon Press, 1963).

28. John Hemming, *Red Gold: The Conquest of the Brazilian Indians, 1500–1760* (Cambridge: Harvard University Press, 1978), p. 147.

29. Marvin Harris, *Patterns of Race in the Americas* (New York: Norton Library, 1974), pp. 18–19.

30. Winthrop Jordan, *White Over Black* (Baltimore: Penguin Books, 1968), p. 11. Spelling and punctuation are modernized.

31. C. R. Boxer, *Race Relations in the Portuguese Colonial Empire, 1415–1825* (Oxford: Oxford University Press, 1963), p. 56.

32. Orlando Patterson, *The Sociology of Slavery: An Analysis of the Origins, Development, and Structure of Negro Slave Society in Jamaica* (London, 1967), p. 9.

33. Daniel C. Littlefield, *Rice and Slaves: Ethnicity and the Slave Trade in Colonial South Carolina* (Baton Rouge: Louisiana State University Press, 1981), pp. 167–168.

34. Thomas Ewbank, *Life in Brazil, or the Land of the Cocoa and the Palm* (London, 1856), p. 266.

35. Frank Tannenbaum, *Slave and Citizen* (New York: Random House, 1946), p. 39.

36. A.J.R. Russell-Wood, *The Black Man in Slavery and Freedom in Colonial Brazil* (London: Macmillan, 1982). This quotation is adapted from that on p. 72. The biographical information is from pp. 73–77 and 101–103.

37. Quoted in Carl N. Degler, *Neither Black nor White* (New York: Macmillan, 1971), p. 16.

Politics
and
Morality

Secular States
and Middle Classes

Americans in the last few years have shown a new concern for morality in politics. While some people have become cynical about the possibility of politics ever being ethical, others have sought ways to instill confidence in government through institutional reforms and the election of politicians with ideals.

In this chapter we try to understand some of our modern expectations about political morality by focusing on the ideas of three extremely important political theorists of the sixteenth and seventeenth centuries: Machiavelli, Hobbes, and Locke. Machiavelli is important because of his formulation of two ideas that are fundamental to our perception of the relationship of politics and morality. The first is the idea that there can be a science of politics, or political science. The second is the idea that the morals of the modern secular state can and must be different from the political ideals of individuals. We live in a world that values not only science and the state, however. We also value the constitutional and legal forms of government that derive from the middle-class, capitalist revolutions of the seventeenth and eighteenth centuries. Thus, we turn to the political theories of Hobbes and Locke because they were among the first to explore the political and moral implications of these middle-class revolutions.

MACHIAVELLI

It is customary for those who wish to gain the favor of a prince to endeavor to do so by offering him gifts of those things which they hold most precious, or in which they know him to take especial delight. In this way princes are often presented with horses, arms, cloth of gold, gems, and such-like ornaments worthy of their grandeur. In my desire, however, to offer to Your Highness some humble testimony of my devotion, I have been unable to find among my possessions anything which I hold so dear or esteem so highly as that knowledge of the deeds of great men which I have acquired through a long experience of modern events and a constant study of the past.

With the utmost diligence I have long pondered and scrutinized the actions of the great, and now I offer the results to Your Highness within the compass of a small volume.[1]

So begins Machiavelli's *The Prince*, perhaps the most praised, damned, and influential "small volume" on political morality ever written. It has been called the work of the devil, the start of political science, a hymn to liberty, a satire, a joke, a warning, a divine inspiration, and a simple description of political reality. Three hundred years after it was written, Napoleon Bonaparte declared that it was the only political book worth reading. Even today, the variety of interpretations seems to multiply. A mere list of the books and articles that have been published on Machiavelli and *The Prince* would be larger than the 80 or so pages of the original "small volume." Although it was written simply and directly, it has given rise to almost as many interpretations as there have been readers. They might all agree only that the book is enormously important.

The opening lines just quoted suggest that Machiavelli viewed his book as a gift to a prince. It was the gift he felt he might best give to Lorenzo de Medici, the new ruler of Florence: a gift of his own knowledge of politics. We might also call this "gift" a letter of application for a job. After 14 years of public service for his beloved city (from 1498 to 1512) Machiavelli had learned a great deal, and now he was out of a job. He had served the "republican" (free, popular) government that had removed the Medici family from power. Although he may not have considered himself anti-Medici, he had commanded the republic's militia, completed diplomatic missions for the republic, and made important contacts with the family's enemies. Thus, when papal armies were able to return the Medici to power in 1512, Machiavelli's name was on a list of possible republican conspirators. He was arrested, tortured, and then released because he was clearly innocent, but he was not asked to carry on his work for the city. For the next 14 years until his death he read, wrote, and attempted to regain the most useful work he knew: service to the city that he "loved more than [his] soul." The great tragedy for Machiavelli was that the Medici never called him back. *The Prince* was largely ignored by the prince it was

Niccolo Machiavelli (1469–1527); portrait by Santi de Tito.

meant to please. The final tragedy of Machiavelli's life was that when the Medici were overthrown again in 1527 and democratic government was restored, his old "application" (of 1513) came back to haunt him. He hurried back to Florence, but the widely circulated manuscript of *The Prince* had made him too many enemies among the republicans. Before the news of the council's rejection came, he was dead.

The Prince is a book of lessons in government, filled with examples from Machiavelli's diplomatic experience and readings in ancient history. As a "how to govern" book, it was similar to dozens of instructional volumes (often called "A Mirror for Magistrates") which rulers had been reading for hundreds of years. But Machiavelli's guide lacked the Christian moral tone of the earlier "mirrors." That was what shocked the council of the Republic of Florence in 1527 and so many readers since.

The lessons that Machiavelli gave were lessons in power and success, grounded in "reality" rather than "imagination":

> For how we live is so far removed from how we ought to live, that he who abandons what is done for what ought to be done, will rather learn to bring about his own ruin than his preservation. A man who wishes to make a profession of goodness in everything must necessarily come to grief among so many who are not good. Therefore it is necessary for a prince, who wishes to maintain himself, to learn how not to be good, and to use this knowledge and not use it, according to the necessity of the case.[2]

The career of Cesare Borgia, whom others viewed as an unprincipled, murderous tyrant, was for Machiavelli most worthy of imitation by a perceptive prince. In discussing how princes could attain order in captured territories, Machiavelli told of Borgia's administration of the Italian territory of Romagna. The province had previously been governed by weak rulers, Machiavelli relates, so that it was "a prey to robbery, assaults, and every kind of disorder." Cesare Borgia "therefore judged it necessary to give them a good government in order to make them peaceful and obedient to his rule." Borgia purposely picked "a cruel and able man" to bring order to the province. Then, after the man had viciously done his job, Borgia "resolved to show that if any cruelty had taken place it was not by his orders, but through the harsh disposition of his minister." Thus, Borgia had his appointed scapegoat "cut in half and placed one morning in the middle of the public square" to satisfy the people's hatred and win their gratitude for himself.

Machiavelli says that Cesare Borgia, whom he had met, sought to preserve in four ways the territories that were given to him by his father, Pope Alexander VI: "[f]irst, by destroying all who were of the blood of those ruling families which he had despoiled," so that none of them could organize to regain their territories; secondly, by gaining allies among the Roman nobles as a check on any future pope who might be hostile; thirdly, by controlling the College of Cardinals so that he could choose his father's successor; "[f]ourthly, by acquiring such power before the pope died as to be able to resist alone the first onslaught." Machiavelli goes on to say that Borgia was almost completely successful in all of these tasks. "For of the dispossessed rulers," he adds, "he killed as many as he could lay hands on, and very few escaped." He had also at least gained veto power in the College of Cardinals over the choice of his father's successor. His only mistake, Machiavelli concludes, was that Borgia let someone he injured become the next pope (Julius II). Otherwise, Machiavelli says:

> I find nothing to blame, on the contrary, I feel bound, as I have done, to hold him up as an example to be imitated by all who by fortune and with the arms of others have risen to power. For with his great courage and high ambition he could not have acted otherwise, and his designs were only frustrated by the short life of Alexander and his own illness.[3]

We get a sense of the limits Machiavelli can accept in the next case he discusses: that of the ancient tyrant of Sicily, Agathocles. First, he dismisses the moral problem by stating that the example of Agathocles is "sufficient for any one obliged to imitate" him. Then, he details Agathocles' "life of the utmost wickedness." Once, for instance,

> he called together one morning the people and senate of Syracuse, as if he had to deliberate on matters of importance to the republic, and at a given signal had all the senators and the richest men of the people killed by his soldiers.[4]

Agathocles was certainly a brilliant strategist and a brave man in surmounting obstacles, Machiavelli says, but we cannot call him virtuous.

> It cannot be called virtue to kill one's fellow-citizens, betray one's friends, be without faith, without pity, and without religion; by these methods one may indeed gain power, but not glory.[5]

But Machiavelli understands that the wicked may be powerful, and their treachery might even increase their power:

> Some may wonder how it came about that Agathocles, and others like him, could, after infinite treachery and cruelty, live secure for many years in their country and defend themselves from external enemies without being conspired against by their subjects; although many others have, owing to their cruelty, been unable to maintain their position in times of peace, not to speak of the uncertain times of war. I believe this arises from the cruelties being exploited well or badly. Well committed may be called those (if it is permissible to use the word well of evil) which are perpetuated once for the need of securing one's self, and which afterwards are not persisted in, but are exchanged for measures as useful to the subjects as possible. Cruelties ill committed are those which, although at first few, increase rather than diminish with time.[6]

Machiavelli's "moral" is that "the conqueror must arrange to commit all his cruelties at once" so that the people will have an increasing sense of security and improvement.

We can see from the way that Machiavelli uses terms like good and evil that he is speaking the language of tactics, not of morality. This was a new and frightening language to his readers who were trained in the Christian culture of moral absolutes. Traditional Christian values were turned on their heads. "It is much safer to be feared than loved." Although every prince should want to appear merciful rather than cruel, he should "take care not to misuse this mercifulness" to the point where disorders arise. *The Prince* is full of such advice: "imitate the fox and the lion"; "be a great pretender and liar"; "be able to do evil."

Statements like these are the cause of Machiavelli's notorious reputation for immorality. But Machiavelli was not immoral. He was simply urging political rulers to recognize the way people really behave, and to act accordingly in the interests of the state. He was rejecting Christian morality for rulers because it would destroy the state. In place of Christian ethics, Machiavelli invented political science—the study of political realities—and created a new version of ancient pagan morality, an ethical system which prized the kingdoms of this world more than those of the next.

Both of these creations—scientific politics and state morality—were Machiavelli's gifts to the modern world. Both were virtually unknown in medieval and Renaissance Europe, and both have shaped our ideas of politics and morality ever since. In traditional Christian society politics and morality were barely separated. The medieval world view recognized a chain or ladder of God's creations, from the lowest to the highest:

> All things whatsoever, spiritual and material things, the archangels, the
> angels, the seraphim and cherubim and all the other celestial legions,
> man, organic nature, matter, all of them are bound in this golden chain
> about the feet of God. There are two different hierarchies; the hierar-
> chy of existence and that of value. But they are not opposed to each
> other; they correspond to each other in perfect harmony. The degree of
> value depends on the degree of being. What is lower in the scale of
> existence is also lower in the ethical scale. The more a thing is remote
> from the first principle, from the source of all things, so much the less
> is its grade of perfections.[7]

In terms of this medieval perspective, ideal and real were not different. The
more "being" or existence a thing possessed the closer it was to God, and the better it was. Humans stood between the animals and angels in both being and value.
The king stood above other men in divine sanction as well as power. Such a perspective did not provide the intellectual tools necessary for examining questions
about the misuse of power or the gaps between ideal and real. Ethics and politics
could barely be conceived of separately.

Machiavelli changed all of that. Or rather, Machiavelli recognized and applauded changes that had begun in Renaissance Italy. Modern secular states were coming into existence. Machiavelli called them "new principalities." They were formed
by men like Cesare Borgia. They were based on naked power. They claimed no
divine justification. They paid no allegiance to higher feudal lords and set themselves free of medieval hierarchies. They claimed the territory that they could control, and they rested their case with the force of arms. They were neither small city-
states, nor divine-right monarchies, nor Holy Roman Empires.

Although secular states proliferated considerably during the Renaissance, many
originated a few hundred years earlier. Perhaps the earliest was the state created by
Frederick II in southern Italy three hundred years before Machiavelli wrote *The
Prince*.

> It was an absolute monarchy in the modern sense; it had emancipated
> itself from any influence of the Church. The officials of this state were
> not clerics but laymen. Christians, Jews, Saracens had an equal share in
> the administration; nobody was excluded for merely religious reasons.
> At the court of Frederick II a discrimination between sects, between
> nations or races was unknown. The paramount interest was that of the
> secular, the "earthly" state.
>
> That was an entirely new fact, a fact that had no equivalent in
> medieval civilization. But this fact had not yet found a theoretical
> expression and justification.[8]

MACHIAVELLI'S MORALITY FOR THE MODERN STATE

Machiavelli provided that theory. He met the issue of political secularism head-on. The church had excommunicated Frederick II twice. Dante, Machiavelli's fellow Florentine, placed Frederick in the flaming ring of heretics in his *Inferno*. Frederick himself justified his state in religious terms, imagining that he had been singled out by divine providence and given the grace of the "highest reason." Machiavelli undercut the needs for religious attack or defense. He questioned the desirability of the Christian state itself. "Our religion," he said of Christianity, "instead of heroes canonizes those only that are meek and lowly." That can never be the basis of a strong state. Pagan religions were much more politically serviceable, he thought. "Pagans deified none but men full of worldly glory, such as great commanders and illustrious governors of commonwealths."[9]

In the new secular principalities, Machiavelli felt, the state could again become the source of religion and morality. As in the pre-Christian ancient world, state gods and official priests could harness the energies of the people on behalf of, rather than against, the political institutions. The namby-pamby Christian ethics of love, prayer, surrender, and escape could be transformed by the new secular states into an ethical system that praised strength, power, independence, and ambition. That was the stuff of successful political life for princes and people alike. Religion was an invaluable tool for the maintenance of a state, but it must be a religion of the state—a religion that created soldiers and patriots, not martyrs who turned the other cheek.

Machiavelli's defense of state religion and state morality was too radical for his time. His fundamentally anti-Christian position was too much for anyone then or since, with the exception of Nietzsche in the nineteenth century. The most ruthless rulers have declared their Christian love and humility. But Machiavelli was right about how things were changing. The secular state has become its own authority. Modern religion has become political loyalty, obedience, and patriotism. We still call ourselves Christians, but our loyalties, our attachments, and our feelings go out to Caesar, to Caesar's state, and to the state's symbols of power. Machiavelli saw that this was beginning to occur in the new principalities of the Renaissance, but it has proceeded much more quickly and decisively in the larger nation-states that have arisen since. By including whole ethnic groups—Italians, French, Germans, or English—in the same territorial state, the nation-state could add the appeal of ethnic pride to its arsenal of brute power. The lip service we still give to Christianity disguises the fact that we now worship the state instead.

The transition from a world in which religion was the chief end in life to one in which religion is either ignored or used to prop up the state took many forms. In France absolute monarchy took shape as the kings gained control of the church. Even French cardinals generally associated their interests more with the French state than with Rome. Cardinal Richelieu, who controlled the government for Louis XIII, combined a policy of Gallicanism—establishing a French, "Gallic" national Catholic church—with the development of a theoretical defense called *raison d'état.* Although Machiavelli did not use the French phrase which means "reason of state," or state morality, it expresses the kind of secular justification of state power that Machiavelli defended. Richelieu attempted to justify Gallicanism and the doctrine of *raison d'état* by having one of his aides write an *Apology for Machiavelli in Favor of Princes and State Officials* (1643). More often, the new monarchs of secular states declared their heated hostility to Machiavelli (as in Frederick of Prussia's *Anti-Machiavelli*) and then proceeded to follow the master's instructions to the letter. That was exactly what Machiavelli would have advised if he were still alive: condemn me publicly, but read carefully.

"States and people are governed differently than individuals." Only Machiavelli's meaning of "states" made that a new thought. Others had accepted the need for governments to engage in certain kinds of behavior that were denied individuals: legislation, taxation, declaring war, even executing an individual. But Machiavelli first used the word "state" in the modern sense—a secular, territorial power outlasting separate governments, whose ultimate justification was not divine will or popular will but force. The idea that the state could do anything that was necessary to maintain its existence was new. Medieval monarchs did not justify anything for the state. Even the existence of the state was second to God's will. Many medieval rulers had no doubt acted as if their rule were all that mattered. But they invariably did so beyond the pale of the church and their own consciences. They still took their Christian ethics seriously. The fear of God was real. The novelty of Machiavelli's small volume is that it brought power politics back into the ethical cosmos. Machiavelli's new pagan ethical system made force and fraud not only acceptable but necessary for rulers who served the state—a goal more "than my own immortal soul." State morality, an anything-goes ethics of power, the defense of the state, the reasons of state—that was what was new. "It was new and it was a monstrosity," the great historian Friedrich Meinecke wrote in his *History of the Idea of Reason of State* which begins with Machiavelli.

When we ask about the abuse of power in the modern state, we almost have to begin by examining the power that we allow that state without calling it "abusive." Abuse of state power can be so destructive today because the accepted power of the state is so enormous. Especially given the fact that we have lost (or transcended—depending on your point of view) the traditional Christian ethical system which kept us honest, our anything-goes ethics make any concentrated power that much more dangerous. The modern state is infinitely more powerful than were the new principalities of Renaissance Europe. Yet, in the name of "national security," "national interest," and "national defense," we allow that state a degree of power over our lives that might make Cesare Borgia blush.

We allow that power to the state, not the particular individuals in the government, of course. But so did Machiavelli. Indeed, Machiavelli assumed more than we do that the ruler would use his power only in the best interests of the state. The problem is that we, like Machiavelli, often leave it up to the particular ruler or government to determine what the national interest or state needs are. The potential for abuse is implicit in the power.

We said before that two modern developments have followed from Machiavelli's separation of politics and morality. On the one hand, morality was determined by the needs of the state: state morality and state religion replaced traditional Christian ethics of government. On the other hand, politics divorced from Christian morality became a science. Now that we have examined Machiavelli's first invention, state morality, let us turn briefly to his other contribution, his scientific politics. They are equally important to an understanding of modern attitudes about the relation of politics and morality. We not only have a tendency to accept whatever the state does as moral, we also tend to think of politics as a scientific rather than an ethical activity.

MACHIAVELLI'S MODERN SCIENCE OF POLITICS

Machiavelli has often been called the father of modern political science. Some of his defenders, in fact, have argued that he was only a scientist: he merely observed how people behaved without imposing his own values. We have said enough to call that interpretation into question. Machiavelli did make value judgments. He applauded Cesare Borgia. He justified state power. The state was in fact his highest value. Machiavelli was unique not only in what he liked but also in his "objectivity" and passion to understand things as they really were. As observer of the human realities behind the veil of sanctimonious rhetoric, Machiavelli was perhaps the first European social scientist. He watched what worked and what did not. He gathered the evidence of the ages and formulated general rules for the power brokers of the future.

Just as Galileo trained his telescope on the heavens and realized that they were made of the same stuff as the earth, Machiavelli turned his perceptive eye to princes and concluded that they behaved just like the beasts of the field. Both "scientists" were more concerned with what "is" than what "should be." In the process of their investigations, both discarded the medieval understanding of an ascending chain of being-and-goodness for scientific laws that applied equally to planets and plows, princes and paupers. Both secularized the world, in order to speak of the capabilities of man. Both tried not to judge in order to understand.

But there were implicit moral judgments in viewing the world without mystery or morals. The scientists insisted that they were only interested in the knowledge that the spectacle of nature offered. Observation was an end in itself. Knowledge was more important than participation and involvement. Though that may have been possible for Galileo the physical scientist (and recent atomic research has raised some doubts), it was not so simple for Machiavelli the scientist of men. He imagined himself to be a mere technician or physician: only showing us how to cure "hectic fevers" in the political body. But even his image of the state as a body or organism had distinct moral implications. If the state is itself a body, it has an instinct for survival which must be satisfied. Part of it is a heart, part a brain, part a stomach, all of which are more important than arms and legs. Disease in the organs might require strong medicine, perhaps even the amputation of a limb. The physician who is willing to prescribe a special diet, bloodletting, or surgery is making definite moral judgements when the patient is the "body politic" of the state.

Sometimes Machiavelli's objective, scientific stance is that of a master strategist who is merely watching the game. This ostensibly amoral spectator's role also has decisive moral consequences. In his illuminating study, *The Myth of the State*, the philosopher Ernst Cassirer shows how the "mere observer" of the human game is necessarily engaged in moral judgments:

> Machiavelli looked at political combats as if they were a game of chess. He had studied the rules of the game very thoroughly. But he had not the slightest intention of changing or criticizing these rules. His political experience taught him that the political game never had been played without fraud, deception, treachery, and felony. He neither blamed nor recommended these things. His only concern was to find the best move—the move that wins the game. . . . Sometimes he shook his head at a bad move; sometimes he burst out with admiration and applause. It never occurred to him to ask by whom the game was played. The players may be aristocrats or republicans, barbarians or Italians, legitimate princes or usurpers. Obviously that makes no difference for the man who is interested in the game itself—and in nothing but the game. In his theory Machiavelli is apt to forget that the political game is not played with chessmen, but with real men, with human beings of flesh and blood; and that the weal and woe of these beings is at stake.[10]

The politics of the modern state has become a science and a game. Moral considerations (except the "morals of state") are set aside for discussions of strategy, "scenarios," and "game plans." While political scientists develop "game theory" and social psychologists explore convincing myths, politicians acquaint themselves with the magic of these new priests and make statesmanship an aspect of public relations and advertising.

It is certainly important to understand human behavior, and the model of scientific understanding is still our best guide. Political science can be a tool for greater knowledge of human needs, a testing ground for possible solutions to political problems. It can also be used, however, as yet another device for manipulation, fraud, and personal advantage.

PROTESTANTISM, ABSOLUTISM,
AND MIDDLE-CLASS REVOLUTION

While Machiavelli argued that politics had nothing to do with ethics, a number of deeply religious "reformers" like Savonarola, Luther, and Calvin insisted that politics must have everything to do with ethics. The Protestant Reformation of the sixteenth century was essentially an attempt to transform the world with the ethics of Christ. Savonarola attempted such a government by God in Florence while Machiavelli was still young. Later Calvin created such a theocracy in Geneva, Switzerland. Luther gained the support of Frederick of Saxony and other German princes in a similar venture to create the holy state.

Although the secular, scientific temperament of Machiavelli was far removed from the religious zeal of the Protestant reformers, and although Machiavelli separated politics from ethics while the reformers sought to reunify them, the results of their labors were almost identical. The Protestants made their states as powerful as any that Machiavelli envisioned. Their states were supposed to legislate the "will of God," but unable to rely on centuries of its interpretation by Catholics, the reformers were forced to interpret it themselves. The results could be only slightly less self-serving than the commands of a secular prince who was mainly concerned with the prosperity of his state. In short, the modern state was created in two forms during the sixteenth century: one secular, the other religious. Both of these enjoyed religious sanction, however, and both were enormously powerful. Protestantism, in fact, served the interests of the national state, the anti-Roman monarch, and the rising national consciousness in some ways better than the state religions that Machiavelli conjured from the pagan past. The patriotism of the English, for instance, was immeasurably deepened by Henry VIII's Protestantism.

In many ways the states that were created between the sixteenth and eighteenth century in Europe, whether encouraged by Machiavellian secular theory or by Protestantism, were ruled by stronger monarchs than any before or since. The eighteenth century was the great age of the absolute monarch and the theory that kings ruled by divine right. After this, the state grew in power, but the rule of the state became legitimized, legalized, and limited. Monarchs were replaced by legislatures, presidents, and parliaments. The rule of the individual was shed for the rule of law.

The unbridled power of the monarch's state became, by the seventeenth century in England and by the eighteenth century in France, too oppressive for the increasingly prosperous middle class to stomach. They revolted to limit the power of the state or open it to themselves. These middle-class revolutionaries spoke the language of new ethical absolutes. It was no longer the absolutes of Christianity or the secular absolutes of *raison d'état*. It was a revival of ancient notions of natural law, a doctrine which again tried to combine the natural and the moral, the actual and the ideal, the political and the ethical. For a brief time—in the midst of revolution—the middle classes of England and France asked that politics be fundamentally moral again. Maybe those in power are always more interested in "political realities," or "the way things are." Those who are deprived of power may be more conscious of what "should be" and less interested in what "is." Rulers call their subjects to face realities. Much of the status quo operates in their favor. They mouth the required moral phrases, but their attention is more practical than ethical. It is the class of people who are excluded from politics, the "outs," the potential revolutionaries who ask sweeping ethical questions and demand moral politics.

Such revolutionaries call for ethics, but they actually want power. Their idea of justice often does not go beyond the admission of themselves and their followers to political power, but at least their dissent and struggle usually involves the raising of basic questions about the relationship of politics and ethics. Sometimes, when the struggle is successful, the result is a new agreement about the moral possibilities and limitations of politics in general.

In brief, this is what happened during the course of the middle-class revolutions of the seventeenth and eighteenth centuries. Beginning in England in the middle seventeenth century (1640s), the European class of merchants, lawyers, professionals, and artisans, which stood midway between the aristocracy and the poor, challenged the dominance of kings and nobles. This middle class developed a wide-ranging body of political theory that was highly moral in tone and purpose. They criticized the idea of the divine right of kings as a guise of tyranny. They condemned the Machiavellian notion of the state as an organic body which set its own ends, and offered instead an image of the state as an artificial creation of people and a means to human ends. They objected to the Machiavellian acceptance of the ruler, prince, or king as interpreter of the public needs and called instead for representative government. They questioned Machiavelli's contention that the exercise of power was always proper and outlined rules and laws which bound ruler as well as ruled. And they went further than Machiavelli in distinguishing between the state, which some still thought to be the eternal sovereign, and the particular governments of that state, which might be replaced at the will of the people.

Similar principles were enunciated continually in the course of the middle-class revolutions: in England in the 1640s and again in 1689, in America in the 1770s and 1780s, in France in the 1780s and 1790s, and in most of the rest of Europe at the end of the eighteenth and beginning of the nineteenth century. Even the revolutions in Russia and Latin America in the early 1800s expressed the new political ethics of the rising middle class: representative government, the rule of law, the limited state, and government as "means" rather than "end."

The most visible feature of these middle-class revolutions was the challenge to monarchy. In England and France the kings were actually executed. Regicide was, however, only one of the possible consequences of the new political and ethical theory. The principles of middle-class theory, which came to be known as liberalism, can be summarized as the limitation of power that had previously been considered absolute and a notion of "ethics as process."

THE ETHIC OF PROCESS

The new ethic of process requires some explanation. Today it is almost part of our "common sense," but three hundred years ago it was a dangerously subversive idea. Remember that in ancient tribal or caste society, as in India, ethics were dependent on clan or caste membership. The Hindu example is probably only an exaggeration of tendencies in other ancient societies. Members of a ruling caste were expected to behave according to different moral codes than the members of a priestly or peasant caste. To a certain extent this social differentiation of ethical systems continued even into medieval society. In general, however, medieval Christian culture and Eastern Buddhism conceived of a unified ethical-political world and argued that ethics were universal. The same set of standards were to apply to rulers, priests, and peasants alike. All were equally divine in the Buddhist view or equal in the eyes of God according to Christian teaching.

The creation of secular states, witnessed by Machiavelli, and of theocratic Protestant states in the Reformation made the state and its rulers, whether prince or prophet, the judge of a new state morality. The state flourished. Its morality, official religion, and political control became virtually absolute. Since the authority of the state was in the person of the ruler, it varied from tyranny to "enlightened despotism." It was sometimes benevolent, but that depended on the particular king. Even the advisory assemblies of nobles which had existed since the Middle Ages lost their ancient power of consent or approval. The Estates General or parliament of France, for instance, was simply not called to assemble from 1614 until 1789, the year of the revolution, and it virtually ignored the middle class anyway. The English Revolution of 1640 similarly had been precipitated by the attempt of King Charles I to govern without Parliament since 1629. Both revolutions made a middle-class parliament supreme. Unlike the kings, these parliamentarians could not govern in their own names as if they were each appointed by God, nor could they argue that God had directed their class to rule.

Representative government was defended on other terms. It was, the middle class argued, the rule of the people and the rule of law. In effect, they made the process of representative government the highest ethical value of politics. We might disagree about the ends of government, they said by their actions, but at least we can give sanction to that disagreement and to an agreed upon means for the resolution of our differences. Machiavelli or Calvin would never have accepted a government concerned with means rather than ends. The notion that means were more important than ends, indeed the idea that the process rather than the goals were the treasure of true citizenship, would have been abhorrent to Machiavelli, Calvin, or the absolute monarchs.

The middle-class revolutionaries really had no other choice. Since government was to be in the hands of the many, there would inevitably be disagreements. Such disagreements could only be resolved in the process of debate, persuasion, bargaining, compromise, and trade-offs. They could never be sure that such a process would always lead to the "right" decision, but they were convinced of fewer absolute "rights" than Machiavelli or Calvin. In effect, they agreed to define the "right deci-sion" as the one which the process of debate and voting produced.

In a strange way the work of Machiavelli and the Protestant reformers led almost inevitably to this modern political ethic of process. Machiavelli led the way by defining politics as a secular activity, but even though he placed the ends of the state above everything else, he was preoccupied with rules, strategy, and process. Much of Machiavelli's work, in fact, was devoted to the examination of political process in the republics of the ancient world. On the other hand, the Protestant reformers were so committed to doing what they perceived as God's will that their only alternative to governing a theocracy was to live as outsiders in a secular state. If their own beliefs were not legislated, then none could be. It was, for example, one of the most religiously committed of American Protestants—Roger Williams—who argued on theological grounds in the 1630s for the separation of church and state and for secular, democratic government. God's law was too precious to be inter-preted by states; mere governments should not pretend to deal in absolutes.

In a secular state where power was to be shared by many, whether each member of the government was an atheist or a different kind of Protestant, the process of decision making had to be valued more highly than particular ends. The political process itself had to be sacred. Nothing was more serious than tampering with the process because nothing threatened the fragile unity of agreement-to-disagree more. No single rule was as important as the inviolability of the system of rule making.

The processes of middle-class government may have originated in medieval cities and parliaments, but they developed rapidly in the course and aftermath of revolution. Majorities, parties, parliamentary rules, elections, voting, caucus, clubs, debates, processes to limit and balance powers, constitutions, separated powers, procedures for everything: these were the safeguards of the new system. Govern-ment became a serious game with complex rules. A brutal struggle of conflicting interests, in deadly earnest and without appeal, it was carried on, at the least, with-out bloodshed. Like the similar middle-class economic marketplace or the new stock exchanges, parliamentary government channeled the most heated confronta-tions of power into peaceful compromise and resolution. What seemed like a fanat-ical adherence to procedure kept tempers cool and disputes from getting too per-sonal.

One of the greater achievements of the middle-class revolutions may have been the translation of civil war into party politics. The Italian city-states of the Renaissance often oscillated between civil war and institutionalized struggle, but the institutions rarely held. The "popular party" was never too far removed from a citizen militia. This was essentially the case in the English Revolution of 1640. The first wide-ranging debates, creating of programs, and gathering of factions or "par-ties" occurred in the revolutionary New Model Army among the soldiers. In the French Revolution of 1789, political parties grew out of middle-class clubs, like the Jacobin club, and crystallized around particular programs in the debates of the leg-islative assembly and the struggles on the street.

At first, political parties were thought to be divisive forces, conspiracies against the rest of the nation. This was particularly the view of monarchists who favored the restoration of a king and those who had absolute solutions to which no one seemed to listen. After Oliver Cromwell's revolutionary Commonwealth government began to come apart and the Stuart kings, Charles II and James II, were restored between 1660 and 1689, party activity fell off in England. Only with the revival of parliamentary power in the Glorious Revolution of 1689 (the second stage of the English middle-class revolution), when Parliament declared the monarchy vacant and selected James's daughter Mary and William of the Netherlands to rule England, did political parties in the modern sense come into being. When real power was in the hands of the many in Parliament rather than of the king or the few, political parties became an essential part of the process of disputing and deciding. This took some time. The parties of 1689—the conservative, country Tory party and the moneyed, urban middle-class Whigs—probably had no more than a few thousand members. Even most of the middle class was still excluded. In the 1760s King George III could still hope to play the role of a popular "patriot king" who could set aside party differences and rule arbitrarily. Not until 1770 did an English political theorist of any influence (Edmund Burke) actually advocate political parties.

Parties were probably the most difficult element of the ethics of process to accept. They would originate in periods of revolution and crisis—when the divisions were very real and very important. These were precisely the times when the goals of the parties were much more important than the acceptance of the process or the rights of the opposition. In times of social harmony, at least among the powerful, process could take precedence over special interest, but then the existence of parties itself seemed destructive. Strong leaders, like George III, George Washington, or Napoleon, were suspicious of parties, but the solution of a Napoleon was often to abolish legitimate opposition and drive it into exile or civil war. The ideas of process involved in the separation of state and government, the acceptance of "the loyal opposition" (loyal to the state but not the ruling party), and the willingness to play by the rules (even, or especially, when it meant losing power) were ideas of the anti-monarchial, middle-class revolution that took a long time to mature.

The differences between Machiavelli's political ethics and the modern ethics of process are sharpest in this light. We accept the latter today, but we still practice the former when we think we can get away with it. The moral failure of the Nixon administration (and, to be fair, of a number of Democratic city machines) was precisely of this kind. The political process itself was undermined. What better examples could there be of the corruption of the political process than the use of state money and personnel to spy on the opposition, harass their contributors and spokespersons with state agencies, and to use the police power and bureaucracy for partisan ends?

SOME UNFINISHED BUSINESS:
THE POLITICAL ETHICS OF LIBERAL MARKET SOCIETY

Just as Machiavelli's secularism and realism had its underside of absolutism and "my country right or wrong" statism, so did the middle-class revolutionary idea of "ethics as process" have its seamier side. To put it as simply as possible, the political process was necessarily closed to all but the propertied class, and (even ideally) the political theory of process offered a sordid, jungle image of humanity and a competitive market idea of society.

Perhaps we can understand these limitations best by examining the political-ethical theory of two of the most famous spokesmen for the English middle-class revolution of the seventeenth century: Thomas Hobbes (1588–1679) and John Locke (1632–1704). Although usually remembered for only two books, Hobbes's *Leviathan* and Locke's *Second Treatise on Government*, they wrote prolifically.

The *Leviathan* was certainly one of the most unpopular books ever written in England. It was rigorously logical and unflatteringly realistic. No party or group accepted the theoretical foundations that Hobbes provided. Most political writers ignored or, like Locke, attempted to refute Hobbes's depressing conclusions. We will look at Hobbes because he was right.

Locke, on the other hand, is interesting for our purposes because of his enormous popularity and prestige. His work became the "common sense" of the eighteenth century. His emphasis on constitutionalism, majority rule, individualism, and limited government inspired generations of middle-class revolutionaries in Europe and America. His very vocabulary was enshrined in our own Declaration of Independence and on American minds ever since. We still speak of "natural" or "inalienable rights" of life, liberty, etc. We still profess the same principles of government. Our justifications of our own "liberal democracy" are still essentially the arguments that Locke worked out to justify the approaching Glorious Revolution of 1689. The rule of law, the consent of the people, the preservation of our liberties, the right of election and even of rebellion—these too are principles of John Locke. In short, Locke defended all of the "good things" that we have come to know as democratic theory. The only problem was his logic and that he was speaking solely for the political liberty of his class—the owners of property.

HOBBES: A GOVERNMENT FOR THE COMPETITIVE JUNGLE

Hobbes did for the middle class what Machiavelli had done for princes. He surveyed the changing scene of English society, noted the new pervasiveness of buying and selling and market mentality, and swept away the old puffy theories of natural law and moral responsibility because they no longer made sense. Since traditional Christian ethical theory, with all its talk of community and commonwealth, of loyalty and obligation, of divine hierarchy and Christian charity, no longer reflected the way people actually behaved, it was useless as a theory of ethics or gov-

The title page of the first edition of Thomas Hobbes's Leviathan, 1651.

ernment. Hobbes based his theory on actuality. He was looking for a justification of newly emerging secular government, which would show people what and why they must obey—without appealing to arguments that had no validity in people's hearts, minds, and guts.

Seventeenth-century England was changing from a feudal, hierarchical society in which the chain of mutual rights and obligations was taken for granted to a capitalist or market society in which rights and responsibilities were bought and sold like everything else. Hobbes recognized the importance of the market. He understood that the elements of market society—private ownership of property, the increasing use of money, and the translation of all relationships into money values—were transforming traditional England. Society was more competitive, less cooperative. Relationships were more fluid, less fixed. Fortunes rose and fell rapidly. Insecurity and war seemed more natural than security and peace.

Hobbes may not have fully realized how new this society was. Seventeenth-century thinkers were still used to thinking, in the style of traditional society, that basic things were always the same, that whatever existed was "natural." Hobbes was the first to accept this new society as the necessary starting point for a viable ethical and political theory. He began with an examination of what he called "the state of nature" which detailed the characteristics of the emerging market society. Only after such a realistic assessment of the way things actually were, he argued, would it be possible to determine what could be. Instead of imposing the "oughts" of traditional theology and natural law, which had worked more or less successfully in traditional society, Hobbes saw the need for a more realistic understanding of the "natural" to suggest the limits of the possible and desirable.

From the vantage point of seventeenth-century market society, the natural state of human life appeared to Hobbes to be "nasty, brutish, and short." Taking market society to its logical conclusion, Hobbes saw a jungle of competitive struggle. Instead of society there were only deals. Instead of creative, emotional, social human beings, Hobbes saw animals with basic appetites—or, more appropriately, rational, calculating machines.

Nothing in Hobbes offended seventeenth-century religious sensibilities more than his materialistic, mechanistic view of humanity. The idea that humans were essentially machines which subtracted potential pain from material advantage before they acted was, no doubt, disconcerting to those who preached love, charity, and spiritual fulfillment. But Hobbes was a realist. The machine model of human behavior made more sense as he looked around him. It also made more sense in terms of the overriding importance of buying and selling decisions in market society.

Hobbes did not use the terms "market society or "capitalism." These are later words. Further, as we said, he thought he was describing the way things naturally were. His generalizations, however, about the natural state of man suggest that he was considering the requirements and possibilities of a society in which the laws and relationships of the market were primary. Human action, for instance, "is either for gain, or for glory; that is, not so much for love of our fellows, as for the love of ourselves." Individuals are like self-directed, self-willed atoms, each alone trying to maximize its wealth, power, or influence. Values, morals, and ethics have no meaning except in terms of the satisfaction of these desires.

> *Honourable* is whatsoever possession, action, or quality, is an argument and signe of Power. . . . Dominion, and Victory is Honourable; because acquired by Power. . . . Riches are Honourable; for they are Power.[11]

In terms of market morality, the right, proper, or good action is that which increases one's power, wealth, or advantage. All people seek to maximize their desires and to increase their possessions. The market works because people are able to ignore emotional issues and to bargain rationally. The best people are those rational machines, which can get the most out of the bargaining process. Value is getting the best price. Since everything is for sale, the best people are those who can command the highest price for their own power.

> The *Value*, or Worth of a man, is as of all other things, his Price; that is to say, so much as would be given for the use of his Power. . . . And as in other things, so in men, not the seller, but the buyer determines the Price. For let a man (as most men do,) rate themselves at the highest Value he can; yet their true Value is no more than it is esteemed by others. [12]

If society is, then, a competitive market, if each man is only out for himself, if power and wealth is its own justification, if everybody has his or her price, and there are no other values than market values, how is it possible for people to agree to any kind of law, ethical system, or government? Hobbes answered that everyone is equally insecure within the market. The market determines not only each person's value and possessions, but also each person's fear that someone will opt for force when he or she loses. As competitive as human relations are in market society, they are still better than open warfare. Some sovereign power is necessary to ensure that people obey the workings of the market without taking things into their own hands. All people, since they are rational, will recognize that an absolute or sovereign power is necessary to enforce the rules of the game: "to appoint in what manner all kinds of contract between Subjects, (as buying, selling, exchanging, borrowing, lending, letting, and taking to hire,) are to bee made; and by what words, and signes they shall be understood for valid."[13]

This is the kind of agreement on politics as process, the agreement to disagree but play by the rules, that we discussed in the previous section. Yet, Hobbes deals squarely with an issue that we only hinted at before. How can we expect a real loser at the social market to continue to play fairly while losing? What is to stop someone from raising an axe or an army when everything is lost? What happens when for some individual or group the controls of market morality and government are more disastrous than the jungle?

Hobbes's answer is twofold. First, remember that he is talking to the property holders. They can recognize that a sovereign power is necessary to ensure the continuance of a market society that allows them private property. Even when they lose some of their holdings, they will still be able to regain and increase their possessions if they have accepted a sovereign power that will permit the game to continue. All property holders, even those who are losing, have a stake in the maintenance of the market system. Secondly, since even a property holder might be made destitute by the market, the sovereign power must be beyond recall, election, or the influence of a particular propertied group. Since the job of the sovereign is to prevent internal war and ensure the opportunity for ownership and gain, it must be subject to none. Its power must be absolute, and it must be self-perpetuating. To preserve the system without yielding to any individual or group, even a majority, it must have no other responsibility. Anything short of this would permit one group to use the sovereign to gain influence or leverage over another group. An electable sovereign would hopelessly divide one property group against another. In a society as fragmented and centrifugal as market society such division among property owners might result in a social revolution and the loss of private property itself. Thus, rational, propertied people would realize that their own interests, individually and as a group, required that they make a compact among themselves to establish an absolute sovereign power that none of them could control. That was the moral basis of government in market society. It was an "ought" that was directly implied in the realities of that society, a moral absolute based on the selfishness of each individual property owner.

It is easy to understand why none of the middle-class groups adopted Hobbes's philosophy. Its assumptions were too unflattering, and its conclusions seemed too severe. But it was logically tight as a drum. If property owners had remained relatively equal in economic power, it would have been necessary for them to put the sovereign beyond the reach of each of them. What Hobbes failed to see was that the same market that created an equality of fear also created inequalities of class. It became possible for classes of property holders to stay cohesive and united enough to minimize the centrifugal pull of the market. Imagine, though, a society in which dozens or hundreds of shipbuilders or cabinetmakers were forced to compete ruthlessly for power. If such owners were the only ones who appointed the sovereign government, imagine how easy it would be for one or a group of them to use that government to their own advantage. An absolute sovereign would be their only protection from other property holders.

Hobbes fully accepted the market morality and ethics of self-interest that was evolving in his time. He used it to show the moral need of the propertied to create and obey a government that maintained the system with absolute power, but, once created, chose its own successors, brooked no objections, and answered to no one. In relation to the sovereign, the kind of political ethics that Hobbes called for was simple obedience. However, since he expected that the sovereign would only enforce the laws of the market, it was the market itself that governed morality. Thus, ethics was the securing of personal advantage, and justice was the striking of a good bargain. Today we call that political corruption. Hobbes might still show us that we can realistically expect little else of market society.

It is interesting that so many modern Americans assume that politics is corrupt but that business is relatively honest. The interesting thing is that by "dirty" or "corrupt politics" we mean just that type of politics that is practiced like business. Political life is "corrupt" for us precisely when it involves buying and selling, when influence is "peddled," when legislators are "bought," when special favors are "sold," in short, when politicians behave like business people or are "too close" to them. We may be justified in our concern that the public trust not be put on the market for sale to the highest bidder. Hobbes would have argued, though, that it is unreasonable for us to reward and expect ambition, aggressiveness, selfishness, drive, competitiveness, wealth, and power in all aspects of life except one and to demand the opposite there. Hobbes might have realistically believed in the seventeenth century that politics could escape the pull of market forces and private interests—but only if the sovereign were absolute and self-perpetuating. Market society has transformed so much of life since then, that his hope sounds as archaic and idealistic as it is oppressive and totalitarian.

LOCKE: A GOVERNMENT FOR CHRISTIAN GENTLEMEN

John Locke told the propertied middle class more of what they wanted to hear. He provided a justification for capitalist or market society that did not dwell on the jungle ethic or the selfish, competitive, market-oriented individual. He spoke a glowing language of absolute rights and resurrected much of the traditional teaching of natural moral laws. He refused to see ethics in totally market or utilitarian terms. He argued for the possibility of limited, representative government in market society. And, more significantly, he offered a positive moral basis for capitalist society with the argument that only the propertied class was capable of full rationality, full understanding, and, thus, full participation in the "natural rights of man."

Locke began with a knotty problem. It had been traditionally assumed that God gave the Earth and its fruits to humanity in common. Locke felt that Scripture and "natural reason" compelled him to accept that traditional assumption, despite the obstacle it posed to a defense of private property.

> But this [that the earth was given to mankind in common] being supposed, it seems to some a very great difficulty, how any one should ever come to have a *Property* in any thing. . . . I shall endeavour to show, how Men might come to have a *property* in several parts of that which God gave to Mankind in common, and that without any express Compact of all the Commoners.[14]

John Locke (1632–1704)

Undaunted by the traditional idea of common ownership, Locke set out to show how private property could be justly created, even without the consent of the common people. First, the fruits of the earth are of no use unless they are appropriated (owned): "There must of necessity be a means to *appropriate* them some way or other before they can be of any use, or at all beneficial to any particular Man." Then there must be a right of individual appropriation. This can be derived from the obvious individual right to own oneself, one's labor, and the work of one's labor: "every Man has a *Property* in his own *Person*. This no Body has any Right to but himself. The *Labour* of his body, and the *Work* of his Hands, we may say, are properly his."[15]

Well then, if individuals have the right to own their own labor and work, they must have the right to sell it: you cannot own what you cannot sell; and the labor class, after all, sells its labor for wages. The problem is that once the laborer has sold his or her labor, it belongs to a new owner; it is no longer the laborer's. Especially after money has been introduced, a society is created where some people own a lot of the fruits of the earth, their own labor, the labor of others, and the goods produced from all of the labor that they own. In other words, the earth has been justly divided among the propertied, society is divided between owners and workers, and neither owe anything to society, because every individual has the right to his or her labor— even to sell it.

From this "labor theory of value," defense of private property, and acceptance of class divisions, Locke goes on to assume, as did most of his readers, that the laboring class could not possibly be fully rational or participate fully in political life. Their labor is owned by others, and they do not have the time and opportunity to understand politics.

The labourer's share [of the national income], being seldom more than a bare subsistence, never allows that body of men, time, or opportunity to raise their thoughts above that, or struggle with the richer for theirs.[16]

Except, Locke adds, in a common disaster when the laborers "forget respect" and "break in upon the rich."

Locke's inalienable rights of life, liberty, and property (Jefferson changed "property" to "the pursuit of happiness") could only be upheld in his terms as long as the propertied class monopolized political power. When he urges, against Hobbes, that "the majority" can rule without a self-perpetuating sovereign, he means the majority of the propertied class. He does not even consider the possibility that the majority would abolish private property. He does not have too. The poor only react in revolution. The purpose of government is to ensure the inalienable rights. The liberty to own and sell property is only inalienable if the propertied rule.

It is usually said that Hobbes saw human morality in the jungle and insisted on a dictator, while Locke felt that men could compose their moral and political laws themselves. As we have seen, they were both talking about government by the propertied class. But the difference is even greater than that. Hobbes accepted the morality he found in market society. Locke clung to the traditional belief that there were certain moral "natural laws" that any reasonable or rational man could recognize. He believed that he could hold certain truths to be "self-evident." We might argue, along with Hobbes, that people no longer took any truths to be self-evident; indeed, that was the problem that called for a new justification of government. But Locke would not listen to that. Certainly, he would say, there are moral absolutes that every rational person would accept. And if we objected to one of these—the absolute right to own property, say—Locke could retort: "You're clearly not being rational."

In short, Locke flavored his defense of the new system with the moral absolutism of traditional Christian theology. He sounded good. But he gave that traditional wisdom a class basis. Only the propertied could fully reason. Only they could understand the natural laws of politics and morals. Only their majorities were fit to legislate the self-evident.

THE UNFINISHED BUSINESS OF BUSINESS SOCIETY: PRIVATE OWNERSHIP OR POLITICAL DEMOCRACY

Locke's language of "inalienable truth" and "natural law" appealed to the eighteenth century. We have become more skeptical since. We are closer today to Hobbes. We are not sure that any moral principle is absolute anymore. We speak today as if morality is "what you feel good after." We fear "value judgments." We shudder at the thought of "imposing our own values." We may not agree with so-and-so but we certainly "defend his (her) right to say it."

All of that is fine, even if it sometimes makes us incapable of outrage. It is all part of the heritage of middle-class liberalism—the Machiavelli-Hobbes variety. One may wish at times that modern Americans expended more effort on moral questions, that they still had the capacity for shock and indignation, that they did not accept so many things with a moral shrug of the shoulders. But no matter. There is value in our tolerance. To that extent we have learned the lesson of the middle-class revolution: we have civilized civil war; we have recognized diversity; and we have moved toward an ethics of process.

At the same time, however, we still live with the legacy of John Locke. It is amazing how many people, like Locke, still deny imposing their own values while they do it all of the time. We no longer speak of "natural laws" but we argue for "objectivity" when we mean "my view of things." We call for "balance" or "the other side" when we mean that we disagree. We find "bias" in everyone but ourselves.

We also still share Locke's specific problem: the moral justification of government. In fact, we have compounded it. Locke may not have fully realized the class basis of his moral absolutes, but he frankly limited government to the propertied. Since Locke, suffrage has become virtually universal. Perhaps the laboring classes refused to read between the lines of the noble Lockeian list of universal rights and freedoms. Some would say that they forced the propertied middle class to turn their rhetoric about such rights into a reality for all. Others would say that the liberal, middle-class promise has still not been redeemed. The freedoms and liberties which middle-class revolutionaries proclaimed for all men (while limiting them to themselves) are still not enjoyed by all.

The problem may go deeper than that, however. It may be, as Hobbes and Locke thought, that the freedoms of the middle-class revolution—especially property ownership—cannot be made available to all. The freedom of uninhibited acquisition cannot be given to everyone. Every person on the block cannot have the freedom to own the block. Once one person exercises that freedom, everyone else has lost it. The freedom to be a millionaire means that a million people are a dollar short.

The problem is how to justify complete economic freedom or independence (with all of the potential exploitation of others that is implied) with the goals of a democratic society. Like Locke we still honor absolutes—freedom of opportunity, free enterprise, freedom of ownership. In practical terms the unhindered enjoyment of these freedoms still may mean the suffering and impoverishment of others. Some are born with more of these freedoms than others, and their increasing use of such freedoms is at the expense of the same freedoms for many others.

We are still grappling with the problem that Hobbes and Locke posed three hundred years ago. How do we defend or justify market society? How can we argue for the continuance of a society of class divisions? How can we give an ethical basis to the conversion of the commons into the preserve of the few? Hobbes made no pretense of democracy. Locke began that pretense. Now that we also accept the language of Locke's revolution, we have compounded the problem. Can we have freedom of economic opportunity and democracy too? How do we justify class or economic differences in a democracy? Which is more important: the rights of private ownership or majority will? What happens if the unpropertied majority wants to abolish the "rights" of private ownership? Like Locke we still assert that everyone enjoys the freedom of economic opportunity—even when we do not exactly mean everyone. Unlike Locke, we think that we can mean everyone. Locke would not have to read Hobbes to say that we were being naive.

As ethics have become relative or at least more relative, so has the nature of politics become less moralistic. We have gone from a politics of goals to a politics of process. In fact, the maintenance of process is the most important, and perhaps the only, goal we can have. That, probably, is the main achievement of democratic theory.

But, as we have observed, the revolution in political and ethical theory that was ushered in by the middle-class revolutions beginning in the seventeenth century also had a darker side. As Machiavelli realized, the state could replace the old religion. As Hobbes recognized, the power of that secular state—especially in market society—might have to be enormous. Locke reminded us of some of the old values of absolutist, but communal, society. Both Hobbes and Locke provided moral justifications for political activity in the new society. But neither Hobbes nor Locke were willing to come to grips with the class divisions and fragmentation that the new economy created.

That problem still remains. We live in a society that makes equal access to the political process its highest ideal. Our political ethic today is democratic process. In part, we said, our problem is that that goal has not yet been fully realized. Our examination of Hobbes and Locke, however, suggests that such a goal was something of a sham from the beginning. Locke glossed over the problem by repeating the high-sounding moral absolutes of the older natural law tradition. The problem, however, persists. If our only possible political ethic is process, our only absolute imperative is that the process be open to all. The other goals of the middle-class revolution, however—market society, individual acquisition, private ownership of the "capital" (productive facilities), and the acceptance of class (owners and workers, rich and poor)—all mean that the political process cannot possibly be open to all. Economic inequality can make political equality meaningless.

Politics is still the clash of differing interests. That is the model of market society. But some interests have much more power than others. Even with only public financing of political campaigns, we cannot expect the weak to be as well represented as the powerful. The large corporations can pay enough people to outwit the best intentions of democratic government. Their staffs are not only frequently larger than those of government, they are often the same. As long as economic power is private, political power cannot be democratic—except for the few. Hobbes and Locke, of course, knew that. They had no objections. Only the "lunatic fringe" on the left wing of the middle-class revolutions, like the radical Diggers in England, thought of democratizing political power fully by democratizing economic power. Perhaps they were both behind and ahead of their time.

OPENING THE PROCESS: FROM LIBERAL TO SOCIALIST DEMOCRACY

"I tooke my spade and went and broke the ground upon George Hill in Surrey, therby declaring freedome to the Creation, and that the earth must be set free from intanglements of Lords and Landlords, and that it shall become a common Treasury to all, as it was first made and given to the sonnes of men." Thus Gerrard Winstanley explained why he led a group of twenty poor men to cultivate the wastelands of Saint George's Hill as communists in 1649. They invited all of England to join them. The middle-class revolutionaries of Cromwell's new government were horrified by these "Diggers" and their threat to the emerging institutions of the market and private property.

Winstanley wrote two years before Hobbes's *Leviathan* and over thirty years before Locke's *Treatise*, but his declaration could have been a direct answer to both as well as to Cromwell. "You are all like men in a mist, seeking for freedom, and know not where, nor what it is," he said with perhaps too much trust in middleclass intentions. "No true freedom can be established for England's peace, or prove you faithfull in Covenant, but such a one as hath respect to the poor, as well as the rich; for if thou consent to freedom to the rich in the City, and givest freedome to the Free-holders in the Countrey, and to Priests and Lawyers, and Lords of Mannours, and Impropriators [owners], and yet allowest the poor no freedome, thou art then a declared hypocrite," Winstanley wrote a bit more pointedly. "Because this buying and selling is the nursery of cheaters. . . . Therefore, there shall be no buying and selling in a Free Commonwealth, neither shall any one hire his brother to work for him."

In the middle of the English seventeenth century an attack on private ownership, buying and selling, market society, classes, and wage labor was both futile nostalgia and bold dreaming. Not until the nineteenth century, when the middle-class revolution had run its course, did new revolutionary movements arise, which found the liberal democracy of the propertied insufficient. Like Winstanley, Marx and the socialists called instead for a radical democracy that would be social and economic as well as political, for the poor as well as the wealthy.

The socialists sometimes seemed to talk as if they rejected the ethics of process. They spoke again of fundamental goals, the priority of ends over means, and they frequently criticized parliamentary process and evolutionary change. In a sense, however, the socialists were asking only that the political process be allowed to operate more fairly, and their attack was implicit in the justifications of middleclass revolution.

The middle class took power from kings and nobles because they were barred from the process of decision making. Implicit in their defense of liberal democracy was the argument that revolution was the only alternative for those who were not allowed to participate. There was nothing unethical or immoral in revolution. It was the only recourse for those whom the process ignored. They created, or recreated, the ethics of process as the most important moral ideal of a politics of full participation. For those who shared access to power, there could be no higher goal than the agreement to follow the rules. That was the only way a shared system of power could work. In that sense, the central core of modern political ethics is the maintenance of a democracy. And in that sense, the democratic socialist parties were in complete agreement. They sought to broaden the process and to make fully representative political decisions more important than those of the market.

FOR FURTHER READING

This chapter explores the origins of modern politics in Europe by focusing on three individuals who were important in shaping our understanding of the state and its relationship to different social forces: monarchs, clergy, elites, the middle class, the nation, and the people. Students should recognize that there are many other ways to search for the meaning of modern politics. There are numerous volumes on the Italian Renaissance and on the English revolution and Civil War that form the background to the ideas discussed here. One could also study the development of constitutional states, middle-class polities, or the "politics of process" by focusing on the French, American, and Atlantic revolutions. There is also increasingly a rich literature that puts the political revolutions of early modern Europe and the Americas into a larger global context. Jack A. Goldstone's *Revolution and Rebellion in the Early Modern World* is a good place to start. Charles Tilly's *Coercion, Capital, and European States* AD *990–1992* takes a longer chronological perspective. William H. McNeill's *The Pursuit of Power* and Geoffrey Parker's *The Military Revolution* emphasize the role of military organization and technology in the rise of the European state system.

To pursue this chapter's approach to modern politics through the great theoretical texts, one should begin with the texts. There are numerous editions of *The Prince* in print, but for a full understanding of Machiavelli, one should also read his *Discourses*, also widely available. Isaiah Berlin's "The Originality of Machiavelli," in his *Against the Current*, is a classic. Sebastian De Grazia's *Machiavelli in Hell* and J.G.A. Pocock's *The Machiavellian Moment* are rich interpretations. Maurizio Viroli's *Nicola's Smile: A Biography of Machiavelli* argues that Machiavelli's life reveals a principled diplomat who was actually appalled by the way in which power politics had been played in the continual wars of France and the Holy Roman Empire over Italy.

For an overview of Hobbes' life and work see R. Tuck, *Hobbes*. For historical background of the period, see Maurice Ashley, *England in the Seventeenth Century*. I have followed the argument of C. B. MacPherson in *Possessive Individualism*. For opposing arguments and different interpretations, see I. Berlin, "Hobbes, Locke and

Professor Macpherson," *Political Quarterly*, 1964, Norberto Bobbio, *Thomas Hobbes and The Natural Law Tradition*, Leo Strauss, *Natural Right and History* and *The Political Philosophy of Hobbes*, Howard Warrender, *The Political Philosophy of Hobbes*, and David Gauthier, *The Logic of Leviathan*.

For a series of essays on both Hobbes and Locke, which is also at variance with this chapter, see *The Social Contract Theorists: Critical Essays on Hobbes, Locke, and Rousseau*, edited by Christopher W. Morris. These essays incorporate a current scholarly appreciation of "contract theory," a view which is most effectively presented in the work of John Rawls' *A Theory of Justice* and David Gauthier's *Morals by Agreement*.

On Locke, I have also followed C. B. Macpherson. For other approaches, Ruth Grant's *John Locke's Liberalism* is an interesting recent interpretation. John Dunn's *The Political Thought of John Locke: An Historical Account of the Argument of the 'Two Treatises of Government'* argues that Locke was primarily a theological thinker. Willmoore Kendall's *John Locke and the Doctrine of Majority Rule* is a conservative classic. Another classic is J. W. Gough's *John Locke's Political Philosophy: Eight Studies*.

NOTES

1. Niccolo Machiavelli, *The Prince*, trans. Luigi Ricci (New York: Random House, 1950), p. 3.
2. *Ibid.*, p. 56.
3. *Ibid.*, pp. 29–30.
4. *Ibid.*, pp. 31–32.
5. *Ibid.*, p. 32.
6. *Ibid.*, p. 54.
7. Ernst Cassirer, *The Myth of the State* (New Haven: Yale University Press, 1946), p. 131.
8. *Ibid.*, p. 137.
9. *Ibid.*, p. 138.
10. *Ibid.*, p. 143.
11. Thomas Hobbes, *Leviathan*, edited by A. R. Waller (Cambridge: Cambridge University Press, 1904), p. 58. Cited in C. B. Macpherson, *The Political Theory of Possessive Individualism* (London: Oxford University Press, 1962), p. 37. Much of the argument is based on Macpherson's stimulating book.
12. Hobbes, p. 55. Cited in Macpherson, p. 37.
13. Hobbes, p. 179. Cited in Macpherson, p. 96.
14. John Locke, *Second Treatise*, in *Two Treatises of Government*, edited by Peter Laslett (Cambridge: Cambridge University Press, 1960), p. 304. Cited in Macpherson, p. 200.
15. Locke, pp. 304–306.
16. Cited in Macpherson, p. 223.

Work
and
Exchange

Capitalism
Versus Tradition

If the modern state poses new questions about morality, the modern capitalist economy raises new questions about reality. The capitalist economy has transformed
modern society perhaps even more than the state.

What is capitalism? Where, when, and how did it originate? What problems of
working and exchanging has it solved? What relation does it have to freedom,
democracy, and our high standard of living? What relation does it have to problems
of inequality, jobs, health, environment, and productivity? Has it made us more
free? Does it create jobs? Does it give us more pay and leisure? We will try to answer
some of these questions in this chapter.

BEFORE CAPITALISM:
TRADITIONAL WAYS OF WORKING AND EXCHANGING

Capitalism has been defined in a lot of different ways. Any useful definition, however, must describe a series of very recent economic developments in Western history over the last five hundred years or so. It will not do to think of capitalism as
an eternal or universal economic system. Nor does it make sense to think of capitalism as the system which satisfied basic or natural human needs. The fact is that

101

a capitalist economic system is the exception rather than the rule. It was a new twist in European history after the Middle Ages and it has matured as a recognizable system only in the last couple of hundred years.

One of the best ways of seeing the uniqueness of our modern capitalist, market, or business civilization is to examine the ways in which economic activities—like working and exchanging—have been carried out in most of the other places and periods of human history. Anthropologists have found an enormous variety of economic activities in tribal and traditional peasant societies. One anthropologist, Manning Nash, has written:

> The economic life of man shows a great variety over time and space. In the New Hebrides islands (in the South Pacific), the main economic concern is the accumulation of pigs. Men raise pigs, exchange pigs, lend out pigs at interest, and finally in a large ceremonial feast destroy the pig holdings of a lifetime. Among the Bushmen of the Kalahari desert (in Southern Africa) there is no private property in productive goods, and whatever the hunting band manages to kill is shared out among the members of the group. In the Melanesian islands every gardener brings some of the yams from his plot to the chief's house. There the pile of yams grows and grows, and eventually rots, to the greater glory of the tribe. The Indians of Guatemala and Mexico live in communities each with its own economic specialty. One group produces pottery, another blankets, another lumber and wood, and the next exports its surplus maize (corn). These communities are tied together in a complex system of markets and exchange.[1]

There is so much variety in the economic lives of pre-capitalist societies that we are sure to find an exception to almost every generalization. Despite this difficulty, however, there are enough similarities among most of these societies to enable us to distinguish between pre-capitalist and capitalist societies.

We have referred to capitalist society as market society. We should be careful of using these terms too loosely. In the passage just quoted Manning Nash pointed to the existence of "a complex system of markets and exchange" in the peasant societies of Mexico and Guatemala. Indeed, there have been markets of some kind in almost all peasant societies, and some of the first cities were essentially markets—especially for exchanging produce of the countryside, crafts of the city, and imports from far away. Despite this, our notion of modern, capitalist society as a market society is still very useful. The reason for this is the pervasiveness of market relationships in capitalist society. To a great extent, all of the relationships of capitalist society tend to be market relationships. Ideally the market becomes in capitalist society a kind of "invisible hand" that supervises and determines all social relations. "Everything is for sale," said a visitor to America in the late twentieth century. "Everyone is treated like a customer—a buyer or seller." That is the sense in which market society was evolving in England in the seventeenth century. That is what Thomas Hobbes noticed in embryo.

PREMARKET EXCHANGE: HOUSEHOLDING, RECIPROCITY, AND REDISTRIBUTION

A market is a system of distribution or exchange. There are other systems too. In fact, for most of human history the market has been only a minor method of distributing and exchanging. Most past societies have relied on systems of exchange which some anthropologists have called "householding," "reciprocity," and "redistribution." In modern, capitalist society the market has replaced most of these earlier forms.

Householding is one of the oldest forms of exchange. The term reminds us of how goods are distributed in the average family household—even to a certain extent today, but much more generally in traditional, farming society. Everyone works, and everyone shares in the produce of the work. This system makes most sense to us in the family. It does not occur to the parents to refuse to feed the children because they do less work; the children have no need to buy or barter their upkeep: it is expected. Prices are not attached to goods and services. The job is done, and everyone benefits.

It may surprise us to realize that householding has been a fairly typical method of exchange in societies much larger than the family. Actually, however, it has worked among extended families, clans, tribes, and other large groups of people throughout history. Householding is essentially the production of goods for use—rather than for sale or gain. In a sense, most pre-capitalist societies have practiced a kind of householding. The ancient Greeks called it *œconomia*—the root of our word for economy. Aristotle insisted that the essence of *œconomia* was the production for the use of the group—householding. He argued that this had nothing to do with producing for gain, money, or profit through the market: such activity was very different from "economics." Today in capitalist society we define economics in exactly the opposite way.

Householding, production for use and distribution within the group, was the norm in the feudal societies of the Middle Ages as well. The medieval manor was a self-sufficient unit of production and distribution. Markets were largely irrelevant outside of the cities. The manor household, like the Roman *familia* or the Greek clan, could operate quite independently of markets. The degree of authority exercised in production and distribution varied considerably. The Roman head of the household was often something of a tyrant. So were many Western medieval lords. But that was not inevitable in householding. The southern Slav *zadruga* households, for instance, were very democratic. The politics of decision making—about who gets what—are very different from the economics of common work for common use. Manors, families, and communes can be anything from tyrannies to democracies.

A society can allocate resources and exchange goods like a large household. Perhaps most societies have. Within that household of society, and with other households or even strangers, societies have traditionally practiced some form of reciprocity or redistribution.

Reciprocity is an anthropologist's word for giving. The members of a group who think of themselves as a household give their work and the fruits of their work to the other members. They expect that the other members will return or reciprocate the gift; and the other members do what is expected. Reciprocity has often worked in tribal societies of many households as well. One of the favorite examples of anthropologists is the custom until recently of the Kwakiutl Indians of the Canadian Pacific. The Kwakiutl astonished American anthropologists, like Ruth Benedict in Patterns of Culture (1934), because their custom of gift giving seemed to be such a parody of American capitalist culture's getting and taking. Kwakiutl Indians achieved prestige in their society by giving away or even destroying more property than their rivals. Periodic festivals, "potlatches," were the occasions for a Kwakiutl to show off great wealth by giving it all away. Anthropologists have interpreted this "riches to rags" custom as a way of distributing the property—boats, beads, fish oil, and more important names, songs, and titles—more equally among the tribe. The potlatch among the Kwakiutl, and similar practices of giving or destroying property among many societies, was a system of exchange and a system of periodic leveling or equalizing. The custom ensured that everyone would be taken care of, and that no one would be too rich or powerful too long.

Reciprocal exchange was perhaps also the earliest kind of foreign trade. The classic example is the Kula ring exchange of the Trobriand Islanders who inhabit a ring of islands in the Pacific near New Guinea. Each exchange of hard goods, like pigs, yams, canoes, and pottery, is preceded by the ceremonial exchange of armbands and necklaces that the traders value much more highly. The necklaces travel clockwise, and the armbands counterclockwise, around the ring of islands. Some of the shell ornaments are highly prized. They are all thought to be much more valuable than the pigs or canoes. The Trobriander would describe the acquisition of one of these ornaments as the real purpose of the trade. But there is no bargaining for them. There can be no hoarding. Everyone has a season to own each object and then pass it on.

Reciprocal giving and taking is most common in the poorest and simplest of societies. But reciprocity is such an ingrained value in primitive and peasant societies that it fades slowly. Even today in parts of South America, Africa, and Asia that have not yet been commercialized by market attitudes and institutions, people work and live without money as if they were part of a large reciprocal family, An Egyptian who grew up in a small village says that he was surprised to learn when his family moved to Cairo that he needed money to pay for haircuts, shoes, or food. In the village the son of the barber was given bread by the baker, the son of the baker had his shoes mended by the shoemaker, and the son of the shoemaker had his hair cut by the barber, all without money, promises, or notations in an accounting book.

In Cairo he needed money, but even there credit, charity, and gifts were a normal part of life. That same Egyptian in the United States struggles today with whether or not to send "thank you cards" when he stays at the homes of other Egyptians in the United States. "To say 'thank you,'" he says, "is an insult because it ends a 'transaction.' We Egyptians are used to taking hospitality for granted. Things that are expected are not 'thanked.'" Perhaps "thank you" is our commercial society's polite, but weak alternative to reciprocity. In the less commercialized countries of the world the words "please" and "thank you" are rarely used. That may be a sign of more mutual concern rather than of less politeness, or maybe politeness itself is a sign that genuine feeling has disappeared—"virtue gone to seed" Ralph Waldo Emerson called it.

Redistribution is a kind of institutionalized reciprocity. Redistribution also involves giving and taking without prices, bargaining, money, or calculation. But redistribution is less voluntary or spontaneous. Normally, it is carried out by the chief, king, ruling officials, or other specialized agencies. Surplus goods are collected, like taxes, and held in a central store, bank, or granary. In the complex bureaucracies of ancient Mesopotamia, Egypt, India, China, and the American kingdoms of the Aztecs and Incas, large storehouses were maintained for grain, wine, pottery, cloth, ornamental objects, art work, and other goods. Frequently in the case of these empires, the goods were used to support the state bureaucracy, soldiers, and the ruling elite, as well as the emergency needs of the people. In less complex feudal societies, with a less oppressive or top-heavy bureaucracy, both collection and distribution were often more democratic. In some tribal societies, without even a feudal upper class, collection was quite voluntary and distribution benefited everyone but the chief. There was a standing joke among early anthropologists who studied American Indian tribes that you could always find the chief by looking around for the poorest man. Apparently the demands of redistribution could be so great that the chief would give away everything he could collect, leaving himself only the prestige of the tribe.

An account of redistribution among the Creek Indians in the eighteenth century shows how democratic the system could be. Before they carry off

> their crops from the field, there is a large crib or granary, erected in the plantation, which is called the king's crib; and to this each family carries and deposits a certain quantity, according to his ability or inclination, or none at all if he so chooses; this in appearance seems a tribute or revenue to the micro [chief], but in fact is designed for another purpose, i.e., that of a public treasury, supplied by a few voluntary contributions, and to which every citizen has the right of free and equal access, when his own private stores are consumed, to serve as a surplus to fly to for succour, to assist neighboring towns, whose crops may have failed, accommodate strangers, or travellers, afford provisions or supplies, when they go forth on hostile expeditions, and for all other exigencies of the state.[2]

Premarket economic systems of exchange—householding, reciprocity, or redistribution—could be voluntary or forced, democratic or imposed. That depended on the degree of social equality or class stratification and on the extent to which power was shared or monopolized. The important difference between all premarket and market systems is that the premarket systems minimized strictly economic behavior. There was really no such thing as economics or economic activity in premarket society. Everything that we would call economics was understood simply as an aspect of social life. Tradition, religion, custom, and human relationships were the cause and context of working, exchanging, providing, and allocating. One did what was expected. Work, produce, and material goods were not ends in themselves, but means to the life that was sanctioned by one's family, clan, tribe, or village.

THE ORIGINS OF CAPITALISM:
MARKETS, LOGIC, AND DESIRE

The theorists of emerging capitalist society, from Thomas Hobbes to Adam Smith, imagined that selfishness, competition, bargaining, and private ownership were eternal traits of human nature, characteristic of all of human history. The discoveries of human diversity and evolving economic institutions, which we discussed in the previous section, were largely discoveries of the nineteenth century. There were forerunners, of course. One thinks of the recognition of diversity and change in the writings of Montesquieu or Vico in the early eighteenth century. But it was probably the experience of the industrial revolution in the nineteenth century that made European thinkers generally aware of the importance of human change—especially economic change. The nineteenth century was the golden age of historical study, the age of the study of evolution and origins, and the first age to suggest that human nature itself might have changed from one age to the next. The world of Darwin and Marx and anthropology could no longer imagine that the inclinations or institutions of capitalist society had existed for all time.

Defenders of the new economy in the nineteenth century—groups like the English Manchester liberals and utilitarians who spoke for the middle class of merchants and manufacturers—developed a new assumption of the naturalness of capitalist ideas and behavior which was more consistent with the historical consciousness of their age. They reasoned in effect that although capitalism had not always existed, the instinctual need and logic of capitalism had always existed, and that history was the development of that desire and logic. Their ideas were so influential that they have become almost the "common sense" of twentieth-century Americans. They imagined that primitive trading had merely become more complex over the years, that people gradually found it easier to attach price tags or money values to the things they bartered, and that local trade led to national and finally international trade as the new knowledge of marketing techniques grew. In effect, these defenders of the new system were arguing that if capitalism had not always existed at least a natural human inclination to barter had become more sophisticated. In many ways this was yet another version of human nature.

Many of us still today assume that capitalism developed logically from the inside out, from the simple to the complex, from the local to the foreign, and from the small scale to the world scale. We assume for instance that barter exchanges among friends led gradually to more efficient money exchanges, that local trade became more monetized as it became more complex, that such capitalist institutions as money, markets, prices, profits, and private property expanded from village to city to state to world as they proved their superiority over simpler ways. There is something very comforting in that assumption. It allows us to think that ideal capitalism began among friends, that it originated in small groups, and that it expanded naturally and gradually because people wanted it to. There is a good deal of comfort in knowing that things have happened in accordance with both logic and human desire.

Actually, however, nothing is further from the truth. One of the most amazing things about the history of capitalism is that most people fought every step of its expansion. The clergyman, the artisan, the farmer, the villager, the worker, the landlord, the tenant, and even many of the slowly emerging middle class fought the expansion of capitalism because it seemed to come from outside to threaten the local and the traditional ways.

The nineteenth-century defenders of capitalism were not completely mistaken, however. There was a kind of logical inevitability in the expansion of capitalism.

The logic was the expansion of markets. Market prices were less debatable than barter, and clearer than haggling. Once certain things were bought and sold, a special effort was necessary to prevent people from buying and selling other things. The quest for profit in one commodity or in one area led to negotiations in others. Markets did not have to expand. In fact most ancient civilizations prevented their expansion. But once they were allowed to expand, all of society was increasingly opened to its logic. For that reason we can trace the evolution of capitalism in the development of market society from the first markets.

Markets existed in the most ancient cities. Caravans of merchants often worked out the first roads that connected one urban civilization with another. But the ways of merchants and markets were never important in the internal economies of ancient civilizations. Outside of the urban market square it is not even correct to talk of economies. The word suggests a separate realm of activity that did not even exist in the rest of the city or the countryside. Working and exchanging in accordance with traditions of householding, reciprocity, and redistribution were simply aspects of the rest of life, subject to the same habits and personal relationships as marrying, worshiping, playing, and feuding.

Market society did not come into existence until the ways of the market permeated the whole fabric of working and exchanging. In traditional agricultural society this was all but impossible. Peasants did not even need the city's market. Those who brought a couple of eggs or a blanket into the city on market day were as happy to return with it as to sell it. If anyone had suggested turning their agricultural lives into a gigantic market where they sold their labor as time, bought and sold land as if it were eggs, or used their tools and their skills to make money, they would have been appalled. Yet it was precisely this commercialization and monetization of labor, land, and capital that did occur.

Medieval Europe of 1000 was as unlikely a seedbed for commercialization as were the ancient empires of a thousand or a couple of thousand years earlier. Just as Aristotle had reflected his age's view of the "life of craftsmen or of traders" as "devoid of nobility and hostile to perfection of character," and just as Cicero had expressed a typical Roman view that "those who buy wholesale in order to sell retail" lead "sordid" lives "because they would gain no profits without a great deal of lying," so did the Christian thinkers of medieval Europe condemn the values and activities of the marketplace. "The merchant can scarcely ever be pleasing to God," was the medieval dictum. "It is wholly sinful," Saint Thomas Aquinas wrote, "to practice fraud for the express purpose of selling a thing for more than its just price, inasmuch as a man deceives his neighbor to his loss. The doctrine of the "just price" (a "fair" price that did not take advantage of scarcity or an intermediary's shrewd-ness), the prohibition against usury (which first meant lending money at any inter-est), and the general medieval suspicion of money and merchants combined with the agricultural self-sufficiency of medieval society limited commercial activity to towns and periodic fairs.

How then did Europe become a market society? Historians point to a number of changes in European society after 1000 to account for the expansion of market ways and values. Cities multiplied, expanded, and increased their hold over the coun-tryside almost continually after 1000 (though urban population declines in the fourteenth-century Black Death may have also spurred technological innovation and commercial experimentation). The Crusades introduced Europeans to Eastern markets, luxury goods, commercial techniques, and enough booty to set up thou-sands of soldiers as entrepreneurs in pepper, spices, and other commodities. Euro-pean navigational, shipbuilding, and gunpowder technology outdistanced the Isla-mic and Chinese by 1500. European kings suppressed local trade barriers, fought rebellious nobles with national armies, and created national economic policies and industries. A whole new middle class of merchants, bankers, and manufacturers, richer than many nobles, bought respectability for their activities, their projects, and their ideals. Poor and perceptive nobles commercialized their lands by con-verting ancient manorial dues into fixed money rents and by enclosing lands that the peasants had used in common (e.g., half of the arable land of England) for their own use as more profitable sheep pasturage. Protective fellowships of medieval craftsmen (called "guilds") became competitive industries hiring landless labor as employees instead of training apprentices and journeymen to eventually take over.

Before 1500 the institutions of market society—money, prices, profits, private property, wage labor, and competition—were developing within the bounds of a feudal society. Feudalism had been a system of laws, customs, and political loyalties that made sense in the decentralized, agrarian, manorial economy of the Middle

Ages. Market society required and encouraged a whole new set of legal, social, and political institutions and ideas which we can call capitalism.

Capitalism was the system which gave legal, political, and social sanction to land, labor, and capital as separate market entities, convertible into money terms or prices. In feudal society, a person did not buy land, sell labor, or invest capital for the most part because they each were aspects of life rather than economic categories. Land was home, fields, or place, not real estate. Labor was activity, chores, or giving birth, not time and effort for sale. "Capital" was not even used to indicate the cattle or plows that were the peasant's or community's investment in future productivity.

When people say that capitalism is a system of private-property ownership, they mean the private ownership of capital—the productive resources of the society. They do not mean the private ownership of personal property like clothes and furniture. That sometimes causes confusion. Almost all societies have recognized the private ownership of personal property. Capitalism recognized the private ownership of what the medieval person would almost call public property—the large scale tools and resources or capital upon which future productivity depended. (Thus, when socialists talk about the abolition of private property they usually mean factories, corporations, banks, and television stations, not televisions, cars, and personal property.) To say that capital is privately owned is to say that it is not owned by everyone, but by the few who are capitalists.

Capitalism did not suddenly replace feudalism after 1500. Even by 1700 the market society had not attained the sanction of laws that legitimated land, labor, and capital as separate economic entities. Serfdom was not formally abolished in France until the revolution of 1789. Guild regulations in England, like the restriction of only two apprentices to each master hatmaker, were in effect until the repeal of the Statute of Artificers in 1813. The English industrial and commercial middle class were not fully represented in Parliament until the passage of the Reform Bill of 1832. Even today in the United States, the most advanced capitalist country in the world, there are still laws which restrict the full commercialization of life: Sunday blue laws in some states curtail shopping time; prostitution is illegal in most places; one cannot use private property or draw up a contract for absolutely any purpose that buyer and seller desire. The market is not even yet entirely supreme legally, politically, and socially. The tendency of capitalism to extend and legitimate the market in all ways of life is still not completed.

We can, however, get some idea of the opposition that capitalism faced in its youth if we look more closely at some of these examples of incomplete development today. Blue laws and anti-prostitution laws are clearly on the way out. There is almost a logical inevitability to the expansion of Sunday shopping and the legalization of prostitution. Opposition almost always seems to counter reason and evolution. If people can buy coffee on Sunday, then why not whiskey? If they can shop on Saturday, then why not on Sunday? Are we legislating what people should drink? Are we penalizing Saturday workers or American Muslims who have a Friday sabbath? The same is true of prostitution. Is not legalization preferable to hypocrisy, turning poor women into criminals, and possibly increasing the spread of venereal disease? The market is imperial. And its expansion is almost always more equitable, rational, and fair. The market eliminates black markets, prejudice, hypocrisy, and inefficiency. But its rush to equalize in commerce also takes its toll of human values: the sanctity of marriage and the family, the need for spiritual renewal, personal loyalty, friendship, and love. We may object to human beings becoming consumers and gamblers instead of sons and lovers, but each step of that protest is as futile, backward, and even illogical as the protests of peasants and artisans centuries ago.

CAPITALISM: WORK AND PAY, PRICES AND PROFITS

We are used to thinking that we work less and receive more in a capitalist economy. But the evidence is not that clear. Anthropologists are often amazed at how little time the people of primitive and traditional societies spend working. More than a hundred days of labor seems to be quite rare. Christopher Hill, the English historian, has computed that the average English worker of 1530 worked only 14 or 15 weeks for the year's needs. Two and a half centuries later, a full 52 weeks of over 12-hour days were fairly typical for the working classes. Similarly, a tabulation of the average real wages of English carpenters from 1250 to 1850 shows interesting fluctuations but no general improvement. The average wages (translated into kilograms of wheat) look like this:

    1251–1300 81.0
    1301–1350 94.6
    1351–1400 121.8
    1401–1450 155.1
    1451–1500 143.5
    1501–1550 122.4
    1551–1600 83.0
    1601–1650 48.3
    1651–1700 74.1
    1701–1750 94.6
    1751–1800 79.6
    1801–1850 94.6[3]

This table shows us that the English carpenter received the same real wages in 1850 as in 1300. His income increased until about 1450, then declined precipitously from 1450 to 1650, and only gradually returned to the thirteenth-century level by 1850. Further, there are indications that this pattern was a European, not just an English, phenomenon. The great French historian Fernand Braudel writes:

From 1350 to 1550 Europe probably experienced a favourable period as far as individual life was concerned. Following the catastrophes of the Black Death [1348–1350] living conditions for workers were inevitably good as manpower had become scarce. Real wages have never been as high as they were then. In 1388, canons in Normandy complained that they could not find anyone to cultivate their land "who did not demand more than what six servants made at the beginning of the century." The paradox must be emphasized since it is often thought that hardship increases the farther back towards the middle ages one goes. In fact the opposite is true, as far as the standard of living of the common people— the majority—is concerned. . . . The deterioration becomes more pronounced as we move away from the "autumn" of the middle ages; it lasted right up to the middle of the nineteenth century. In some regions of Eastern Europe, certainly in the Balkans, the downward movement continued for another century, to the middle of the twentieth.[4]

Braudel's magnificent *Capitalism and Material Life 1400–1800* is full of statistical and literary evidence to support this conclusion. To take only two examples on the single issue of the consumption of meat—so dear to the stomachs of Europeans: there were 18 butchers in the small town of Montpezat in 1550, 10 in 1556, 6 in 1641, 2 in 1660, and only 1 in 1763; and after 1550 there were far more than the usual accounts of the "good old days" when "tables at village fairs and feasts sank under their heavy load," and "we ate meat every day."[5] Whether we mark the decline from 1450, 1500, or 1550 (and it certainly varied from place to place), one thing is clear. The standard of living of the majority of Europeans declined drastically with the rise of a capitalist or market economy. For this was precisely the period in which the ways of the capitalist market replaced those of traditional feudal society.

It would be foolish, of course, to date the origins of capitalism at 1492 because of Columbus's voyage or at 1494 because of the Italian invention of double-entry bookkeeping. A single year, even a single century, is too precise dating for anything so complex. Karl Marx, who began the historical study of capitalism, saw the first beginnings of capitalist production as early as the fourteenth or fifteenth century, sporadically, in certain towns of the Mediterranean but marked the capitalist era from the sixteenth century. The year 1500 may be useful, but symbolically.

Recently economic historians have turned their attention to charting price movements since they are usually a fair indicator of economic activity, and this course seems more fruitful than searching for specific beginnings. Furthermore, old ledgers and account books are full of the prices of things, and modern computer techniques make their compilation and comparison relatively easy. This is what they have discovered, From about 1150 to 1300 there was a rapid rise in prices. As we have seen, this was a period of general prosperity. Population increased, new lands were opened for cultivation, and economic production rose—but all pretty

The spread of gin drinking in England in the eighteenth century was both a result of and a metaphor for the spread of market society. Gin oiled the way to social irresponsibility in much the way money did. And it destroyed the poor before it atomized the entire society. This is William Hogarth's famous "Gin Lane" etching of 1750. (The Metropolitan Museum of Art, Harris Brisbane Dick Fund, 1932)

much within a feudal economic and social system.

Then from 1300 to 1450 prices fell. Marxists, who are keen on revolutionary "turning points" where one historical stage dies before another is born, refer to this period as the crisis of feudalism. The figures seem to support something very much like that. The feudal economy may have reached a point (like the Roman slave economy a thousand years earlier) where the system had passed its capacity for exploiting. Feudalism, according to the Marxists, had lasted as long as the feudal barons and clergy could extract an increasing economic surplus (work, food, dues, etc.) from the peasantry in order to keep themselves in the style to which they had become accustomed—often a style of lavish waste. After the depopulation that accompanied the Black Death (1350), the remaining commoners were more powerful. In fact, there were numerous peasant revolts in this period, and we have seen from Braudel and von Bath that the commoners' living standard peaked. Unable to get more work from the peasants, and without a machine technology to replace them, the feudal ruling classes may indeed have reached the limits of the system. As feudal incomes declined, the nobility sent their sons on interminable wars in search of land and booty and borrowed heavily from the new class of merchants and bankers that we spoke of before. Thus—and the Marxist argument is still convincing here—power may have begun to shift from the old feudal class to the new entrepreneurial money class.

It is clear, in any case, that the period from 1450 or 1500 to 1650 was one of phenomenal price rises (inflation). This had a lot to do with the influx of gold and silver from the Americas. The kingdoms of the Aztecs, Mayans, and Incas were ransacked by feudal sons from Spain. Then more gold and silver were mined in Mexico and South America by imported African slaves. Much of the gold, silver, and treasures filled Spanish and Portuguese royal treasuries. But there was so much left for commercial circulation that it fueled one of the greatest inflations that the world had ever known. The bullion probably saved feudalism in Spain and Portugal, but by raising the price level throughout Europe it forced the destitute lords of England and France to deal in the money men and commercialize their own estates. Landlords who were smart enough to adopt the values of the market saved themselves by cutting corners. They studied new methods of cultivation and new ideas of property management. They cut their costs, improved their yields, and brought their surplus to markets for profit. But the easiest corners to cut were the plots of their tenant farmers. In England, the Netherlands, and France (where population increased as quickly as prices) the feudal obligations of numerous peasants were converted into rents. Common lands that had for centuries been used by the villagers and tenants were taken over (or enclosed) by the landlords. Peasants who had barely survived with small plots and an animal or two on the commons found themselves unable to continue. A new class of landless workers was created—people without ancestral rights who could work only for others and for money. In Eastern Europe, the squeeze came as a renewed second serfdom. There peasants were not freed to be poor; their feudal obligations increased with their poverty.

We have seen how the living standard of European farmers and workers was wrecked by the drastic inflation of the long sixteenth-century price revolution. The bullion of the Americas was crucial in inflaming the inflation. But neither gold nor inflation must necessarily destroy the well-being of the people. If the European class structure had been egalitarian enough so that the new bullion could be distributed evenly, all Europeans would have been richer at the expense of the American losers. European peasants would have been able to use the gold to buy Arabian coffees, Indian teas, or Chinese spices and silks. Alternatively, their mercantilist governments would have been able to use the bullion to develop national industries that could have made the lives of all Europeans easier. But the bullion did not enter an economically democratic society. It entered a society where the old feudal ruling class was in debt, and neither they nor the royal governments were as wealthy as the evolving merchant, financial, and industrial classes. As usual in a class-divided society, the new wealth went to the old wealth. And the entrepreneurial class that knew money and its uses used the new money effectively. Merchant adventuring companies and joint stock companies were created to establish new mines and plantations, build ships, carry on trade, and eventually create the factories and goods of the industrial revolution.

Fernand Braudel noticed the crucial fact about the European expansion that began after 1492: "the gold and silver of the New World enabled Europe to live above its means, to invest beyond its savings."[6] No society develops economically or technologically without saving some of the productive capacity of the present in order to build capital for the future. Merchant ships, machines, or factories can only be built if people consume less (or spend less of their energy and resources on immediate consumption). Investment in future productivity requires savings. Thanks largely to the resources and inhabitants of the Americas and the inhabitants of Africa, Europe was able to invest beyond its savings. The gold and silver savings of centuries of American Indian labor, and the forced labor of native Americans and Africans in mines and plantations, allowed some Europeans to begin the massive investment in future productivity that culminated in the industrial revolution.

Since the more a society saves and invests, the more productive it becomes, and consequently the more it is able to save and invest, some historians have spoken of "takeoff" stages of economic growth. Western Europe experienced its first takeoff into sustained economic growth in this period, 1500–1650. Although much of the bullion was wasted in an economic sense (that is, not invested in future productivity), much of it also fueled economic and technological development. This was especially true of England, so much so that historians have frequently noticed a first industrial revolution in England between 1540 and 1640 that preceded the great industrial revolution by over a century.

"During the last sixty years of the sixteenth century," the historian John U. Nef has written, "the first paper and gunpowder mills, the first cannon foundries, the first alum and copper factories, the first sugar refineries, and the first considerable salpetre works were all introduced"[7] into England. "Between 1540 and 1640," he adds, "the process of iron-making assumed a new and highly capitalistic form," iron output increased several times, coal output increased at least eightfold, and the issue of mineral rights became as much of a political issue as the enclosures of farm land. Private mills and manufactures which employed a thousand workers were not uncommon.

Thus, the period from 1500 to 1650 was one in which a general rise in the price level of three or four times (15 times on the Paris wheat market) both reflected and fueled a capitalistic economic takeoff. In this period capitalists commercialized agriculture, incorporated huge trading companies, banked the mercantilist policies of monarchs, and began applying their fortunes to large-scale industrial production. In this period Europe became the richest and most powerful amalgam of states in the world. Royal, national, and private fortunes were made that had been rare for emperors of the past. And yet—remember von Bath and Braudel—this was precisely the period in which the income and standard of living of the average European declined drastically. The English carpenter had less than a third of the real income in 1650 that he had enjoyed in 1450. Like the African, the American Indian, and the serfs of the European periphery, the common people in the core of capitalist economic growth paid for that growth while others reaped the profits.

We can see the same contradiction between capitalist economic growth and popular living standards if we follow the historians of price movements from 1650 to 1850. Very roughly, the period from 1650 to 1750 was one of falling prices accompanied by declines in population, food production, economic activity, and profits. It was, however, a period in which the English carpenter doubled his real income. Conversely, the period from 1750 to 1850 witnessed rapidly rising prices, population, production, and profits. This was the period of gigantic increases in energy, income, and technological productivity—the full industrial revolution. And average incomes remained constant despite the fantastic new wealth. The conclusion seems inescapable. Capitalist economic productivity has thrived on the sacrifices of the mass of people in order to benefit the few.

After 1850, of course, the industrial technology itself was more than adequate to provide a rising standard of living for descendants of those who made the important initial sacrifices. It did that for some Europeans and North Americans. That it did not do so for the rest of the inhabitants of the world market economy may have been due more to the failures of the economic system than to the limits of the technology.

CAPITALISM AND THE INDUSTRIAL REVOLUTION

The capitalist economic growth of 1500–1650 was mainly agricultural and commercial rather than industrial. The countryside was transformed into large estates geared to production for market while peasant farmers were dispossessed, often becoming landless day laborers for wages. The largest fortunes, besides those of the landlords, accrued to merchants, traders, and their financial backers, rather than to industrialists as yet. Commercial capitalism was supplanted by industrial capitalism

European colonization in the sixteenth and seventeenth centuries provided the bullion, plantations, and trading stations that later enabled European industrialization and global dominance.

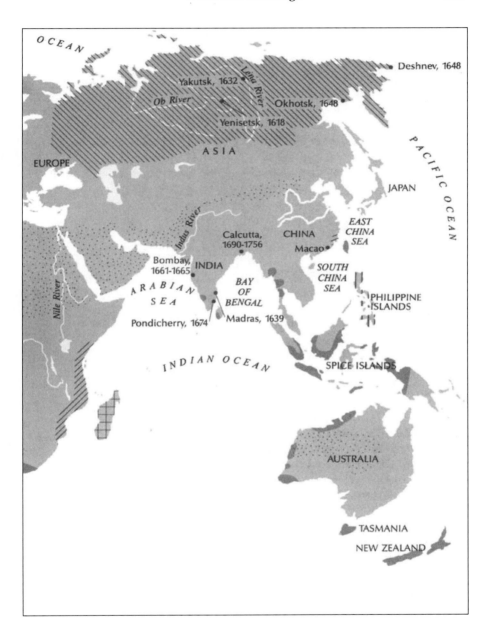

in the process of the great industrial revolution that began after 1750.

We have only to look at the countries of the contemporary developing world to see how difficult it is to conduct an industrial revolution on a capitalist basis. Over and over again, in Russia, China, and the Third World, industrialization has taken a collectivist or state-sponsored form. How, then, was it possible for the emerging nations of the eighteenth century to industrialize when no one imagined what an industrial revolution might be (the term was not invented until the 1820s), and when the competing interests of capitalist society fought against collective, planned action?

The answer lies in the peculiarities of Britain at the end of the eighteenth century, because it is unlikely that the first capitalist industrialization would have occurred anywhere else. The English had a government that was sympathetic to the interests of private capitalists and industrial development. English agriculture was efficient enough to support a large class of potential workers. Population pressure had been steep enough (and enclosure movements ruthless enough) to ensure a vast quantity of cheap labor after 1750. But, perhaps most significantly, Britain emerged victorious from two centuries of military and naval conflict (first with the Spanish and Dutch, and then with the French) by 1763, which gave it access to the markets and resources of most of the world from India to the Americas.

England in the 1780s (even after the political loss of the United States) was in a position similar to Spain in the 1500s. But while the Spanish nobility choked itself on the booty of colonialism, the English industrial class made money. The British cotton industry was the key. It grew with the English conquest of India, the slave trade, the cotton plantations of the Caribbean and the Americas, and the huge market of its colonies. Indian cottons (calicos) were recognized as the finest in the world. The English East India Company (agents of the older style commercial or trading capitalism) sold the Indian cloth throughout Europe. Some of the profits went from Liverpool into the slave trade and the Caribbean plantations. Eventually the merchants of Liverpool were outfoxed by the textile mill owners of Lancashire. When Indian revolts interrupted the calicos, Lancashire bought Caribbean cotton and gradually took over the trade. The old vested interests of the East India Company and Liverpool merchants were finally undermined as the producers secured from Parliament import bans on calicos. Industrial capitalism took over. Between 1750 and 1769 British cotton exports increased over ten times. By 1820 the British were exporting over 200 million yards of cotton. By 1840 they exported that much to Europe alone, and over another 500 million yards to the colonies. Even the ancient Indian industry was systematically deindustrialized to become a market for Lancashire cotton. India took 11 million yards in 1820 and 145 million by 1840.[8]

Cotton was more appropriate to lead an industrial revolution than anyone could have known at the time. With slave labor on the plantations the cost of raw materials was miniscule. Slaves did not have to be paid anything close to the value of their work. English spinners and weavers were numerous, disorganized, and consequently also cheap. Under the earlier domestic "putting out" system, many had learned spinning and weaving at home in order to augment their incomes. Then there was no overhead for the merchants who simply brought them raw materials and bought the finished products. But domestic production was never extensive enough to trigger an industrial revolution. It would never have developed into the mass production which creates its own demand. The worldwide English markets offered the possibility of seemingly insatiable demand. Every slave, every Indian, every South American could be sold a shirt. Thus, cotton, combined with world dominion, was one industry where goods could be produced cheaply on a massive scale. Conversion from domestic to factory production was also relatively simple and cheap. The construction of factories, spinning wheels, and weaving looms could be financed out of profits, because the profits were enormous. Robert Owen started with a borrowed £100 (about $200) in 1789, and twenty years later he was able to buy out his partners with £84,000 in cash. Even the technology of cotton was ideally suited to an industrial takeoff. It benefited enormously from slight improvements. The spinning jenny, the water frame, and later the power loom were adaptations of existing machinery that required little scientific insight and paid for themselves in vastly increased production.

Far more than any other new industry, cotton propelled the British industrial revolution. In 1830 the words "industry" and "factory" were practically synonymous with cotton production. In 1833, 1.5 million people were employed in cotton production. Between 1816 and 1848 cotton amounted to 40 or 50 percent of British exports. Cotton was both wind and weather vane of the British economy. It caused and signaled the successes and contradictions of capitalist industrialization.

Its successes were extraordinary. The world was supplied with cotton clothing in vastly greater quantities and at cheaper prices than would ever have been thought possible before. Between 1785 and 1850 British production of cotton cloth increased from 40 million to over 2 billion yards per year. While production increased over 50 times, the price of cloth dropped to about one-tenth of the 1785 level. Competition not only exploded output and trimmed prices, it also forced an endless series of inventions. In cotton spinning alone there were 39 new patents between 1800 and 1820, 51 in the 1820s, 86 in the 1830s, and 156 in the 1840s. Creative energies were unleashed that transformed human productivity more completely in 50 years than in the previous five hundred—perhaps even five thousand.

CAPITALIST CONTRADICTIONS AND CONTRACTIONS

But in the midst of success, there began to appear contradictions in the capitalist economy which were also of imposing scale. The age-old cycle of economic expansion and contraction, which had previously been caused by long-term fluctuations in population growth or by natural catastrophes and agricultural failures, was intensified, shortened, and given artificial human causes. For the first time productivity, rather than want, caused economic contraction. Success in the competitive market depended on continually expanding growth. Without coordination or planning, with only market prices as a guide, entrepreneurs were inevitably drawn to what was momentarily the most profitable enterprise. In the early nineteenth century that was cotton. Because the cotton industry was competitive, many could enter with modest capital; and many did because the profits were so high. But competition cut prices. Costs were more constant. So profit margins shrank. In 1784 the selling price of a pound of spun cotton yarn was 11 shillings, the raw cotton was 2 shillings, leaving a profit margin of 9 shillings. That margin tempted so many that by 1812 the selling price had been trimmed to 2-1/2 shillings, but the cost had been reduced to only 1-1/2 shillings, leaving only a single shilling profit. And since businesses are easier to enter than leave, each entrepreneur had to sell nine times the quantity of 1784 to do only as well. For many that was actually possible in 1812. Expansion was enormous, but a saturation point always loomed on the horizon. By 1832 the selling price had been cut to 1 shilling and the cost of raw cotton to a little more than half a shilling, leaving a profit margin of less than half a shilling. Volume had to increase 18 times, and that was asking too much. By the 1830s and early 1840s, the market that seemed so insatiable was becoming absorbed. The falling rate of profit could no longer be compensated by multiplied sales. The competitors had priced each other out because the market could not continue to expand at a multiplying rate. Indeed, no market can.

There were also social contradictions to this competitive struggle. The gradually tightening profit squeeze forced entrepreneurs to try to cut costs by improving machinery and reducing wages. As a result, the technological capacity of the society (its wealth, power, and energy), and the wealth of the already wealthy, increased as the wages of the poor declined. The average weekly wage of the hand-loom weaver in Bolton declined from 33 shillings in 1795 to 14 shillings in 1815, and then to 5-1/2 shillings in 1829–1834.

Poverty amidst affluence: that was the hallmark of capitalist industrialization. By the late 1830s and early 1840s the saturated cotton market brought about the first industrial depression, forcing five hundred thousand handloom weavers to starve and a much smaller number of successful entrepreneurs to find a place to invest fortunes which totaled about 60 million pounds a year. Some of the capitalists spent their profits on luxuries and large estates and mansions in an attempt to ape the style of the aristocracy. But far more of this new money class were savers rather than spenders. That is how they had been successful (even when they were forcing others to save), and that is what they hoped to continue to do. If they had all behaved like aristocrats, the windfall profits might have left England in the 1850s not much more productive than Spain in the seventeenth century.

RAILROADED TO THE RESCUE

The industrial takeoff continued because cotton profits were invested—almost by chance—in an industry which would create a stock of capital goods that would transform the world and keep the process going. That industry was railroads. The railroad solved a problem of capitalist industrialization that few could have foreseen at the time. More accurately it answered a whole series of questions that sprung from the contradictions of capitalist expansion. Looking back now we can ask those questions. How is it possible for a private enterprise economy to develop a capital goods capacity (that complex of iron- and steelworks, heavy machinery, transportation and communication networks that full industrialization requires) when individual investors, unlike governments, compete in already existing markets for the greatest immediate return? How can individual investors be induced by the market to sink their money into expensive productive facilities that are socially useful but not very profitable? How to keep the economy going, so that it can rebound from each depression? And, what can be done with all of that money that was made by a few—even in the midst of economic collapse?

From the standpoint of the investors of the 1830s and 1840s the question was what to do with their money—that £60 million per year. Giving it to the poor was out of the question, of course, and that would not be a good investment even in a social sense: it wouldn't increase productivity. South American loans were big in the 1820s, but by the 1830s many of them were worthless pieces of paper. Railroads seemed an unlikely alternative. They returned not the hundreds or even thousands percent profits of early cotton expansion, but only 3.7 percent in 1855. The answer is that rails were really the only alternative. There was simply too much money to invest in any other way. And, as John Francis said in 1851, the railroad's "absorption of capital was at least an absorption, if unsuccessful, in the country that produced it. Unlike foreign mines and foreign loans, they could not be exhausted or utterly valueless."[9]

No doubt the otherwise irrational "railway manias" of investment in 1835–1837 and 1844–1847 were also enflamed by promoters and speculators who catered to the fantasies of the new class for speed and power. The railroad became the symbol of the age and its movers. Even the shrewdest, most calculating investor sometimes puts his money where his heart is. Actually, the market may have played only a secondary role in luring investment where it was needed. And in the United States it was government subsidy (including land grants of over 130 million acres or 7 percent of the nation) combined with Congressional bribes that made rail investment profitable.

Private enterprise, public enterprise, or passion—whatever the reason—the railroad was just what was needed to channel huge profits into productive investments, create a capital goods industry and a transportation network, revive the economy, and send it soaring. Between 1830 and 1850 world railroad mileage rose from a few dozen to 23,500. In the same period British output of both coal and iron tripled. The techniques for the mass production of steel followed naturally in the next decades.

The history of the English industrial revolution between 1780 and 1850, its formative stage, reminds us of the difficulties of capitalist industrialization. We have grown so used to crediting the wealth of industrial society to capitalism, that we have to be reminded from time to time that capitalism and industry are not synonymous. It is possible that the first industrial revolution could not have been achieved in a noncapitalist economy. The power of even the strongest mercantilist rulers in the eighteenth century was probably not sufficient to bring about collectivist industrialization—and besides, the middle class was too willing to play a role. But capitalist industrialization was not entirely a private affair. National mercantilist policy, tariffs, and encouragement were essential. And the private free enterprise aspects of the capitalist industrialization were often mindlessly unplanned and socially disastrous. The highly organized state-planned industrializations of Russia and China in the twentieth century may have sacrificed a generation of workers and peasants. But the unplanned, chaotic, profiteering industrializations of England and the West may have been just as humanly expensive over a longer time.

FOR FURTHER READING

The subject of this chapter is one of the most contentious among world historians today. All agree that the economic rise of the West (Europe and North America) has been a major factor in modern world history, but the timing and causes of that development are widely debated. At one extreme stands the traditional argument that this process of Western economic growth, the *European Miracle* as Eric Jones called it, began long ago and had its roots in distinctive European ideas and institutions. The best statement of this position is David Landes's very readable *The Wealth and Poverty of Nation*. At the other extreme are books like Andre Gunder Frank's *ReOrient* and Kenneth Pomeranz's *The Great Divergence*, which argue that the European economy did not eclipse the Chinese until the nineteenth century, and that even them it was based on a certain amount of luck and plunder rather than any long term European cultural advantage. In support of this position, James Blaut's *The Colonizer's Model of the World* disputes every claim to Europe cultural precociousness and traces the rise of Europe to its conquest of the Americas. More temperately, R. Bin Wong's *China Transformed* shows how Chinese development before 1850 was on a different, but not necessarily slower, track than Europe's.

For medieval and early modern Europe, Robert S. Lopez's *The Commercial Revolution of the Middle Ages, 950–1350* and Carlo Cipolla's *Before the Industrial Revolution: European Society and Economy, 1000–1700* are excellent introductions. Lopez's *The Birth of Europe* as well as Cipolla's *Money, Prices and Civilization in the Mediterranean World* are also very valuable. Robert-Henri Bautier's *The Economic Development of Medieval Europe* is especially well illustrated.

The alternative to these studies which stress early European capitalist economic development has not been to deny it, but to put it a global context, a process that began with Fernand Braudel's magnificent three volume *Civilization and Capitalism: 15th–18th Century*. Janet Abu-Lughod's *Before European Hegemony* outlined the global economy from 1250–1350. K. N. Chaudhuri's *Asia Before Europe* painted layers of material civilization across the Indian Ocean region before European colonization. Philip Curtin's *Cross-Cultural Trade in World History* called attention to trading "diasporas" in Asia. James Tracy's *The Rise of Merchant Empires* brought together essays on long-distance trade between 1350 and 1750. Dennis Flynn and Arturo Giraldez's collection of essays in *Metals and Monies in an Emerging Global Economy* demonstrated the degree to which the global economy was integrated by silver flows before 1800. For a recent brief summary of much of this work, see David Ringrose's *Expansion and Global Interaction 1200–1700*.

Still, for most historians, the industrial revolution was unequivocally European and the decisive launch for the rise of the West. For introductions to the industrial revolution as a stage in technological history see James E. McClellan III and Harold Dorn's *Science and Technology in World History*, Arnold Pacey's *Technology in World Civilization*, and Joel Mokyr's *The Lever of Riches*.

For the social and political background of industrialization, E. J. Hobsbawm's *The Age of Revolution 1789–1848* is a classic. Changes in social class are discussed in Peter N. Stearns's *European Society in Upheaval* with almost startling clarity. On England, E. P. Thompson's *The Making of the English Working Class* is the classic.

World historians have begun to study the industrial revolution as a global process. Peter Stearns's *The Industrial Revolution in World History* is a useful starting point as is his brief pamphlet *Interpreting the Industrial Revolution*.

NOTES

1. Manning Nash, "The Organization of Economic Life," in *Horizons of Anthropology*, ed. Sol Tax (Chicago: Aldine, 1964), p. 171.
2. Adapted from William Bartram, *The Travels of William Bartram*, ed. Francis Harper (New Haven: Yale University Press, 1958), p. 326.
3. Slicher van Bath, *Agrarian History of Western Europe* A.D. *500–1850*, trans. Olive Ordish (London: Edward Arnold, 1963), tab. 1, p. 327.
4. Fernand Braudel, *Capitalism and Material Life 1400–1800*, trans. Miriam Kochan (New York: Harper Row, 1967, 1973), pp. 129–130.
5. *Ibid.*, pp. 130–31 and pp. 195–96, respectively.
6. Braudel, "European Expansion and Capitalism: 1450–1650," in *Chapters in Western Civilization*, 3rd ed. (New York: Columbia University Press, 1961), vol. 1, p. 285.
7. John U. Nef, "The Progress of Technology and the Growth of Large Scale Industry in Great Britain, 1540–1640," *Economic History Review* 1 (1934), reprinted in *The Industrial Revolution in Britain* (New York: Heath, 1958), p. 8.
8. These figures and much of the following discussion are drawn from E. J. Hobsbawm, *The Age of Revolution 1789–1848* (New York: New American Library, 1962), pp. 56–66.
9. *Ibid.*, p. 67.

Chronological Table of a Unified World, 1500–1800

Europe	Americas	Africa and Islamic World	Asia
			Chinese Ming dynasty 1368–1644
Machiavelli 1469–1527 (w. *The Prince* 1513)			Japanese Warring States 1467–1600
Martin Luther 1483–1546			Wang Yangming and neo-Confucians 1472–1529
Western naval superiority a. 1500	Decline of American empires b. 1500	Ismail Safavi becomes Shah 1500	
Rise of capitalism a. 1500	Destruction of Native American empires 'by arms and disease a. 1500		
Drastic inflation 1500–1650	Gold, silver taken, mined 1500–1650		
John Calvin 1509–1564	Cortés conquers Aztecs 1519	Suleiman the Magnificent r. 1520–1566	
Shakespeare 1564–1616 (w. *Othello* 1604)		Indian Akbar r. 1556–1605	Japanese "sword hunt" and Christianity banned by Toyotomi Hideyoshi 1556–1598
		Revival of Kanem-Bornu by Idris Alawamo r. 1575–1610	
Hobbes 1588–1679 (w. *Leviathan* 1651)		Persian Shah Abbas the Great 1588–1629	

Europe	Americas	Africa and Islamic World	Asia
Mercantilism 1600–1789	North European colonization; Iberians lose monopoly 1600–1648	Moroccan conquest of Songhay 1590	Japanese Tokugawa 1600–1868
Locke 1632–1704 (w. *Two Treatises* 1690)		Indian Shah Jahan r. 1628–1657	Japan closed to foreigners 1630
English Civil War 1640–1649			Dutch defeat Portuguese at Malacca 1641
	English ascendance 1655–1763		Chinese Qing dynasty 1644–1911
English Glorious Revolution 1689			Kangxi r. 1662–1722
Peter the Great's Russian reforms (r. 1682–1725)		Rise of Ashanti in West Africa c. 1700	
		Decline of Safavid Empire 1737–1747	British defeat French in India at Plassey 1757
English Indian empire and cotton a. 1763			
Adam Smith 1723–1790 (w. *Wealth of Nations* 1776)	Declaration of Independence 1776	Spread of Islam by Fulani in Africa 1776–86	Qianlong r. 1776–1798
Industrialization, rising prices, profits, productivity 1750–1850			
French Revolution 1789–1800			
Whitney's cotton gin 1792	Rise in cotton slave plantation a. 1792		Chinese White Lotus Rebellion 1796–1804
	Simón Bolívar 1783–1830		

a. = *after*   *b.* = *before*   *w.* = *wrote*   *r.* = *ruled*

Auguste Rodin, Le Penseur [The Thinker], 1888. Bronze.

✖ II ✖

An Industrial World

1800–1914

German engine factory near Berlin, 1847

Preview of the Period
1800–1914

If a Martian who had visited the earth two hundred years ago were to return today, what changes would be most startling? Certainly the sheer number of people and the extent of human settlement would be a shock. In 1800 world population was under a billion. Today it is about six billion. In 1800 there were large areas of the world uninhabited or sparsely settled by humans. The Martian would wonder what had happened to the forests and the animals, all apparently replaced by people.

There would be many other surprises as well. Temperatures are warmer than they were in 1800. People are taller. There are more old people and more fat people. Most people look healthier and are better clothed.

Two other facts would leap at the visitor. The first, and most obvious, is the number of *things* in the world today. Big things and little things, personal things and public things, things ranging from pocket radios and wristwatches to airplanes and skyscrapers have multiplied like cancer cells since 1800. The other fact, which would require a little travel to notice, is that the placement of these things is not even throughout the world. In fact, the differences between the average household possession of things vary enormously. This was not the case in 1800. One measure of this, "standard of living," which was roughly equal in most parts of the world in 1800, is now said to be eight times higher in the "industrial" world than in the "developing" world.

The Industrial Revolution. If one had to designate the three most important turning points in world history, they would be the agricultural, urban, and industrial revolutions. If one had to designate the hallmark of modem society, it would be industrialization. We introduced the subject in the previous unit because the industrial revolution began to

129

define Western society before 1800. Initially an English phenomenon, industrialization rapidly became a European, an Atlantic, a Western, and, after 1900, a global phenomenon. In one sense, it was a global event from the start, unlikely to occur without the slaves of the Caribbean, the control of India, and the access to the world markets and material of the British Empire. While Britain's empire and inventions often take pride of place, North America was an important part of that empire even well into the nineteenth century. It was part of the British labor supply, and depot of capital and labor.

The history of the English industrial revolution is often recounted in terms of the particular inventions that made it possible. Among these are James Kay's flying shuttle (1733), James Hargreave's spinning jenny (1765), James Watt's steam engine (1769), Richard Arkwright's water frame (1769), and Eli Whitney's cotton gin (1791). This is a useful catalog. We might learn more about the process of industrialization, however, by concentrating on some of the larger forces at work. Although their dates are less certain, these would include the displacement of farmers and farm laborers, the growth of a class of urban workers, the replacement of household industry by factories, and the explosion of mass-produced goods at fiercely competitive prices and wages.

Few countries have purposely avoided industrialization. Its promise of material improvement is attractive to all. The appeal of the British model of industrialization, however, is less universal. Even the industrialization of the United States and Western Europe departed somewhat from the British model. Abundant land and labor played a more significant role in the United States. The peasantry (small landholding farmers) stayed on the farms longer in France. The landed aristocracy was stronger in Germany. Both peasantry and aristocracy slowed the speed of industrialization, urbanization, and the spread of middle-class values. While North American and continental European industrialization began a generation after the British, by the mid-nineteenth century most industrial societies were going through canal and railroad building, depressions, financial concentration, and mass-market merchandising together. By 1914, in fact, the later industrializers had a youthful edge. After the destruction of European labor and capital during World War I (1914–1919), the United States became the preeminent industrial power in the world.

The state played a greater role in the industrialization of Germany in the nineteenth century than elsewhere in the West. State direction was even more significant in the industrialization of Japan and Russia. While both began the process in the later nineteenth century (Japan after the Meiji Restoration in 1868 and Russia under Count Sergei Witte in the 1890s), the Japanese victory in the Russo-Japanese War (1904–1905) showed that Japan was further advanced.

Western Dominance. The industrial revolution enabled Europe and North America to colonize and dominate the world. Colonialism advanced on ships, roads, and rails, with Bibles and muskets, from the Pacific islands to the African interior. By the end of the nineteenth century European powers were absorbed in a feverish competition for foreign colonies in which diplomats, and later armies, placed considerable national stake. But the result of European and North American dominance was to internationalize the world, to teach the same values and build the same furnaces from Maui to Malacca.

It is useful to distinguish between two stages of Western dominance between 1800 and 1914. Between 1800 (actually, 1776 might be a better date) and 1873 we can speak of an age of a "free trade empire." In this period, first Britain and then other Western powers found it most satisfactory to dominate their colonies with a minimum of outright political control. Adam Smith's *The Wealth of Nations* and the American Revolution (both in 1776) showed that the principles of free trade were sufficient for a stronger economic power to dominate the weaker. Ownership of colonies was both unnecessary and expensive. When, as in the case of England, one ran the "workshop of the world," there was no need to encourage trade barriers or worry about competition. This was a lesson that took the English a while to learn after the initial loss of the American colonies. But it soon became clear that those former colonies would continue to need British goods and capital long after independence.

Increasingly, however, the state had to step in. Troops

had to be sent to China when the Chinese refused to allow the British to sell opium (in the Opium War of 1839–1842). The British East India Company, faced with an Indian "mutiny" (1857), had to relinquish control to the British government, and India became the jewel in the crown of Queen Victoria's British Empire. A second form of dominance arose.

Since Western government control was extended over many of the former free trade colonies after the European depression of 1873, the age of "new imperialism" (1873–1914) has often seemed to have been an attempt to secure foreign economic markets. However important such economic needs were, the political and military seizure of colonies in this period was fueled by militant nationalist propaganda (that in 1914 led to World War I). Between 1880 and 1914 most of Africa was partitioned by Britain, France, Germany, and even Italy. Spheres of influence and "foreign concessions" were carved out of China. The French secured French Indochina, today's Vietnam, Laos, and Cambodia (1885). The United States secured control of Cuba, Puerto Rico, the Philippines (in the Spanish-American War, 1898), and the Hawaiian islands (in a separate action the same year). Even industrializing Japan began its expansion into Taiwan (in the Sino-Japanese War of 1894–1895), Russia's Sakhalin island (1895), and Korea (1905).

The new imperialism was the high point of military occupation, territorial acquisition, and imperial dominion by the West. It rested on enormous technological superiority: machine guns over Zulu spears, steam-driven metal battleships against wooden Chinese junks. It unified and divided the world, making the European war of 1914 the First World War. Imperialism did not end with the war, however. It merely abated. It is not until after the Second World War (1939–1945) that we can speak of an age of decolonization.

Colonial Worlds. Not all the non-Western world was colonized between 1800 and 1914. As we have seen, Japan joined the colonizers. The Ottoman Empire governed the Middle East and North Africa with a different kind of colonialism. Few countries—Siam (Thailand) was one—escaped colonization completely. There were many similarities in the lives of the colonized: the surprising brutality and philanthropy of the colonizers, the tensions between traditional and Western culture, the appeal and seduction of Western material life, language, law, and liberalism, and all of the gnawing contradictions of "improvement" by the overseer in "preparation" for self-government.

But the colonies were also different areas, each with its own culture before colonization and after. Thus, we must look at each of the culture areas separately.

Latin America. Most of Latin America achieved political independence from Spain and Portugal between 1807 and 1830. Much of Latin American economic life, however, was determined by Britain until 1900 (despite the pleas of the Monroe Doctrine in 1823) and by the United States afterward. Latin America was the classic free trade empire in the middle of the nineteenth century. It produced wheat, beef; tropical products, such as coffee and bananas; and raw materials, such as copper, nitrates, and guano (for fertilizer) at prices determined by the free market (and European demand). In return it received manufactured goods made by industrialized Europe. As a result, there was no industrialization in Latin America, and the economy became increasingly agrarian, devoted to a few export crops, and dependent on the large landowners and foreign markets. When these markets collapsed in the 1920s, Latin America had no mixed economies or industrial structure to rely on.

Politically, Latin American countries flirted briefly after independence with liberal republics. But popular leaders like Bernardo O'Higgins of Chile (r. 1818–1823) threatened vested interests of property and church and were replaced by conservative *caudillos*, usually leaders from the army who ensured that no social revolution would occur. The exceptions to this rule were Brazil, where the reign of Emperor Pedro II (from the Portuguese royal family, 1830–1889) was followed by a republic and the dictatorship of Getúlio Vargas (1930–1945), and Mexico, which underwent a social revolution in 1910.

The Mexican revolution followed a series of inept rulers including Antonio López de Santa Anna (r. 1822–1855), the emperor Maximillian (r. 1864–1867), and Porfirio Díaz (r. 1876–1911). Before 1911 there were only brief moments of liberal reform, most notably under Benito Juarez (1861–

1864). The popular leaders of the revolution were Emiliano Zapata (1879–1919) in the south and Pancho Villa (1874–1923) in the north. They were controlled by the liberal Francisco Madero, who was killed by the United States–backed General Victoriano Huerta in 1913. After a bloody civil war, a wealthy landowner with the support of U.S. President Wilson, Venustiano Carranza wrote a constitution that consolidated a modest revolution (1917). In 1934 Lázaro Cárdenas was elected president and carried out extensive land reform and the nationalization of oil.

Argentina was dominated by the large cattle ranchers even into the early twentieth century as the city of Buenos Aires filled with immigrants from Europe. The *caudillo* who gave voice to the urban working class was Juan Perón (1895–1974), who had the support of military leaders who were favorably impressed with European fascism.

Thus, in most of Latin America there was no social revolution to accompany political independence. As a result, the landholding class increased its power throughout the period, and the peons sank further into debt. Only in racial policy could Latin America be considered liberal. Slavery was abolished by 1855 everywhere except for Brazil (where it continued until 1888).

The real powers remained, however, the large landowners, the military, the church, and foreign corporations and governments. These powers came later to Central America, where there was less Spanish settlement, slavery, and plantation agriculture in the colonial period. Not until coffee farming was introduced, in the mid-nineteenth century, were many Indians expelled from communal lands in Central America. Later, large tracts of land were assembled by wealthy cotton and sugar planters from small corn and bean plots that had made peasants self-sufficient. This later consolidation of power came when the United States was the chief power of the hemisphere, and it thus depended on U.S. corporations and arms. U.S. troops landed in Honduras five times between 1905 and 1925; they landed in Panama four times between 1908 and 1918. The United States controlled Nicaraguan trade revenues between 1911 and 1949, and repeatedly occupied the country between 1912 and 1932. The U.S. policy of "dollar diplomacy" supported the interests of U.S. companies, like United Fruit, and allied unpopular dictators against popular peasant and plantation-worker uprisings. This reimposition of political and economic control on countries that were politically independent is sometimes called neo-colonialism.

North Africa and the Middle East. If Latin American countries went from independence to neo-colonialism between 1830 and 1914, the countries of the Islamic world of North Africa and the Middle East went from one kind of colonialism to another. They passed from the hands of the Ottoman Empire to those of western Europe. This process began even before 1800, with Napoleon's invasion of Egypt in 1798. He was defeated in 1815, but French influence in the Middle East remained strong until the defeat of Napoleon III by Germany in 1870. Then, except for continuing French influence in Algeria, England and Russia dominated the Middle East (the former in Egypt and Persia, the latter in northern Persia and Turkestan).

The Ottoman Empire was close enough to Europe, and yet still sufficiently independent, to borrow successful European techniques and adapt them to its own defenses. This included early movements (after Peter the Great of Russia) to "Westernize." There were different forces of Westernization. Balkan orthodox merchants were a force for Westernization that the Ottoman Arab dominions (except Syria) generally lacked. More typically, the rulers of the provinces of the Ottoman Empire attempted modernization from the top down. Turkey developed a Western army at the direction of Sultan Selim III (r. 1789–1807), but the Janissaries regained power. Then Mahmud II (r. 1808–1839) reintroduced a Western army, and the Tanzimat legislative movement (1839–1860) introduced Western-style schools, press, and political forms. From the army came the Young Turks of 1908 and the radical Westernization of Mustafa Kemal "Atatürk" (r. 1922–1938) after World War I. The reforms of Atatürk (the abolition of Muslim courts and Islam's official role, and the adoption of the Swiss civil code and woman's suffrage, among others) made Turkey the most secularized of former Muslim states.

Similar efforts were made in the mid-nineteenth century in Persia and Egypt. The relatively independent governor (or *pasha*) of Egypt, Muhammad Ali (r. 1805–1849), introduced aspects of Western army organization, agriculture, industry, and education that set Egypt on a clear

Western course, but his successors' spending led to a financial crisis and outright British occupation for forty years (1882–1922).

Not all Muslim leaders preferred Westernization. Some intellectual leaders, like al-Afghani (1839–1897), argued that Muslims should adapt Western accomplishments to Islam. Muslims should study Western science, he said, because "science belongs to no nation," its only parents being proof. At the same time, al-Afghani rejected Western materialism and secularism. Other Muslims urged the entire rejection of the West, root and branch, and the return to fundamentalism, or the authority of the *ulema*.

Sub-Saharan Africa. As in the Middle East, European imperialism generally followed Muslim cultural domination in Africa south of the Sahara. Before the European partition of Africa in the 1880s, Muslim powers extended their influence in the Sudanic area almost as far south as the equator. Some of these movements were Muslim *jihads*, led by charismatic reformers like Usman Dan Fodio (1754–1817), who directed the conquest of most of the Hausa lands of Nigeria. Others were African "secondary empires" that took advantage of European weaponry and military styles, like Muhammad Ali's conquest of the Sudan.

European settlement of Africa before 1880 was limited, for the most part, to the French in Algeria and the Dutch (and some French Protestant Huguenots) in South Africa. Between 1880 and 1914 European governments cut the entire continent up into colonies, showing no concern for traditional African ethnic boundaries.

There was very little difference in practice between the British system of "indirect rule" through selected intermediaries (which the British called chiefs) and the French direct rule of Africans. There was a difference, however, between those colonies with a large European population and those that were only lightly settled. European settler states were often more developed, and more repressive toward Africans, than colonies that were not heavily settled. The most extensive European settlement was in South Africa, where Europeans made up about 10 percent of the population; Rhodesia had 5 percent, and Kenya 1 percent before World War II.

The wrenching experience of colonialism for individuals was in some ways greater in Africa than elsewhere. This is because of the relative importance in Africa of limited and stateless societies. More of the colonial experience in Turkey or China may have been cushioned by indigenous states. In African cities, European tongues, religion, money, and manners became the media for communication with other Africans as well as with the Europeans in authority. As a result, Westernization was less voluntary and less questioned outside of Muslim areas.

European Colonial Empires in Asia. European colonialism was more complete in Asia than in Latin America or the Middle East, but probably not as severe as in sub-Saharan Africa. The impact of Europe varied. The British completely colonized India. English became the second language of all educated Indians; the British educational and legal systems prevailed; the subcontinent was entirely reshaped politically. The French were as thorough in colonizing French Indochina. The Dutch in Indonesia played a similar role. At the other extreme of European influence was Japan: the country ended its isolation after the landing of Commodore Perry in 1853, but managed its own modernization after Tokugawa in the Meiji Restoration of 1868. The colonization of China lay in between. China was never conquered by European powers, but Western (and Japanese) spheres of influence, concessions, and port cities sapped China of any possible independence.

The story begins in India. The British East India Company received a charter to trade in "the Indies" in 1600; it set up its first warehouse on the Indian coast in 1608. A series of military victories over Indian rulers and French colonials gave Britain supremacy by 1763. Until 1772 Company administrators plundered India for their own benefit. A parliamentary reform act in 1773 placed the first regulations on the company, which, thanks to the enlightened administration of Warren Hastings (1772–1784) as governor general, became more solvent and extended its control from Bengal throughout northern India. An Indian rebellion in 1857 by their Sepoy soldiers finally led the British crown to take over the *raj* (rule) of India.

If Britain in the eighteenth century robbed India of much of her capital (treasures, jewels, and precious metals), nineteenth-century Britain undermined her industrial potential and self-esteem. If British industrialization did not depend on the accumulated capital of the eighteenth century, it certainly benefited from the restriction on Indian textiles and the borrowing of Indian clothes and dyes in the nineteenth century. Increasingly after 1800, Britain saw her role in India as that of guardian rather than plunderer. At the same time, the earlier policy of the East India Company to respect Indian culture and religion was reversed. English education was introduced in 1835. English and Indians were increasingly segregated as Britain undertook its mission to civilize and enlighten.

Paternalism backfired. As British policy became more aggressively "protective" of Indian interests, and more committed to "Westernizing" India, Indian grievances mounted. By the end of the century tens of thousands of Indians had attended colleges, many in Britain, where they were educated as British gentlemen. On their return they had little opportunity to exercise the citizenship they had studied. In 1885 the Indian National Congress was formed. Its leaders, Gopal Krishna Gokhale (1866–1915), Mohandas Gandhi (1869–1948), and Jawaharlal Nehru (1889–1964) worked toward the gradual realization of independence and self-government. Gandhi, through force of will and personality, steered the congress and nation with a radically disarming policy of passive resistance to British authority. In his hands, a simple act like scooping salt from the ocean took on revolutionary meaning in the context of a British salt tax and a march to the sea by millions. Gandhi embraced the untouchables and Muslims, but independent India was to contain the former and not the latter. Muhammad Iqbal (1873–1938), Muhammad Ali Jinnah (1876–1949), and other Muslim spokesmen found it impossible to choose secular nationalism over Muslim commu-nity. Thus, the independence of India and Pakistan in 1947 was accompanied by mass migration and murder as Muslims struggled to get to Pakistan and Hindus to areas in India.

The effects of European colonial policy in China were different in degree and speed of execution rather than in kind. The Opium War is an important part of the story. The British were losing silver in the unfavorable balance of trade that brought British products to India, Indian cotton to China, and Chinese tea to Britain. Not until Britain found a product with an ever-increasing demand—opium

Commodore Perry meeting with the Japanese to make a trade agreement, 1853. (New York Public Library)

—did the balance reverse and silver begin flowing from China to Britain. In 1836 the Chinese banned the sale of opium, closed the dens in which it was smoked, and demanded death sentences for opium dealers. In 1839 Commissioner Lin Zexu [Lin Tse-hsu], sent to Canton to enforce the ban, proved so effective that the British went to war. The Opium War raged from 1839 to 1842. British cannon bombed Chinese ports, and British troops occupied Chinese cities, forcing the Chinese to surrender. The Treaty of Nanking in 1842 gave the British Hong Kong and access to five other ports, and gave British citizens protection under British law (extraterritoriality). In 1844 similar treaties were signed with the United States and France that also permitted Protestant and Catholic church activities.

The humiliation of China and the concessions to Western governments led to the Taiping Rebellion (1850–1864), probably the largest mass revolt in world history. Between twenty million and thirty million people died (in addition to thirty million who died in Muslim rebellions and natural disasters during the same period). The Taipings used a combination of ancient Chinese writings and Protestant tracts to call for a "Heavenly Kingdom of Great Peace" where all the "foreigners" would be thrown out and all Chinese, women as well as men, would be equal and uncorrupted. While the Manchu government was eventually successful in defeating the rebels, it never fully recovered.

Another anti-colonial rebellion, the Boxer Rebellion in 1900, was more specifically directed against the Western occupying powers, gained the partial support of the dynasty, and was suppressed by foreign troops who then occupied Beijing [Peking]. As a result of the defeat by the Japanese in 1895 and the increasing power of the rural Chinese gentry (large landlords), the Manchu dynasty fell on October 10, 1911.

Japanese history is a story of colonialism avoided. The policy of closing Japan to foreign influence had been successful during most of the Tokugawa era (1600–1868). After 1800, however, American whaling ships and merchant vessels bound for China made Japanese isolation increasingly difficult. In 1853 the American Commodore Perry appeared. The following year he returned with a quarter of the United States navy (eight ships), asking for ports to be opened for trade. A treaty was signed in 1858. Britain wanted the same treatment. A British official was murdered by samurai. Western ships were fired upon. It was less than twenty years after the opening skirmishes of the British Opium War in China, and so things could have gone badly. The Japanese were unaware of events in China and of the significance of the American ships. But, perhaps fortuitously, internal events in Japan were bringing an end to the feudal Tokugawa system and leading to the restoration of the Meiji emperor in 1868. Perhaps also fortuitously, about half of the leaders of the new government in 1871 decided to travel to Europe and the United States to get the unfavorable treaties rescinded. When they returned in 1873, after visiting Western factories, schools, and parliaments, they were committed to modernizing Japanese society along Western lines. In rapid succession, they abolished the samurai class and created a national draft army, converted the old grain tax to a money tax, created national and local assemblies and political parties, and adopted a constitution (based on the conservative Prussian model of 1850).

In 1894 Japan finally ended extraterritorial rights for foreign residents. But perhaps nothing impressed the West as much as the succession of Japanese military victories after 1890: first the Japanese use of modern naval tactics in sinking the Chinese fleet in the Sino-Japanese War (1894–1895); then the effective participation of Japanese troops, along with European troops, in suppressing the Boxer Rebellion; and finally the Japanese defeat of Russia (1904–1905). These convinced Western powers that Japan was to be counted among the colonizers rather than the colonized. In 1910 Japan formally annexed Korea, and by the early 1930s it occupied Manchuria and much of northern China.

✣ 5 ✣

Energy
and
Environment

Industry
and Capitalism

What is responsible for the disregard of nature that has led to our environmental and energy problems? Here we focus on the most obvious, immediate causes of the modern problem: industry and capitalism. The industrial revolution, almost everyone agrees, has been the basic underlying cause. By suggesting that capitalism may be an alternative explanation, we do not mean to suggest that industrialization is not significant. The question is only whether or not capitalism aggravated the dramatic rupture with nature that industrialization brought about.

The problem is a practical one. Hardly anyone seriously proposes a return to pre-industrial, handicrafts industries. Even if a few North Americans can put up with that, the masses of people in the developing world will not. They want industrialization. So the question is how we can continue industrialization in a less exploitative way. That is why we ask about capitalism. Is it possible that a less capitalist industrialization could be more careful of limited energy supplies and less hostile toward the environment?

THE INDUSTRIAL REVOLUTION IS RESPONSIBLE?

Almost everyone agrees that the rise of modern science (after about 1500) made possible the series of inventions that we call the industrial revolution. Lewis Mumford, who shows how the early scientists attempted to subject all of organic nature to mechanical laws, puts it this way:

> What was left was the bare, depopulated world of matter and motion: a wasteland. In order to thrive at all, it was necessary for the inheritors of the seventeenth century idolum to fill the world up again with new organisms, devised to represent the new realities of physical science. Machines—and machines alone—completely met the requirements of the scientific method and point of view: they fulfilled the definition of "reality" far more perfectly than living organisms. And once the mechanical world-picture was established, machines could thrive and multiply and dominate existence: their competitors had been exterminated or had been consigned to a penumbral universe in which only artists and lovers and breeders of animals dared to believe. Were machines not conceived in terms of primary qualities alone, without regard to appearance, sound, or any other sort of sensory stimulation? If science presented an ultimate reality, then the machine was the true embodiment of everything that was excellent. Indeed in this empty, denuded world, the invention of machines became a duty. By renouncing a large part of his humanity, a man could achieve godhood: he dawned on this second chaos and created the machine in his own image; the image of power, but power ripped loose from his flesh and isolated from his humanity.[1]

The scientists stole the life from nature in order to understand it. Then they were forced to fill the world with creatures, and the only creatures they understood were those which followed scientific laws—that is, machines. That's a bit simple, perhaps. But Mumford's analysis at least emphasizes the historical link between modern science and its offspring, the machine technology of the industrial revolution. It is true that the scientists were interested primarily in knowledge while industrialization was a process of harnessing knowledge for practical results. But even the most religiously motivated scientists imagined their work led to an increase of human power. One of the first modern European scientists, Sir Francis Bacon (1561–1626), insisted that knowledge was, after all, power. We might understand the world so that we could control it. The proof of science, ultimately, was in the technology it produced.

The industrial revolution would also have been impossible without the two guiding ideas of modern science: that humans were separate from nature, and that they could control this separate natural world. The industrial revolution was the application of modern science to technology. Machines could only take over human work after the machine became the model of the natural world. This required not only viewing the objects of the organic world as machines, but also the elimination of the human element from the organic world of time and space.

INDUSTRIALIZATION: MECHANICAL TIME VERSUS ORGANIC TIME

Lewis Mumford suggests that the first requirement for the creation of a machine age was the invention of mechanical time to take the place of organic or natural time. Time had to be understood in terms of its component parts; it had to be divided up. This was accomplished by the invention of the clock.

> The clock, not the steam-engine, is the key-machine of the modern industrial age. For every phase of its development the clock is both the outstanding fact and the typical symbol of the machine: even today no other machine is so ubiquitous. . . .
>
> The clock . . . is a piece of power-machinery whose "product" is seconds and minutes: by its essential nature it dissociated time from human events and helped create the belief in an independent world of mathematically measurable sequences: the special world of science. There is relatively little foundation for this belief in common human experience: throughout the year the days are of uneven duration, and not merely does the relation between day and night steadily change, but a slight journey from East to West alters astronomical time by a certain number of minutes. In terms of the human organism itself, mechanical time is even more foreign: while human life has regularities of its own, the beat of the pulse, the breathing of the lungs, these change from hour to hour with mood and action, and in the longer span of days, time is measured not by the calendar but by the events that occupy it. The shepherd measures from the time the ewes lambed; the farmer measures back to the day of sowing or forward to the harvest: if growth has its own duration and regularities, behind it are not simply matter and motion but the facts of development: in short, history. And while mechanical time is strung out in a succession of mathematically isolated instants, organic time is cumulative in its effects. Though mechanical time can, in a sense, be speeded up or run backward, like the hands of a clock or the images of a moving picture, organic time moves in only one direction—through the cycle of birth, growth, development, decay, and death—and the past that is already dead remains present in the future that has still to be born. Around 1345, according to Thorndike, division of hours into sixty minutes and of minutes into sixty seconds became common: it was this abstract framework of divided time that became more and more the point of ref-

erence for both action and thought, and in the effort to arrive at accuracy in this department, the astronomical exploration of the sky focused attention further upon the regular, implacable movements of the heavenly bodies through space.[2]

As a piece of machinery, the clock was certainly not as powerful as the steam engine. It could not move thousands of tons of railway cars. But the clock produced an attitude toward time which made the steam engine and the railroad and the factory possible. This new attitude was more than punctuality and consciousness about time. It was the feeling that time existed on its own—separate from the world of human need and natural processes. Like the mechanical laws of the new science, time was thought to be an abstract standard, which humans were expected to conform to. Mechanical time was more demanding than natural time had been because mechanical time could be used efficiently or wasted. As long as medieval workers thought in terms of the "time it takes to make a table" or the "time for a walk into town" they could never be inefficient or late. There was no way of saying that they made a table in more or less time than "the time it takes to make a table"; it would have been absurd to ask someone to make two tables in that time. That became possible only with the invention of seconds, minutes, and hours—of abstract time. When abstract, measurable time existed independently of human activity, human activity could be timed. Timing permitted jobs to be standardized and coordinated. The modern factory would otherwise have been impossible.

The world could be filled with machines only after time was precisely measurable in nonhuman terms. Machine parts had to do things exactly on time—like "clockwork." But the machine parts also had to be designed and constructed precisely. This meant that each part had to be measured exactly. Standard, abstract measurements of space and weight (meters and centimeters, pounds and ounces) were as necessary as standard amounts of time.

INDUSTRIALIZATION: STANDARD SPACE AND INTERCHANGEABLE PARTS

In the Middle Ages (as in almost every other society before the industrial revolution) the few machines that existed (like water mills and windmills or potters' wheels) were all custom-made, as we would say. No two machines were ever exactly alike. Each was made according to the needs or whim of the artisan or the people who would use the machine. One gear would have to mesh with another of course, but there was no standard-size gear or screw or lever or anything else. Each machine was made for the particular job to be done, and the challenge of each new job frequently stimulated the creativity of the artisan.

The unique achievement of the industrial revolution was the mass production of products by the standardization of machines. Goods could be produced on a mass scale because they were made by machines—each one just like the other, the only way machines can make things. Even the machines were identical so that two machines could produce exactly the same products. This meant that machine parts had to be standardized so that they were interchangeable. Exactly similar interchangeable parts were first invented for muskets to meet the needs of war or expected war. This happened almost at the same time in France in 1785 (before the French Revolution) and in the United States in 1800, by Eli Whitney.

We can get some sense of the significance of the invention of interchangeable parts if we recall Thomas Jefferson's amazement when the French inventor LeBlanc gave Jefferson (then U.S. minister in France) the locks of 50 guns, all taken apart. "I put several together myself," Jefferson wrote home, "taking pieces as they came to hand, and they fitted in the most perfect manner. The advantages of this when arms need repair are evident."

The first mass-produced goods were the muskets, and later the uniforms, of Western armies. There were no other organizations in Western society around 1800 that could demand the enormous quantities of goods that required machine production. But although the new industrial technology was the child of war, it became (by the early twentieth century) an Aladdin's magic lamp of undreamed-of quantities of consumer goods. Today machines produce everything from shirts and ballpoint pens to airplanes and houses. It is difficult to buy anything made by hand any more. The advantage of machine production is not only that spare parts are always available because the parts are identical, as Jefferson realized. It is also cheaper for a machine than for an army of medieval artisans on starvation wages to produce a great quantity of identical goods.

There is no way of disputing the human value of machine production over hand manufacture. This is so obvious that it would not be said if it were not for some of the excessive claims of "handicraft" enthusiasts and "back to nature" people. We may complain about the inferior quality of some machine-made products, and we may enjoy making some things ourselves (there can be a real sense of accomplishment in that). But a machine can do anything that an artisan (or even an artist) has done because it is only a mechanical duplication of human labor. And industrial society does not prevent us from doing things ourselves if we like. The machine is only a shortcut for human labor. As such, it is of unquestionable value in doing things more quickly than we can by hand, and in doing more things than human and animal labor are capable of alone.

ENERGY SOURCES:
WIND AND WATER VERSUS COAL AND IRON

The almost "magical" characteristic of machines (doing things automatically, by themselves) is due to the fact that they harness sources of energy other than human and animal muscle. The oldest machines, like the waterwheel, which originated over two thousand years ago, and the windmill (in use for the last thousand years), use sources of energy which can never be depleted. Rushing streams and wind are inexhaustible, if sometimes unpredictable. They can never be used up. Their power is not even diminished after their energy has been used. The Dutch countryside of the seventeenth century never faced an energy shortage as more and more windmills were erected. Some of the more rapidly moving streams of England and New England in the eighteenth century could power as many water mills as there was room for.

The central ecological fact about the full-scale industrialization that began in the West in the 1800s is that irreplaceable energy resources were used. Instead of increasing the efficiency of wind and water as power sources, industrialists turned to the fossil fuels of the earth—especially coal, oil, and gas—which could never be replaced because of the time nature took to duplicate them.

Coal, oil, and gas were formed over millions and millions of years by the action of the sun on living organisms, carbon dioxide, and water. It is as if this treasure of energy were suddenly discovered in the last couple of hundred years and immediately used up. The average age of gasoline in your car's fuel tank is about 70 million years. It is estimated that half of all of the easily recoverable oil in the world will be consumed by 2010. The generation of Americans born after World War II will have consumed 70 percent of American oil reserves in a single generation.

It is possible, of course, that we will find new sources of energy to replace these fossil fuels. But we have taken the easy way out. We are squandering our treasure as if there were no tomorrow, and it is by no means certain that the new discoveries will come in time or that they will be sufficient to maintain our rate of growth.

Coal, asphalt, oil, and natural gas were occasionally used in ancient times for heating and lighting—but in miniscule amounts. Perhaps we began to live on borrowed time when, during the eighteenth century, the English faced a shortage of wood and found it easier to mine coal in large quantities. By 1800 the world mined about 15 million tons of coal per year. By 1850 the amount had increased to over 100 million, and by 1950 to almost 1,500 million tons per year.

From the early 1800s the rise in coal production was tied to the fortunes of the steam engine. The steam engine was first used to remove water from the mines, and the coal from the mines kept the engines going. Coal-driven steam engines were then used to power the first railroad cars, which were used to transport the coal from the mines.

Coal and steam built the iron civilization of the nineteenth century. Coal was the most available and most effective fuel for smelting iron ore as well as for producing steam. The vast new quantities of iron were used to build larger steam engines, railroads, and blast furnaces (requiring more coal to produce more iron).

The civilization based on mining—the industrial West of the nineteenth century—was fundamentally at war with the natural environment. As Mumford has remarked, "mining is a robber industry." The mine robbed the earth of its accumulated energy. It robbed future generations of the savings of eons. It robbed the miners of light and healthy lives, and it robbed their families of clean air and water. The psychology of mining civilization was most evident in the "rushes" of the nine-

The worst abuses of mining civilization were suffered by the children who worked in the low tunnels—before illustrations like this in a British parliamentary report brought some reform with the Coal Mines Act of 1842. (Radio Times Hulton Picture Library)

teenth century. Gold, iron, copper, and oil rushes were races to reckless exploitation. The lawless, antisocial life of the mining camp was only the logical conclusion of mining civilization. The get-rich-quick mentality and wasteful destruction of nature in the mineral rushes was only an extension of the feverish, impatient mindlessness of the larger society.

Iron and coal colored every aspect of nineteenth-century industrialization. The color varied from black to shades of gray. Even, Mumford notes, the formal dress of the industrialists—black tie, black suit, black boots, black stovepipe hat—reflected the blackness of coal country, called in England "the Black Country." The gray iron buildings and bridges, the great achievements of mining civilization, were blackened with the soot and cinders of blast furnaces that wastefully belched out as much useful black fuel as they consumed. By 1850 the whole civilization from Pittsburgh to the Ruhr Valley in Germany seemed to be in mourning.

Pollution and waste were two sides of the same coin. Benjamin Franklin had suggested that the soot and smoke that polluted the air might be trapped and reused in the furnaces to provide more energy and keep the air clean. Industrialists realized that their excess smoke and gas was only unburned energy, but they rarely bothered to conserve it. It was always cheaper to dig another well, open another mine, or level another mountain than it was to improve the efficiency of what they had. The symbols of power meant more than the quality of the environment. The smoking factory chimney which shut out natural light with a permanent fog over company towns was a symbol of prosperity. The noise of Watt's original steam engine was preferred as a sign of power—despite Watt's own attempts to quiet the machine just as automobile engine noise was later increased by manufacturers for its symbolic value.

The nineteenth-century industrial revolution assaulted the environment of Western countries in a number of ways. The mines scarred the countryside, the waste products and smoke of furnaces, refineries, and factories polluted the air and rivers, and railroads cut through forests and farms to make whole countries part of the same industrial system. Perhaps it was the gigantic scale of the new industry, which had the most serious ecological effect. When water, wind, and animal power had been the main sources of energy, up until the eighteenth century, mills and factories could be operated on a relatively local scale and each locality could engage in a number of varied occupations. Maybe they did not have to be overconcentrated. There were iron works in the eighteenth century which simply used the iron in local bogs. They were often inefficient, but when they emptied their slag in local streams, they did little environmental damage because they were so few. The miners of the nineteenth century, however, exploited large deposits; they mined whole mountains for their ore or fuel. As a result, industries became concentrated in areas near these rich deposits. Places like Pittsburgh and Detroit became industrial centers because they were close to the source of raw materials or energy. Farming and the smaller industries of these areas became secondary. The concentration of industry near these areas meant a wholesale deterioration of the environment. The discharge from these mines and mills was too much for the surrounding area to absorb. Huge cities were erected near these sites. The human sewage just increased the impossible strain on the atmosphere and rivers.

In some ways the industrial revolution of the twentieth century overcame the handicaps of the earlier industrialization. The discovery of electricity as a power source made it possible for every town or even farm to generate its own power. All that was needed was a small wind or water source of power which could be turned into a local electric generator. Even the cleanliness of the older age of wind power and waterpower could be regained. The possibility was there, but it was rarely employed.

Electricity was also easier to transmit than coal energy. High tension wires lose little power over long distances, and the power can be transmitted much more cheaply than the cost of shipping coal on railway cars. Further, electricity is easily converted into motor energy to do mechanical work, light, and heat. An increase in size does not increase efficiency nearly as much as with the steam engine. When a water turbine is used, the costs of producing energy are reduced to almost nothing. Even when electricity is generated by central power stations, the system can work very efficiently. The current is not wasted when it is not used, and it is relatively simple to provide current to those areas that need it most in times of emergency. Electric power could also allow local areas to satisfy their own needs for food and a complex assortment of industrial goods without making a particular area dependent on a single industry.

In short, the twentieth century provided new sources of energy (some of which, like the water turbine and solar energy and the energy inherent in the different temperatures of the earth's layers, were never adequately exploited) which would not have required the elaborate system of roads and railroads which came into being. The discoveries of the twentieth century allowed industry to become decentralized, but those who were in control of the older energy sources merely added the new sources to their stables, and things changed very little.

CAPITALISM IS RESPONSIBLE?

The industrial revolution which has transformed the Western world in the last few hundred years was based on an organization of the economy and society which was capitalistic. This means that most of the decisions were made in the interests of private profits. This may not have been inevitable. The Russians, the Chinese, and other societies that call themselves socialist have more recently attempted to industrialize on the basis of public, rather than private, ownership and decision making. They have been more or less successful. They have certainly not been free of environmental pollution, depletion of resources, or other affronts to the environment. Their failures and their successes may be a result of their socialistic economy—or possibly of something else. This is very difficult to determine. Perhaps all that we can do is attempt to determine to what extent our own environmental crisis has been caused or aggravated by our particular type of economic organization.

We might put the question in a number of ways. Is our problem the machine or the way a capitalist economy organizes and uses its machinery? Or, if we agree that the machine has done its share of damage (as well as of good), is it possible that a more public or socialized use of the machinery could have averted some of our more serious problems, or that it still might? Lewis Mumford states the case for the prosecution pretty clearly:

> It was because of certain traits in private capitalism that the machine—which was a neutral agent—has often seemed, and in fact has sometimes been, a malicious element in society, careless of human life, indifferent to human interests. The machine has suffered for the sins of capitalism; contrariwise, capitalism has often taken credit for the virtues of the machine.[3]

The real question when we compare the ravages of the machine with the disadvantages of capitalism is which of the two (if either) is dispensable. This is the issue that Mumford comes to grips with. He concludes that the machine is neutral, that it can be used for good or bad, that it can revitalize or destroy our ecology. If we accept his conclusion, we are forced to ask why the machine has been used primarily to exploit nature and why it has been used so callously and wastefully. The answer may lie in the social and economic organization of our society.

Mumford and other social critics have blamed capitalism for our ecological problems for a number of reasons. Their strongest argument is that capitalism is ideally a system of private enterprise, control, and profit, whereas ecology is ideally a public concern, perhaps our most important public concern. In other words, when capitalism works at its best, and with least interference, all decisions about the use of resources and the production of goods are made privately by those who own them, and they make their decisions solely in terms of what will bring them the most profit. There are times, of course, when private profit can serve public, even ecological, needs. Some private companies today, for instance, make all of their profits by producing and selling antipollution devices. But the critics of capitalism argue that such cases are exceptions to the rule. Normally, they insist, a system of private ownership and profit runs counter to social or public needs. At the very least, they argue, a private enterprise system becomes engaged in social or public causes only when the potential profit is greater than in other activities. These critics would like to see enterprise and industry devoted to social needs all of the time, not just when there is the possibility of a higher profit.

The defenders of capitalism have sometimes argued that the public interest is best served when each individual acts independently in pursuit of his or her self-interest. The Scottish economic philosopher Adam Smith wrote in *The Wealth of Nations* in 1776 that the capitalist market, operating according to the law of supply and demand, would always ensure—like some "invisible hand"—that public and private profit were the same.

> Every individual . . . neither intends to promote the public interest, nor knows how much he is promoting it. . . . [H]e intends only his own security . . . only his own gain. And he is in this . . . led by an invisible hand to promote an end which was no part of his intention. . . . By pursuing his own interest he frequently promotes that of society more effectually than when he really intends to promote it.[4]

According to Smith, manufacturers would always be forced to give society exactly what it wanted at the price it was willing to pay as long as all buyers and sellers acted independently and selfishly. When society wanted more gloves, the prices of gloves would rise so that new people would enter the industry, make more gloves, and eventually lower the price. When the profit on gloves was lower than the anticipated profit on shoes, glove manufacturers would selfishly go into shoemaking. Shoe manufacturers who raised their prices too far beyond the demand price would be forced out of business by new people who undersold them. Manufacturers who tried to underpay their workers would lose them to another company. Each manufacturer could only stay in business as long as he or she produced exactly what society wanted at a price only slightly above costs. Collusion among manufacturers was always impossible; if they artificially inflated prices, there would always be someone else along to undersell them.

Adam Smith's model of capitalist enterprise must have made some sense in 1776 or he would not have been taken seriously. It was a finely balanced scheme. The idea of unbeatable market laws made a lot of sense to Europeans who had recently become accustomed to thinking that the earth and heavens were subject to the clockwork laws of nature. Manufacturers were enthralled with a philosophy that made their selfish behavior into a social virtue. In a sense, Smith's philosophy was even true. The early industrial economy of England was made up of a large number of fairly competitive manufacturers. The technology was simple enough to allow workers and manufacturers to change jobs when the demand shifted. The large number of manufacturers in any one field made competition intense. It must have seemed to many of these enterprising manufacturers that they were acting on the orders of invisible laws, dictated by society's needs. Prices fluctuated rapidly. Fortunes seemed to follow. Individuals went from rags to riches, and back.

There were, however, at least two problems with Adam Smith's model of capitalist society. First, its assumption that everyone had equal buying and selling power never applied to the workers or the poor, even if it were true of a large number of manufacturers. Second, the manufacturers did not stay relatively competitive very long. Some of the more wealthy were able to use their resources, political power, and prestige to prevent challenges by younger, more aggressive companies. They were able to fix prices, pad expenses, monopolize an industry, and use the government for their own ends. Ironically, it was the most successful early capitalists who undermined ideal capitalism. Very shortly after Adam Smith proposed a society regulated entirely by the free market without government intervention, successful manufacturers built national governments stronger than those Adam Smith had complained about. Manufacturers used these governments to charter banks, provide land and resources, subsidize expenses, offer tariff protection, and protect the big companies from possible competitors.

Adam Smith's model may have worked if everyone started with about the same amount of money, and if it were absolutely impossible for the temporarily rich to become permanently rich by converting their money into political power. But everyone did not start on an equal footing, and the market was not the only regulator or the only source of power. Capitalist society has never been a society of equal, independent producers. There were monopolies in Smith's day. (Indeed, his book was written to oppose the monopolies of such companies as the East and West Indies trading companies.) And there have been monopolies since. It is possible that a free market where everyone had the same access to research, patents, manufacture, the courts, the banks, and today the media and advertising might have prevented fantastic accumulations of power by the few. But that is something that the successful have never allowed to happen. Consequently, when we talk about capitalism in the real world we must consider the effects of class differences, inequality, and economic concentration. We can no longer rest assured that the invisible hand of the market will see to the harmony of selfish and public interests. Private profit is no longer (if it ever was) the profit of each of us independently. Private profit is the profit of the few who own most of the stock or manage the boards of the major corporations. We must ask if those who own and direct these corporations act for all of us when they act for themselves. That is a very different question.

ECOLOGY AND IDEAL CAPITALISM

Before we try to answer that question, we should consider one other alternative. What if we were able to make Adam Smith's model really work? The fact that it does not and has not is beside the point. It is at least theoretically possible that we could reform present society by making it *more* capitalistic than it is presently. Some conservative philosophers and politicians have suggested this. In fact, much of the trust-busting legislation and court decisions since the end of the nineteenth century have been directed toward such a goal. What if we could find a foolproof way of avoiding economic concentration, giving everyone a relatively equal opportunity to become rich, and ensure, with something like a 100 percent inheritance tax, that each generation would start at roughly the same line? At the very least, we could force each plant or division of large corporations to become independent, we could eliminate government assistance or force the government to aid small businesses with the same fervor that it aids the aerospace giants. To be more specific, what if General Motors could only make cars, or what if each Chevrolet factory were independent, and forced to compete with the others for workers, steel, and advertising space? What if it were still possible for the small company with ideas and energy to enter a major industry without having to face the corporate power of the giants?

In that kind of society certain social needs might be served much more readily. It would be impossible for the automobile manufacturers to conspire against the public demand for cleaner engines. They would not be able to buy up socially desirable inventions for the sole purpose of squashing them. They might not have the resources to throw away millions in an effort to drive more efficient, but less wealthy, competitors from the market with expensive court cases (that only giants can afford to lose) or temporarily lower prices in the line of products that was challenged. Greater competition would certainly make corporations more responsive to changing public needs.

But there is a problem with this ideal capitalist society which strikes at the root. The more equal, and the more competitive, and the more independent each unit, company, or individual was, the more it would wastefully duplicate efforts and consume common resources. Let us take a simple example. Imagine a piece of pastureland owned by the inhabitants of a village in the Middle Ages. In this precapitalist society, the villagers often made all major decisions about the use of the pasture as a group because they considered the land to be the responsibility of the whole group. The pastureland was recognized as a common resource. It was usually, in fact, called "the commons." If the cows were owned separately by each villager, the villager would still make group decisions. They might, for instance, take turns bringing in all of the cows in from grazing, avoiding any unnecessary duplication of effort. They would also agree on certain procedures to prevent soil erosion, and they might agree on a maximum number of cows for each villager. In short, they would organize to preserve their precious, but limited, resource, the pasture.

Now imagine what would happen if these villagers thought like modern capitalists, each looking out for his or her private profit and competitive advantage. Without any common organization each villager would realize that it was to his or her personal advantage to increase his or her own number of cows. Each additional cow would be an added burden on the limited pasture, but the owner would share that burden with each of the other villagers, and he or she alone would reap the profit from the additional cow. In other words, private interest would force each villager to graze as many cows as possible. Public interest, however, would dictate some limitation on the number of cows to prevent exhaustion of the resource. If everyone acted only in terms of private profit the commons would eventually have more cows that it could support. Ultimately they would starve. Each villager might see the long term disaster, but it would still seem to be in his or her own best personal interests to get as much as possible. If he or she did not, someone else would.

With limited resources, private gain must always be a public loss. Even in an ideal capitalist society where each person has the same economic power, each will gain more than he or she loses individually by depleting the commons.

Think of nature as the commons. The fish in the seas, the trees in the forest, the oil and gas underground, the mineral resources, are all finite, as we have only recently realized. But they have been exploited privately, and competitively. For years, whaling companies have realized that the whale is becoming extinct. But because each company acts independently, they have been unable to avoid the eventual extinction of their own source of profit. In fact, they continue to bring about their own doom as an industry because they attempt to maximize their own profit before it is too late. They hurry their own end because it is profitable (for each separately) to do so.

In ecological terms, private exploitation and private ownership seem to mean the destruction of the commons. The social costs of depletion or pollution or extinction are always shared. Private profit never is. That is why it always pays the private enterprise to be wasteful.

We have recently realized that nature is not inexhaustible, that it is a fixed legacy for all. But it is difficult for us to think of the land, game, energy sources, and mineral resources as common property. In modern capitalist society, especially the United States, everything is privately owned. Even the airwaves are bought and sold privately with the exception of one or two public stations. But it was not so long ago that even Americans thought primarily in terms of the commons. Though Colonial America was rapidly exploited by private individuals and companies, the young Republic maintained an earlier tradition which the historian Henry Steele Commager calls "devotion to the commonwealth."

> It was devotion to the commonwealth that inspired the generation of the Founding Fathers; it was the sense of obligation to the new nation, to mankind, to posterity that animated Franklin and Washington, Jefferson and Hamilton, John Adams and Tom Paine, John Jay and James Madison, and others who are now part of the American Valhalla. From their earliest youth they gave themselves to serve the common-

wealth; they exhausted their energies, their talents, and their fortunes in service to the commonwealth. Modern day politicians and civil servants seem to do pretty well for themselves; it is pertinent to remember that Washington had to borrow $500 to go to his own inauguration; that Jefferson died a bankrupt after fifty years in the public service; . . . that Tom Paine, who served his country well, and France, too, died a pauper. A society obsessed with the vindication of private enterprise does not nourish a generation dedicated to public enterprise. Without that dedication, the commonwealth is betrayed and lost.[5]

ECOLOGY AND MODERN CAPITALISM

So much for ideal capitalism and "ideal selfishness." Let us return to our earlier question about the possibility of social and ecological welfare under modern capitalism. From what we have just said about the ideal of equally independent producers, we might conclude that we are better off today with a high degree of economic concentration. We have beaten the problem of the isolated villagers on the commons. The economic units of modern society, for the most part, have achieved a scale of organization and cooperation that Adam Smith would have found as impossible as it was undesirable. Instead of thousands of competing auto manufacturers, each depleting the public resources by needless duplication, we have only about a dozen globally. Instead of hundreds of telephone companies crossing wires at each corner, there are a few. We have, in short, avoided some of the fantastic waste of resources that would have occurred, and to a certain extent did occur, in Adam Smith's ideal of many independent competitors.

Perhaps an ecologist could have told Adam Smith that economic concentration was bound to occur. Modern ecologists, at least, realize that small-scale competitive units are normally replaced by monopolies:

> A cornerstone of ecological theory is the competitive exclusion principle. Simply, this principle states that competing species cannot coexist indefinitely. If two species are utilizing a resource that is in short supply, one of them will be eliminated as a competitor, either by being forced out of the ecosystem or by being forced to use some other resource . . . Again and again, the evidence seems to indicate that competition reduces the number of competitors. . . . Competition in economic systems has the same effect as competition in ecosystems. It reduces the number of competitors. The more efficient or larger producers force the less efficient or smaller out of business or buy them out, resulting in monopoly. . . . The number of competitors continues to become smaller, prices and profits increase, and the huge corporations and conglomerates are more difficult if not impossible to manage efficiently.[6]

This process was almost completed in the United States by the end of the last century. In the first decades of the twentieth century, all that was needed was for the major corporations to induce the federal government to stabilize their dominant position by creating regulatory commissions that would police the upstart competitors. The historian Gabriel Kolko has shown in a fascinating book called *The Triumph of Conservatism* that this is exactly what happened. Under the guise of regulating business, the administrations of Theodore Roosevelt and Woodrow Wilson created commissions which gave large corporations the monopolies that they had become too fat to gain on their own.

By World War II American corporations had become "public" in their power and responsibility. With the assistance of commissioners in Washington, they were able to avoid most of the excesses (and drawbacks) of competitive capitalism. They planned production and sales like governments in Scandinavia, often with more resources at their disposal. It was possible again to talk of the commons that these corporations controlled and administered. The only difference—and it was crucial—was that these new public overseers of government funds and common resources were privately owned, and operated accordingly. They ran the commons with unanimity, at least, but entirely to increase their own profits.

FOR FURTHER READING

There are a couple of very good introductions to the history of human energy use. Vaclav Smil's *Energy in World History* is the best introduction. Clive Ponting's *Green History of the World* is a useful survey. Carlo M. Cipolla's *The Economic History of World Population* is a classic that offers a brief overview. Fred Cottrell's *Energy and Society* develops in a more leisurely fashion the effect of the industrial revolution. Lewis Mumford's *Technics and Civilization* is still a fountain of ideas and interpretations. Jared Diamond's *Guns, Germs, and Steel* is a magnificent ecological history.

There is a rich literature on ideas of nature, especially in the Western tradition. Clarence J. Glacken's *Traces on the Rhodian Shore* is the classic for Western thought through the 18th century. Keith Thomas's *Man and the Natural World* mines the literature of 17th- to 19th-century Europe. Simon Schama's *Landscape and Memory* shows how every landscape is a human construction. For more specific studies of ecological ideas, see Donald Wooster's *Nature's Economy*, especially on Thoreau and Darwin, and Ramachandra Guha's *Environmentalism: A Global History*. Vera Norwod's *Made From This Earth* surveys American feminist environmentalists.

On the scientific revolution, Alfred Crosby's *The Measure of Reality* is a superb brief study of the culture of measurement in Western society, 1250–1600. Carolyn Merchant's *The Death of Nature* is a classic feminist treatment.

For the history of technology see James E. McClellan III and Harold Dorn's *Science and Technology in World History* and Arnold Pacey's *Technology in World Civilization*. Other interesting interpretations include S. Giedion's *Mechanization*

Takes Command, Elting E. Morison's *Men, Machines, and Modern Times*, and the essays in Arthur O. Lewis, Jr.'s *Of Men and Machines*.

On the issue of capitalism and industrialization, Eric Hobsbawm's *Industry and Empire* is a useful history. See also Robert Heilbroner's *Business Civilization in Decline*, Barry Weisberg's *Beyond Repair: The Ecology of Capitalism*, and Martin O'Connor's *Is Capitalism Sustainable?: Political Economy and the Politics of Ecology*.

A number of very good books explore the relationship between imperialism and ecology. The classics are Alfred Crosby's *Ecological Imperialism: The Biological Expansion of Europe, 900–1900* and his path-breaking *The Columbian Exchange*. More recent are Richard Drayton's *Nature's Government: Science, Imperial Britain, and the "Improvement" of the World* and Richard H. Grove's *Ecology, Climate, and Empire: Colonialism and Global Environmental History, 1400–1940*.

NOTES

1. Lewis Mumford, *Technics and Civilization* (New York: Harcourt Brace Jovanovich, 1963), p. 51.
2. *Ibid.*, p. 14–16.
3. *Ibid.*, p. 27.
4. Adam Smith, *An Inquiry into the Nature and Causes of the Wealth of Nations*, ed. Edwin Cannan (New York: Modern Library, 1937), Book IV, Chapter 2, p. 423.
5. Henry Steele Commager, "America's Heritage of Bigness," *Saturday Review*, 4 July 1970, p. 12.
6. Bertram G. Murray, Jr., "What the Ecologists Can Teach the Economists," *New York Times Magazine*, 10 December 1972, pp. 64–65.

❧ 6 ❧

Economics
and
Revolution

Socialism
and Capitalism

"Socialism" in our contemporary world is so identified with twentieth-century communism that it is difficult to understand the appeal that socialism had for many people before our own age. When most contemporary Americans think of socialism they think of communist secret police, single-party governments, and failed economies. But this was not always the case. In fact, for most of the early history of socialism, from the period of the French Revolution of 1789 to the Russian Revolution of 1917, socialism was a vision of a prosperous but more humane society than the one increasingly shaped by capitalism (private property and the market).

It is often said that socialism was a belief in equality whereas capitalism was a belief in liberty. This distinction has a lot of value. Certainly all advocates of the capitalist free market have professed greater interest in liberty than in equality and all socialists have been more concerned with equality than with liberty. But, at least between 1789 and 1917, most socialists believed that inequality was not only unsatisfactory in itself but that it was also unsatisfactory because it limited people's liberties. "What liberties did the poor enjoy?" these socialists asked rhetorically, "except the liberty to starve."

Probably every society (at least since the agricultural revolution) has had its rich and poor. And every one of these has had some people who were more interested in equality and others more interested in liberty. But certain periods of history have produced greater divisions between rich and poor (and greater tensions between the "haves" and "have nots") and the period of the French Revolution was one of these.

THE FRENCH REVOLUTION:
LIBERTY AND EQUALITY

The rallying cry of the French Revolution in 1789, "Liberty, Equality, and Fraternity," points to the agreement between prosperous proponents of liberty and more radical advocates of equality in the early stages of the revolution. Even the desire for "fraternity" (meaning "brotherhood") indicates a presumed unity of purpose among all of the people, rich or poor, in 1789. This was because the poor were united with the prosperous middle-class—bourgeoisie—in their combined opposition to the king and the nobility. According to political practice before 1789, all of the poor (in city and country) and all of the bourgeoisie together, comprising almost 99 percent of the population, were represented by only a third of the representatives in parliament. A cynic might say it didn't matter because the king had not called a meeting of the parliament since 1614. Nevertheless the old constitutional system which divided France and its parliament into three estates rankled the far more numerous body of the Third Estate. The minute fraction of nobility constituted the First Estate, the only slightly larger body of priests, mainly bishops and cardinals, the Second. So when Louis XVI had to summon parliament in 1789 to pay his debts (mainly owed to bankers from the Third Estate), all of the Third Estate, rich and poor, bankers and debtors, united to declare that the Third Estate should not meet in the old-fashioned way by which each estate had one vote, but that members of each estate in the Estates General ought to be counted as individuals.

The idea that individuals, and not estates, should have equal votes was a revolutionary idea in France in 1789. It led to the formation of an alternative governing body, made up only of the Third Estate, called the National Assembly. Since that body included "the people" and "the people with money," they immediately replaced the Estates General as the parliament of France.

The alliance of the poor and the prosperous lasted as long as the king, clergy, and nobility retained power, which is to say not very long at all. By August of 1789, much of the financial base of the nobility and church had been undercut by a bill abolishing ancient rents and obligations that originated in feudalism. By January of 1793, the king and queen were executed.

The influence of the urban poor, the most vociferous champions of equality, increased between 1790 and 1794. But the French Revolution was never a socialist revolution. Middle-class lawyers, business people, and professionals, along with a few liberal nobles, were in charge even in the most radical days of 1793–1794. The strength of the Parisian poor was not in governance, but in applying pressure on the changing parliaments with street demonstrations and occasional riots.

The class that enabled the bourgeoisie to ignore the urban poor was the rural class of farmers, the peasantry. Many peasants dropped out of the revolution as early as August of 1789 when feudal dues were abolished. But the Constituent Assembly (1789–1791) and the Legislative Assembly (1791–1792) were sufficiently businesslike to sell church lands and demand that peasants pay their old feudal lords for the land they tilled. The most radical government, the National Convention (1792–1795), eased the payment requirement, but lost any remaining peasant support by executing the king and conducting a European war that required enormous sacrifices in the countryside, including the confiscation of crops for soldiers and urban workers. The Parisian poor, on the other hand, benefited from the confiscation that kept them from starving, as well as from maximum prices on some commodities, and the Constitution of 1793 which gave them suffrage for the first time.

It may have been essential to fight the war to prevent the failure of the revolution. The kings of Europe would have reimposed a monarchy with a vengeance (even after the execution of Louis). But the necessary war destroyed the revolution. The drain on soldiers, food, and energies created a militarized society that by 1794 made the old regime seem like the good old days. French revolutionary society during the war years was transformed, like modern wartime societies since, into a barracks warfare state that took good care of its soldiers and forced even the richest and laziest to contribute their share, even when that could only be accomplished by means of official surveillance and terror. Some of the middle-class radicals approved of the rough equality that the terror produced, and the national mission that powered it. But as the ruling Committee of Public Safety under Robespierre failed to put the Constitution of 1793 into effect, and proceeded to devour the children of the revolution as well as royalists, it met the combined opposition of popular leaders on the left and the more moderate elements on the right. Robespierre, who as Director of Public Safety came to personify the worst excesses of the revolution, was himself executed in the summer of 1794, and the revolution was over. A counterrevolutionary White Terror followed Robespierre's revolutionary Red Terror, the conservative Constitution of 1795 replaced the radical, but unused, document of 1793, and a corrupt, cynical Directory government (1795–1799) replaced the radical firebrands of the National Convention.

GRACCHUS BABEUF AND THE CONSPIRACY OF EQUALS: THE FIRST COMMUNISTS

One of the radicals who rejoiced at Robespierre's downfall because he thought it marked a chance for the revolution to continue, rather than its end, was Gracchus Babeuf. Disillusionment led him and others to form in prison and underground a secret Conspiracy of Equals. It can be called the first communist organization.

Under the conditions of the Directory it was necessarily secret, conspiratorial, and revolutionary. It planned to continue the revolution with a popular uprising, direct-ed by its own members. After seizing the government they intended to abolish pri-vate property and create (with whatever force was necessary) a society of equal work and equal rewards.

We know Babeuf from the newspapers and posters he wrote to bring about the insurrection between 1795 and 1797, and from the description of organizational structure and strategy which his comrade, Philippe Michele Buonarroti, passed on to revolutionary organizations in Europe in 1828. But we know him best from the three days of testimony he gave in April 1797, on trial for his life. His defense was a summary of a life of revolutionary activity, a review of some of the most radical philosophy of the prior century, and a look ahead to a new age.

Babeuf was arrested with 46 associates, mostly workers or *sansculottes* (which meant literally people "without breeches"—a whole class described by the unique-ness of their working clothes: pants). They included people who gave their profes-sions as printer, goldsmith, shoemaker, clockmaker, weaver, lace worker, and em-broiderer, among others. They were tried by a special 16-man jury under a law of April 1796 that was passed specifically to stem the rising tide of revolt under the Directory and the Constitution of 1795. The law decreed the death penalty for any-one advocating (even verbally) the overthrow of the government, the reestablish-ment of the Constitution of 1793, or the division of lands. The state was able to produce agents who had infiltrated the Conspiracy, but even without testimony on the organization's activities Babeuf's words were sufficient for conviction. Conse-quently his defense centered on denying the legitimacy of the law itself on the grounds that it would mean the execution of many of France's greatest philoso-phers, respectable bourgeois revolutionaries, and even of some of the leaders of the Directory, who at one time had said the same things that Babeuf was accused of saying.

Babeuf referred to one count of the indictment—an article that he had written in his newspaper, *The Tribune of the People*—and told the court that it was true that he had published the allegedly inflammatory language, but that it had been copied word by word from the great philosopher Jean-Jacques Rousseau (1712–1778). "The progress of society depends upon all having enough and none too much," Babeuf said, quoting Rousseau. "You are lost if you forget that the fruits of the earth belong to all, the earth itself to none."[1]

Babeuf continued. Was it not Diderot, the philosopher of nature who wrote the *Encyclopedia*, who declared that it was private property that caused human selfish-ness? You cannot improve the condition of man one whit, Diderot said, "if you do not lay the ax to the tree of private ownership."[2]

Without notes, books, or the use of a library, Babeuf quoted a whole age of philo-sophic speculation. But while the philosophers he quoted had engaged in specula-tion, Babeuf grew up in a world, after the American Revolution, where speculation overthrew governments.

Babeuf was a conspirator for revolution (despite his courtroom denials to protect his friends). Ideas had become weapons. It is in that light that we date the origins of communism in the 1790s with the Conspiracy of Equals, and not with Rousseau or Diderot. But it was still too early in the 1790s to define a revolutionary communist program in great detail, or to take account of the emerging industrial system, or to gain a mass or working-class following. In practice Babeuf's program would have meant little more than leveling incomes, and thus equalizing poverty. Nobility and clergy would have to work like everyone else. All goods produced would be collected and distributed by a "common store" with "scrupulous fairness." Babeuf pointed out that this was the procedure for provisioning "twelve armies with their 1,200,000 men. And what is possible on a small scale can also be done on a large one."[3] There was no talk of socializing large-scale industry, because in the 1790s none existed. The private property that would be commonly owned were the possessions of the rich, the food and things produced, and of course the land. At times Babeuf seemed to be suggesting that land be periodically redivided. At his trial, however, he clearly went beyond this traditional peasant dream to a notion of common ownership and farming. In any case his urban movement was more concerned with the private wealth of the middle and upper classes—which is what "property" meant to the Parisian poor. Even the revolutionary 1790s was still an age of generalities, broad outlines, and guiding principles.

On 24 May 1797, Gracchus Babeuf was found guilty by the High Court of Vendôme of advocating the reestablishment of the Constitution of 1793. On 26 May he was sentenced to die. "I feel," he wrote his wife and children, "no regrets that I have given my life for the best of causes. Even if all my efforts have been in vain, I have done my duty."[4] He was executed the following day.

The ideals and strategies of the Conspiracy of Equals were carried throughout Europe by the deported Buonarroti to surface again in 1830 and 1848. By then socialism had developed new roots among the industrial working class, but communism had come to mean the most radical, communal form of socialism.

A NEW OLD IDEA OF WORK:
THE SOCIALISM OF FOURIER

Charles Fourier (1772–1837) is often dismissed as one of the madmen of early utopian socialism. Mad, he probably was. But his madness was akin to the poet's vision and the romantic's lust for human values which the sober bourgeois, industrial world mocked. It is easy to make fun of his suspicion that the stars had intercourse or that the oceans could be turned into lemonade, but such fantasies should not distract our attention from Fourier's radical critique of the separation of work and life in capitalist industry or from "his prophetic warning that real progress was something other than the mechanical confection of instruments for destroying human happiness."[5]

Fourier grew up in a comfortable middle-class home during the French Revolution. He was given enough of the family wealth on his twenty-first birthday in 1793 to set up his own business as a cloth merchant and importer in the southern French city of Lyon. After a few months he joined Lyon's insurrection against the revolutionary government in Paris, a move that cost him much of his fortune, and almost his life, when Lyon was recaptured. So Fourier was no revolutionary. His socialism did not emerge from the working-class experience of Paris or from the radical politics of journalists and intellectuals like Babeuf.

> If the Lyon insurrection disgusted Fourier with revolutionary politics, it was the financial chaos of the Directory that shaped his economic views. The brief Jacobin experiment in a directed economy was followed by a complete relaxation of economic controls; and the Directory was a period of skyrocketing inflation, industrial stagnation, and widespread food shortages. Fortunes were made overnight through speculation in paper money, profiteering in military supplies, and the creation of artificial shortages. As a commercial employee Fourier saw these abuses at first hand and occasionally participated in them. They strengthened his conviction that there was something wrong with the whole economic system based on free—or as he called it "anarchic"— competition. He began to formulate a general critique of commercial capitalism which emphasized the parasitism of the merchant and the middleman as the chief cause of economic ills.[6]

By 1799 Fourier had arrived at the main outlines of his system for solving social and economic ills. He felt he had discovered the laws of human "natural association," a "geometrical calculus of passionate attraction," and a scheme for organizing a new community in which people would work harmoniously at socially useful jobs because they wanted to. However, less than a year later, Fourier had exhausted the rest of his fortune and was forced in June 1800 (shortly after Napoleon took power from the Directory) to return to "the jailhouse of commerce."[7] For the remaining 15 years of Napoleon's rule Fourier filled his notebooks for a few hours every evening "after having spent my days participating in the deceitful activities of the merchants and brutalizing myself in the performance of degrading tasks."[8] His book-length announcement of his discoveries in 1808 was met with derision, as was his offer to Napoleon that the emperor become his "founder of Harmony."[9] Ignored, he declared he would withhold his discoveries until a million troops had been lost in Napoleonic wars.

In 1815, after Napoleon's final exile, Fourier used an inheritance from his mother to quit his clerical and traveling sales jobs to write full time. He devoted himself to his investigations of passion, love, and sexuality. He refined his blueprint for social organization in a community of passionate work. And he began to publish the thousands of pages of his *Grand Treatise* in different versions in 1822.

The question of work was central to Fourier's personal life and to the emerging industrial society in which he lived. The bourgeoisie justified its claim to power by making its own preoccupation with work a virtue. They criticized the poor and some of the unproductive nobility and clergy for not working. They sought ways of indoctrinating the whole society with a work ethic. But the kind of work that they offered in their factories and offices Fourier viewed as a new kind of slavery. Work in chemical plants and glass works often seemed a form of murder. In textile mills even the easiest manual labor constituted 12 to 15 hours of disciplined, soul-wrecking boredom. The "little people" of the lower middle class were often further removed from physical starvation, but they were prey to the same anxieties, insecurities, and regimentation. In fact the emotional starvation of the clerical worker whose body rotted in shuffled paper was often more severe since the work showed no tangible product.

It is no wonder, Fourier noticed, that work itself was despised. Work had become divorced from life. It was necessary then *"to find a new Social Order* that insures the poorest members of the working class sufficient well-being to make them constantly and passionately prefer their work to the idleness and brigandage to which they now aspire."[10] Fourier, of course, was convinced that he had found the new social order, and solved the problem of work.

The solution lay in Fourier's recognition that almost everyone in society had a passion to do something that someone else called work. So instead of concentrating (like the factory owners) on forcing people to work against their instincts at the particular jobs which profited the owners, Fourier suggested the construction of societies which gratified those instinctual needs. Instead of shaping the person to the job, the jobs would be the agencies of passionate, sensual gratification. Society would work to satisfy instincts instead of repressing that deepest and most spontaneous emotional energy for useful work. Fourier could almost define useful work as the work that people would instinctively do, not only because he had faith in human nature, but also because he prized human diversity.

Such a society (even, or perhaps especially, in an experimental form) must have certain preconditions to be possible. Everyone would have to own a share in the community to feel part of it. The working places and residences would have to be comfortable and attractive. And a minimum standard of living would have to be guaranteed to all so that work was clearly spontaneous. Then the diversity of human instincts would allow each person to find his or her most expressive working opportunity. The important thing would be to allow the fullest expression of one's passion. Even a bloodthirsty tyrant like the Roman emperor Nero would be happy as a butcher. His passion expressed, rather than repressed, the young Nero raised in a phalanx (Fourier's name for the community) "would have begun by the age of four to satisfy twenty other penchants" which his Roman teachers would have stifled "for the sake of morality."[11]

But the Nero type is only the most extreme of 810 personality types that Fourier characterized. A phalanx should have at least one man and one woman of each type. Every passion or combination of passions can be put to use in socially valuable work. The passion of some children for dirt is no exception:

Two-thirds of all boys have a penchant for filth. They love to wallow in
the mire and play with dirty things. They are unruly, peevish, scurrilous
and overbearing, and they will brave any storm or peril simply for the
pleasure of wreaking havoc. These children will enroll in the Little
Hordes whose task is to perform, dauntlessly and as a point of honor, all
those loathsome tasks that ordinary workers would find debasing.[12]

Among these are "sewer-cleaning, tending the dung heap, working in the
slaughter-houses," and keeping "the roads of Harmony lined with shrubs and flowers and in more splendid condition than the lanes of our country estates."[13] (We
might remind ourselves that Fourier was writing in an age when young children
were commonly caged in factories and mines for over 12 hours a day.)

Few passions are so strong as to commit one to the same work all day, every day.
Many people have multiple passions. And many have a "butterfly passion" which
requires that they "flutter about from pleasure to pleasure." Consequently, these
people will be aided in designing as often as necessary their preferred series of work
attractions. A maximum period of two hours at any job would probably be desirable. Thus a typical summer day of one Harmonian might include five meals, mass,
two public functions, a concert, an hour and a half at the library, and eight tasks:
hunting, fishing, gardening, and tending pheasants in the morning, and the afternoon at the fish tanks, the sheep pasture, and in two different greenhouses. Finally,
he would spend an hour before supper at the "exchange" to plan the next day's
activities.

Fourier's revolutionary method of asking what people want instead of what has
to be done enabled him to surpass, he felt, even the efficiency of capitalist industry. This is because even the most humanitarian factory owner must repress the
worker's source of productive and creative energy—the instincts. A smart owner
might be able to find a worker who has the proper physical or temperamental inclinations for a particular job, but the work would always be grudgingly performed as
long as it were done for someone else. The problem with work in commercial industrial society (which Fourier called civilization) is that it must inevitably suppress
rather than liberate the passions. And not only is that humanly crippling, it is also
socially inefficient.

It is easy to compress the passions by violence [he wrote]. Philosophy
suppresses them with a stroke of the pen. Locks and the sword come to
the aid of sweet morality. But nature appeals from these judgments; she
regains her rights in secret. Passion stifled at one point reappears at
another like water held back by a dike; it is driven inward like the
humor of an ulcer closed too soon.[14]

How inhuman, and how wasteful to deny such elemental forces with the violence of morality. Human passions always have value when they are allowed expres-

sion in a nonrepressive, social setting. Civilization outside of the phalanx makes the error of rejecting and repressing human feelings in the interests of morality or efficiency. But it is wrong on both counts. A morality that ignores human needs must depend on locks and swords, and such institutions of oppression yield a very low level of efficiency.

So far we have described Fourier's system without much attention to its social dimension. This was appropriate because Fourier began with an analysis of passions—an essentially psychological issue—and he sometimes spoke of human society in the idiom of bourgeois liberalism as a collection of separate atoms. Liberals from Adam Smith to John Stuart Mill (and twentieth-century conservatives) looked for social harmony in the competing self-interest of each isolated atomistic individual. Similarly, Fourier argued that his community of Harmony would emerge from "rivalry, self-esteem, and other stimuli compatible with self-interest."[15] The difference is that the liberal defenders of capitalist industrial society interpreted self-interest in narrowly economic terms, and Fourier's psychology led to an idea of self-interest that was deeply emotional, sexual, and social. Liberalism posited an abstract social harmony derived from individuals competing in the marketplace and the job market. Fourier (and most socialists) sought the social harmony that derived from individual drives toward intimacy, cooperation, love, and participation.

Work was to be accomplished in Harmony not only because each individual would give vent to his or her personal passions, but also because it would be performed by individuals who were as attracted to each other as to the work itself. Love, even sexual love, was not to be an obstacle or "a recreation which detracts from work; on the contrary it is the soul and vehicle, the mainspring of all works and of the whole of universal attraction."[16]

Whenever possible work would be done in groups. These voluntary associations would change personnel, but they would always be comprised of men and women of similar inclinations. Working would thus provide occasions for meeting new people, developing relationships, and creative social interaction. Groups could compete with others and individuals could show off their talents without creating permanent divisions. Fourier chose to discuss "one of the most difficult administrative problems of civilization: the recruitment of armies" to show how even in the most extreme case love could motivate work. Harmony would recruit young men and women to its training maneuvers and athletic contests with "magnificent feasts" of food and love. In the process of a season's military campaigns the young women would choose partners from the suitors who competed in valor for their attention.[17]

Fourier's discussion of armies touched on a subject that he kept hidden in his notebooks, which he called *The New Amorous World*. Here he imagined a future stage of Harmony which offered complete instinctual liberation with a guaranteed sexual minimum that enabled the inhabitants to transcend sexual scarcity in the same way that the economic minimum allowed spontaneous work. Marriage was to be allowed. But Fourier castigated enforced monogamy for separating love from sexuality and limiting sexuality to copulation or procreation. Christian civilization, Fourier argued, had deprived productive work and civic life of its eroticism by restricting the enjoyment of sexual pleasure to the marriage bed. Harmony's Court of Love would guarantee enough opportunities for sexual gratification so that in the new society of abundance sex would not be a single obsession, but an ever available enjoyment of life. All work was to be passionate play.

VARIETIES OF SOCIALISM:
THE LEGACY OF THE FRENCH REVOLUTION

What makes Fourier a socialist? His criticism of capitalism (which he called commerce or civilization) certainly qualified him, especially since he proposed the creation of a common cooperative alternative to competitive capitalism. His insistence that work serve the interests (indeed, the passions) of the workers (instead of the profits of capital) was socialist. So was his antipathy to markets, sales, production for profit, and his placement of Harmony outside of market society. But perhaps the most socialist aspect of Fourier's philosophy was his radical, revolutionary confrontation of bourgeois civilization. He asked different questions: What are human needs? How can society be organized to satisfy human needs? He made different assumptions: Human nature is various and good; all repression of instincts is destructive.

Fourier's socialism had its peculiarities. He actually sought capital investment in his community, for instance. Shares in the community were to be given to capital, labor, and talent. After the minimum subsistence was paid, the remaining dividends were to go four-twelfths to capital, five-twelfths to labor, and three-twelfths to talent. He also naively expected his program to be adopted by Napoleon or some wealthy financier. That was a peculiar misunderstanding of the revolutionary nature of his proposals. He had little appreciation of the way in which industry was transforming society and creating even more ghastly "jailhouses" of work. His agricultural vision of utopia was becoming outdated as he wrote. Yet, in another sense he was far ahead of his time. The instinctual liberation through creative work that he imagined possible in the 1830s has only recently appeared on the agenda of social reformers, often as a product of modern technology. Fourier would probably find modern innovations of flexible working hours, home offices, worker participation in management, as feeble steps in the right direction.

The varieties of socialism in the first half of the nineteenth century were enormous. There were dozens of Fourierist colonies alone, each with its own version of the master's voice and all understaffed and undercapitalized, on four continents. There were also utopian communities modeled on the socialist theories of Etienne Cabet, Robert Owen, and many others. Etienne Cabet (1787–1856), in his *Voyage to Icaria*, conceived of a communist society on a national scale, with industry supporting a population of a million. Icaria was to exclude private property and eliminate any social inequality. All citizens were to labor equally, and receive from the common store equally, "each according to his needs." And because Cabet grew up in a French society where, even after the Revolution of 1789, clothes designated status, the inhabitants of Icaria were to dress alike. Cabet's ideal society reflected much in his own personality, It was austere, authoritarian, almost harshly fair, and deeply Christian. Communism did not become associated with atheism until after 1848. In that year Cabet introduced communism to the United States, but in the form of experimental communities like those of Fourier and Robert Owen (which he had criticized as so inadequate).

Claude-Henri de Rouvroy de Saint-Simon (1760–1825) was one of the most interesting men of his time. Yet it was his disciples who turned a rather ambiguous legacy into a socialist movement throughout Europe and beyond. Saint-Simon was not only an aristocrat who survived the French Revolution and then went on to launch socialism. He also fought in the American Revolution, undertook canal projects through Central America and in Europe, and renounced his title (but not his knack for making money) in becoming Citizen Bonhomme ("Goodman") of the French Revolution. He was arrested and nearly executed by Robespierre, became rich under the Directory, found himself an inmate at Charenton insane asylum under Napoleon, became unofficial spokesman for the banking and industrial liberal bourgeoisie in the restoration of constitutional monarchy between 1815 and 1830, but found himself ignored by his former banking friends (who eventually took power in 1830) because at some point in the last decade of his life he had crossed the line from liberalism to socialism without knowing it.

Saint-Simon's route from bourgeois spokesman to socialist was marked not by a change in his own outlook but by a continued effort to carry the arguments of the bourgeois revolution to their logical conclusions. As long as the banking-industrial class was politically weak after the defeat of Napoleon and the restoration of the monarchy in 1815, Saint-Simon's insistence that power belonged to the "producers" satisfied them. They would have preferred Saint-Simon to argue for the power of "property" rather than "producers," but it was clear enough that Saint-Simon meant them. But as France industrialized, it became increasingly clear that the real class of "producers" were not the owners but the workers. Nevertheless, it was Saint-Simon's followers who created a socialist movement. It was the Saint-Simonian journal, *Le Globe*, which popularized the word *socialisme* in February 1832. For them the new word meant not the abolition of private property so much as the assumption that property was social and could therefore be called to public account.

Unlike Fourier and the utopians, the Saint-Simonians almost uniformly embraced the national industrial system. In France they were greater proponents of technology than the capitalists. Like Cabet, Saint-Simonian socialists were also religious. Many thought of themselves as disciples preaching "faith" in the "new Christianity." Thus, the combination of religious commitment and the acceptance of an inevitable, centralized industrial state could have profoundly authoritarian tones. On the other hand, the Saint-Simonians saw the exploitation of nature (through industrialization) as a way of ending the exploitation of human beings, and they were leading proponents of the rights of women and the dispossessed. They pioneered prison reform, employment of paupers, and treatment for the insane. Like the followers of Fourier, they spoke little of economics, aside from criticizing private property, market relations, and inequality, but argued for a general human liberation that, however utopian, began with human needs for creative expression and social participation.

THE ORIGINS OF MARXISM

On the eve of the abortive French social revolution of 1848 there was still no major socialist movement outside of France. German liberals were allied with a few socialists in an effort to create the parliamentary system, national unification, and middle-class freedoms that France had achieved in the revolution of 1789 and England had been developing since 1689 or even the 1640s.

By 1848 Britain had created the world's only industrial society. Consequently, British thinkers were in a much better position to survey the economics of the new order. The "movement" in England before 1848 was Chartist and Owenite. Robert Owen was a successful Fourier. He turned his own textile mill into a model community for the benefit of his workers, aided the creation of utopian worker cooperatives in Britain and America, and pioneered a consumer cooperative, and the organization of British trade unions which eventually became the Labour party.

British Chartism was a larger mass movement than all of French socialism, but only a few of the Chartists considered themselves socialists. The People's Charter that the Chartists wanted passed would have given working men the vote and the possibility of serving in parliament. But even with petitions bearing the signatures of half of the adult males of Britain, the charter was overwhelmingly rejected by Parliament. It took another 80 years before the demands of the charter were passed.

We are left then with something of a paradox. The country which pioneered the industrial revolution, the most advanced capitalist economy of the nineteenth century, the patent office and workshop of the world, waited in the 1840s for a German (or rather two Germans) to fuse the new study of political economy with the socialism of Owen, and to turn the mass working-class movement from liberal to socialist goals.

In fact, Karl Marx and Friedrich Engels not only studied the workings of the new economy and the conditions of the new working class, they also changed the meaning and importance of socialism for ever.

Marxism is the fusion of French socialism, German philosophy, and British political economy. For Marx the starting point was the philosophical climate at the University of Berlin in the 1830s. Under Napoleonic occupation, German philosophers had largely turned away from exterior political issues of nationhood and freedom, and they had consoled themselves with intense speculations about such "interior" problems as knowledge, morality, being, reason, judgment, and consciousness.

Factory with mechanical looms, England, 1835

Marx studied philosophy but bridled at the fashionable mind games. He wanted to spend his life working to improve the welfare of humankind, he wrote as early as 1835 at the age of 17 on a final examination. But he noted that people's actions are to some extent already shaped by their social relationships.

To recognize what is socially determined, and yet to seek to make a better world—this was the problem that Marx set himself and pursued for the rest of his life. In doing so, Marx enlarged his culture's understanding of the depth of necessity and the possibilities of freedom by showing people how to think historically about human societies.

"History" in the Germany of the 1830s and 1840s meant the philosophy of Hegel. Hegel taught Marx that history is a process of conflict, and that conflicts transform the world in understandable ways. The idea that there was a logic to history had been developed in the French Enlightenment of the eighteenth century. But this had led to Saint-Simon's and his follower August Comte's idea of distinct historical stages, with little thought given to the actual process of change. Hegel, and then Marx, found a motor or propeller of social change in human labor. "The great thing in Hegel's *Phenomenology*," Marx wrote in his *Economic-Philosophical Manuscripts of 1844*, "is that Hegel conceives the self-creation of man as a process and that he therefore grasps the nature of labor and comprehends objective man as the result of his own labor."[18]

Karl Marx (1818–1883)

In his early writings, Marx developed a philosophy of history and a rudimentary sociology that saw human labor as the creator and beneficiary of history. Through practical activity or labor, Marx argued, people produce themselves and their world. And it works both ways. Human labor creates new environments which then transform human beings. Human productivity continually transforms human needs, feelings, beliefs, and dreams as it transforms the external world.

Thus, Marx turned his history of human labor into a criticism of labor in capitalist society. Workers created the world. but they did not inherit it, Marx argued. And because the laboring classes worked for others, and not themselves, their work was not allowed to be spontaneous, social, creative, and useful. The most fundamental human need—that of expressive activity—was thwarted by capitalist markets and profits. Workers became alienated (cut off) from their own work and their own bodies.

> What constitutes the alienation of labor? First, that the work is external to the worker, that it is not part of his nature; and that, consequently, he does not fulfill himself in his work but denies himself, has a feeling of misery rather than well being, does not develop freely his mental and physical energies but is physically exhausted and mentally debased. The worker therefore feels himself at home only during his leisure time, whereas at work he feels homeless. His work is not voluntary but imposed, *forced labor*. It is not the satisfaction of a need, but only a *means* for satisfying other needs. Its alien character is clearly shown by the fact that as soon as there is no physical or other compulsion it is avoided like the plague. External labor, labor in which man alienates himself, is a labor of self-sacrifice, of mortification. Finally, the external character of work for the worker is shown by the fact that it is not his own work but work for someone else, that in work he does not belong to himself but to another person.[19]

Marx believed that this alienation of labor was new to capitalist society. In earlier ages of household production for use, people enhanced their identities by producing things for themselves and their families. But, just as these products once affirmed their existence, abilities, desires, and identity, now under capitalism the products of human labor testified to human enslavement.

Under capitalism, Marx argued, laborers are alienated from an expanding world of objects which "oppose them." They are alienated from their own powers, from their creative selves. And separated from the objects of their labor, without the self-esteem of making, forming, and shaping, they, themselves, are treated like objects. Bought and sold like pieces of a machine, they think of themselves as objects and treat others similarly.

Thus, under capitalism according to Marx, it is not only work but all of life that is alien to human needs. The "principal thesis" of capitalism, Marx wrote:

> is the renunciation of life and of human needs. The less you eat, drink, buy books, go to the theater or to balls, or to public houses, and the less you think, love, theorize, sing, paint, fence, etc., the more you will be able to save and the greater will become your treasure which neither moth nor rust will corrupt—your *capital*. The less you *are*, the less you express your life, the more you *have*, the greater is your alienated life and the greater is the saving of your alienated being.[20]

1848: THE COMMUNIST MANIFESTO

Marx the philosopher should not obscure Marx the revolutionary. Philosophy and revolution were not separate occupations for Marx. "The philosophers have only *interpreted* the world in different ways," Marx wrote in 1845, "the point is to *change* it."[21] But an uninformed, mindless desire for change was, for Marx, no better than sterile philosophizing. Successful revolution required a firm philosophical and historical foundation that Marx found lacking in the visions of utopian socialists and the ranting of suicidal revolutionaries.

The Communist Manifesto was written in the winter of 1847–1848 by Marx and Friedrich Engels, who was both a businessman and a communist, as the platform of the Communist League. It was a schizophrenic document for a schizophrenic age. In part it looked to the completion of the bourgeois revolution that had only begun in France since 1789 and had barely gotten under way in Germany. And in part it looked to the future socialist revolution that appeared only in embryo in the "hungry forties."

If Marx and Engels had mistaken the birth pangs of bourgeois capitalism in 1848 for its death throes, it was a fault of their broad historical vision. They were able to discern the future developments of the new economic and social system so well that they sometimes imagined it had already occurred. That is why the *Manifesto* exaggerates both the achievements and the failures of bourgeois society in 1848. *The Communist Manifesto* exaggerates the *achievements* of capitalism?

[Capitalism] has been the first to show what man's activity can bring about. It has accomplished wonders far surpassing Egyptian pyramids, Roman aqueducts and Gothic cathedrals; it has conducted expeditions that put in the shade all former Exoduses of nations and crusades.

The bourgeoisie cannot exist without constantly revolutionizing the instruments of production, and thereby the relations of production, and with them the whole relations of society. . . . All fixed, fast frozen relations, with their train of ancient and venerable prejudices and opinions, are swept away. . . .

The need of a constantly expanding market for its products chases the bourgeoisie over the whole surface of the globe. . . . In place of the old local and national seclusion and self-sufficiency, we have intercourse in every direction, universal interdependence of nations. And as in material, so also in intellectual production. The intellectual creations of individual nations become common property. National one-sidedness and narrow-mindedness become more and more impossible, and from the numerous national and local literatures there arises a world literature.

The bourgeoisie, by the rapid improvement of all instruments of production, by the immensely facilitated means of communication, draws all, even the most barbarian nations into civilization. . . . It has created enormous cities, has greatly increased the urban population as compared with the rural, and has thus rescued a considerable part of the population from the idiocy of rural life. . . .

The bourgeoisie, during its rule of scarce one hundred years, has created more massive and more colossal productive forces than have all preceding generations together. Subjection of Nature's forces to man, machinery, application of chemistry to industry and agriculture, steam-navigation, railways, electric telegraphs, clearing of whole continents for cultivation, canalization of rivers, whole populations conjured out of the ground—what earlier century had even a presentiment that such productive forces slumbered in the lap of social labor?[22]

Now, certainly all of that had not happened by 1848. National seclusion had not yet been opened to "multinational corporations." Local provincialism and "rural idiocy" had not yet completely disappeared. National "narrow-mindedness" had not yet been replaced by "world literature." But Marx and Engels were able to elaborate the distant future implications of bourgeois capitalism because they understood its dynamic.

The same is true of their exaggeration of the new society's failures. They recognized the transforming potential of the new system and expressed their prophecy in the past tense.

The bourgeoisie, wherever it has got the upper hand, has put an end to all feudal, patriarchal, idyllic relations. It has pitilessly torn asunder the motley feudal ties that bound man to his "natural superiors," and has left no other nexus between man and man than "cash payment." It has drowned the most heavenly ecstasies of religious fervor, of chivalrous enthusiasm, of Philistine sentimentalism, in the icy water of egotistical calculation. It has resolved personal worth into exchange value and in place of the numberless indefensible chartered freedoms, has set up that single, unconscionable freedom—Free Trade. In one word, for exploitation, veiled by religious and political illusions, it has substituted naked, shameless, direct, brutal exploitation.

The bourgeoisie has stripped of its halo every occupation hitherto honored and looked up to with reverent awe. It has converted the physician, the lawyer, the priest, the poet, the man of science, into its paid wage laborers.

The bourgeoisie has torn away from the family its sentimental veil, and has reduced the family relation to a mere money relation.[23]

Again, the future tense would have been more appropriate. European society in 1848 still had significant feudal elements. Serfdom had not entirely disappeared. Aristocracies were still powerful. People had not converted all social relationships into business ones. Cash had not everywhere replaced honor, duty, generosity, and morality. Religion had not completely disappeared. Priests were still honored. Everyone, even physicians, did not work only for money. Absolutely everything was not for sale. Family life was still important. The market economy had not commercialized all of life by 1848.

But today? Just call your doctor and ask. The genius of Marx and Engels was in recognizing the revolutionary nature of the new market, business, or commercial society. They were able to chart the way things were changing by focusing on what was new and elaborating its consequences. They recognized that capitalist or bourgeois society was unleashing forces that would radically change the world—indeed, create a single world. Their historical vision suggested that this world would be immeasurably more productive than the past one—the feudal age. But their studies of social classes suggested that the enormous productivity of the new society would also contain the seeds of its own destruction, just as the feudal age had.

The *Manifesto* speaks only generally about these "seeds."

It is enough to mention the commercial crises that by their periodical return put on its trial, each time more threateningly, the existence of the entire bourgeois society. In these crises a great part not only of the existing products, but also of the previously created productive forces, are periodically destroyed. In these crises there breaks out an epidemic that, in all earlier epochs, would have seemed an absurdity—the epidemic of overproduction."[24]

The question of capitalism's crises of periodic depressions was to occupy an important part of Marx's later work for *Capital*. In 1848 it was sufficient to point to the history of commercial crises, and to stress the absurdity of a society drowning in its very productivity because the owners didn't pay the workers enough to buy what they produced.

At times Marx and Engels seemed to agree with their contemporaries that the actual income of the working classes would decline. But they always insisted that the amount of money available to the workers was not the issue. Workers who did not collectively own the factories and other productive means would always be exploited. Private ownership would always mean that the profits of the new productivity would be monopolized by the owning class. Capitalist society would continually increase the gap between owners and workers, but far more importantly it would increase the gap between the potential of its new productivity and its performance. The absurdity of poverty in affluence would deepen, but the absurdity of meaningless, obsolescent, and destructive production would offer no remedy.

SOCIALISM AND COMMUNISM

The Communist Manifesto had virtually no effect on the revolutions that swept European society in 1848. The socialist revolution could not be put on the agenda until the bourgeoisie had completed its own revolution and developed capitalist society to the limitations of its power and its contradictions. Despite their exaggerations of the maturity of bourgeois civilization, Marx and Engels realized that the time for socialism was still far off. Later they were to talk of the need to wait possibly 50 years before capitalism had worked itself to death. In 1848 the *Manifesto* spoke of the distant future as if it were the past but concluded with specific proposals geared to the needs of the present. The communists should ally themselves with the bourgeois parties, the *Manifesto* insisted. Only after assuring bourgeois supremacy could the fight against bourgeois society begin.

For a moment after the failure of the revolutions of 1848 Marx and Engels flirted with the idea of speeding up the process. But by 1850, and for the rest of their lives, they were committed to a gradual process of study, education, and struggle. Marx worked on *Capital* in London until his death in 1883 and poured his energies into the analysis of the capitalist system. The revolution became increasingly a work of organizing the labor movement and labor parties. Gone was the rhetoric about spontaneous insurrection that had marked some of their writings before 1848. Gone also was the talk of secretive parties and a temporary "dictatorship of the proletariat" that sometimes seemed the only hope in the despair of 1849. The Marxist vision of socialism after 1850 was thoroughly democratic (as it had been before 1849). It awaited the achievements and the contradictions that the *Manifesto* described.

Capitalism recovered from the depressions of 1873 and 1893 with whole colonial territories to lift the burdens of exploitation from the European and North

Revolution returned to France and much of Europe in 1848. In Paris, thousands of workers dismissed from their jobs built barricades. Their revolt was suppressed by the army under General Cavaignac, the conqueror of Algeria in the 1840s, soon to be known as the "Hangman of Paris."

American working classes. The class struggle was abated at home as it became internationalized. Working classes were allowed unions, better wages, social insurance, mass education, and even suffrage as long as they gave their lives to preserve the international imbalance.

The European socialist parties of 1914 screamed that they would never go to war against their brothers in the international working class in order to preserve the colonies that kept capitalism alive. And when war came they enlisted and died in the millions. Modern propaganda created nationalist appeals that no singing of *The International* could drown out.

The Russian Revolution of 1917 offered a foolish moment of hope to the suicidal European movement. Things might have been different if the German socialists had succeeded. But they failed. Socialism and communism became identified with Soviet bureaucracy, Stalinism, and the secret police. European socialists had themselves to blame for accepting the credentials of the Russian Marxists in the first place. They forgot the essence of Marx's historical vision when they imagined that a genuine socialist revolution might occur in the most feudal country of Europe. In 1917 only England and the United States had approached the mature capitalism that would be productive enough to junk oppression. And their colonies gave their system an extended lease on life. Further, the Russian confusion of collectivist industrialization with Marxist socialism allowed the benefactors of Western capitalism to call themselves the democracies and identify socialism with slavery, insolvency, and stupidity. Even Russian industrialization, although more rapid than capitalist, could be compared unfavorably to Western. "See? That's what happens when there's no incentive." Never mind that the Russians were only a generation removed from serfdom.

The collapse of capitalism in 1929 seemed to be the final failure that Marx had predicted. Socialist and communist parties regained some of the strength and prestige they had enjoyed before 1914. But capital had one final option: war. The military state solved the problem of underconsumption (which they called overproduction) by forcing workers to produce things they would never want to buy: bombs.

Capitalism recovered from the Great Depression of the 1930s through militarization. Soviet Communism never recovered from Stalinism and militarization. Whether socialism can recover from its identification with Soviet communism will depend on whether or not future generations find value in the ideas of people like Babeuf and Fourier, Marx and Engels.

FOR FURTHER READING

There are a number of good general histories of socialism. George Lichtheim's *The Origins of Socialism* is a scholarly history of utopian and Marxist socialism that parallels most closely the period (1789–1848) that we have chosen in the chapter. Albert S. Lindemann's *The History of European Socialism* is a useful overview through the twentieth century. Edmund Wilson's *To the Finland Station* is a literary as well as interpretive jewel that traces the tradition back to the philosophy of history of Vico and Michelet and engages the reader with an extensive anecdotal and critical biography of Marx. Michael Harrington's *Socialism* is a demanding, persuasive history of Marxist and democratic socialism.

For the French Revolution, the best introduction is Jack Richard Censer and Lynn Hunt's *Liberty, Equality, Fraternity: Exploring the French Revolution*, available in CD format as well as book. Simon Schama's *Citizens* is a more challenging and interpretive account. For a conservative view see François Furet, *Interpreting the French Revolution*. For a sympathetic interpretation of the Jacobins, see Patrice L. Higonnet's *Goodness beyond Virtue: Jacobins during the French Revolution*. Georges Lefebvre's *The Coming of the French Revolution* and *The Thermidorians* are classics. Among other classical interpretations are George Rude's *The Crowd in the French Revolution*, Alfred Cobban's *The Social Interpretation of the French Revolution* and A. de Tocqueville's *The Old Regime and the French Revolution*. For an understanding of the roots of communism in the French Revolution, *The Defense of Gracchus Babeuf*, edited and translated by John Anthony Scott, has been invaluable.

For Fourier, Jonathan Beecher and Richard Bienvenu's *The Utopian Vision of Charles Fourier* is excellent. Barbara Taylor's *Eve and the New Jerusalem: Socialism and Feminism in the Nineteenth Century* is a good introduction to Owenite utopian socialism and early feminism.

On Marx and Marxism, Francis Wheen's biography *Karl Marx: A Life* is the best recent introduction to the man. Isaiah Berlin's *Karl Marx: His Life and Environment* is a good, readable, more conservative interpretation; George Lichtheim's *Marxism: An Historical and Critical Study* is a thorough one-volume analysis. Robert Tucker's *Philosophy and Myth in Karl Marx* is an interesting theoretical study. G.A.A. Cohen's *Karl Marx's Theory of History* is a thoughtful defense.

For interpretations of particular aspects of Marxism, Erich Fromm's *Marx's Concept of Man*, published with a translation from Marx's *Economic and Philosophical Manuscripts* by T. B. Bottomore, is an excellent introduction to the early Marx. Herbert Marcuse's *One Dimensional Man* integrates Fourier and Marx. Istvan Meszaros's *Marx's Theory of Alienation* is a subtle, thorough treatment of the subject, as is Bertell Ollman's *Alienation*. Schlomo Avineri's *The Social and Political Thought of Karl Marx* is a more general statement.

NOTES

1. *The Defense of Gracchus Babeuf Before the High Court of Vendôme*, ed. and trans. John Anthony Scott (New York: Schocken Books, 1967), pp. 63–64.
2. *Ibid.*, p. 73.
3. *Ibid.*, p. 57.
4. Quoted in *ibid.*, p. 11.
5. George Lichtheim, *The Origins of Socialism* (New York: Praeger, 1969), p. 32.
6. Jonathan Beecher and Richard Bienvenu, *The Utopian Vision of Charles Fourier: Selected Texts on Work, Love and Passionate Attraction* (Boston: Beacon Press, 1971), pp. 6–7.
7. *Ibid.*, pp. 8–9.
8. *Ibid.*, p. 10.
9. *Ibid.*, pp. 14–15.
10. *Ibid.*, pp. 30–31.
11. *Ibid.*, p. 304.
12. *Ibid.*, p. 317.
13. *Ibid.*, pp. 317–318.
14. *Ibid.*, p. 40.
15. *Ibid.*, p. 8.
16. *Ibid.*, p. 59.
17. *Ibid.*, p. 53.
18. Adapted from *Economic-Philosophical Manuscripts*, trans. T. B. Bottomore, in Erich Fromm, *Marx's Concept of Man* (New York: Ungar, 1961, 1966), pp. 176–177.

19. *Ibid.*, pp. 98–99.
20. Quoted in Herbert Marcuse, *Reason and Revolution: Hegel and the Rise of Social Theory* (Boston: Beacon Press, 1960), p. 144.
21. Karl Marx, *Thesis on Feuerbach*, no. xi. Included in T. B. Bottomore, ed. and trans., *Karl Marx: Selected Writings* (New York: McGraw-Hill, 1964), p. 69.
22. Karl Marx and Friedrich Engels, *The Communist Manifesto*, ed. Samuel H. Beer, trans. Samuel Moore (Northbrook, Illinois: AHM Publishing Corporation, 1955), pp. 12–14.
23. *Ibid.*, p. 12.
24. *Ibid.*, p. 15.

The Cuban Revolution of 1869: proclamation of the Cuban Republic.

7

Race
and
Class

The United States
and South Africa

It is particularly ironic that racial barriers were constructed in the United States and South Africa at the very time that class differences were increasing—during the period of rapid industrialization between 1870 and 1914. Normally the process of capitalist industrialization creates social classes: workers and employers; skilled and unskilled; manufacturers and miners; industrial and service personnel; rich and poor. Normally capitalist industrialization erases all inequalities except class: it makes money, wages, income, and property more important than race, gender, nationality, religion, or background. While such changes occurred among most white workers in the United States and South Africa, the presence of black Africans (or African-Americans) altered that process for whites as well as blacks. Racial identity was often more important than class identity. People often thought of themselves (and others) as members of a race, rather than as representatives of a particular social class, income group, religion, or even gender. The white boss (a redundancy in itself) saw the African first as a black, then as an individual who happened to be Christian, poor, or male.

The purpose of this chapter is to try to understand why this happened in the United States and South Africa. A comparison of these two bastions of white

181

supremacy helps us to understand both the causes and the direction of change in the two countries.

SOUTH AFRICA AND NORTH AMERICA:
COLONIES AND CONQUEST

There are striking parallels in the early history of race relations in North America and South Africa. Both areas were settled by Europeans in the seventeenth century. In each case there was an initial confrontation with indigenous inhabitants—the Native Americans of North America and the Khoikhoi (or Khoisan) of South Africa. In North America the land was taken for European settlement, and the Native Americans were virtually annihilated. In South Africa the Khoikhoi surrendered both their land and their labor to the Europeans.

The process of European conquest was slower in South Africa than in North America. The South African settlement at the Cape of Good Hope was originally intended by the East India Company of Holland to be a supply station for the Dutch ships en route to the East Indies. The company initially discouraged settle-

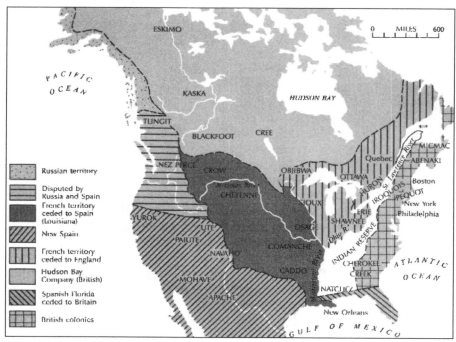

North America in 1763, after the Seven Years' War

ment beyond Cape Town, feeling that a larger colony would be too difficult to govern. The Khoikhoi were pastoralists who provided the Europeans with cattle. But as the European colony grew, its demand for meat outstripped Khoikhoi ambitions or intentions. The area of white occupation increased tenfold between 1703 and 1780 as former company employees seized Khoikhoi land for their own farms and pastures. Those Khoikhoi who were not killed by war or smallpox epidemics (as many Native Americans were) became the herders and wagon drivers for the new Dutch masters (called Boers).

Thus, in one important respect the racial situation in South Africa was different from that of North America around 1770. While most coastal American Indians had been annihilated, sent to the West Indies as slaves, or pushed beyond the Appalachians, the survivors among the original Khoikhoi inhabitants of the Cape region of South Africa became a class of subordinate servants.

Initially neither North American nor South African colonists justified their dominance in racial terms. Rather, they justified European settlement economically. The North American colonists drew on Lockeian theories of labor and private property to assert that agricultural work was more desirable than hunting because agriculture involved the addition of one's own labor to nature. Thus, according to this rationale, Europeans were improving the land, while Native Americans were only draining it. This rationale ignored the fact that Native Americans were also agriculturalists and concentrated on their more marginal hunting and gathering activities. In the case of South Africa both the Boers and the Khoikhoi were pastoralists, so the Boers could not make the same argument. Instead, the Boers maintained that by taking Khoikhoi land they were spreading Christian civilization, a claim that became louder (if not more accurate) with the passage of time. These economic and religious justifications suggest the absence of racist feelings in the early stages of colonization. Indeed, the Native Americans were called noble savages and portrayed as bronzed Europeans. Intermarriage between Boers and Khoikhoi was not uncommon, and the Khoikhoi did not experience racial discrimination.

WHITE SETTLERS AND INDIGENOUS PEOPLES

Settler movement beyond the initial frontiers occurred in both North America and South Africa around 1770. In both cases the government had hoped to keep the Europeans and indigenous peoples apart. In North America, when the British defeated the French in the French and Indian War in 1763, the British issued the Proclamation of 1763, which prohibited European settlement beyond the Appalachian Mountains. In South Africa the Dutch East India Company had originally attempted to keep the Europeans in Cape Town. When that effort failed, they attempted to restrict Europeans' movement to the area bounded by the Great Fish River. By then Boer and Khoikhoi mixed as masters and servants. There were, however, different, less Westernized Africans beyond the Great Fish River that the

Dutch (and after 1795 their successors, the British government) wanted to keep separate. These were the Bantu peoples (generally taller, darker-skinned Africans who had migrated south from the Sudan for over a thousand years). The Bantu peoples constituted many nations. In 1800 the Zulu, Swazi, and Basuto emerged as the strongest in southeastern Africa beyond the Great Fish River.

The Bantu peoples were a more formidable barrier to European migration than either the Khoikhoi or the Native Americans. The Bantu were far more numerous. Further, since the great Bantu migration had originated on the southern edge of European settlement and trade in Sudanic Africa, these peoples had already developed immunities to European diseases, which devastated the Native Americans.

The American white settler economy was also more expansive than the Boer South African. While the American economy provided important shipping supplies for the enormously productive West Indian sugar plantations of the British empire, the Cape Colony of South Africa remained essentially a subsistence pastoral economy and a food supplier for passing ships until the discovery of gold and diamonds at the end of the nineteenth century. The American settlers were therefore more powerful politically than their Boer counterparts. While there were sporadic Boer rebellions against Dutch, and later British, control of the frontier, there was nothing approaching an American Revolution in South Africa. In the end, the American settlers were successful in displacing the Native Americans because of the American Revolution. Thomas Jefferson and other early presidents insisted on protecting the Native Americans by incorporating them into American civilization. But by the 1828 election of Andrew Jackson, a veteran Native American fighter, the policy of the federal government was to remove the Native Americans in order to make way for white settlement. Even Native American nations that had attempted to adopt the ways of the white society were unceremoniously forced to move; the Cherokee, for example, were sent on a forced march to Oklahoma that was so brutal that four thousand out of fifteen thousand died along the way.

The Boers, unable to convince the Dutch before 1795 of their expansionist needs, became greatly suspicious of the British administration that took over after 1795. In the frontier conflicts with the neighboring Xhosa and Bantu peoples, the Boers believed that the British government was on the side of the Africans. In the period of the 1820s to 1850s many Boers took matters into their own hands in a different way than did the North American revolutionaries. They left British protection entirely by driving their wagons, families, cattle, and Khoikhoi herders beyond the Great Fish River and north to the high plains (or Meld) outside the colony. This migration became the national epic of the Boers, the equivalent of the American War of Independence. But the story of the Great Trek also resembles the later North American stories of war with the Native Americans: wagon trains in a circle to fend off attacks; crossing deserts and mountains with only Bibles, muskets, and determination; establishing "free" and independent states that depended on the expulsion of the original inhabitants.

RACE AND SLAVERY

We have said nothing so far of slavery. There was, of course, slavery in both North America and South Africa, but neither the Native Americans nor the South African Khoikhoi became slaves in great numbers. Even most of the South African Bantu remained outside the system of slavery. The Khoikhoi were indentured servants, as were many Europeans who came to America in the colonial period. The Bantu (like the Native Americans) could not be easily captured, enslaved, and assimilated. The slaves of South Africa were the mixed group of Asian and African peoples that South Africans bought from slave markets or imported from other Dutch colonies (especially Indonesia). Since these slaves were not drawn from a particular racial or ethnic group, slavery was not identified with race. Thus, slavery in South Africa actually had little to do with South African racial ideas.

If South African slavery was less racially specific than North American, it was also more widespread. There were more slaves, and more white slave owners. Slave ownership was more "democratic" (if such a word can be used): in 1750 half the whites in South Africa owned slaves, a higher percentage even than in Southern colonies of British America. Further, most South African slave owners owned only a few slaves. This was because South African slavery was not plantation slavery. There were no large estates equivalent to the sugar, coffee, and cotton plantations of the Americas. South African slaves worked in smaller units on farms, on the range, and in the city, usually under a single, extended family. They worked alongside Khoikhoi servants and employees—that is, among dependent workers of varying races and obligations.

Thus, ironically, though slavery was more widespread in South Africa than it was in the United States, white South African society was less dependent on it. Slavery was just one of the many systems of dependent labor in South Africa. For that reason the British abolition of slavery between 1834 and 1838 met with less diehard resistance than the abolitionist movement in the Southern United States. South African whites had become accustomed to having their menial work done by nonwhites, but slavery was not the only way of accomplishing that. While the plantation owners of the American South went to war to preserve slavery, some Boers turned to other methods of labor control. Others took their slaves, families, and herds on the Great Trek out of the country.

THE AMERICAN CIVIL WAR

There are historians who will tell you that slavery was not the main cause of the Civil War in America. They will tell you that the South seceded from the Union in order to preserve states' rights, not slavery. They will say that Lincoln went to war to preserve the Union, not to end slavery. And they will say that most Northerners did not want to fight a war to force the South to abolish slavery.

It is possible that a majority of white Southerners thought they were fighting a war of independence and principle. It is also possible that a majority of Northerners were against freeing the slaves when the war broke out in 1860. But majorities, like individuals, often delude themselves or get lost in the rush of events.

What does seem indisputable is that there were two social systems inhabiting the body politic of the United States in 1860, and those two systems had become increasingly incompatible. Whether we call those systems "free" and "slave," as Lincoln did, or "competitive" and "paternal," as Southern slaveholders did, the difference in labor systems was the point of conflict for the powerful in the North and the South. The expanding industry of the North depended on a wage labor system, and the Southern plantation depended on slavery. As both groups eyed the new territories in Texas and the West, these contrary systems, each of which seemed to exclude the other, offered more than economic competition. As the conflict intensified, each system came to stand for a way of life. Slavery meant agriculture, Southern gentility, honor, the traditions and values of past generations of planters. Wage labor meant free labor, free land, free men, opportunity, progress, and industry. And as these world views diverged and hardened, the future states of the American West represented the political battleground in which the national government would be won or lost. Lincoln's election victory in 1860 signaled the ultimate loss of that battleground, the government of the Union, for Southern planters. It seemed to them the defeat of their class and their way of life—if they remained to accept it.

It might have been possible for a slave system and a capitalist wage labor system to exist side by side indefinitely. The growth of capitalism in the North, and in England, owed much to the slave labor of the cotton plantations in the South. The initial stages of capitalist industrialization depended on cotton and slavery. In many ways the plantation owners of the South even operated like capitalists. "A great plantation was as difficult to operate as a complicated modern factory, which in important respects it resembled. Hit-or-miss methods could not be tolerated, endless planning and anxious care were demanded."[1]

Different economies, even class systems, might have remained compatible. The cultures, values, ideals, and ideas that those social systems engendered proved less open to compromise. The war of nerves that preceded the war of armies was waged with words. As tensions increased, Northern publicists and politicians became more indignant about slavery, and Southern planters revived older visions of agricultural harmony, natural order, and civilized grace, which they contrasted with the money-grubbing ways of the North. Some Southerners saw Northern moralistic rhetoric as a program to abolish Southern property.

The Civil War was a radical revolution. Charles Beard, the great American historian, called it "the Second American Revolution." In some ways the Civil War was even more radical than the "first" American Revolution. The Revolution of 1776 has often been called a "conservative revolution" because it transferred power from an English ruling class to a colonial ruling class. The Civil War enshrined the conviction of the Revolution that "all men are created equal." It took seriously the

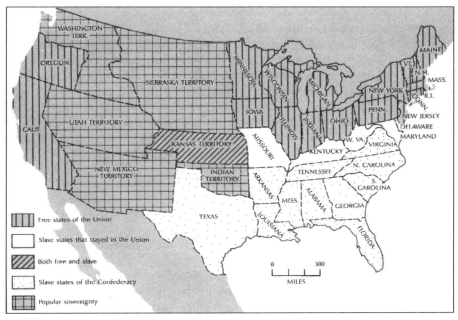

The United States during the Civil War

radically democratic message of the middle-class capitalist revolution. It drew on the resources of the most egalitarian elements of capitalism. Not coincidentally was a Midwestern lawyer the candidate of the new Republican party in 1860. Lincoln spoke for frontiersmen who had become successful farmers. By the 1850s they had created a third America, as agricultural as the South but without slavery. Instead of siding with the South, the new West found its allies in the more radical spokesmen of the Northeast.

The union of frontier farmer and Northern capitalist did not, however, last much beyond the war. Only a few of its statesmen were willing to unseat the ruling elite of the South once they had been defeated. Fewer still were willing to break up the old plantations and distribute the land to the former slaves so that they might become independent farmers themselves. A small band of radical Republicans that did not include Lincoln saw slavery as a remnant of a dying world of feudalism and sought to "reconstruct" the South according to the Northern principles of "free speech, free toil, schoolhouses, and ballot boxes." Thaddeus Stevens, their most eloquent spokesman, proposed that the large plantations be confiscated to provide forty acres for each former slave family, a measure that had been carried out on a smaller scale by the Union army in the last year of the war. Horace Greeley, editor of the *New York Tribune* and a former abolitionist, spoke for many when he answered Stevens's bill: he objected to what he saw as warfare on Southern property; he praised the wealthier class of Southerners as enlightened and humane; and he warned against social upheaval. A radical revolution, even a democratic capitalist one, was not to endure.

Still, the accomplishments of the era of Reconstruction (1865–1877) were considerable. The Thirteenth Amendment to the Constitution freed the slaves in 1865. The Fourteenth Amendment gave the freedmen citizenship and civil rights by 1868. The Fifteenth Amendment provided the vote by 1870. Civil rights legislation and the radical wing of the Republican party guaranteed blacks full political participation. There was, however, no social revolution for the former slaves. The plantations were not divided to give freed slaves "forty acres and a mule." Without land or capital, former slaves became tenant farmers and sharecroppers who had to mortgage their futures for seed.

The reason that Stevens's bill failed in Congress and no other attempt was made at land redistribution for the former slaves was that there was simply no consensus, even in the North, for fully integrating the former slaves into American society as equals. There were other drawbacks, to be sure. The confiscation of Southern land struck fear into the hearts of others besides Horace Greeley. There was also a long-standing belief in Anglo-American political thought, going back to John Locke, that legal equality and the ballot box were all anyone needed to compete on life's playing field and that government should provide nothing more. However, since Northern businessmen were persuading the government to give them tariffs, a strong central banking system, railroads, and a huge chunk of federal land, we cannot take such principles too seriously. The more important reason Congress rejected the bill seems to be a general unwillingness to integrate independent blacks into American society.

DOMINATIVE VERSUS AVERSIVE RACISM

In a book called *White Racism: A Psychohistory*, Joel Kovel suggests a distinction between two kinds of racism, which he calls dominative and aversive. Dominative racism, he says, is the racism of slave society. Domination is legal and accepted. Slaves know their place, even if they resent it. In some cases the domination is so complete that it goes unquestioned, thus allowing whites to view the slaves as good-humored children grateful for their protection. In these cases bonds of loyalty and affection can develop between masters and slaves, who pretend to ignore the reality of domination because it is so complete, legal, and unquestioned. Then, when breaches occur, they are punished with the most severe brutality, almost as if a sacred trust has been violated, and the very inequality of the relationship is revealed.

The vice president of the Confederacy, Alexander Stephens, sounded the tune of dominative racism in 1861:

Many governments have been founded on the principles of subordination and serfdom of certain classes of the same race; *Such were, and are, in violation of the laws of nature.* Our system commits no such violation of nature's laws. With us, all the white race, however high or low, rich or poor, are equal in the eyes of the law. Not so with the Negro. Subordination is his place. He, by nature, or by the curse against Canaan, is fitted for that condition which he occupies in our system. . . . Its foundations are laid, its "cornerstone" rests upon the great truth that the Negro is not equal to the white man, that slavery—subordination to the superior race—is his natural or normal condition.[2]

Aversive racism is different from dominative racism, according to Kovel. Aversive racism is the racism that existed in the North before the Civil War and became the American attitude, North and South, after the war. The aversive racist accepts the notion of legal equality, at least reluctantly. Unable to achieve "legal distance," he or she seeks "physical distance" from blacks. The aversive racist has an aversion to blacks and attempts to turn away and avoid them. This is the racism of segregation, legal and "voluntary." It is the racism of those who wish the blacks would "just go away." As a psychological state of avoidance it is more difficult to confront than dominative racism. The aversive racist can also turn away from the recognition that his or her own behavior is racist. It is part of the avoidance to insist that "I'm not racist, but . . ."

Not everyone in the North was an aversive racist, but many of those who were antislavery were also antiblack and hoped to get rid of blacks as well as slavery. Many Republicans, including Lincoln, answered charges by their opponents in the election of 1860 that they were in favor of racial equality and amalgamation by declaring their support of plans to deport the black population. Indeed, the colonization of Liberia in Africa was supported by Northern abolitionists as well as Southerners.

It was racial segregation, however, that was the core practice of aversive racism, just as slavery was the core of dominative racism. And it is racial segregation that unites South African and United States history, because both societies made an important investment in racial segregation in the twentieth century. We might date the reign of racial segregation in the United States from the Supreme Court decision of *Plessy v. Ferguson* in 1896 to that of *Brown v. Board of Education* in 1954, although it began earlier and has continued in residential and other "voluntary" forms since. In South Africa we may date segregation from shortly after the founding of the Union of South Africa in 1910 to the collapse of the apartheid regime in 1989.

SOUTH AFRICA, 1834–1910

We have already seen that there was no South African equivalent of the Civil War. When slavery was abolished by the British government in 1834, the Boers had already developed alternative forms of forced labor. The end of slavery did not mean the end of cheap black labor, and so it could be tolerated. What was more galling to the Boers was the British insistence that blacks and whites be treated equally before the law. British humanitarianism they could not stomach. And so, while they did not go to war, some ten thousand Boers between 1836 and 1846 walked away from British authority in their Great Trek. The Boer governments of the Orange Free State (after 1848) and the Transvaal, or (officially) South African Republic (after 1880), were sufficiently independent of British authority that we must speak of a number of South Africas before the Union of 1910.

The Boer republics received British recognition on the condition that they not revive slavery. They complied in word only, replenishing their stock of "apprentices" with "orphans" captured in Bantu wars. Their constitutions were unabashedly white supremacist. One declared there would be "no equality between colored people and the white inhabitants of the country." Another barred political participation to anyone of mixed race "down to the tenth degree."

The British colonies, on the other hand, professed racial equality while allowing discrimination. The British government of Natal declared "there shall not be in the eye of law any distinction of color, origin, race, or creed; but the protection of the law, in letter and substance, shall be extended impartially to all alike."[3] It proceeded to exclude the majority Zulus and other Africans from any citizenship by beginning the process of ruling them in separate "homelands." Only in the Cape Colony were Africans theoretically allowed to vote, and there a property qualification limited the suffrage to a token few. While whites and blacks were presumed to be equal before the law, the Cape Colony passed a series of "Masters and Servants" laws, which dictated strict control and punishment of unruly "servants," all of whom, of course, were black.

A union of such divergent societies and racial policies seemed unlikely at mid-century. There could be no South African civil war because there was no South African Union. The establishment of Boer republics and African homelands was a process of fragmentation rather than unification. Two events changed all that. One was the discovery of diamonds in 1867. The other was the discovery of gold in 1884. Both discoveries in Boer republics required African labor and British capital. They provided an industrial base that required a far more extensive transportation and communication network than the rural and landlocked Boer republics could build on their own. Gold and diamonds created a unified South Africa by 1910.

The "Union" of South Africa that was created was a union of whites: British and Boers. The Africans paid the bill for the new white harmony. The Boer model of racial policy, not that of the British colonies, became the national model for the Union, despite the fact that British arms had imposed unity in the Boer War

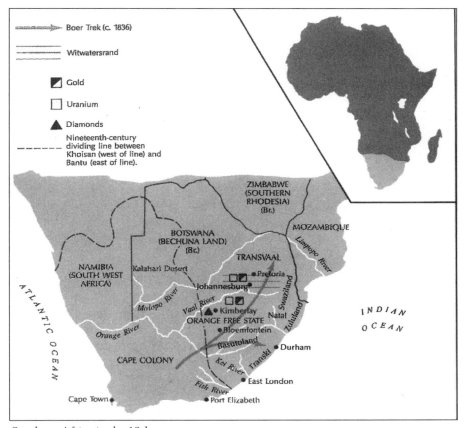

Southern Africa in the 19th century

(1899–1902). One might say that the British won the war but gave away the peace. But that is not quite accurate. By 1902 the British were not as concerned about racial equality as they had been in the 1830s. By accepting Boer racism they were not giving up very much.

That judgment might be more true of the defeat of radical reconstruction in the Northern United States. The North, which won the Civil War in 1865, gave away the peace in 1877. In the United States, as in South Africa, a peace was made between white ruling classes that excluded blacks. In the United States in 1877 and in South Africa in 1910, national unions were forged for whites only. There lie the origins of racial segregation and subordination in each.

FROM RECONSTRUCTION TO SEGREGATION:
UNITING THE STATES, 1877–1914

The disputed presidential election of 1876, in which Rutherford B. Hayes ran against Samuel Tilden, provided an opportunity for the conservative white South to regroup to aid the conservative Republicans of the North. They elected Republican Hayes, and he pledged his presidency to undo the work of the radical wing of his own party and to return the South to the whites. Federal troops were withdrawn from the South, and the federal government looked the other way as one Southern state after another began to restrict the civil rights of blacks.

Segregation, the hallmark of aversive racism, began in the North before the Civil War, but it was made into a system of race relations in the 1870s. This occurred in the South in new cities, such as Birmingham, not in the older plantation-area cities, such as New Orleans. Until the 1890s, "social contact between the races persisted, particularly at New Orleans, in a variety of sports, on the beaches of Lake Pontchartrain, and in some churches and bars," writes C. Vann Woodward.

> One source of leadership and strength that Louisiana Negroes enjoyed and that blacks of no other state shared was a well-established upper class of mixed racial origin in New Orleans with a strong infusion of French and other Latin intermixtures. Among the people were descendants of the "Free People of Color," some of them men of culture, education, and wealth, often with a heritage of several generations of freedom. Unlike the great majority of Negroes, they were city people with an established professional class and a high degree of literacy. Their views found expression in at least four Negro newspapers that existed simultaneously in New Orleans in the 1880s. By ancestry as well as by residence, they were associated with Latin cultures that were in some ways at variance with Anglo-American ideas of race relations. Their forebears had lived under the *Code Noir* decreed for Louisiana by Louis XIV, and their city faced out upon Latin America. This group had taken the lead in fighting for Negro rights during Reconstruction and were in a natural position to resist the tide of legal segregation. When it touched their shores they were the first to speak out.[4]

But touch their shores it did. On 10 July 1890, a bill requiring separate railroad for blacks passed the Louisiana state legislature, despite the work of militant leaders and eighteen black members of the state legislature (as well as the railroad, which regarded segregation as an added expense). The opposition organized to challenge the constitutionality of the law under the Fourteenth Amendment. Homer Adolph Plessy, a black, bought a ticket in New Orleans and sat in the car reserved for whites. He was arrested and convicted before Judge John H. Ferguson of the Criminal District Court of the Parish of New Orleans. The case *Plessy v.*

SCÈNE DE LYNCHAGE AUX ÉTATS-UNIS
Un nègre fusillé sur une scène de théâtre

Dominative racism did not disappear with slavery. Between 1882 and 1927 in the United States, 4,951 black men were lynched. Most were acts of mob violence. Sometimes official executions were equally grotesque. Here the opera house of Livermore, Kentucky, was the site of a public execution by the audience. Holders of orchestra tickets were given six shots; balcony tickets got one.

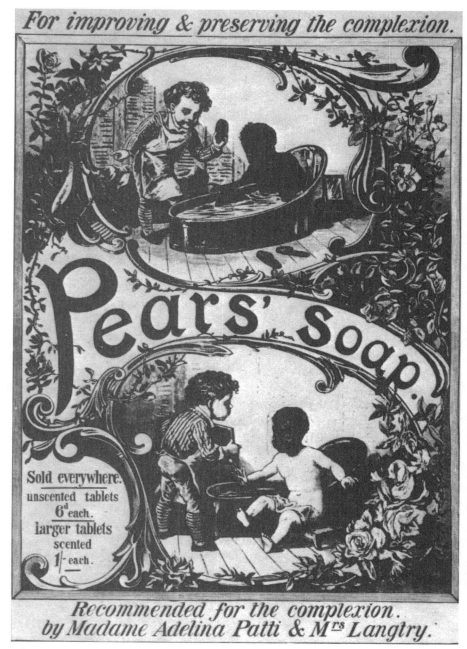

This Pears' soap ad, from The Illustrated London News *of 1885, penetrates (as ads often do) the deeper emotional meaning of aversive racism.*

Ferguson came to the U.S. Supreme Court. "Justice is pictured blind and her daughter, the Law, ought at least to be color-blind," Plessy's attorney, Albion Tourgee, argued. "Why not require all colored people to walk on one side street and the white on the other?" he asked scornfully.[5]

With the Supreme Court's decision on *Plessy v. Ferguson*, in May 1896, Tourgee's taunt became a reality. White segregationists cheered the decision of Justice Henry Billings Brown for the majority that "separate but equal" facilities were constitutional. By 1900 all Southern states had separate railway cars, and segregation was spreading to stations, streetcars, public parks, hospitals, and prisons. Some towns prohibited blacks altogether. Many cities imposed compulsory residential segregation. North Carolina and Florida required white and black students to use different textbooks in the public schools. New Orleans even created separate districts for white and black prostitutes.

Segregation measures were sometimes executed with platitudes of enlightened liberalism. President Woodrow Wilson told blacks in the campaign of 1912 that he wished to see "justice done to the colored people in every matter; and not mere grudging justice, but justice executed with liberality and cordial good feeling." Then when elected he segregated the eating and toilet facilities of federal civil service workers.

Blacks were systematically disenfranchised as well in the decades after *Plessy*. Poll taxes, "general understanding" tests, "good character" tests were among the obstacles used to prevent blacks from voting. In 1896 there were over 130,000 registered black voters in Louisiana. By 1904 there were fewer than 1,350.

Frenzied racist propaganda led to "white supremacy elections," in which white mobs attacked and destroyed black neighborhoods and engaged in widespread lynching and looting. Between 1890 and 1920 four thousand blacks were put to death without trial. The brutal violence of dominative racism did not disappear in the age of aversive racism. Intimidation and separation, domination and aversion, were often employed together by whites concerned with "keeping blacks in their place."

Blacks too learned the survival skills of a white supremacist society. "Just the other day my Laura started getting sassy about white children," one black mother told an interviewer much later:

> "My husband told her to hold her tongue and do it fast. It's like with cars and knives, you have to teach your children to know what's dangerous and how to stay away from it, or else they sure won't live long. White people are a real danger to us until we learn how to live with them. So if you want your kids to live long, they have to grow up scared of whites; and the way they get scared is through us; and that's why I don't let my kids get fresh about the white man even in their own house. If I do there's liable to be trouble to pay. They'll forget, and they'll say something outside, and that'll be it for them, and us too. So

I make them store it in the bones, way inside, and then no one sees it. Maybe in a joke we'll have once in a while, or something like that, you can see what we feel inside, but mostly it's buried. But to answer your question, I don't think it's only from you it gets buried. The colored man, I think he has to hide what he really feels even from himself. Otherwise there would be too much pain—too much."[6]

Booker T. Washington expressed that attitude for many American blacks in the generation after the Civil War. Born a slave on a Virginia plantation in 1859, he worked his way to become head of a new college for blacks, the Tuskegee Institute of Alabama in 1881. Convinced that Southern whites would not accept education for blacks if it challenged white supremacy, Washington dismissed academic education as dangerous. Instead he urged vocational training and imbued his students with conservative values. He wrote in his 1901 autobiography, *Up from Slavery*:

"We wanted to teach the students how to bathe, how to care for their teeth and clothing. We wanted to teach them what to eat, and how to eat it properly, and how to care for their rooms. Aside from this, we wanted to give them such a practical knowledge of some one industry, together with the spirit of industry, thrift, and economy, that they could be sure of knowing how to make a living after they had left us. We wanted to teach them to study actual things instead of mere books alone."[7]

In an age when blacks were being excluded from trades as well as professions Washington's gradualism had its supporters. By the 1890s, it also had its critics. William Edward Burghardt Du Bois was born into a middle-class black family in Boston three years after the Civil War. In his *Souls of Black Folk* (1903) Du Bois accused Washington of making a compromise that relegated blacks to a new slavery. He urged confrontation instead of compromise. In 1909 he called for the organization of a committee for racial equality, the right to vote, and full education. The following year that committee became the National Association for the Advancement of Colored People. In the pages of *Crisis*, its monthly journal, Du Bois lashed out at everything from American imperialism overseas to the timidity of black preachers at home. An internationalist, he organized Pan-African congresses that brought African and American blacks together, and he taught his readers both critical citizenship as Americans and a wider African cultural heritage. His own struggle between a defensive black nationalist separatism and a cosmopolitan, international democratic socialism continued to be a principal concern of black intellectuals after the war.

SEGREGATION IN SOUTH AFRICA:
BOER WAR TO WORLD WAR I

While the Anglo-Boer War in South Africa pitted one group of whites, the British, against another, the Dutch-descended Boers, it was not like the American Civil War, because British and Boers had never been part of the same society. And although British racial policy was more liberal than Boer, the war was not fought on behalf of the Africans. There was in fact a kind of white gentlemen's agreement not to arm the Africans on either side. Britain was victorious because, like the North in the American Civil War, it enjoyed a superior economy and technology and was ruthless (including devising the concentration camp for its Boer prisoners). The defeat of the Boers in 1902, like the defeat of the South in 1865, did provide the opportunity for a commitment to racial justice. As we have seen, that commitment was made, if incompletely, by Northern Republicans between 1860 and 1877. It was barely made by the British in South Africa at all.

Perhaps postwar radical reconstruction was never possible in the Transvaal or Orange Free State in 1902. The "white man's peace," the Treaty of Vereeniging in 1902, required the Boers, or Afrikaners, to become British citizens but limited citizenship to whites and allowed some Afrikaner soldiers to retain their rifles for defense against Africans. The enormous numerical superiority of Africans (70 percent) and "coloreds" (10 percent) over whites was enough to ensure compromise.

Alfred Milner, the postwar British governor of the two Afrikaner colonies, had the power to dictate some racial reform. Instead, he chose to convert the defeated Afrikaners to the fact of British administration by aiding their economic development. That meant an alliance with wealthy farmers and mining magnates and involved assistance in their quest for cheap labor.

Conquered Africans had provided cheap labor as squatters on Afrikaner farms since the Great Trek. Heavy work had generally been seasonal, however, and it was never organized on a massive scale. The mines were different. The discovery of diamonds in 1867 and gold in 1884 transformed the interior economy (especially the Transvaal) infinitely more than partial industrialization had changed the American South in the 1890s. The Witwatersrand, the gold-mining area of the Transvaal, demanded 42,500 African workers in 1894 and nearly 100,000 in 1899.[8]

Further, the poor quality of gold made its extraction expensive. The problem for the mine owners was how to ensure that an increasing number of Africans would work in the mines for the extremely low wages that would make it profitable. In fact, Africans in the years after the war "were staying at home in large numbers, somehow contriving to support their families on their small plots, unwilling to come out to work for the reduced level of wages that mining magnates, industrialists, large farmers, and government officials all agreed 'the country' in such straitened circumstances could afford to pay."[9]

There were many answers to the labor problem after the war. Milner himself was interested in importing Chinese laborers (and did in fact bring in fifty thousand between 1904 and 1910).[10] Others, like the defeated Afrikaner general and future

prime minister Louis Botha, insisted that African labor would be ample if only sufficient force were applied. Taxes might be increased, especially on the unemployed.
But Botha, a farmer who had always relied on African squatters close at hand and
attentive to his needs, said nothing about segregation when he addressed Milner's
Transvaal Labour Commission in 1903. The word was first used about 1910 by
future Nationalist party leader J. B. M. Hertzog. Segregation was still a new idea in
1903.

"I would like you to give me your opinion on this scheme." Mr. Thompson,
member of the Native Affairs Commission, was questioning the Reverend B.
Kumalo and other African members of the Native Vigilance Association of the
Orange River Colony on September 23, 1904. "If the Government of the Orange
River Colony were today to move you all . . . to a spot a couple or three miles out
of Bloemfontein, there right out of town, away from the white people, would that
meet your idea?" Mr. Kumalo's "idea" had been that Africans ought to hold property and vote. "Not fully," he replied, "because that would not give the black man
the right to buy land in town. He ought to have the right to buy land in the town
even, and to speculate if he wishes to."

"But answer this first," Mr. Thompson interjected. "Would you not like to see,
in the first place, all the Natives moved from these slums and all about, and put a
couple of miles out of the town, with a proper railway system to bring them out in
the morning, and take them back at night, ring the curfew bell at night, at nine
o'clock, and keep them in their town. Do you not think that would be in the interests of the Natives as a whole round Bloemfontein?"[12]

A proper railway to bring them to work in the morning and return them at
night: who could ask for anything more? Segregation was the recommendation of
the Native Affairs Commission in 1905 because the commissioners had found a
way of combining physical separation with labor control. On the farms, Africans
had to be close by to be useful. Whole separate towns could be built for Africans
near the labor-hungry mines. "Plots of half-acres" might not be affordable after all.
The ghetto was to be a more appropriate model.

Actually the territorial segregation the Native Affairs Commission envisioned
led to two types of ghettos. One was the separate black "townships" suggested by
the commission to get blacks out of the cities. The second was the barrack compounds near the mines for black workers, men forced to live for weeks or months
without women or families. The mine compounds were barely disguised prisons.

> Eight, twelve, or sixteen men slept in concrete bunks stacked four deep
> along the walls. Their washing hung from string tied to the top bunks,
> so that you had to duck and plough your way to the door. The single
> light bulb was always burning. . . . Men came and went at all hours
> . . . the food was prepared and dished out to tin plates by shovel in the
> cookhouse.[13]

The townships, designed not for the sleeping hours of contract workers, but as the homes of families lured or forced from the cities, were less obviously prisons. Typically the government built thousands of identical small cement houses arranged in rows for miles in each direction with only a single road for entry or exit; transit into or out of the townships required the presentation of a pass at the guard house.

The restriction of blacks to mining camps and special townships that deprived them of rights and basic amenities was part of a larger plan to accomplish two contrary goals. South African whites wanted blacks to be readily available to provide cheap labor in the mines, cities, and farms throughout the country, but they wanted them to disappear after work. Outnumbered by blacks almost ten to one, South African whites sought a way to live off black labor in a white country. The Native Land Act of 1913 declared that certain designated black reserves were the only places blacks could live, unless whites gave them temporary permission to live elsewhere. "The town is a European area," the Native Affairs Commission of 1921 declared. "The native men, women, and children should only be permitted within municipal areas in so far and for so long as their presence is demanded by the wants of the white population," another commission added the following year. The Natives (Urban Areas) Act of 1923 and succeeding amendments established a system of "influx controls" and "passes." Based on the disingenuous assumption that all blacks reside in the 13 percent of South African territory designated as reserves or tribal homelands, these laws required permission and passes for blacks to be in the towns, cities, and mining areas—the only areas where white South Africans allowed them to work. An African without a proper pass could be imprisoned, sent to a remote "resettlement camp," or forced into convict labor.

Since it is "inconceivable" (as Jan Hofmeyr, a deputy prime minister in the 1940s, put it) for whites to do without black labor and "just as inconceivable" for blacks to find sufficient work in the homelands, the existence of these homelands as anything but a labor reserve is a convenient fiction. Thus, when the South African government began in the 1960s to give "independence" to these "Bantu homelands" and assign South African blacks to "citizenship" in these tribal reserves, it strengthened its claim that the blacks were alien "guest workers" in South Africa. Blacks who were born in the cities of South Africa and declined to move to remote homelands or accept "tribal citizenship" were often deprived of internal passes, passports, and any remaining rights. One South African recounted:

> I'm a Zulu, but I was born and raised in Johannesburg. My grandparents and mother are buried in Johannesburg. The [officials] wanted my father, brothers and sisters, and I to go to what they called a Zulu homeland. First they refused to give me a passport. Then they just destroyed our home. I came back one day and it had been bulldozed to the ground: our furniture was on the street.[14]

APARTHEID AND SEGREGATION

Apartheid was enshrined as official South African policy by the Nationalist party government after its victory in 1948. As official government policy, apartheid led to increasing discrimination against blacks and an escalating level of protest, culminating in the violence in Sharpeville in 1960, Soweto in 1976, and throughout South Africa until it was abandoned in 1989, the year in which Nelson Mandela was released from prison and the ban on his African National Congress party was lifted. Finally, in 1994, Mandela was elected President of South Africa, and the country has struggled to create a multi-racial democracy since.

The comparison of South African apartheid and North American segregation illuminates some issues and confuses some others. The comparison points out the similar turn to racial discrimination in two parts of the world at about the same time. That is instructive. Both developments were products of white settler societies after a period of slavery when they were beginning to industrialize and required large numbers of workers. But the comparison falls short when we push it further. In South Africa, apartheid, or "separate development," was part of a system of beliefs that became official government policy. It gained its "philosophical" defenders. Commissions, studies, and books were presented to argue that "separate development" was better for blacks as well as for whites. South Africa, they argued, was a country of minorities, different tribes, "white and black," each of which should be allowed to go its own way. The white tribes were urban, the black tribes rural. Each of the black tribes had unique native traditions that, they argued, should be preserved rather than mixed in a melting pot.

The "melting pot" became an American ideal, at least for whites. Segregation in America was rarely defended as anything but a pragmatic solution (usually temporary) to a difficult problem. It's not that Americans were unable to be philosophical racists. Southern slaveholders had produced their share of books and speeches proving the superiority of slavery over wage labor. But America took segregation less seriously. American segregation was equivalent to what South Africans called "petty apartheid," the smaller, less important signs of separation: the "whites only" facilities from washrooms to cemeteries that dotted the landscape of both countries in the middle of the twentieth century. For South Africans the issue of separate washrooms was always a minor matter compared with the issues of exclusion from the cities; restriction to homelands, camps, and townships; lack of citizenship or the vote; and the need for all blacks (but no whites) to carry passes. Thus, as blacks were removed from the white cities and neighborhoods, segregated facilities became less necessary.

One of the main differences between South African and United States history is that in North America the Europeans annihilated the native inhabitants (intentionally or not) and took the land. The "American Bantu" were quickly decimated, and their descendants were put on reservations. They never approached a majority of the population. The second main difference follows from this. The American Indians could never provide the abundant and inexpensive labor necessary for economic growth and industrialization. African slaves played that role in the very important agricultural stage of American economic growth, but the American Civil War created a society with a different set of needs and values. It is true that some of the freedmen of the South were employed in the new Southern mill towns after the Civil War, especially in new cities, such as Birmingham. By and large, however, by the 1880s most former slaves were relegated to a new kind of serfdom as tenant farmers and sharecroppers. They became indebted, often to their old masters, on the land they had formerly worked as slaves. In this respect, their participation in the second stage of American industrialization was curtailed.

The workers who built America between the Civil War and the First World War were, for the most part, immigrants rather than former slaves. Successive waves of new arrivals came (especially from Europe) with the hope of making a better life for themselves in the New World. Only after 1920, with the large-scale internal migration of blacks to Northern cities, did blacks again play a crucial role in the industrial work force, and that created new racial tensions. In effect, the captains of American industry chose to import masses of cheap immigrant workers at about the same time that South African mine owners decided to employ native blacks. Both societies created color lines. In South Africa blacks were the unskilled laborers and whites were skilled. In the United States blacks were left with marginal subsistence on the farms, while each new wave of immigrants was brought in to struggle with its predecessor.

The tensions between the waves of immigrants were often racial, their sentiments racist. This was the case even when one ethnic group opposed another ethnic group of the same "race," and perhaps especially true in the conflicts over Chinese labor. But since such "racism" could be directed against Irish or Italians as easily as against Indians or Chinese, it was less a matter of race than of class.

FOR FURTHER READING

The comparative study of racism in the United States and South Africa was initiated with the appearance in the early 1980s of George M. Fredrickson's *White Supremacy: A Comparative Study of American and South African History* and John W. Cell's *The Highest Stage of White Supremacy: The Origins of Segregation in South Africa and the American South*. Since then, the subject has grown considerably. Fredrickson has contributed *Black Liberation: A Comparative History of Black Ideologies in the United States and South Africa* and, more recently, collected essays in *The Comparative Imagination: On the History of Racism, Nationalism, and Social Movements*. His earlier study of the development of racism in the American south, *The Black Image in the White Mind*, has also been reprinted. Another recent comparative study by a political scientist, Anthony W. Marx's *Making Race and Nation*, adds Brazil to the comparison, attributing much to the role of the state in all three cases.

Among other useful comparative studies are Stanley B. Greenberg's *Race and State in Capitalist Development: Comparative Perspectives* and Carl Degler's *Neither*

Black nor White on Brazil and the United States. Somewhat more introductory is Pierre L. van den Berghe's *Race and Racism: A Comparative Perspective*. The subject is put in different comparative contexts in Louis Hartz, ed., *The Founding of New Societies*, Robert A. Huttenback's *Racism and Empire*, Philip Mason's *Prospero's Magic: Some Thoughts on Class and Race*, Leo Kuper's *Race, Class, and Power: Ideology and Revolutionary Change in Plural Societies*, Joel Kovel's *White Racism: A Psychohistory*, and Barrington Moore's *Social Origins of Dictatorship and Democracy: Lord and Peasant in the Modern World*. For the history of South Africa, a useful introduction is T. R. H. Davenport's *South Africa: A Modern History*. A much more thorough volume is the *Oxford History of South Africa*, edited by Monica Wilson and Leonard Thompson.

South Africa might, however, be more easily approached through its novels, plays, and short stories. Alan Paton's *Cry the Beloved Country* has long served that purpose admirably. That and his other novels capture a moment painfully lost. The novels of Nadine Gordimer and those of J.M. Coetzee introduce us to a bleaker, more current South Africa. The mystery novels of James McClure are candidly informative. Andre Brink's *A Chain of Voices* is a rich novel of slavery set in 1825. The novels of Peter Abrahams, like *Mine Boy*, offer an internal view of black society. The plays of Athol Fugard are deeply moving. There are also memoirs and biographies which are valuable, especially Albert Luthuli's *Let My People Go*, Donald Woods' *Biko*, and John Ya-Otto's riveting *Battle-Front Namibia*.

For studies of race relations in America, a good place to start is Francis Jennings, *The Conquest of America: Indians, Colonialism and the Cant of Conquest*. An equally valuable introduction to early American race relations is Gary B. Nash's *Red, White and Black: The Peoples of Early America*. European ideas of the "Indian" are presented in Robert F. Berkhofer, Jr., *The White Man's Indian: Images of the American Indian from Columbus to the Present*.

American ideas of races are explored in *Lost Tribes and Promised Lands: The Origins of American Racism* by Ronald Sanders, *Race: The History of an Idea in America* by Thomas F. Gossett, Winthrop Jordan's *White Over Black*, and William Stanton's *The Leopard's Spots*.

C. Vann Woodward's *The Strange Career of Jim Crow* is the classic introduction to the late-nineteenth-century development of segregation. Joel Williamson's *The Crucible of Race* is a lengthy account of racism in the South since Reconstruction. Diane McWhorter's *Carry Me Home* is a rich account of the civil rights struggle in Birmingham, Alabama. The correspondents of the *New York Times* recently compiled an excellent series of articles under the title *How Race is Lived in America*.

Some of the most interesting recent work on racism in the United States is on the construction of "white" identity. These include Noel Ignatiev's *How the Irish Became White*, Theodore W. Allen's two-volume *The Invention of the White Race*, David R. Roediger's *The Wages of Whiteness*, and Grace Elizabeth Hale's *Making Whiteness: The Culture of Segregation in the South, 1890–1940*.

NOTES

1. Allan Nevins, *Ordeal of the Union*. Volume 1: *Douglas, Buchanan and Party Chaos, 1857–1859* (New York: Charles Scribner's Sons, 1950), p. 438.
2. George M. Fredrickson, *White Supremacy: A Comparative Study in American and South African History* (New York: Oxford University Press, 1981), pp. 161–162.
3. Fredrickson, *op. cit.*, p. 176.
4. C. Vann Woodward, *American Counterpoint: Slavery and Racism in the North-South Dialogue* (Boston: Little Brown, 1971), pp. 213–214.
5. *Ibid.*
6. Robert Coles, *Children of Crisis* (New York: Dell, 1968), p. 66.
7. Booker T. Washington, *Up from Slavery* (New York: Lancer Books, 1968), p. 129.
8. Martin Legassick, "The Analysis of 'Racism' in South Africa: The Case of the Mining Economy" (presented at IDEP/UN International Seminar, Dar es Salaam, 1975).
9. John W. Cell, *The Highest Stage of White Supremacy: The Origins of Segregation in South Africa and the American South* (Cambridge: Cambridge University Press, 1982), p. 46.
10. Terence O'Brien, *Milner* (London: Constable, 1979), p. 216.
11. Cell, *op. cit.*, pp. 47 and 49.
12. Minutes of Evidence, South African Native Affairs Commission, 1903–1904. Extracts in Sheridan Johns III, *Protest and Hope, 1882–1934*, p. 39. This is the first volume of Thomas Karis and Gwendolen M. Carter, *From Protest to Challenge: A Documentary History of African Politics in South Africa, 1882–1964* (Stanford: Hoover Institute Press, 1972)
13. John Ya-Otto, *Battle-Front Namibia* (Westport, Conn.: Lawrence Hill, 1981), p. 14.
14. Interview with anonymous informant, July 1984.

Foreign Troops enter Beijing (Peking) following the Boxer Rebellion, 1900.
(New York Public Library)

✕ 8 ✕

Nationalism and Internationalism

Imperialism and Independence

• The newly independent nation of East Timor chose Portuguese as its national language instead of the more widely spoken language of its colonial occupiers from 1975 to 1999, Indonesian, or the local language, Tetum. The Portuguese occupied the island from the early 1550s until 1975. The official currency is the American dollar. The national phone company is Australian.

• "Look for the union label when you are buying a hat, coat or glove. . . . It means it's made in the good old U.S.A." That "Buy American" commercial was the message of an organization called "The *International* Ladies Garment Workers Union."

• The automobiles produced by some Japanese-owned companies in the United States have more American-made parts than some cars made by General Motors and Ford.

• When European integration reaches the point of abolishing separate national currencies and passports, extreme nationalist political parties win voters to their anti-immigration and anti-foreign policies.

All of these events suggest the confusion of nationalism and internationalism in the world today. Nationalism might best be defined as a primary commitment to

205

the nation—for example, the French, the English, the Polish or the Japanese nation—by a member of that nation. A French nationalist is one who thinks first of the French, is usually particularly proud of French culture, the French language, and of everything French, and often believes that the French are superior to other nations. Internationalism might be defined as a primary commitment to a larger international unit than the nation. An internationalist is first concerned with the world, the global environment, the United Nations, or the people of the world.

Nation and nationalism, like race and racism, are fuzzy terms. A nation is not always a country. Not all of the French are in France. Some are in French Canada, some in Italy, some in Africa, and some in the United States, for instance. So a French nationalist could be found in France who would have very different ideas from a French nationalist in Canada (except for their agreement about things French). Their commitment to the French nation may, or may not, mean allegiance to a particular state. Only in the last few hundred years (and this is part of the story of this chapter) have nations become identified with particular states. Many nations (like the French Canadians) identify with a state (Canada) that is not just their own nation state but is the state of other nations as well (primarily the English Canadians, but including other nations from all over the world). There are also nations that have no separate nation-state of their own: the Basques in Spain, the Ibo of Nigeria, Armenians in Turkey, and the Navajo in the United States are among the many.

Nationalism and internationalism are opposing tendencies but neither is pursued to the exclusion of the other. Even the most extreme nationalist sees the need for alliances with other nations. Even an internationalist force like the United Nations asserts the right of all peoples to national self-determination. The question for all people is how to define the extent of their nationalist and internationalist allegiances. To what extent are internationalist feelings preferable to nationalistic ones? Where should one draw the line? These are questions that each person has to answer independently.

Modern society has in the last two hundred years made virtual religions of both nationalism and internationalism. Why did they both develop at the same time? That internationalism is a modern idea is understandable. Modern society requires greater international coordination, cooperation, and organization than ever before. The threat of nuclear annihilation, environmental pollution, limited global resources, international travel, trade, and communications, call out for international agreement, law, and, perhaps, government.

Nationalism may be a bit older than internationalism, but it is also a modern force. Before the industrial revolution, people lived local lives in which knowledge of kin, craft, and community was sufficient. Industrialization created national states with flags, newspapers, and road and rail networks. In addition, armies, laws, taxing authorities, and government administrators needed legitimacy. In the age of mass media, electoral governments, and mobile job markets, local identities are too limited.

National identity is normally thought to be old, even ancient, but historians have recently recognized that many national "traditions" were invented in the nineteenth century. The disruptions of industrialization caused people to create "imaginary communities" in their minds that they might hold as ancient models to emulate. Unlike the modern nation state, most of the empires of the ancient and traditional world were quite cosmopolitan.

What makes people nationalistic? What makes them internationalistic? What have been some of the ways in which nations have cooperated internationally? Is nationalism increasing? If so, is that a problem? Is greater international cooperation possible? How would it occur? These are some of the questions that prompt this chapter. In order to better understand these issues we will look at the history of nationalism and international cooperation in the last two hundred years.

THE RIGHTS OF ENGLISHMEN AND INDIANS

The American colonists in 1776 did not think of themselves as Americans. They declared their independence from Britain because, they said, their rights as Englishmen had been abridged by the crown. Thomas Jefferson's Declaration of Independence lists the colonialists' grievances against King George III. There were disagreements with Parliament, to be sure, but chief among these was Parliament's taxation without representation. The rights of Englishmen meant representation by Parliament or English recognition of colonial legislative bodies.

These "rights" were ignored by King and parliament because England saw the colonies as part of a mercantilist empire in which colonies were created to enhance the wealth of the metropolis. The Navigation Acts made this clear as early as the 1660s. The colonies would supply raw materials to England. England, not the colonies, would engage in manufacturing. The colonies would purchase the products of English manufacture, transported in English ships.

Adam Smith said that the colonials profited from the English mercantile system. But the colonials did not see it that way. To them, a system in which they provided the raw materials for England's manufacturing was not a level playing field. They recognized that the profits came to those who converted raw materials into finished products, not those who supplied the raw materials. Economic prosperity and political power came through manufacturing. So the Continentals went to war for economic and political independence, and to preserve the "rights of Englishmen."

No such revolution occurred immediately on the other side of the British empire in India. There were few British settlers in India, and no independent group of European settlers like the Boers of South Africa. For the most part, the Indians themselves did not think of themselves as a nation. The most articulate spokesman of Indian interests was Rammohan Roy (1772–1833), founder of a number of newspapers, who thought of himself as a Hindu, a Brahman, and a Bengali (resident of Bengal). Insofar as he identified with a larger Hindustan (or India), Roy stands

Rammohan Roy (1772–1833).
(Victoria and Albert Museum)

at the beginning of an Indian national movement. But most of his work was as an Indian officer in the British East India Company and as a champion of Hindu reform. He led a campaign against *sati* (the ritual burning of a widow on her husband's funeral pyre), and spoke critically of the introduction by the English of Christian missionaries into India.

On some issues, however, Roy's criticism of the English sounded very much like that of the North Americans in 1776. In 1823, when the English proposed a bill to restrict freedom of the press in India, Roy wrote that a rejection of the bill would "permit the natives of this country to continue in possession of the civil rights and privileges which they and their fathers have so long enjoyed under the auspices of the British nation, whose kindness and confidence they are not aware of having done anything to forfeit."[1]

NATION, LANGUAGE, AND COLONY

One of the reasons why the North American colonials were successful in organizing a revolution against the British is that they spoke the same language. The situation in India was much more complicated. Not only were there numerous local languages in India (as there still are) but there were also a number of general and colonial languages—Sanskrit, the Persian of the Mughals, and European languages. Rammohan Roy was unusual in mastering Sanskrit, Persian, and English, as well as his local Bengali.

This issue of language caused a major debate among both colonized and colonizers. For the governors of India in the East India Company, the question was whether English education ought to be introduced into India. Some governors feared that an English education might eventually lead to a demand for "the rights of Englishmen." Others followed the arguments of Thomas Macaulay that the teaching of English would make the teaching of modern knowledge and science easier and thus produce a class of Anglo-Indians who could serve as middlemen in British administration. Rammohan Roy agreed with Macaulay. He objected vehemently in 1823 when the government decided to establish a college of Sanskrit studies. His criticism of the proposal aided the eventual shift to English education in 1835. For Roy, English education would provide the knowledge necessary for Indians to eventually govern themselves. In effect, he urged Indians not to cultivate the languages of India, but to create a new nationalism based on the language and culture of the colonizer. This has remained a difficult issue for the colonized in other countries ever since. (Today, for instance, there are Philippine nationalists who want to revive Tagalog, which is spoken nowhere but the Philippines, in opposition to English, which is already spoken by many Filipinos and much of the rest of the world.) On the one hand there is a certain loss of cultural self-respect in accepting the language and culture of the colonizer. On the other hand the colonizer's language may be more useful because it provides greater access to books and people. Roy's decision to teach the "international" language probably led to an earlier nationalist movement in India than would have occurred with the pursuit of an Indian national language. But it is always a difficult decision. As Macaulay had hoped, many Indian administrators in the twentieth century behaved more like Englishmen than Indians.

THE INTERNATIONALISM OF FREE TRADE

British mercantilism was a very nationalist doctrine. It put British wealth and welfare above all others. When Adam Smith challenged mercantilism in his important book, *The Wealth of Nations*, in 1776, he argued that British wealth need not be obtained at the expense of other nations. International free trade, he said, might increase the wealth of Britain and other nations at the same time. Free trade became a very popular idea in Britain at the end of the eighteenth and beginning of the nineteenth century. Politicians and poets sang its praises. Many thought that a world of free trade would benefit all mankind. Each nation would produce what was most suitable to its particular mix of natural resources and abilities. Why should all nations produce the same things? advocates of free trade asked. Specialization would be more efficient. Then every nation could benefit by the specialization of each if they traded their products without import duties or restrictions.

In a sense, the doctrine of free trade was the expression of a market economy that was becoming international. In calling for efficiencies on a global scale, the advocates of free trade were speaking for the most advanced sectors of capitalism. They were challenging the view of mercantilists that national prosperity could only come at the expense of one's neighbors. They were echoing the protests of British colonialists in North America and the Caribbean who saw no reason why they should not trade with the Dutch, French, or Spanish when it suited them. Free trade, carried to its logical conclusion, would make colonies superfluous. Like Adam Smith's "invisible hand" in the domestic marketplace, free trade offered the prospect of international harmony without conflict or inefficiencies.

FREE TRADE FOR WHOM?

The ideal espoused by free trade theorists often meant something less than international equality, however. It should come as no surprise that the most fervent advocates of free trade were the British, or that they developed the idea at the very moment their manufactured goods were becoming cheaper than the handmade products of most other countries. Clearly, the hidden agenda of free trade was that Britain would supply the world with manufactured goods and the world would supply the raw materials. "The great interest of India," according to the president of the Manchester Chamber of Commerce, "was to be agricultural rather than manufacturing and mechanical."[2]

Adam Smith's *The Wealth of Nations* and the American Declaration of Independence (both dating from 1776) made England realize that colonies could be exploited even when they were not politically controlled. As the strongest manufacturing economy in the world, a policy of free and open worldwide trade would insure the victory of English manufactures over those of less-developed countries. This was not, however, immediately the case with India. The Indian textile and shipbuilding industries were world leaders in the eighteenth century. Textiles were manufactured in every area of India. One textile center, the city of Dacca, was described by Robert Clive in 1757 as "extensive, populous and rich as the city of

Tea generated an international market for China in the eighteenth century. Here we see young plants.

London." But by 1840, according to testimony before a Parliamentary Select Committee, the population of Dacca had "fallen from 150,000 to 30,000 and the jungle and malaria are fast encroaching upon the town....Dacca, the Manchester of India, has fallen off from a very flourishing town to a very poor and small town."[3] At least one of the reasons for the victory of Manchester's textile production over India lay in the tariffs imposed by Britain on it's colony's production. The tariff of 1814 levied duties of 2 to 3-1/2 percent for British textiles imported into India while the duty of Indian textiles imported into Britain was a prohibitive 70 to 80 percent. India's textile industry had been destroyed, according to a British colonial historian of the time,

> by reason of the outcry for free trade on the part of England without permitting to India a free trade herself. This suppression of the native for British manufacture is often quoted as a splendid example of the triumph of British skill. It is a much stronger instance of English tyranny, and how India has been impoverished by the most vexatious system of customs duties imposed for the avowed object of favoring the mother country.[4]

FREE TRADE OR ELSE: THE OPIUM WAR

China was another matter. The Ching dynasty had limited foreign trade to the southern port of Canton when George III sent his envoy Lord Macartney, loaded with goods, to expand trade. Macartney was himself embarrassed when he toured the 50 pavilions of the emperor which were "furnished in the richest manner . . . that our presents must shrink from the comparison and hide their diminished heads."[5] In response to the request for greater trade the emperor Qianlong (or Ch'ien Lung) wrote to the King that the "Celestial Court" had already received presents from the four seas. "Consequently," he said:

> there is nothing we lack, as your principal envoy and others have themselves observed. We have never set much store on strange or ingenious objects, nor do we need any more of your country's manufactures. . . . [6]

The British were importing large amounts of Chinese tea. It is estimated that the average English worker spent 5 percent of the household budget on tea. The British needed a product to sell to the Chinese in return. Otherwise the unfavorable balance of trade would drain English reserves of bullion. The answer was the opium grown in India. It was a miracle product for English trade. The more they sold, the greater the demand. *Hunt's Merchants' Magazine* of New York estimated that opium was probably "the largest sum given for any raw article supplied by one nation to another, if we except the cotton-wool exported from the U.S. to Great Britain."[7] Perhaps 10 percent of the Chinese population used opium by the end of the nineteenth century. The impact of the drug on China was enormous. Not only did it debilitate a large number of Chinese workers, but it also reversed the flow of silver bullion from China to England. Aware of the damage the traffic was causing China, in 1838 the emperor sent Lin Zexu (or Lin Tse-hsu) to Canton to stop it. Commissioner Lin acted vigorously. Addicts were rounded up and forcibly detoxified. Dealers were harshly punished and foreign supplies were confiscated.

The last measure infuriated British opium merchants and their representatives in Parliament. Secretary of War Macaulay (the same who furthered English education in India) fired Parliament with a speech that spun confiscated opium into the "innocent blood" of English gentlemen whose "victorious flag" would avenge their loss. *The Times* of London called it the "opium war" and found it regrettable but necessary to open China to free trade. The naval bombardments (1840–1842) were almost as one-sided as imagined in a British stage comedy of the time. Britain won handily. The Treaty of Nanking in 1842 brought an end to the war. The British were guaranteed trading rights in five Chinese ports, granted the island of Hong Kong, and given control over Chinese tariffs and trade. The treaty began a process of dismemberment of the Chinese empire that was to lead eventually to the fall of the Qing dynasty in 1911.

The *Illustrated London News* summarized the benefits of the treaty with a self-satisfied tone of almost cynical self-interest:

> It secures us a few round millions of dollars and no end of very refreshing tea. It gives an impetus to trade, cedes us one island in perpetuity, and in short puts that sort of climax to the war which satisfies our interests more than our vanity and rather gives over glory a preponderance to gain.[8]

Macaulay's flag-waving speech shows how national symbols could evoke the desired Parliamentary vote. But the summary of the *Illustrated London News*, with all of its emphasis on dollars and tea, points to a society of men moved more by calculation than feelings of national pride or patriotism. Nationalism was still a young force in Europe in 1842.

NATIONALISM IN EUROPE

Nationalism and internationalism were products of the Industrial Revolution in Europe. Industrialization both integrated the world and intensified ethnic, linguistic, and national identities. European nationalism emerged with the French Revolution (1789–1795) and Napoleon's conquest of Europe (1795–1815). The French revolutionaries contributed the first national flag, anthem, and draft army. The Napoleonic armies that occupied Spain, Italy, Austria, and Prussia prompted nationalist movements against France in those countries. In 1815 the Congress of Vienna reimposed the rule of European kings and aristocracies who, because they

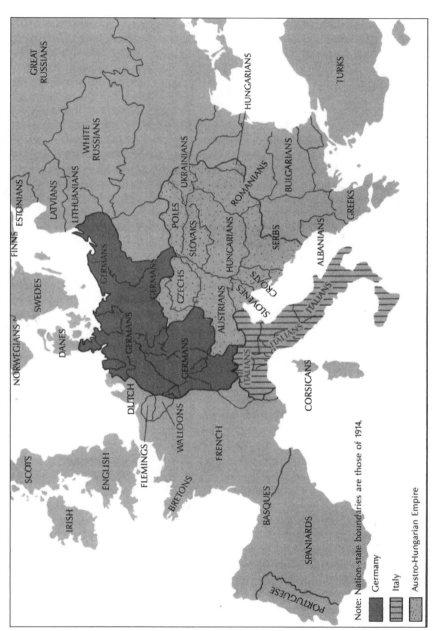

Nations and Nation-states in Europe in the Nineteenth Century.

Note: Nation-state boundaries are those of 1914.

Germany

Italy

Austro-Hungarian Empire

British warships and cannon overwhelmed the junks of the Chinese Navy during the Opium War. This sea battle may have been the British invasion of the port of Canton on January 7, 1841. (National Maritime Museum)

were all related, tended to favor international harmony.

Until 1850 nationalism tended to be a liberal, and at times even revolutionary, idea. There was no "Italy" or "Germany." The unification of the various peoples who spoke Italian or German was to come later. At first, it was nourished by poets, composers, and writers who cultivated common myths, and revived or "invented" ancient traditions. In 1848 national unity was one of the demands of middle-class, liberal revolutionary movements all over Europe, along with the demand for more democratic, parliamentary governments. The revolutions of 1848 were brutally suppressed in 1849 and 1850. After 1850, nationalism was taken over by kings and aristocracies as a cause that could strengthen the state and prevent greater democracy. Ironically, these movements to create "nation-states" were frequently carried out by conservative "internationalist" aristocrats who were afraid of popular nationalism and suspicious of the nationalism of the middle-class. Thus, the unifications of Italy (1848–1861) and Germany (1861–1871) were conservative rather than liberal. In Italy, the moderate Count Cavour (who initially only wanted to enlarge his native state of Piedmont) unified the states of northern Italy in 1859 with the help of Napoleon III (1851–1870) of France. In 1860 he avoided an Italian republic by forcing the popular democrat, Garibaldi, who conquered much of the south with his people's army, to submit to Victor Emmanuel as king.

Similarly, Bismarck (1815–1898), seeking a large Prussia, achieved a small Germany (one that did not include Austria). Using the superior Prussian army, Bismarck separated the duchies of Schleswig and Holstein from Denmark in 1863, annexed Hanover after a brief war with Austria in 1866, and added Austrian Bavaria and French Alsace and Lorraine after a war with Napoleon III's France in 1870. King William of Prussia was proclaimed German Emperor at Versailles in 1871.

Nationalism was a force unleashed, or repressed, elsewhere as well. Austria remained a multinational empire of Germans, Slovenes, Serbs, Slovaks, Croats, Czechs, Hungarians, Poles, Romanians, and Italians until the volatile mixture exploded and touched off World War I. The Russian and Ottoman empires were multinational entities that were more troubled by social and economic problems than they were by ethnic demands.

NATIONALISM IN MULTINATIONAL SOCIETIES

The most diverse multinational society that was formed during the nineteenth century was the United States. Before 1860, it was also multieconomic, consisting of slave and free labor. That disparity was abolished by Abraham Lincoln in a Civil War (1861–1865) that created a unified capitalist society. Unlike Cavour or Bismarck, Lincoln and the northern armies ensured the victory of a liberal, middle-class nationalism. After 1865, the ethnic tensions were more severe. In addition to the wide variety of European immigrants were Africans, Asians, and surviving native Americans. Such a diverse society created a surprisingly strong nationalism that depended not on the folk traditions of any ethnic group, but on an almost religious sense of mission that combined two ideals sometimes at odds: political democracy and economic opportunity.

It is ironic that the age of European nationalism (1845–1914) was also the age in which Europe dispersed 41 million people to the Americas, 35 million of whom went to north America, 33 million settling in the United States. Perhaps national feeling intensified in ethnic communities overseas, in letters home, in promises to return. Perhaps nationalism was also a useful device for organizing national armies, creating a literate citizenry, or gaining the loyalty of uprooted immigrant workers.

For some, of course, nationalism in the nation of immigrants was an expression of gratitude for citizenship, especially for those whose only relationship to government in the "old world" had been subjection. Mary Antin, a Russian Jewish immigrant to the United States, expressed this most effectively in her autobiography, *The Promised Land*:

> Where had been my country until now? What flag had I loved? What heroes had I worshiped? The very names of these things had been unknown to me. Well I knew that Polotzk [Russia] was not my country. It was *goluth*—exile. The beautiful Passover service closed with the words, "Next year, may we be in Jerusalem." . . . For the conditions of our civil life did not permit us to cultivate a spirit of nationalism. . . .
>
> So it came to pass that we did not know what *my country* could mean to a man. And as we had no country, so we had no flag to love. It was

by no far-fetched symbolism that the banner of the [ruling Russian] House of Romanoff became the emblem of our latter-day bondage in our eyes. Even a child would know how to hate the flag that we were forced, on pain of severe penalties, to hoist above our housetops, in celebration of the advent of one of our oppressors. And as it was with country and flag, so it was with heroes of war. We hated the uniform of the soldier, to the last brass button. On the person of a Gentile, it was the symbol of tyranny; on the person of a Jew, it was the emblem of shame.

So a little Jewish girl in Polotzk was apt to grow up hungry-minded and empty-headed; and if, still in her outreaching youth, she was set down in a land of outspoken patriotism, she was likely to love her new country with a great love, and to embrace its heroes in a great worship. Naturalization, with us Russian Jews, may mean more than the adoption of the immigrant by America. It may mean the adoption of America by the immigrant.[9]

EUROPEAN SETTLER SOCIETIES AND NATIONALISM

The United States was the largest of many multinational settler societies of the nineteenth century. Others were Canada, Argentina, Brazil, South Africa, Australia, and New Zealand. The distribution of nationalities in these settler societies was considerably greater than in Europe. French immigrants had long constituted a significant minority of Canadians. Italian immigrants to Spanish Argentina often outnumbered Spanish immigrants. Both shared a new nation with Native Americans and African-Americans. Dutch and British immigrated to South Africa. Irish and Italians could be found everywhere.

But most European settler societies did not develop the unbridled nationalism of the United States. There were far fewer Mary Antins in Canada and Brazil, for instance. It is not that European immigrants to Canada or Brazil did not expect the streets to be paved with gold. Some of them did. There are letters from Italian immigrants in Buenos Aries which express the same enthusiasm for the new land as Italian letters from New York.[10] While the fortunes of immigrants varied widely, many did in fact prosper in whichever settler society they made their home. The observation of an Englishwoman in New Zealand might be made for the immigrants to many of these settler societies:

> The look and bearing of the immigrants appear to alter soon after they reach the colony. Some people object to the independence of their manner, but I do not; on the contrary I like to see the upright gait, the well-fed, healthy look, the decent clothes (even if no one touches his hat to you), instead of the half-starved, depressed appearance, and too often cringing servility of the mass of our English population.[11]

Why then was the United States, the most multinational of settler societies (and thus the one with the least national identity), the most nationalistic? The answer to this paradox may lie in the very diversity of the United States immigrant population. In Canada, Australia, and New Zealand the overwhelming proportion of immigrants were from the British Isles. They remained in the situation of the North American colonies in 1776, demanding the rights of Englishmen. Their common English (or Scots or Irish) background made the development of a new nationality less necessary and their absence from "the mother country" made them more zealous about their Englishness. Anthony Trollope commented on this phenomenon in his *Australia and New Zealand* in 1873:

> It may be well to notice here that as Auckland considers herself to be the cream of New Zealand, so does New Zealand consider herself to be the cream of the British empire. The pretension is made in, I think, every British colony that I visited. I remember that it was insisted upon with absolute confidence in Barbados . . . that it was hinted at in Jamaica with as much energy as was left for any opinion in that unhappy island; and that in Bermuda a confidence in potatoes, onions and oleanders had produced the same effect. In Canada the conviction is so rife that a visitor hardly cares to dispute it. In New South Wales [Australia] it crops out even in those soft murmurings with which men there regret their mother country. . . . But in New Zealand the assurance is altogether of a different nature. The New Zealander among John Bulls is the most John Bullish. He admits the supremacy of England to every place in the world, only he is more English than any Englishman at home. He tells you that he has the same climate,—only somewhat improved; that he grows the same produce,—only with somewhat heavier crops; that he has the same beautiful scenery at his doors,—only somewhat grander in its nature and more diversified in its details; that he follows the same pursuits, and after the same fashion,— but with less of misery, less of want, and a more general participation in the gifts which God has given to the country. . . . All good things have been given to this happy land, and, when the Maori has melted, here will be the navel of the earth.[12]

That last remark about the Maori melting suggests another important element in the nationalism of settler colonial societies. The Maori are the original inhabitants of New Zealand. Like the Native Americans and Australian aborigines and South African blacks, the Maori were the people in the way of the European settlers. These original inhabitants were perceived by the European settlers as an obstacle to the development of their national identity. If nationality involves an identity of people and place, the original inhabitants must be included. But only rarely was this seriously considered (as in the notion of the Mexican identity as

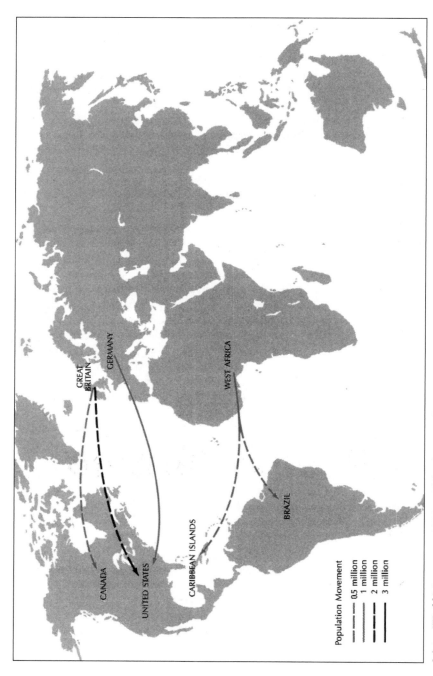

Major World Migrations, 1830–1855. This map shows the impact of the Irish potato famine from 1846 to 1851 and the replacement of Africans by northern Europeans in the Americas.

"bronze," i.e.. Spanish and Indian). More frequently, the settlers eliminated the original inhabitants—in actuality or in their minds. But their continued visibility or the historical memory of their betrayal often made the colonial revert to an extreme identification with the mother country. Thus, as Trollope says, the English colonial feels more English than the English. Perhaps a better example is the extreme French nationalism of the French colonialists in Algeria. Called the *pieds noirs* (black feet) after generations in Africa, they felt themselves Algerians or (like the Boers) Africans. But as a European minority in Algeria they were unable to develop an Algerian nationalism because it would spell their eventual downfall. Thus, they became more French than the French.

WORKERS OF THE WORLD DISPERSE

Europe was not the only donor of immigrants in the nineteenth century and the Americas were not the only recipients. British control of India and victory over China in the Opium War gave access to millions of workers displaced in Dacca or drugged in Canton. Indians were sent by the British to work the tea plantations in Assam, Bhutan, and Ceylon and to labor further afield in the British empire: the British West Indies and British Guyana, the island of Fiji in the South Pacific, British Natal in South Africa, the island of Mauritius off East Africa, British Burma and Malaya. In many of these areas (Guyana, Mauritius, and Fiji) Indians constitute a majority of the population today. In Trinidad they number 40 percent.

The British victory in the Opium War in 1842 removed the Chinese barriers not only to opium but also to the emigration of Chinese workers. Elaborate networks of contract laborers, called the "coolie trade," were developed to channel millions of Chinese workers to Malaya and Singapore (where today they constitute a majority of the population). Hundreds of thousands of Chinese workers were sent to California to pick fruit, mine gold, and build the railroads. A hundred thousand Chinese were sent to Peru. Tens of thousands were sent to Cuba, Guyana, Hawaii, Tahiti, Australia, and South Africa to work in mines and plantations.

Typical was the case of Hawaii. The ethnic Hawaiian population numbered about 300,000 in 1778 when the first white people, Captain James Cook and his crew, appeared. They were quickly decimated by diseases brought by foreigners so that by 1852, when Europeans were clearing ground for sugar plantations, there were only 71,000 Hawaiians. The planter-sponsored Royal Hawaiian Agricultural Society called for "coolie labor from China to supply the places of the rapidly decreasing native population." Planters were well aware of their role in an international labor market. In 1874 they complained that the continual decrease in Hawaiian labor made them pay each worker $12 per month "which is somewhat more than the price of labor in Mauritius, the Philippine Islands, Java, Cuba, and other sugar producing countries." Planters were also very aware of the advantages of a multiethnic labor force. One plantation manager was quite explicit: "Keep a variety of laborers, that is different nationalities, and thus prevent any concerted

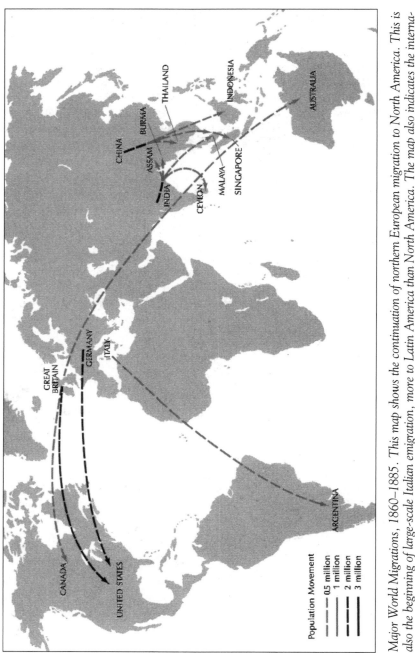

Major World Migrations, 1860–1885. This map shows the continuation of northern European migration to North America. This is also the beginning of large-scale Italian emigration, more to Latin America than North America. The map also indicates the international labor market of the British Empire, which sent Indians to Fiji, Natal, and the Caribbean as well as to the destinations shown on the map. We see also the opening of China to international labor demands after the Opium War. There were many other migrations of Chinese labor that fell short of a half million (including those to California, Hawaii, Peru, and Cuba).

action in case of strikes, for there are few, if any, cases of Japs, Chinese, and Portuguese entering into a strike as a unit."[13] In response to a developing racist reaction, the United States passed the Chinese Exclusion Act in 1882 which ended Chinese immigration to the United States. Australia, South Africa, and British Malaya soon followed suit. When Hawaii was annexed by the United States at the behest of planter interests in 1898, one of the drawbacks was that the planters had to scramble for non-Chinese workers. Concerned about the number of Japanese on the plantations, they looked to Korea, the Philippines, Puerto Rico, Portugal, Italy, and the blacks in the southern states of the U.S. The world had become a single international labor market.

NATIONALISM FOR THE COLONIES?

Both nationalism and internationalism profited the owners of plantations, mines, and factories. An international labor pool offered better bargains than a national one. A multinational labor force was less likely to strike than a national one. It was even profitable to encourage the ethnic identity and nationalist feeling of Italians, Poles, Filipinos and other immigrants. It made them less likely to unite.

A divide-and-rule strategy made even more sense in the colonies. The colonial power benefited by undermining any sense of common identity among the colonized. This was Macaulay's goal in teaching Indians English: "to form a class who may be interpreters between us and millions whom we govern; a class of persons, Indian in blood and color, but English in taste, in opinions, in morals, and in intellect." It was the goal of Lord Minto in establishing separate electorates for Hindus and Muslims. It was the reason for recruiting Gurkhas from Nepal as loyal troops in India and using minority hill tribes in Burma to control the majority Burmans. It was the strategy of the French in Indochina in placing minority Catholics in positions of power and the reason why the Dutch in Indonesia and the British in Malaya favored the Chinese.

How then did nationalism develop at all in the colonies? The answer is "slowly and with great difficulty." The major nineteenth-century revolts against colonial rule show only sporadic and embryonic nationalism.

INDIAN NATIONALISM AND THE REBELLION OF 1857

The development of Indian nationalism was at first an inadvertent British creation. It was the work of the East India Company's governor-general Dalhousie from 1848 to 1856 that unified numerous kingdoms and territories both by military conquest and with the new technology of rail, post, and telegraph. It was Dalhousie who initiated the policy of "lapse" which declared that anytime an Indian ruler died without a natural son, his kingdom would "lapse" and the British would take over.

Dalhousie doubled the area of British India. But equally important was his

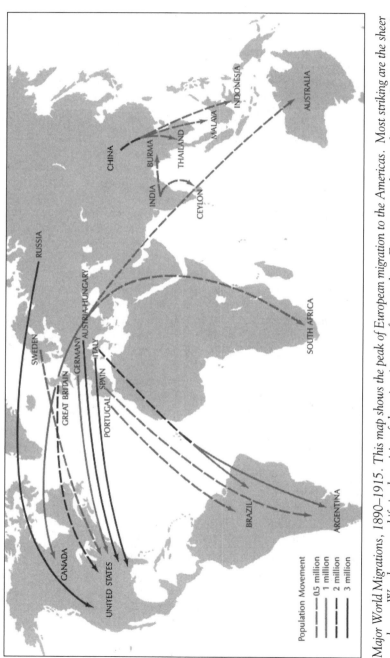

Major World Migrations, 1890–1915. This map shows the peak of European migration to the Americas. Most striking are the sheer numbers. We also see a shift in the origin of these immigrants—from northern Europe to southern and eastern Europe. South America, South Africa, and Australia were also significant European settler societies. We also see the continued export of Indian and Chinese labor, despite the exclusion of Chinese immigrants from the United States in 1882 and its territories (Hawaii and the Philippines) in 1898. Seasonal Indian and Chinese labor migration was much higher than these figures suggest. To give only one example, over a quarter million Indians were sent to Burma each year after 1900 as seasonal workers.

attempt to modernize India. Beginning in 1850 he built railroads that connected the coastal cities of Calcutta, Madras, and Bombay and from Calcutta to Delhi and on to the Northwestern frontier. This enabled the British East India Company to move troops or British imports into the interior and transport raw materials like coal and cotton to the sea. At the same time Indian cities were connected by tele-graph wire allowing immediate confirmation of an import order or a war. For the average Indian, however, the most significant innovation was probably the Indian postal system. It provided India with its first efficient and remarkably inexpensive means of communication, united the subcontinent with letters and newspapers at less cost than in England, and stirred the hunger for literacy and ideas. Had Dalhousie left India in 1855, the historian Stanley Wolpert suggests,[14] the com-bined impact of his policies might have earned him the ironic title of Father of Indian Nationalism.

For, despite selfish British desires, he left India with the technological base for a modern South Asian nation. But Dalhousie stayed on for one "lapse" too many, and it led to a rebellion that brought an end to the Company's rule and almost proved sufficient to remove the British entirely. The "lapse" he declared a bit presumptu-ously was that of the loyal king of Oudh. When he sent *sepoys* (Indian soldiers) from Oudh to enforce his acquisition, he lost the support of key elements in the Indian army. His successor compounded the distrust of the *sepoys* by insisting that troops could be assigned anywhere. But the most serious issue hinged on the use of pig and cow fat to grease the cartridges of the new Enfield rifles. The troops had to bite the cartridge to make it fire quickly. In doing so Muslims swallowed forbidden pig fat and Hindus tasted the fat of sacred cows. *Sepoys* refused. The British arrest-ed them. Whole battalions of Hindus and Muslims mutinied, marched on Delhi, and declared the Mughal Empire restored.

There was widespread support for the rebellion. Half of the quarter million *sepoys* joined the rebels. Only a quarter remained loyal to the 40,000 British troops. But they were hardly enough to govern two hundred million Indians. At the same time peasants rebelled in a number of areas. Some Indian rajas declared their sup-port and urged others to join in.

The rebellion failed, however, not only because the British were able to use the technology of the railroad, telegraph, and Enfield to their advantage. The rebellion failed because there was not a national movement. Rajas and wealthy families did not subordinate personal ambitions and jealousies to national interests. Many princes, wealthy merchants, and privileged groups supported the British. India was still not a nation.

THE RANI OF JHANSI AND INDIAN NATIONALISM

The development of Indian nationalism can be followed in the story of the Rani of Jhansi, sometimes called the Joan of Arc of India. Like the young Joan who led a French army against the British in the fifteenth century, the young Rani defended

Jhansi in central India against the reimposition of British control during the rebellion of 1857.

Without formal training, but literate in Persian, the young Rani Lakshmibai became an expert equestrian, and on the death of her husband the Maharaja in 1853, took control of Jhansi at the age of eighteen. She was an effective rani (ruler); she opened a mint, distributed food and clothing to the poor, and kept the peace.

The problem was that Lord Dalhousie had decided that Jhansi had "lapsed" to British control on the death of the Maharaja. Dalhousie ignored precedents of other female rulers succeeding their husbands, unwilling to accept anything less than the Rani's capitulation. She refused, politely at first in letters that pledged her loyalty to the British, and expected the decision to be reversed.

Events at Jhansi were overtaken, as they were throughout northern India, by the Rebellion of 1857. At Jhansi, sixty-six Europeans were massacred by rebels who were probably also a threat to the Rani. When the rebels withdrew, the British commissioner asked her to restore order. She obliged by recruiting soldiers and manufacturing cannon and other weapons. But when the British commissioner was replaced, the new governor-general, Lord Canning, revived Dalhousie's charges and ordered a trial.

Gradually, but inexorably, the Rani realized that her only hope lay in opposing the British, militarily if necessary. She prepared her defenses as the British-led India Field Force attacked. Just as they were about to breach her fort at Jhansi she escaped on horseback, eluded her pursuers, and joined rebel leaders, Tarya Tope and Rao Sahib, both of whom she had probably known from childhood. Together they attempted a last daring attack on the British. The three marched their armies against the British forces at Jhansi in the hope that another maharaja's armies would join them. In the ensuing battle on June 17, 1858, at the age of twenty-three, the Rani of Jhansi, dressed as a man, swinging her sword with both hands while "holding the reins of her horse in her mouth," was struck from her saddle and killed.[15]

It is unlikely that the Rani gave any thought to the national independence of India before the last months of her life, if then. Between 1853 and 1857 she was a loyal subject of the British. She merely wanted the British to recognize her rule in Jhansi. But in death, the Rani of Jhansi became a martyr of developing Indian nationalism. Popular stories songs celebrated her defiance of the British. By the 1920s, just to say her name was an act of rebellion. In the 1940s her name was given to the woman's regiment of the Indian National Army, formed by Subhas Chandra Bose, with Japanese support, to wrest independence from the British. Today her story is part of Indian national consciousness.

CHINESE NATIONALISM AND THE TAIPING REBELLION

The Taiping Rebellion (1850–1864) was the greatest of many rebellions that swept China in the wake of the opium war. Like the Indian Sepoy rebellion it was directed against the foreigners. Like the Sepoy rebellion it showed widespread and deepseated resentment and dissatisfaction. And like the Sepoy rebellion, it failed because there was no national movement, organization, or coherent national plan.

The Taipings had an effective leader (unlike the reluctant and ineffectual Mughal heir in India). Hong Xiuquan [Hung Hsiu-ch'uan] (1814–1864) was an obsessed visionary able to mobilize enormous numbers and slake many thirsts. At first his combination of Christian fundamentalism and ancient Chinese egalitarianism found eager ears in the cities of Eastern China. Even Westerners were favorably impressed at first. Commodore Perry, in Shanghai in May 1853, thought the Taipings were like the Mormons "gallantly fighting for a more liberal and enlightened religion." Some Westerners saw the Taipings' Christianity and discipline as an avenue to fuller and more regular trade relations. Most Chinese were more attracted to Hong's anti-foreign sentiment. Even those who did not believe that Hong was the second son of God and brother of Jesus or that his mission was to exterminate all of the foreign devils of the world (a group that included Buddhists, Taoists, and Confucians as well as more obvious foreigners) must have been attracted to his opposition to China's ruling "foreign" dynasty, the Manchus. Others applauded the promise of land reform or of equality for women or the banning of opium, tobacco, and alcohol.

But as the rebellion spread and dragged on, Westerners complained of the interruption of trade. U.S. exports shrank sevenfold between 1853 and 1855. The British rankled at the ban on opium, a particular annoyance after fighting a war in order to sell the drug. New trading ports won in a concession by the Manchu government in 1860 convinced Western powers that it would be better to put an end to the rebellion which was, according to the U.S. representative, William Reed, "regarded now as a mischievous convulsion."[16] Western military, financial, and technical assistance to the Manchu government helped end the rebellion. The cost at the end of fifteen years was at least thirty million dead. Another thirty million died in other rebellions and natural disasters during the period. But by 1864 the Manchu government was propped up and ready to stand for almost another fifty years.

NATIONALISM AND ANTICOLONIALISM

While the two great Asian rebellions of mid-century lacked national cohesion and direction, their failure showed the need and prompted the growth of nationalist movements. In both cases, these movements were increasingly directed against the European colonizing power. In China, though the Manchu regime was temporarily revived, it became increasingly clear that it survived at the sufferance of the

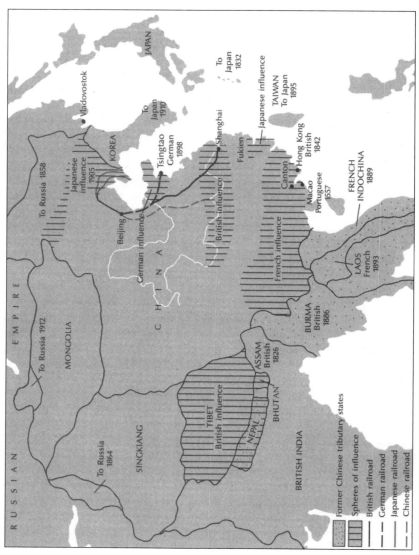

The Dismemberment of the Chinese Empire, 1842–1911. By 1911 the principal European powers and Japan controlled China with territorial acquisitions, spheres of influence, occupation of the major ports and operation of the major railroads.

Western imperial powers. Revolts in the second half of the century were more clearly directed against the European powers. The Boxer rebellion of 1900 was directed explicitly at foreign missions in Peking and it brought on the intervention of foreign troops that sealed the final fall of the Manchu dynasty by 1911. In India, the rebellion of 1857 led to the decision of the British government to rule directly in the wake of the failure of the East India Company. The experience of the Sepoy rebellion opened a chasm that could never be breached. The British closeted themselves in their segregated clubs and look-alike suburban Tudor cottages. Their increasing disdain, ignorance, and racist attitudes led step by step to the forging of the Indian nationalist movement. Nationalist sentiment developed in the Indian National Congress Party after its founding in 1885 as a public service and loyal debating society. By the end of the century important members had settled on the ultimate goal of national independence.

Leaders of the Boxer Rebellion being tried in the High Court of China, 1900. (New York Public Library)

FROM FREE TRADE TO NEW IMPERIALISM

The era of (mainly British) free trade imperialism ended in the 1870s. Free trade had been a policy which was supposed to provide world prosperity at the same time it allowed Britain, as the strongest world manufacturing country, to dominate the economies of many lesser powers without having to own them outright as colonies. As we have seen, Britain was not entirely averse to expanding its empire. When the East India Company proved unable to run India without British troops, Britain took over. It was often said that the British came upon an empire in the reign of Queen Victoria (1837–1901) "in a fit of absentmindedness." Nothing could be further from the truth. Between 1800 and 1875 Britain added an average of 83,000 square miles of colonial lands each year. (The total area of Britain in 1914 was only 120,000 square miles.) The era in which the doctrine of free trade prevailed was hardly anti-colonial. After 1875, however, many European powers adopted protectionist trade policies and sought colonial territories. Between 1875 and 1914 Britain added an average 240,000 square miles each year. Continental Europe followed suit.

The period from 1875 to 1914 has been called the age of "new imperialism" because of the sudden shift during this period toward the idea of colonial conquest. Before the 1870s most Western countries agreed with the British that colonies were too expensive. By 1885 they were all scrambling for colonies. By 1914 they had divided Africa, the Pacific, and much of southern Asia among them. By 1914 Britain had 55 colonies comprising 12 million square miles and 400 million people. France had 29 colonies comprising 4 million square miles and 60 million people, and Germany had 10 colonies with over 1 million square miles and 13 million people. The United States was in the same league as Germany, as were tiny Belgium, Portugal, and the Netherlands. Italy was not far behind.

WESTERN NATIONALISM AND THE
INTERNATIONAL ECONOMY

Why did Western countries suddenly compete in conquering the world between 1875 and 1914? Why did political control of colonial territory suddenly become so important? Different historians emphasize different reasons. There were important technological factors. The steamship, machine gun, and telegraph gave the West the technological superiority that made conquest possible, and sometimes easy. Even some medical advances, like the use of quinine against malaria, were crucial in Africa and the tropics.[17] There were strong nationalist rivalries between the English and the French which dated to the Napoleonic period, and between the French and the Germans that had recently surfaced in the Franco-German war of 1870. Queen Victoria's ability to marry her daughters to the German Emperor Frederick III and to Czar Nicholas II did not quell all nationalist rivalries. Nationalism had become a popular fever, fanned by penny newspapers and manipulated by special interests. While colonialism was not popular before 1875, the threat of competing foreign empires was often enough to sell newspapers and win votes for the imperialists. According to one historian, the sudden threat of Bismarck's claim in 1884 for German colonies in Africa was enough to panic the rest of Europe into making their own claims.[18] Other historians have emphasized the fearful, defensive frame of mind of late Victorian officials who looked "above all to the preservation of what they held . . . lest this great heritage should be lost in the time of troubles ahead."[19]

These nationalist jealousies and official fears were not entirely new. But they occurred in a world which had radically changed in less than a hundred years. The European industrial revolution demanded resources, labor, and markets on an unprecedented global scale. We have already seen the impact of this international labor market in the new multinational states. In the early part of the century when England was still the "workshop of the world" she could afford to integrate the ports of the "East Indies" and the West Indies at her own pace. But by the 1870s England was not the only country that controlled the genie of industrialization. France, Germany, Belgium, the Netherlands, and the United States each had its own bottle. Each of these newly industrialized countries required the enormous resources and markets that had propelled England to world dominance. They had multiplied the world's productive capacity overnight.

But there was a catch. The economic transformation had been so swift, there was not enough time to make the political and social adjustments that would enable the world to benefit from the boon. (Some would say the world still has not adjusted.) Europe and North America created a single world economy with enormous productivity, far beyond the dreams of past ages. But these industrial countries did not create the world government or international order that might prevent chaotic competition between industrial countries. Instead they intensified national competition, economically and politically, coming close to war on numerous occasions before finally doing so in 1914.

In 1873, at the height of their technological productivity, Western economies collapsed. The crisis of 1873 like the earlier industrial crises of 1837 and 1857 was a result of producing more than people could afford to buy. This time, however, the problem of "overproduction" had become, according to one historian, "a permanent nightmare."

> The spread of industrialization had made the international struggle for markets more intense. British exporters, accustomed to enjoying a virtual monopoly in many markets, now found themselves up against German, American and other foreign competition. Moreover, the industrializing countries were competing on an unprecedented scale in each others' home markets.[20]

The national economies of Europe and North America slipped into a global depression that lasted from 1873 to 1896. It was not a depression in the living standard of the average worker. The real wages of workers in Great Britain and France rose 40 percent between 1870 and 1900.[21] This was because of the enormous increase in productivity and the development of unions. Nor was there high unemployment in this period. It was, rather, a depression in prices, profit margins, and profits due to increased competition. It was a "time of troubles" for the businessman in a new era of international competition.

Its effects could be softened by cheap labor. This was the age of mass migrations and the "coolie trade." Many industrialists thought their profit margins could be bolstered by protective tariffs. This was the age of tariffs and protectionist legislation (except in England). Another solution seemed to lie in reducing competition. This was the age of the rise of cartels and trusts, the age of "monopoly capitalism." It also seemed to demand the control of cheaper sources of raw materials and more extensive and more predictable markets. This was the meaning of the new imperialism. The West had created an international economy in which Western national interests prevailed to the detriment of international interests or colonial national interests.

THE PARTITION OF AFRICA

The primary theater for the exercise of the new imperialism was Africa. Between 1884 and 1924 the entire continent of Africa was carved up into colonies by the major European powers. Unlike the "free-trade imperialism" of an earlier era or the attempt to partition China into "spheres of influence," the African colonies of the era of new imperialism were administered directly by the European powers.

Much has been written on the question of whether these new colonies satisfied mainly political or economic needs. Certainly they satisfied both. Politically, European powers had begun to cultivate the patriotism of their urban workers, recently eligible to vote and potentially subject of military enlistment. Economically, European workers were being pacified with costly benefits of the welfare state: union recognition, higher wage, and insurance against disability, old age, and unemployment. This was necessary to undermine socialist parties at the very moment of intense economic competition and contraction. If colonies were expensive, they were deemed a necessary expense. They instilled national pride at the same time that they seemed to offer a new economic frontier.

If the creation of African colonies fueled the nationalist feelings, and filled the empty pockets, of the European working classes, it postponed the development of African nationalism for decades.

One has only to look at a map of modern Africa to see how African nations were ignored. The boundary lines between modern African states are the legacy of the partitioning of Africa by the European powers between 1884 and 1914. The boundaries appear to be drawn at 90 degree angles from the sea, as if charted from the beach. They take little notice of what might be considered the natural boundaries of rivers and mountains and they completely ignore ethnic or national boundaries

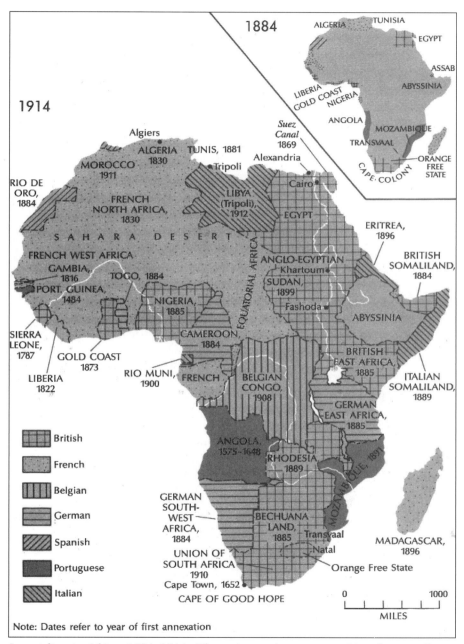

Imperialism in Africa, 1884–1914. The entire continent was partitioned among European powers in thirty years. The map of Africa was drawn with little regard for African ethnic boundaries.

of African peoples. The example of the Somalis was typical. They were divided among four sovereignties: French, British, Italian, and Ethiopian. In such densely populated areas as the Niger delta in West Africa and the area of Lake Victoria in East Africa, many nationalities were forced into the same colony. Often traditional enemies became subjects of a common European power. Such boundary lines settled disputes between European rivals but made no sense from an African perspective.

The legacy of these colonial boundaries has been mixed for modern Africa. Many of the national disputes since independence, such as that between the Ethiopians and Somalis, or between Ibos, Hausa, Fulani and Yoruba in Nigeria, can be traced to these artificial boundaries. Nevertheless, since independence most African states have agreed to accept such arbitrary boundaries as definitive, rather than risk future conflicts. In that respect, modern African states may be more inclined to international cooperation than most other states. However, their lack of nationalism may also hinder their ability to develop economic independence.

AFRICAN ECONOMIC DEPENDENCE

Africans were the first "workers of the world." As slaves they were the first peoples to be systematically exploited for their labor in both Eastern and western hemispheres. At the end of the nineteenth century they were the first people to be slated exclusively as producers for the world market. Indians and Chinese were viewed by Europeans as customers as well as workers. Africans were seen essentially as workers. The different perception may have been due, in part, to the lesser population of Africa after the slave trade ended. It may have also been due to the tendency of Westerners to focus on the rich natural environment of Africa instead of the people. (Even today, Western film and travel concentrate on the animals and scenery rather than the people.) In any case, Africans were the first peoples to be colonized in order to work.

Given the international nature of the economy in the 1880s, Africans were forced to work at export industries, especially in mining and farming, that brought little return to their own societies. Cocoa, coffee, peanuts, tropical fruits, diamonds, and gold were among the major exports. While many of these products had been enjoyed by Africans before the 1880s, under European colonialism production was organized only for the world market. Further, since African ethnic and national identities were frustrated by the colonizers, African workers often lacked the common language or culture necessary to perceive their plight or organize resistance.

We might distinguish three different ways in which Europeans secured control of African land and labor for the production and export of food and raw materials in Africa. One was the development of colonial control over peasant farmers, mainly in West Africa. A second was the development of concessions to European companies of land, principally in the rain forest of the Congo. The third was the creation of whites-only plantations, mines, and states in East and South Africa.

DOMINANCE OVER WEST AFRICAN PEASANTS

West Africa was very densely populated. There were many different ethnic groups, speaking many different languages, in a wide variety of political arrangements. There were kingdoms like the Mande-speaking kingdom ruled by Samori Toure (1830–1900) inland between the Senegal and Niger rivers, and there were smaller kingdoms and numerous small "stateless societies" (with a relatively decentralized political structure). The first European contacts with the smaller kingdoms and stateless societies of the West African coast usually took advantage of conflicts between different groups.

Two controls on labor developed in West Africa that became typical of colonialism everywhere. By placing a high value on certain key export crops, the Europeans played a significant role in directing African peasant farming to the world market. This meant a change from varied subsistence crops consumed locally to a few select products grown in vast amounts for export. This "monoculture" (single crop) production tied African peasants to the world market. It need not have been disastrous. Free trade advocates had long taught the advantage of geographic specialization and exchange. But the exchange was never equal. Africans did not control the terms of trade. Europeans set the price of their commodities and monopolized the trade. Once converted to monoculture, the Africans had to import many food products they had previously produced for themselves. Europeans controlled this trade as well.

Africans were also made dependent on Europeans by means of taxes. Head taxes and hut taxes were imposed by European administrators partially to cover the expenses of colonial administration. Most colonies were expected to pay for themselves, and most did. Not only the cost of railroads and port facilities but even the cost of occupying troops and colonial wars were charged to the colonies. There was an additional reason for taxes, however. The payment of taxes forced the Africans to get money. Money was not necessary in the traditional African village. Self-sufficient farmers could produce all they needed or barter for anything they were unable to produce. To require Africans to have money was to require their participation in the larger economy, either by raising products for sale or by selling their labor.

DOMINANCE OVER CENTRAL AFRICAN PEOPLES

King Leopold II of Belgium (r. 1865–1909) was an early proponent of colonies. He took the financial success of the Dutch in Indonesia as his own model. Since other European powers and his own government would have opposed him, he acted secretly to build a personal empire along the Congo River in central Africa. In 1876 he called an international geographical conference and founded an association to raise money for exploration of the Congo. The resulting organization was a corporation entirely owned by Leopold which pretended to be an educational and research institute. In 1879 he sent the British explorer Henry Morton Stanley (1841–1904) to the Congo. Stanley had captured the imagination of the Western world in an African search sponsored by the New York *Herald* in 1871 for David Livingstone (a missionary who was not aware he was "lost") with the words "Dr. Livingstone, I presume." Just as the explorer had unwittingly sold newspapers in 1871, in 1879 he bought real estate for King Leopold while imagining that he was negotiating treaties for a philanthropic organization. Thanks to his efforts, Leopold could claim "title" to almost a million square miles south of the Congo River and an African population of about 20 million in 1884.

The kingdom of the Bakongo in the sixteenth century had controlled much of this area. It was a rich, sophisticated kingdom. Bakongo kings were converted to Christianity by Portuguese missionaries and sent their sons to school in Lisbon. But the Bakongo and other central African kingdoms had been decimated by the slave trade and were in disarray by 1884. Leopold made the necessary alliance with the Arab power in the north. The United States granted recognition at an opportune moment after Leopold made contact with leaders of American business. The Berlin conference of 1885 made the "Congo Free State" official.

From the beginning it was a business proposition for Leopold. Concessions were granted to companies (most of which Leopold controlled) to exploit the available resources and labor without any regard to humanitarian concerns. The invention of rubber tires for bicycles and automobiles made the gathering of wild rubber extremely profitable. Rubber exports increased from 80 tons in 1891 to 1600 tons in 1897 to 6000 tons in 1901.[22]

So brutal was the administration of Leopold between 1885 and 1908 that the population of the Congo declined from twenty to ten million. Many were shot. Many fled. Many were mutilated. Women and children were held as hostage while the men gathered the rubber. If they did not meet their quotas, the women would be raped or the children's hands or feet would be cut off. Baskets of hands would be preserved by smoking and brought to the authorities for proof.

The world uproar over these acts pressured the Belgian government to take over the colony from the king in 1908 and govern it more humanely.

DOMINANCE OVER EAST AND SOUTH AFRICAN PLAINS

A third method of control, more typical of the high plains in East and South Africa, was for the Europeans to remove the Africans from the land, labeling it "white man's country" because of its cool climate, fertility, or mineral wealth. The first step was for the Europeans to establish political control. Chief Kabongo of the Kikuyu people describes this process:

> A Pink Cheek man came one day to our Council. . . . He sat in our midst and he told us of the King of the Pink Cheek who was a great king and lived in a land over the seas. "This great king is now your

king," he said, "and this land is all his land, though he has said you may live on it as you are his people and he is your father and you are his sons." This was strange news. For this land was ours. . . . We had no king, we elected our Councils and they made our laws. . . . With patience, our leading Elders tried to tell this to the Pink Cheek, and he listened. But at the end he said, "This we know, but in spite of this what I have told you is a fact. You have now a king . . . and in the town called Nairobi is a Council or government that acts for the king. And his laws are your laws."[23]

Once the Europeans had secured political control over the high lands of East and South Africa, they forced the Africans off the better land. But depriving the Africans of their land was not enough. The secretary of the Kenya Colonial Association argued as follows in 1908:

It is grossly unfair to invite the white settler to this country as has been done, to give him land under conditions which force him to work, and at the same time to do away with the foundation upon which the whole of his enterprise and hope is based, namely, cheap labor, whilst the native is allowed to retain large tracts of land on which he can remain in idleness.[24]

Another white settler in Kenya, Colonel Grogan, put it more bluntly when he said of the Kikuyu people: "We have stolen his land. Now we must steal his limbs. Compulsory labor is the corollary of the our occupation of the country."[25] This was accomplished by head taxes, as in West Africa, which forced the Africans to work in order to pay the tax. It was also accomplished, especially in the mining areas of Rhodesia (Zimbabwe) and South Africa by depriving the Africans of any land in which to support themselves thus forcing them to work in the mines. In little time, African work on European farms and mines became an article of faith. "I am prepared to state definitely," the Governor of what was shortly to become Kenya said in 1917, "that we desire to make of the native a useful citizen, and that we consider the best means of doing so is to induce him to work for a period of his life for the European."[26]

IMPERIALISM AND NATIONAL ECONOMIES

The result of the new imperialism in Africa was to deprive the Africans of national economies in order to inflate the economic power of the international corporations of the colonizing countries. In some cases a single foreign company ran the colonial economy. In Liberia, for instance, the income of the Firestone tire and rubber company in one year was $127 million while that of the entire country was $175 million.[27] One might be tempted to applaud these companies for their contribution to the African economy until one sees what happened to the profits. The profits went back to the international corporation, headquarterd in London, Paris, or New York. Some of them might be plowed back into the plantation or mine in Africa, but the corporation determined its investments on the basis of international considerations. The copper industry of colonial Northern Rhodesia (now Zimbabwe) in one year made payments to Rhodesia and Rhodesians of £12 million (including wages to white and black workers, expenses, taxes and custom duties) while the value of the copper they mined was £36 million. Thus, the international companies and their shareholders took out of Rhodesia double what they contributed. (In Rhodesia the companies increased the odds against any national unity by paying the average white worker twenty times the wages of the average black.)

There is a long-running debate among historians about the relationship between the economic development of the Western countries and the lesser development of former colonial countries like those of Africa. Some historians argue that Western development was the product of underdevelopment in the colonial world, that the West is developed today because the rest of the world is not.

Whether or not this judgement is accurate, it would be simplistic to assume that there is no connection between rich and poor countries. And while one could make a good case for the value of African prosperity to the West, it may have been to the advantage of some Western countries and companies to exploit and, thus, prevent the development of Africa.

A SMALL EXAMPLE

Let us take one small example. For as long as anyone in Africa can remember (which is pretty long), the cola nut has been a sign of hospitality and a second wind—the equivalent of the American coffee break (which, by the way, is another African story). When one African visits another, out comes the cola nut which is cut and offered to the guest. The nut is tasty and rich in caffeine. It enlivens the conversation. Things go better with cola nuts. Now, along comes an American company that discovers it can use the properties of the cola nut in a soft drink. The Coca Cola company becomes so successful with its "secret formula" that it is able to produce and market its drink all over the world. Coca Cola, of course, is for sale in Africa like everywhere else.

Now, the question to ask is what effect does this have on African economies? Regardless of the price paid by the Coca Cola company for the nuts, or the wages they pay the growers, Africans are going to be paying for a product which is grown in Africa and sold to them by an international corporation. Perhaps an even more important question to ask is what would happen if Africans decided to make their own cola drinks? Would Coca Cola, or Pepsi or the other companies, let them? Certainly they would not encourage it. They might undersell any competition to put them out of business. They would have enormous resources to ensure that it did not happen. And why should it? The international companies already make a popular product. Anyone who has tasted the version that was made by China until a few years ago can easily understand why they opened their doors to the international brand. The point is that this is one manufacturing route effectively closed to Africans. We can safely predict that no country in Africa is going to create a cola drink company unless it is a disastrous, spiteful, nationalist act that everyone soon regrets.

"So what?" one might say. We started by saying this was a small example. It is small, at least, from an American perspective. But it is symptomatic of the problem of African economic development precisely because the cola nut is so important to Africans. If Africans cannot develop their own cola drink industry, then what can they develop? What avenue has the West left open? Certainly an automobile industry is out of the question. French speaking Africa has its Peugeots, English speaking Africa its Minis, and the Toyotas have replaced the Fords everywhere. A Cameroonian or Kenyan car would be silly. What, then, would not? In the market place one sees clothes made in Hong Kong by American or British companies. Reliance on the European economy defies all rhyme or reason: city stores in Cameroon carry only French bread and butter flown in from Paris. One looks in vain for a product that has not already been overproduced by the industrial economies of the West and, increasingly, the Asian rim.

WAYS AND WORDS

One favorable legacy of colonialism for the national economies of Africa (and the rest of the former colonial world) is the infrastructure of roads, railroads, phone and mail service created during the colonial period. But in general, the results are less happy for Africa then they were for Dalhousie's India. Instead of integrating national and regional economies, all railroads lead to Rome or Paris by way of the seaport. Phone and plane connections between nearby cities that happen to have a different colonial heritage have to be routed through Europe. Mail follows a similar route. An African's letter to another African can be stopped by a strike in Paris.

As in India, the legacy of a common language is also a mixed blessing. There were 200 languages in Cameroon before the Germans arrived. The Germans were replaced by the British and the French after World War I. Now all citizens speak English or French. Students are expected to speak both. Children often speak both their mother's language and father's language if they are different, and a third local "market" language if it is different from the parental languages. There could not be a nation with 200 languages; it is difficult enough with two or three.

WHO NEEDS NATIONALISM?

On one level, the North African Frantz Fanon once said, it may seem as if Africans do not need nationalism. Traditional African ethnic identities are frequently divisive forces in the modern state. Modern African national boundaries are artificial. Further, as a reaction to colonialism, nationalism is off the mark. For the European colonist "the Negro was neither an Angolan nor a Nigerian, for he simply spoke of 'the Negro.'"[28] Thus, when the African intellectual seeks his own cultural roots, Fanon continued, he "never does so in the name of Angola or Dahomey. The culture which is affirmed is African culture."[29] But ultimately this response is a blind alley, Fanon concluded. History structured the oppression of Africans according to particular institutions in particular states by particular European powers. To attain economic and cultural independence, Africans needed first to achieve political independence, and this was a struggle of each colonized people against each colonizer. In short, nationalism was necessary for those whose nations were colonized.

BUY AMERICAN?

Is nationalism necessary for the colonizers as well? Is nationalism a useful force among the independent and industrialized countries? Or does nationalism simply prevent the realization of greater global harmony and integration? Histories cannot be shaped to provide easy answers to big questions like these. But perhaps one conclusion we might draw from our brief survey of nationalism and internationalism in the nineteenth century is that any nationalist stance by an internationalist power is apt to be rife with contradictions, if not outright hypocrisy. Indeed, the free trade crusade of Britain in the century suggests even internationalist positions might be more self-serving than disinterested.

Regardless of what one makes of the argument that Western development was the other side of colonial underdevelopment, the increasingly international needs of the nineteenth century economy are clear. Even if one approves of the use of colonies to export domestic economic problems and import cheap labor or raw material, it was not simply nationalistic. When Hawaiian planters imported Chinese workers, they were not "buying American." Capital, labor, materials, and production—all the elements of the capitalist economy—were international in the nineteenth century, and they have been ever since. It is therefore both cruel and futile for one national labor group to campaign against another.

THE SOCIALIST INTERNATIONAL

Such was the policy of the Socialist International. At its congress in Stuttgart in 1907 and again at Basel in 1912 the International faced the issue of nationalism and internationalism in its most difficult form—the conflict between national defense and socialist internationalism. As the nationalist conflicts of the European powers were coming to a head, the International adopted a resolution sponsored by Rosa Luxemburg and V.I. Lenin which called on all socialist parties to try to prevent the outbreak of war. But if war should come, as many feared it would, the resolution called for socialists to do all they could to oppose it, including taking advantage of "the economic and political crisis created by the war to arouse the population and hasten the overthrow of capitalist rule."[30]

Such was not to be. Even in 1912 the International was breaking up into patriotic nationalist factions. A proposal for a general strike in the event of war was rejected by most German socialists because they thought the German socialists were better organized to cripple the German war machine than the Russian socialists were to cripple the Russian army. Therefore, they reasoned, a general strike would just result in the Russian army overrunning Germany. Internationalist principles were further compromised by the fact that Russia and France were allies. It was the German military's plan in the event of a Russian mobilization to quickly conquer France (as in 1870) so they could concentrate on the Russian front. Thus, German socialists talked themselves into supporting an invasion of France at the first sign of a Russian mobilization.

In fact, Lenin and Rosa Luxemburg were part of a minority of left-wing socialists who opposed the war in 1914. The German socialists in parliament voted for war because, as they said, they were afraid if they did not they would have been beaten up by their supporters. The working classes, socialist and not, were proud of their patriotism and marched off to war eagerly. In a meeting of left-wing socialists in Switzerland in 1915 Lenin opposed any argument for national defense. Since the fundamental cause for the war was the imperialist striving of all capitalist governments there were no "aggressors" and "defenders." The only proper response, Lenin insisted, was to end imperialism by ending capitalism. Lenin was anything but naive. He recognized that most workers were patriotic. He believed that imperialism was also the cause of worker patriotism. The high profits of imperialism, he thought, enabled Western capitalism to "buy off" a large section of the working class. A Western "worker aristocracy" was thus created which benefited from colonialism and opposed revolution. Whether or not Lenin was correct, war came in 1914. Five years later neither nationalism nor imperialism had been buried with millions of bodies.

FOR FURTHER READING

Ernest Gellner's *Nations and Nationalism* offers a concise and readable theoretical approach. Eric Hobsbawm's *Nations and Nationalism since 1780* is a brief historical study of European nationalism. Benedict Anderson's more global essays in *Imagined Communities* shows how nationalist identities are constructed, as does Hobsbawm's more difficult *The Invention of Tradition*. More introductory approaches, if a bit dated, can be found in Hans Kohn's *Nationalism: Its Meaning and History* and Louis L. Snyder in *Varieties of Nationalism*. Anthony D. Smith's *Nationalism* is a useful recent reader. More demanding theoretical treatments can be found in *Nationalism and the State* by John Breuilly, *Theories of Nationalism* by Anthony D. Smith, and Toward a Marxist Theory of Nationalism by Horace B. Davis. On internationalism see Boyd C. Shafer's *Nationalism and Internationalism* and Sandi Cooper's excellent collection, *Internationalism in Nineteenth Century Europe*.

For specific studies on the development of nationalism in Europe, see Eugen Weber's *Peasants into Frenchmen*, David Avrom Bell's *The Cult of the Nation in France: Inventing Nationalism, 1680–1800*, and Rogers Brubaker's *Citizenship and Nationhood in France and Germany*.

On British colonialism and nationalism in India, Geoffrey Moorhouse's *India Britannica* is a well-illustrated, lively history of British rule. D.A. Low's *Lion Rampant* is a rich exploration of some interesting themes. On "free trade imperialism" see B. Semmel's *The Rise of Free Trade Imperialism*, F. Clairmonte's *Economic Liberalism and Underdevelopment*, and P. Harnetty's *Imperialism and Free Trade: Lancashire and India in the Mid-Nineteenth Century*. Partha Chatterjee's *The Nation and Its Fragments* is mainly concerned with Indian nationalism, but raises broader issues about nationalism in former European colonies in Asia and Africa.

Among the readable histories of the opium war are Peter Ward Fay's *The Opium War 1840–1842*, Hsin-pao Chang's *Commissioner Lin and the Opium War*, and Jack Beeching's *The Chinese Opium Wars*. James M. Polachek's *The Inner Opium War* looks at the internal Chinese debate with a critical eye toward Commissioner Lin. Carl A. Trocki's *Opium, Empire and the Global Political Economy* puts the opium trade in the larger context of the expanding empire. John King Fairbank's *The Great Chinese Revolution 1800–1985* is an excellent introduction to Chinese history. Two recent interpretations of Chinese economic history argue for its vitality and strength: Kenneth Pomeranz's *The Great Divergence* and R. Bin Wong's *China Transformed*. Jonathan Spence's *God's Chinese Son* is a rich and vivid history of the Taiping rebellion.

On multinational societies and the great migrations of the nineteenth and early twentieth century, most histories deal with the Europeans who came to the United States. Two classics are John Higham's *Strangers in the Land* and Thomas J. Archdeacon's *Becoming American*. The extent to which these were labor migrations is well demonstrated in *Labor Migration in the Atlantic Economies*, edited by Dirk Hoerder. There are also excellent studies of other important migration movements. Maxine Hong Kingston's *The Woman Warrior* and *China Men* are rich personal evocations. Ronald Takaki's *Plantation Life and Labor in Hawaii* is a moving history. Among personal accounts of immigration, Mary Antin's *The Promised Land* is a classic, as is *The Letters of Rachel Henning* from Australia.

On the new imperialism in Africa, Harrison Wright gathers some of the classic interpretations in *The "New Imperialism"*. Raymond Betts does the same for *The "Scramble" for Africa*. Robert O. Collins' *Europeans in Africa* is a short overview. Daniel Headrick's *The Tools of Empire* reveals some of the technological factors. Ronald Robinson and John Gallagher's *Africa and the Victorians* is a classic. Walter Rodney's *How Europe Underdeveloped Africa* is a more critical account.

Among useful interpretive studies of imperialism, Tony Smith's *The Pattern of Imperialism: The United States, Great Britain, and the Late-industrializing World since*

1815 is a vigorous and demanding comparative study. Edward Said's *Orientalism* is a demanding classic, recently challenged by David Cannadine's *Ornamentalism*. For a much debated new interpretation, see Michael Hardt and Antonio Negri's *Empire*.

NOTES

1. Wm. Theodore de Bary, ed., *Sources of Indian Tradition*, vol. 2 (New York: Columbia University Press, 1958), p. 34.
2. Cited by P. Harnetty, *Imperialism and Free Trade: Lancashire and India in the Mid-Nineteenth Century* (Vancouver: University of British Columbia Press, 1972), p. 6.
3. Cited by F. Clairmonte, *Economic Liberalism and Underdevelopment* (London: Asia Publishing House, 1960), pp. 86, 90. Quoted in L. S. Stavrianos, *The Global Rift: The Third World Comes of Age* (New York: William Morrow, 1981), p. 247.
4. *Ibid.*
5. Frederick Wakeman, Jr., *The Fall of Imperial China* (New York: Free Press, 1975), p. 101.
6. S. Y. Teng and J. K. Fairbank, *China's Response to the West* (Cambridge: Harvard University Press, 1954), p. 19.
7. Hsin-pao Chang, *Commissioner Lin and the Opium War* (New York: Norton, 1964), p. 30.
8. Cited in Peter Ward Fay, *The Opium War* (New York: Norton, 1964), p. 30.
9. Mary Antin, *The Promised Land* (Boston: Houghton Mifflin Company, 1912), chapter 11, "My Country," passim.
10. Samuel L. Baily, *Immigrants in the Lands of Promise. Italians in Buenos Aires and New York City, 1870 to 1914* (Ithaca: Cornell University Press, 1999).
11. Cited in Keith Sinclair, *A History of New Zealand* (Harmondsworth: Penguin, 1959), p. 97.
12. Cited in *ibid.*, p. 213.
13. Cited by Ronald Takaki, *Pau Hana: Plantation Life and Labor in Hawaii 1835–1920* (Honolulu: University of Hawaii Press, 1983), pp. 22, 23, and 24 respectively.
14. Stanley Wolpert, *A New History of India* (New York: Oxford University Press, 1977), pp. 231–232.
15. Christopher Hibbert, *The Great Mutiny* (New York: Penguin, 1980), p. 385.
16. Cited by S. Y. Teng, *The Taiping Rebellion and the Western Powers* (London: Oxford University Press, 1971), p. 116.
17. A good case for the importance of these and other technological factors is made by Daniel R. Headrick in *The Tools of Empire: Technology and European Imperialism in the Nineteenth Century* (New York: Oxford University Press, 1981).
18. D. K. Fieldhouse, *The Colonial Empires from the Eighteenth Century* (New York:

Dell, 1966), p. 209.

19. Ronald Robinson and John Gallagher with Alice Denny, *Africa and the Victorians: The Climax of Imperialism* (Garden City, N.Y.: Anchor Books), p. 472.

20. Tom Kemp, *Historical Patterns of Industrialization* (Harlow, Essex, England: Longman, 1978), pp. 102–103.

21. F. Sternberg, *Capitalism and Socialism on Trial* (New York: John Day, 1951), p. 27. See also L. S. Stavrianos, *The Global Rift*, p. 267.

22. Edouard Bustin, "The Congo," in Gwendolen M. Carter, *Five African States* (London: Pall Mall, 1963), p. 28.

23. Cited by David Killingray, *A Plague of Europeans* (Harmondsworth: Penguin, 1973), p. 72.

24. *Ibid.*

25. Cited in Walter Rodney, *How Europe Underdeveloped Africa* (Washington, D.C.: Howard University Press, 1982), p. 165.

26. Sir Henry Belfield, *Proceedings of the East Africa Protectorate Legislative Council*, 1st session, 1917, p. 3. Cited in D.A. Low, *Lion Rampant* (London: Cass, 1973), p. 66.

27. G. I. Beckford, *Persistent Poverty* (London: Oxford University Press, 1972), p. 131. Cited in L. S. Stavrianos, *The Global Rift*, p. 273. The year is 1967–68.

28. Frantz Fanon, *The Wretched of the Earth* (New York: Grove Press, 1968), p. 211.

29. *Ibid.*, p. 212.

30. Carl E. Schorske, *German Social Democracy, 1905–1917* (Cambridge, Mass: Harvard University Press, 1955), p. 83. Cited in Albert S. Lindemann, *A History of European Socialism* (New Haven: Yale University Press, 1983), p. 189.

✣ 9 ✣

Culture
and
Change

Beyond Certainty
and Relativity

During the last hundred years Western culture—the ideas, values, mentalities, and feelings of men and women in the most industrialized part of the world—has gone through a profound change. It might not be too simplistic to call it a change from certainty to relativity. Over a hundred years ago people were certain about almost everything. God, progress, truth, beauty, human motivation, morality, sexuality, marriage, civilization, war, economics, and nature were all clear concepts about which certain definite, often absolute, statements could be made. Today such certainty is no longer possible.

We live today in what has been called an age of uncertainty and anxiety, of relativity and cynicism. This chapter will look at how this change to relativity came about. It begins with a survey of the development of modern culture in just one of its many forms—painting from 1863 to 1913. This leads to an investigation into the development of modern ideas of change and culture—one of the sources of modern uncertainty and relativity. Then, our chapter focuses on some of the confrontations with relativity in the twentieth century and some of the attempts to understand it and overcome it. In essence, our concluding chapter asks how we are learning to live with these conclusions.

MODERN PAINTING:
A VISUAL BAROMETER OF CHANGE

One of the best ways to see the change to modern culture in the last hundred years is to walk through a museum or thumb through a history of painting. Whether you begin with European painting in the Renaissance, the seventeenth century, the eighteenth century, or even the beginning of the nineteenth century, you see (despite changes in style) the same things. You see objects, landscapes, and people. They are identifiable as such. They are shown in three-dimensional perspective: things get smaller and fuzzier the further they recede into the background, just the way we see. They show shadows all going in the same direction. Usually they look beautiful, but even when they show violence or warts it is to look noble, dramatic, or uplifting. They convey messages like "how enchanting," "so real," or "how coura-geous Napoleon was"; they tell stories and show what things look like. There are exceptions, of course, but almost all paintings from the Renaissance to the end of the nineteenth century reflect these interests in visual accuracy, beauty, and "objec-tive" truth. The paintings themselves are framed, rectangular "windows" on the world. As we approach the paintings of the late nineteenth century all of this changes: colors seem wrong; objects are not recognizable; nothing looks like any-thing anymore. What happened?

We would have been able to see the beginning of this revolution if we had attended the Salon des Refuses ("Room of the Rejected") at the "Exposition des Beaux-Arts" in Paris in 1863. The mere existence of such a room was something of a revolution. The French emperor, Napoleon III, had stepped in on behalf of the artists whose work had been rejected from the official exhibition. He ordered the creation of an annex which would contain the rejected work so that the public could decide for themselves if the official jury had acted wisely. The reaction of the public was derisive laughter and renewed faith in the official jury. Only a few who came to laugh left "serious, anxious, and troubled" or struck by "a certain sincerity . . . novelty and singularity," as two reviewers noted.[1]

The painting which most outraged the public, the jury, and the critics was Edouard Manet's *Le dejeuner sur l'herbe* (*Luncheon on the Grass*). Most professed to be disgusted by the appearance of a nude woman in a public park with two well-dressed gentlemen. The emperor, who had a string of mistresses in private, was said to have been shocked. At least one critic complained of the unconventional tech-nique: the lack of three-dimensional depth, and the flatness of perspective in clothes that seemed to hang without bodies, "boneless fingers and heads without skulls," and "side whiskers made of two strips of black cloth." Most, however, com-plained of the subject matter. A visiting English critic was impressed by Manet's attempt to translate the Renaissance subject into modern French, and he pardoned its "fine colour," but he too found the subject of "doubtful morality."

The revolution of modern art began as an attack on traditional subject matter. Manet's nude at a picnic could not be dismissed as a classical goddess: she seemed to come out of the Parisian underworld. She was hardly a fitting subject for a great

Edouard Manet's Le dejeuner sur l'herbe *(Luncheon on the Grass)*. *(Louvre, Jeu de Paume)*

work of art: that is what shocked the critics.

From the perspective of today, however, the most visible shift in the history of modern art occurred not with the new subjects of the Salon des Refuses, but with the new styles of the next decades: Impressionism and Expressionism. The flatness of Impressionism was already implicit in Manet's work of 1863, and the young group of French Impressionists gathered around Manet in the next decade. The paintings of Claude Monet, Auguste Renoir, Edgar Degas, Camille Pissarro, and Paul Cézanne that were gathered together in the first Impressionist exhibition in 1874 were attacked more for a lack of drawing than a lack of decency. Today we can praise their bold use of color, their meticulous perception of light, their imaginative way of capturing the impermanence of a rapidly changing world, their willingness to paint outdoors, their joyous spontaneity in the ordinary and the transient, or their almost instinctive search for new perceptions that would not be outdone by the developing technology of the camera (the first exhibition was held in a famous photographer's studio). In 1874 the critics treated the show as if it were a hoax: "Do you recall the Salon des Refuses?" the paper *La Patrie* asked. Well, that was the fine museum of the Louvre compared to the paintings of the Impressionist exhibition. "Looking at the first rough drawings—and rough is the right word—you simply shrug your shoulders; seeing the next lot, you burst out laughing; but with the last

Claude Monet's impressionistic Rouen Cathedral. *This is one of many paintings Monet did of the Cathedral at different times of day to capture momentary changes of light. (The Metropolitan Museum of Art, The Bequest of Theodore M. Davis, 1915)*

Paul Cézanne's Modern Olympia *(Musée Jeu de Paume).*

ones you finally get angry."

The critics saved most of their venom for Cézanne's *A Modern Olympia.* Cézanne had taken a classical theme—the reclining goddess Olympia—which Manet had already modernized in 1865, to the consternation of the Parisian art world. Manet's *Olympia* pictured the goddess as a Parisian prostitute in a setting that looked all too much like a brothel. (Manet's *Olympia* was called the first work of modern art because it was the first to require police protection.) Cézanne modernized the theme and style of *Olympia* much further. The goddess became a willowy dream, unveiled by her black attendant for the artist on the couch as flowers exploded with expectation overhead.

Cézanne's dreamy confrontation with Olympia, a painting which was already beyond the boundaries of Impressionism, was described over and over again as the work of a madman. Cézanne was to lead the next generation of Western painting into an expressionist style that made the work of the Impressionists look "pretty" and "quaint."

While the Impressionists were still concerned with capturing an objective reality of color and light, if only for an instant, the Expressionists turned inward to express the emotional dimension of the artist's experience. While the Impressionists had relished the flickering, endless changes of their world, the Expressionists (perhaps overwhelmed by change) sought universals in their own personal feelings, the symbols of dreams, and the abstract structure of materials. In this broad sense, almost all Post-Impressionist art was Expressionist, and remains so even today.

We can get a more manageable idea of the extent of this change if we look at a few of the works displayed at one landmark exhibition of the twentieth century. The work displayed at the American Armory Show of 1913 reflected a more radical idea of art than that suggested by the canvases of the nineteenth century Salon des Refuses or the Impressionist exhibition. They made Manet's *Dejeuner sur l'herbe* and even Cézanne's *A Modern Olympia* look like continuations of the Renaissance. And we understand the radical departure of modern art even more fully by noticing the responses of the critics and the public to this twentieth-century exhibition. Not only do the paintings seem to come from another planet, but they were also accepted without much of the shock and scandal of the more modest departures of 1863 and 1874.

The organizers of the American Armory Show of 1913 attempted to bring to New York City "the most complete art exhibition that has ever been held in the world during the last quarter century." Allowing for American exaggeration, they were pretty close to the truth. Many of the major Post-Impressionists were represented. There were works by Vincent van Gogh, Paul Gauguin, and Pablo Picasso (as well as Cézanne) which were still shocking for their flat perspective, sketchy outline, bright, broad patches of color, and almost cubist, geometrical shapes. But the most radical departures from traditional painting, and the most heatedly debated of the show, were the paintings of Henri Matisse and Marcel Duchamp. Matisse's *The Blue Nude* seemed to assault the viewer's traditional expectations with the pose, look, and setting, but especially the blue color of the model. Duchamp's *Nude Descending a Staircase* showed neither staircase nor nude, but almost a blurred study of machinelike parts in rapid movement.

The reviewers and public had a lot of fun with the more radical exhibits. Almost all tried out their wit at the expense of Duchamp: one concluded that it was actually "a staircase descending a nude." Another called it "an explosion in a shingle factory."

> The jibe was perceptive, up to a point. The figure is indeed shattered into shinglelike planes that merge and overlap in a pattern of great energy. But the jibe falls short in that the shattered figure is not chaotic. Contrarily, it is reassembled into a pattern of great order and vivacity, more expressive of bright descending movement than an imitative painting of a nude descending a staircase could be.[2]

Henri Matisse's The Blue Nude. *(The Baltimore Museum of Art, The Cone Collection, formed by Dr. Claribel Cone and Miss Etta Cone of Baltimore, Maryland)*

The public was infuriated by playful titles, cubist studies of structure and movement, and expressionist uses of color and line. They resented artists who challenged or made fun of their expectations. But given the radical divergence from traditional art, and keeping in mind the charges of scandal, hoax, and madness in 1863 and 1874, the remarkable thing is the good-natured character of the criticism and the degree of public and critical acceptance of these most avant-garde works.

Few viewers responded as sensitively as the American painter John Sloan, who described the exhibition as:

> The beginning of a journey into the living past. The blinders fell from my eyes and I could look at religious pictures without seeing their subjects. I was freed to enjoy the sculptures of Africa and prehistoric Mexico because visual verisimilitude was no longer important. I realized that these things were made in response to life, distorted to emphasize ideas about life, emotional qualities about life.[3]

Few were as sympathetic as Stuart Davis, the younger American painter, who recalled:

Marcel Duchamp's Nude Descending a Staircase. *(Philadelphia Museum of Art)*

I responded particularly to Gauguin, Van Gogh, and Matisse, because broad generalizations of form and the non-imitative use of color were already practices within my own experience.[4]

But eighty-seven thousand admissions were recorded in New York, and by the time the show had returned from Boston and Chicago, three hundred thousand Americans had been introduced to modern art. Many of the paintings (including those of Duchamp) were purchased by collectors. There were even many favorable reviews of the exhibition. Surprisingly, it was a great success. But why?

The paintings in the 1913 exhibition were far more radically modern than those of the Paris exhibitions in 1863 and 1874. Not only had modern painting distinguished itself more from the traditional in those 40 years, but many Americans were viewing "modern art" for the first time, while Parisians were shocked at slight departures of a few years or a decade. Why, then, did Americans in 1913 respond so much more tolerantly (and even enthusiastically) to much greater changes?

Part of the answer is provided by one of the most notable visitors to the New York Armory, President Theodore Roosevelt. Roosevelt's personal taste in art ran to drawings of wild animals. He admitted that the more extreme paintings in the Armory show were beyond him. He made fun of people who called themselves Cubists. It seemed to him something like calling themselves "Knights of the Isosceles Triangle, or Brothers of the Cosine." He preferred Navajo rugs to Duchamp's Nude. But—and here is the point—he insisted that the organizers of the show "are quite right as to the need of showing to our people in this manner the art forces which of late have been at work in Europe, forces which cannot be ignored." He welcomed "newness" and "progress" and agreed that "there can be no life without change, no development without change, and that to be afraid of what is different or unfamiliar is to be afraid of life."[5]

This was the faith of the progressive era of the early twentieth century. It was also a recurring American faith. But, perhaps most significantly, it was one of the only possible attitudes to the sheer enormousness of change that had swept Western society in the preceding half century.

We see, then, a number of things in Western art in the 50 years before World War I. We see the sudden transformation of a traditional, centuries-old style of painting. In 50 years artists abandoned the models of centuries. We see that the artists themselves were responding to, and attempting to show, the changes sweeping their world. We see increasing public acceptance of the artists' radically new perception. But we also see that the public was accepting change more than they were understanding the new art.

If the critics of 1863 and 1874 rejected new departures for the wrong reasons or without understanding them, by 1913 the critics and even much of the general public were accepting modern art for similar wrong reasons, without understanding them. In fact, the critics and public of 1863 and 1874 probably understood more of what was happening than did either group in 1913. Art had changed fundamentally. It ceased to communicate with the educated populace. It would have been absurd in 1913 for the president of the United States to urge the public to judge the jurors (as Napoleon had done in 1863). The organizers of the Armory exhibition had even hoped originally to hang everything submitted. Jury selection, artistic criticism, aesthetic standards no longer seemed to make any sense. Change had been so rapid that there were no standards available. The new artists had fought against the traditional standards, but their experimentation with new forms was so varied that no new standards were possible. A public that accepted change for its own sake smiled, satirized, or bought, but without understanding what the artists were saying.

THE DISCOVERY OF CHANGE AND CULTURE

The idea that change is one of the fundamental ingredients of life (perhaps, in fact, the only one) is very recent. It is an idea which was whispered in the eighteenth century, but has become popular only in the last century. Even today, many people who recognize that everything changes are as unaware of the implications of that idea as was Teddy Roosevelt.

All societies since the Neolithic revolution have recognized that seasons change. Even earlier societies knew that people changed, at least in growing older. But almost all societies before the last hundred years thought that human continuity was much more basic than human change. The ancient Hebrews were probably the first society to understand themselves in terms of change. Their Bible was a history book because they believed that God revealed his promises and commands through the history of his chosen people. Christians continued to believe that God acted through history: the period after Christ was fundamentally different from the period before; Christ would at some revealed time return; the temper of the times had to be understood in order to understand God's design for man. The Christians also placed a premium on the individual's capacity to change: although everyone was born with original sin, conversion gave one a new life, indeed an eternal life. These ideas were quite different from those of Asia, Africa, the Americas, and even Greece and Rome. The Greeks, Romans, Chinese, and some other societies wrote histories, but in order to understand what had always been, not to understand how things were changing. They believed that time was a succession of repeating cycles and that human nature was always the same. Their history writing was for them a source of moral examples that would show a ruler how to govern and the people why they should behave. In classical Greece and Rome this "exemplar history" became quite sophisticated in explaining the causes of events and the motivations of people—but always in terms of what was imagined to be human nature.

Actually, Christian consciousness of change became subordinate in the Middle Ages to the church's control of revelation and interpretation. Medieval Christian history was limited to "lives of the saints," which taught the same examples by telling the same stories. The potential of Christian culture to grapple with change as a fundamental reality lay dormant until the influence of the church was challenged by secular science and the Protestant Reformation.

Western historical writing regained some of the sophistication of the classical world during the Renaissance, partly because historians like Machiavelli and Guicciardini modeled their work on classical histories. We have seen in our reading of Machiavelli, for instance, how he borrowed examples from classical Greece or his contemporary Italy as if both periods were the same in all essentials. He recognized differences, to be sure. In fact, he wrote *The Prince* with an eye to what he saw as the superiority of pagan religion over Christianity. But he imagined that Italians could adopt pagan values because he did not understand that Christianity had brought about fundamental changes. He saw religions, like political strategies, to be interchangeable, because he believed that all people were essentially the same.

But the Europeans of Machiavelli's time were beginning to discover that some people in the world were very, very different. The first letter of Columbus (written on the return voyage of the Nina in 1493) was printed throughout Europe and (according to legend) sung on the streets of Italian cities.

> The people of this island, and of all the other islands which I have found and of which I have information, all go naked, men and women, as their mothers bore them, although some women cover a single place with the leaf of a plant or with a net of cotton which they make for the purpose. They have no iron or steel or weapons, nor are they fitted to use them, not because they are not well built men and of handsome stature, but because they are marvellously timorous. . . . They are so guileless and so generous with all they possess that no one would believe it who has not seen it. They never refuse anything which they possess, if it be asked of them; on the contrary, they invite anyone to share it, and display so much love as if they would give their hearts.[6]

The immediate European response to the discovery of vastly different peoples was to place them in the legendary golden age of classical mythology which corresponded somewhat to the Christian idea of the time "before the fall" of Adam and Eve. But this was a literary and mythological solution, not an historical or anthropological one. Eventually, however, the persistent questions which were posed by the existence of such peoples led Europeans to discover "culture" and change," the inventions of modern anthropology and history. Three thinkers of the eighteenth-century Enlightenment stand out in the European discovery of culture. They are Montesquieu, Voltaire, and Vico. Both Montesquieu and Voltaire tried to account for the similarities and differences among the world's peoples within an overall framework that would do for human society what Newton's scientific laws had done for the physical world. Both realized that there were certain connections or relationships which taken together made up a people's culture (today we often use the word "lifestyle"). There were, to use Columbus's information as an example, certain connections between going naked and having no steel or iron weapons, and possibly even a relationship between both of these and the native American's habit of generosity. The ingredients of a particular culture fit together. They were not completely arbitrary or accidental. It would be highly unlikely, for instance, to find a society whose inhabitants went around naked and also forged steel.

The reader will not find this idea surprising. Much of this book has shown how certain kinds of thought and behavior fit together. We have, for instance, pointed out the "fit" between ideas of individuality and both Protestantism and Neo-Confucianism, between the rise of the European middle class and ideas of politics as a process, and between class society and aversive racism, to name just a few. When we point out how people of a similar background often think in similar ways, we are speaking about "culture."

Perhaps because people like to think that they are themselves free to do whatever they want and, in fact, feel the anxiety of choice every time they do something, they often do not recognize how much their culture determines their very options and choices. As a result, they are slow to recognize the existence of culture as a set of forms which both limits and permits certain kinds of walking, talking, dreaming, and doing. Europeans like Montesquieu, Voltaire, and Vico were beginning to understand this in the eighteenth century.

Both Montesquieu and Voltaire, however, stopped short of allowing their discovery of culture to lead them to a discovery of fundamental change. Montesquieu developed a modern comparative method for outlining the internal relationships of cultures. He organized new information about different peoples into what Max Weber later called "ideal types" or abstract shorthands about cultural forms. But he held to a faith in human nature by suggesting that every cultural variety was a product of a particular "spirit of laws," and that there were only three fundamental types of such spirits. Voltaire argued that a history of customs would reveal more about people than any history of kings and battles, but his own historical writing treated peoples of every age as if they had the same values, motivations, and attitudes as the eighteenth-century French. Both Voltaire and Montesquieu, for instance, refused to believe the observations of the classical historian Herodotus about certain sexual customs of the classical world.

Giambattista Vico's *The New Science* (1725) was the first modern anthropology and the first modern history in that it accepted the uniqueness of primitive and ancient cultures and recognized that all ideas and institutions (even the most sacred) had human histories. It was the first study of culture and change that denied the constancy of human nature. Vico found similarities and even cyclical repetitions in human history, but they were the cycles of the spiral, not of the circle. For Vico, human history changed fundamentally because it was a cumulative process created by human beings. Each age had its own culture—its own morals, myths, and language. Each age created the preconditions for the next, but could only be understood fully on its own terms. For Vico, the recognition of cultural variety led to the recognition of change. It was not enough to explain cultural types in terms of particular environments (as Montesquieu was to do in *The Spirit of Laws* in 1748), because each new environment was a human creation that changed. Human history had a direction that humans determined, consciously or not. Nothing was eternal or natural.

Vico's radical discoveries went unnoticed until the French and industrial revolutions made change a commonplace. After 1789 European intellectuals engaged in a series of studies that developed some of Vico's preliminary insights more fully. The French Revolution stimulated a secular version of the Christian idea of linear, rather than cyclical, time. The growth of human knowledge seemed enough (without religious considerations) to suggest that each age was an improvement on those past. The late-eighteenth-century idea of progress became for some in the nineteenth century an idea of human perfectability (both ideas would have been blasphemous earlier). The French Revolution also encouraged nationalist movements in Europe, which sought support from studies of the uniqueness of each national culture and the origins of national identity in medieval folk traditions and myth. In Germany, the study of myth and language led to the systematic study of cultural change that we traced from Hegel to Marx, and to the professional analysis of historical documents in the productive German historical schools of the nineteenth century.

The French historian Jules Michelet actually rediscovered the writings of Vico in 1824, and proceeded to write the history of France as the work of the French people. Both Michelet and the German historians and philosophers insisted that the writing of history was possible only by reliving the experiences of the past. Like Vico, they believed such reliving to be possible because there were still "traces" of older mentalities in the modern mind. But the swiftness of change in the nineteenth century and the logical analysis of philosophers like David Hume in England and the German historicists made that task increasingly difficult.

The full realization that every culture was unique, and that life is nothing but change—which was historicism's philosophical position in the nineteenth century, and which has become one of our basic assumptions today—was, and is, devastating. It was fought against continually. As we have noticed over and over again, each age wishes to believe that its values and behavior reflect human nature. A belief in human nature was perhaps even more essential for the upholders of market society in the nineteenth century. As we have seen in our discussion of Hobbes and Locke, the defenders of modern market society invented a whole new set of certainties about "human nature" and "natural law" in order to ward off the centrifugal pull and atomistic, fragmenting tendencies of a society modeled on the marketplace.

Many of the new "certainties" that they invented were disputed by the new anthropological discoveries and methods of logical analysis as soon as they were proposed. That had happened since the seventeenth-century beginnings of liberal market theory. In the seventeenth century, Blaise Pascal made a mockery of René

Descartes's simple faith that "God has so established the order of things that even if every man were to be concerned only with himself, and to show no charity to others, he would still, in the normal course of events, be working on their behalf."[7]

The varied customs of men showed Pascal that "theft, incest, infanticide, parricide" had all been considered "virtues" by some cultures. To "found the order of the world on the caprice of each individual" seemed a kind of madness. For Pascal the laws of human nature changed with each season and with each crossing of a river. To assume that justice could come from a society without charity, community, or tradition was nonsense. The empty, self-centered morality of the postmedieval world was as frightening as "the eternal silence of infinite space" posited by postmedieval science.

At the end of the eighteenth century, Adam Smith repeated the faith of Descartes. His vision of naturally "economic man" was also refuted by the anthropological knowledge of Columbus. His assumption that the laws of supply and demand and the "natural" human acquisitive instinct would provide a natural harmony of interests was already challenged by David Hume's insistence that the logic of cause-and-effect was much too limited for such generalizations.

Yet nineteenth-century British utilitarians and European positivists had to learn the same lessons again. The need for a society run like a market conspired with the success of machines and science to suggest new laws of human nature—which turned out to be just like the old laws of Descartes, Locke, and Adam Smith. The utilitarians (Jeremy Bentham, James Mill, and the young John Stuart Mill) attempted to find human nature in the supposed universal ability to rationally calculate pleasures and pains of every atomistic individual. They imagined that "the greatest good for the greatest number" of people could be the goal of social policy, just as the maximization of individual pleasure could be the measured goal of individual action. Positivists like Hippolyte Taine in France went so far as to argue that "virtue and vice are products like sugar and vitriol."

The nineteenth-century versions of human nature and natural law were even less tenable than earlier versions. Opposition was more intense. A lonely Pascal had been replaced by an entire romantic movement of artists, poets, and philosophers whose insistence on the power of passion, irrationality, emotion, and culture could not be ignored. The emerging professional studies of anthropology, sociology, and history brought forward too much evidence of cultural variety to permit universal laws of human nature. The path from the recognition of cultural differences to the recognition of fundamental change had been well cleared and was easier to follow for people raised on Christian time with a faith in progress. But there was still one last refuge from relativity. For at least one generation in the nineteenth century, the crisis of modern consciousness could be averted. Evolution preserved whatever certainty was left.

EVOLUTION: CERTAINTY'S LAST STAND

In *Evolution and Society* J. W. Burrow wrote:

> The evolutionary method in social thinking triumphed, not only or
> perhaps even primarily because it was in tune with that of the vogue
> sciences of the period, but because it offered a way of coping with new
> kinds of experience and new methods of interpreting them—methods
> which had been germinating throughout the earlier part of the cen-
> tury. . . . The proceedings of the [British Anthropological] Society, dur-
> ing its short life, reveal the impasse reached by mid-nineteenth-centu-
> ry positivism once it had abandoned, for various reasons, the belief that
> a science of man and society could be deduced from a few cardinal
> propositions about human nature. The way out of that impasse—in a
> sense, for the Victorians, the only way—was by some kind of evolu-
> tionary theory.[8]

Since it was no longer possible to believe in human nature, one could at least
find security in orderly, predictable, almost providential change. Evolutionary theory satisfied sociologists, anthropologists, and historians, as well as geologists and
biologists, in the nineteenth century because it kept the lid on suspicions of relativity. In fact, it was a solution which accorded well with the traditional Christian
belief that God revealed himself and his design in time. The century that accepted
evolution as the fundamental fact of life was the most Christian of centuries in its
thought and culture. Sociology was hailed as the new Christianity. Primitive societies could be studied sympathetically without implying criticisms of life in the
modern world: primitive and traditional peoples simply represented an earlier stage
of human evolution (or of God's revelation).

The furor over Darwin's theory of evolution was largely misdirected. Christian
fundamentalists (especially in the United States) found themselves stuck with a
particular Biblical literalism (the first parents, the relatively short list of later generations that collapsed the human time scale, and images of world catastrophes like
the Flood that seemed to make sudden geological changes and a special human creation tenable). They accepted the same predicament for themselves that the
Catholic church had accepted for itself in its conflict with Galileo: since the Bible
literally says that Joshua made the sun stand still, that "the foundations of the earth
are fixed so firm that they cannot be moved," and that the sun "runneth about from
one end of the heavens to the other," it is impossible that the earth revolves around
the sun.

By 1859 (the date of publication of Darwin's *Origin of Species*) there were sufficient intellectual tools to understand the Bible as an historical document which
reflected a thousand years of Judeo-Christian attempts to understand their God and
world (Vico had shown the way). It was even possible to understand the Bible as
"the divine revelation" necessary for the particular time and level of understanding

that had been achieved in the ancient Near East. God's gradual, historical revelation could still be more fundamental than the Bible. Indeed, if God were a living presence, the revelations of the Bible would have to be dated. But nineteenth-century Christians were often more committed to a literal interpretation of the single revelation of the Bible than they were to the more traditional Judeo-Christian idea of God's continuous revelation throughout history.

FROM CERTAINTY TO RELATIVITY

If the idea of "evolution" could have been hailed as the culmination of the Christian vision of time, the idea of "natural selection" posed more difficulties. Darwin's work had argued that evolution occurred through a process of natural selection. This meant that nature normally and randomly threw off mutations. Some of these mutations would survive, but only those that were "fittest" or most adaptable to the rest of nature. The problem was that God seemed to have nothing to do with the process. Everything happened spontaneously in nature, according to nature's own laws. One English critic of Darwin noticed this problem when he remarked: "Upon the grounds of what is termed evolution God is relieved of the labour of creation; in the name of unchangeable laws he is discharged from governing the world."[9] To this Herbert Spencer replied that the same objection could be leveled at Newton's law of gravitation, the science of astronomy, or, indeed, any scientific laws. The American scientist Asa Gray argued that natural selection was simply an explanation of God's method. God created a nature so that it would produce new species itself. But many wondered if such scientific laws of nature did not remove God too far from his accustomed place of immediate involvement in the world. And Herbert Spencer's reminder that this was the effect of all scientific knowledge was not answered.

Evolutionary theory by natural (or "supernatural") selection did not disprove the existence of God. But like the rest of science, it made (as one French philosopher had said in the eighteenth century) that "hypothesis" less necessary. It replaced the certainty of divine intervention with the certainty of human discovery. But in removing the supernatural further from human life, it made humans more dependent on their understanding of nature. And, in at least one way, the new evolutionary sciences of geology and biology offered less certainty. They were not predictive. The methods of nature could be reconstructed retrospectively, but it was impossible to gauge which one of the millions of new mutations would succeed. A nature evolving according to its own laws was a trip without a destination, or, with a continually changing destination. Even the religious had to study science to chart the course.

Much the same could be said about the triumph of the evolutionary method in the "human sciences." Human "selections" were as difficult to predict as natural selections. And increasingly, throughout the end of the nineteenth and the beginning of the twentieth century, Westerners realized that human selections were infinitely more complex, and less predictable, than the positivists and utilitarians had recognized. Philosophers like Arthur Schopenhauer, Friedrich Nietzsche, and Henri Bergson ridiculed the positivist belief that man was a rational, thinking machine. They insisted, instead, that human beings were essentially bundles of animal drives. Will, instinct, energy, and drive were the human motivators. Humankind was swayed more by power, myth, and lies than by reason and evidence. Sigmund Freud found evidence that human behavior was essentially irrational, rather than rational. Sexual urges, the accumulated drives of the subconscious, were what made people do what they do. Reason, in fact, was a tool for self-delusion and confusing others. Rationalizations (or rational, but false, explanations) of our behavior were the defenses of a subconscious able to hide. Since we prevent ourselves from understanding ourselves, how can we possibly understand others? No wonder that one of the frequent themes of drama in the twentieth century was that people do not communicate with one another.

Just as philosophers and Freud revived the insights of romantic poets and artists concerning the irrational in individuals, sociologists became increasingly aware of the irrational fabric of society. People did not create society with a "social contract" as the positivist thinkers had imagined. No one ever agreed to join society as one joined the A.S.P.C.A. Society was like religion, Emile Durkheim pointed out. One accepted its myths and powers because one was a member. One did not choose membership in human society. Society and culture gave one (as Socrates had known and Locke had forgotten) one's humanity and individuality. Similarly, Max Weber noted, people did not obey laws because they agreed to. Often people obeyed leaders because they were magical and charismatic, or they obeyed laws out of traditional thoughtlessness or bureaucratic apathy. Knowledge of the importance of irrational factors in society led some sociologists (from Vilfredo Pareto to modern public relations and advertising) to teach manipulation and mystification. Others (like Georges Sorel) exploited popular myths as a tool of social revolution.

To see that a behavior was socially determined had the same relativistic implications as the anthropologists' discoveries that much of human life was culturally determined. Knowledge itself was subjected to such analysis in the emerging discipline of "the sociology of knowledge" in the twentieth century. Based on Marx's discovery of the ideologies of social classes, Durkheim's investigation of "collective mentalities," and Weber's theoretical and historical studies, sociologists like Karl Mannheim showed that even knowledge was relative (or, as he preferred, related) to the social position of the knower. Different classes developed different kinds of knowledge. Though there might be ways of determining whether a particular piece of knowledge was true or false, the important thing to recognize is that it was knowledge for a particular class in a particular historical situation. Thus, the whole tradition of modern Western scientific investigation reflected the needs of an emerging, individualistic, market-oriented class in its concern for separated observer and observed, its tendency to atomize and particularize, and its emphasis on quantification. The knowledge of Chinese science and the structure of Chinese language, for instance, reflected the different needs of a bureaucratic class of intellectuals. There are an infinite number of types of knowledge. One's social and cultural position determined what one would know.

BEYOND CERTAINTY AND RELATIVITY:
UNDERSTANDING AND MAKING HUMAN HISTORY

Karl Mannheim in writing what could be called the "Manifesto of Historicism" declared that this intellectual force epitomizes the world-view of modern man: historicism is of extraordinary importance both in the social sciences and in everyday thinking. Today it is impossible to participate in politics, even to understand a person, without recourse to historicist principles. Modern man, be he social scientist or layman, must treat all realities confronting him as having evolved and as developing dynamically. For also in daily life people use concepts with historicist implications, such as cultural behavior, capitalism, social movement, and so forth. The modern mind copes with these phenomena as potentialities that are always in flux, moving from some point in time to another. Even in our everyday thinking we strive to locate our present situation within a dynamic field and to tell time by the "cosmic clock of history."[10]

We live in a world which is continually changing. Its change is our only certainty. We cannot understand ourselves or our present without understanding these changes, because that is all we are. But the more things change, the more difficult they are for us to understand. We are most able to understand sameness and continuity, but our survival depends on understanding change.

This was the problem that historicism began to confront at the end of the nineteenth and the beginning of the twentieth century. Philosophers (Wilhelm Dilthey, Friedrich Nietzsche, Benedetto Croce, R. G. Collingwood) pushed the problem of historical understanding to the brink of uncertainty. Each age—indeed each event and individual—is unique. To understand it fully we have to transcend our own uniqueness and participate in its particularity. But our reliving of it is necessarily our own. We never fully lose the self. Every explanation and interpretation is, despite our efforts, our own. Understanding the past as an objective reality is absurd. Each person sees it from his or her vantage point or self. The same is true of understanding the present, but the past (beginning a moment ago) is even more lost for us. Thus, there is no such thing as the past, but only as many understandings as there are people in the present. History is thinking about the past. Though we can determine if a particular fact is true after careful consideration of what that means, there are an infinite number of facts which can be viewed from an infinite number of perspectives. We choose those that interest us because they interest us. Each age rewrites the past in the interests of the present. Every individual does so, and changes it. Myth, memory, nostalgia, and history are only alternative ways of grounding ourselves in time. "Objective" history has no meaning aside from following the rules of verification of the present. That helps us discount errors, but gives no advice in choosing the facts. History is only our imaginative reconstruction of the past in terms of the present.

The recognition that everything changes was possible only in a society that changed everything—the disposable society. But once recognized, it was valid for every society. Many twentieth-century thinkers found the conclusion of historicism so uncomfortable that they sought refuge from change in religion, mythology, or the immediate. Some concluded that since history was not final, it was not worth knowing, or that since everything changed, there was no point in knowing how.

Others found (as Michelet did in reading Vico) an enormous freedom in the discovery that humans make, and continually remake, themselves. For them, the universality of change meant not throwing up one's hands in disgust and confusion, but the opportunity for fresh understanding and planning new directions. This book is written for them.

FOR FURTHER READING

Two books with the same title aptly introduce the goals of this chapter. The title is *The Shock of the New*: one by Ian Dunlop used here, and a more popular one by Robert J. Hughes that deals with a slightly later period and was the basis of an excellent television series. In addition there are numerous useful histories of modern art, among them Norbert Lynton's *The Story of Modern Art*, H. Horvard Arnason and Marla F. Prather's *History of Modern Art*, John Canaday's *Mainstreams of Modern Art*, and Herbert Read's *A Concise History of Modern Painting*. In addition, Diane Kelder's *The Great Book of French Impressionism* is a useful introduction to that subject.

This chapter, however, is concerned more with the social history of art and with art as a social or historical indicator. The classic introduction is Arnold Hauser's *The Social History of Art* (especially vol. 4, *Naturalism, Impressionism, the Film Age*). For recent studies in the social history of art, see Richard R. Brettell's *Modern Art, 1851–1929: Capitalism and Representation* and Jane Mayo Roos's *Early Impressionism and the French State: 1866–1874*.

For studies of modern culture more generally, see H. Stuart Hughes's *Consciousness and Society: The Reorientation of European Social Thought 1890–1930*, Stephen Kern's *The Culture of Time and Space*, Raymond Williams's *The Politics of Modernism*, Peter Burger's *Theory of the Avant-garde*, and Monique Chefdor et al., *Modernism: Challenges and Perspectives*. In addition, Roger Shattuck's *The Banquet Years: The Origins of the Avant-Garde in France, 1885 to World War I* is an engaging study of four artists of the period. Renato Poggioli's *The Theory of the Avant-Garde* is a challenging analysis. Equally challenging are John Berger's *Ways of Seeing* and Raymond Williams's *Culture and Society, 1750–1950*.

NOTES

1. These and other quotations in this section are from Ian Dunlop's *The Shock of the New* (New York: McGraw-Hill, 1972).
2. John Canady, *Mainstreams of Modern Art* (New York: Simon & Schuster, 1959), pp. 469–470.
3. Van Wyck Brooks, *John Sloan*, quoted in Ian Dunlop, *op. cit.*, p. 197.
4. Walter Pach, *Queer Thing, Painting*, quoted in *ibid.*
5. Quoted in *ibid.*, pp. 184–185.
6. Quoted in Howard Mumford Jones, *O Strange New World* (New York: Viking Press, 1964), pp. 15–16.
7. Letter of 6 October 1646 to Princess Elizabeth of Bohemia, quoted in Lucien Goldmann, *The Hidden God* (London: Routledge & Kegan Paul, 1964), p. 28.
8. J. W. Burrow, *Evolution and Society* (Cambridge University Press, 1966), p. 136.
9. William Ewart Gladstone, quoted in A. D. White, *A History of the Welfare of Science with Theology in Christendom* (New York: Dover, 1960), vol. 1, p. 76.
10. Gunter W. Remmling, *Road to Suspicion: A Study of Modern Mentality and the Sociology of Knowledge* (Englewood Cliffs, N.J.: Prentice-Hall, 1967), p. 95.

Chronological Table of
the Industrial World
1800–1914

Europe	Americas	Africa and Islamic World	Asia
		Usman Dan Fodio 1754–1817	
Industrial revolution a. 1780			Indian nationalist Rammohan Roy 1772–1833
Napoleon r. 1800–1815			
Utopian socialism 1800–1848	Britain ends slave trade 1807	Ottoman Sultan Mahmud II r. 1808–1839	
	U.S. ends slave trade 1809		
	Independence of most of Latin America 1810–1828		
First railroad 1825	Monroe Doctrine 1823	French settle in Algeria 1830s	
		South African Boers "Great Trek" 1836–1838	
Chartist movement 1838–1848		Muhammad Ali of Egypt r. 1805–1849	Opium War 1839–1842
Revolutions of 1848		Decline of African slave trade 1840–1863	
Communist Manifesto 1848			
Unification of Italy 1848–1870			

a. = after   *r. = ruled*

Europe	Americas	Africa and Islamic World	Asia
Napoleon III r. 1852–1870	Brazil ends slave trade 1851		Taiping Rebellion 1851–1864
			Opening of Japan 1854
			Sepoy Rebellion in India 1857
			British government rules India 1858
Mill's *On Liberty* 1859			
Darwin's *Origin of Species* 1859			
Russian emancipation of serfs 1861	U.S. Civil War 1861–1865	Egyptian cotton boom 1861–1865	
Salon des Refusés 1863	U.S. Emancipation Proclamation 1863		
	U.S. era of Reconstruction 1865–1877	Opening of Suez Canal 1869	Meiji Restoration in Japan 1868
Paris Commune insurrection 1870			
Impressionism 1870–1890			
Internal-combustion engine 1876	Telephone 1876	Egyptian bankruptcy and European control 1876	
	Development of legal segregation in U.S. 1877–1954	Al Afgani 1839–1897	
	Brazilian emancipation of slaves 1888	Partition of Africa begins 1884	Organization of Indian National Congress 1885
Post-Impressionism a. 1890	U.S. finance capitalism a. 1890		

a. = after   r. = ruled

Europe	Americas	Africa and Islamic World	Asia
Expressionism a. 1893			
Discovery of X ray 1895	*Plessey v. Ferguson* 1896		Japan defeats China 1894–1895
Wireless telegraph 1899		South African Boer War 1899–1902	
Freud's *Interpretation of Dreams* 1900	U.S. Progressive movement 1901–1916		Boxer Rebellion in China 1900
Cubism a. 1903			
Russian Revolution of 1905		Segregation in South Africa begins 1905–1907	
Einstein theories 1905–1910		Establishment of the Union of South Africa 1910	Japan defeats Russia 1904–1905
	Mexican Revolution 1911		Chinese Revolution 1911
	N.Y. Armory Exhibition 1913		Sun Yat-sen becomes first President of Republic 1912

a. = after   r. = ruled

Alexander Archipenko, Woman Combing Her Hair. [1915] Bronze, 13-3/4" high. Collection, The Museum of Modern Art, New York. Acquired through the Lillie P. Bliss Bequest.

A Divided World

1914–1945

Poster by Walter Crane, 1889, created for May 1, International Labor Day—an ideal destroyed by World War I.

Preview of the Period
1914–1945

Between 1914 and 1945 the world was split twice by wars that were fought worldwide. The fissures that split Europe and then the world were only the most obvious ones. The world was also divided between rich and poor, colonizers and colonized, capitalists and socialists, and between industrialized and agricultural societies.

The First World War and the Russian Revolution (1914–1921). The First World War was more than a European civil war. Battles were fought in Africa and Asia, and the commitment of colonial troops involved an implicit promise, and training, for their own independence. The Russian Revolution also was a global event. Its impact on China and emerging nations in Asia and Africa was as great as its impact on the Western world. In many ways the Russian Revolution cost Europe its colonies, though it took another world war before the colonies achieved independence and European world dominance came to an end.

Nationalism and colonial rivalry were among the more important causes of the First World War. It began in the boiling cauldron of nationalistic aspirations in the multiethnic Balkans and Austro-Hungarian Empire. At a time when the empire was attempting to keep the lid on the nationalistic feelings of its many subject populations, a Bosnian Serb shot and killed the heir to the throne, Archduke Ferdinand. The result was more than a war between Serbia and the Austro-Hungarian Empire because of the intricately balanced European alliance system. Germany had agreed to back the empire. Russia backed Serbia. France had an alliance with Russia, and England with France. The war became a *world* war because European powers were now world powers with colonies throughout Asia and Africa, and because, besides the colonies, other non-European powers became involved, including the United States and the Ottoman Empire (as an ally of the Austro-Hungarian Empire and Germany).

While there were battles between French and German colonies in Africa in which Africans were expected to die for the Kaiser or for La France, and an attempted invasion of the Ottoman Empire in which many Australians died during an attack on Gallipoli, most of the fighting took place in Russia and France. The war began in 1914 with a quick German advance through Belgium to the Marne River in France. Because the French were able to hold at the Marne and prevent the Germans from marching the remaining twenty miles to Paris, both sides dug in, and a war that might have ended in a few months (like the Franco-Prussian War of 1870) dragged on for four years. The death toll in suicidal attacks on each side's fortified trenches was in the millions. New weapons, such as gas and machine guns, were as deadly as the rats and disease in the muddy trenches. The deaths of gallant aristocrats dueling in flimsy biplanes offered the only contrast to mass slaughter.

The turning point in the war came in 1917 with the entry of the United States on the side of Britain and France, largely in response to a renewal of German submarine (U-boat) attacks on British-American shipping. Despite the withdrawal of Russia from the Triple Entente (with Britain and France) and the new Soviet Union's suit for peace in the Treaty of Brest-Litovsk (March 1918), the war came to an end on 11 November 1918.

Before the war ended, President Woodrow Wilson of the United States had offered "14 Points" for peace. ("The Good Lord only had ten," the feisty French Prime Minister Clemenceau jibed.) Wilson wanted to let bygones be bygones and end all war with a so-called League of Nations (even though the U.S. Congress did not support his position). Clemenceau and France (whose casualties numbered thirty-six times the American total) wanted an admission of guilt from Germany, a huge payment of reparations, and the dismemberment of much of Germany and the Austro-Hungarian Empire. Wilson and Clemenceau compromised, with British Prime Minister Lloyd George's acquiescence, by writing both French and American positions into the Treaty of Versailles (1919), despite the inconsistency.

Lenin and Trotsky (saluting) in Red Square in Moscow in 1919.

German resentment at the admission of guilt, the occupation of its industrial heartland in the west, and an impossible payments schedule contributed to the rise of Hitler and the Second World War.

World War I vastly changed all Western societies. Governments became much more involved in people's lives, and as the bureaucracies expanded they also became more centralized. First as a wartime emergency, and then out of force of habit, political expediency, or public desire, government activity embraced entirely new areas of economic planning and public welfare. Sometimes the need for new sources of workers during the war had profound effects. In the United States, southern blacks came to northern industrial cities to take up jobs in armament and war-related industries, beginning a mass migration that continued into the 1920s and made the entire United States a biracial society. Similarly, the employment of women during the war did much to bring women the vote in England in 1919 and in Germany and the United States a year later.

No country, however, was changed more by World War

I than Russia. The war was probably the most important immediate cause of the Russian Revolution of 1917, both the March stage and the final November Revolution. While the war was popular in the beginning, as it was throughout Europe, its toll was enormous. In the midst of military defeats and bread riots in Petrograd (Saint Petersburg), Czar Nicholas II (1868–1918) abdicated, turning power over to a provisional government. Headed by Alexander Kerensky (1881–1970) during most of the summer, the provisional government proved unable to deal with the most serious problems facing the people. A moderate socialist, Kerensky was unable to initiate land reform or end the war. Vladimir Ilyich Lenin (1870–1924), the leader of the majority Bolshevik wing of the Social Democratic party, arrived from exile and seized the opportunity to carry out a second revolution, seizing power from the provisional government and turning it over to the *soviets* (workers' councils). The result was the establishment of the Union of Soviet Socialist Republics, which emerged at the end of a civil war that lasted until 1921.

Depression, Totalitarianism, and World War II (1922– 1945). The Western economic collapse, culminating in the Great Depression of the 1930s, also had its origins in the First World War. Not only did the war kill 1.4 million French, 1.8 million German, and 1.7 million Russian soldiers (and many more civilians), it also wiped out much of the industry, mines, and ports that made Europe prosperous. Even more significant, perhaps, was the enormous German war debt that France insisted on collecting for its own industrial revival and the loans owed by the Entente allies to the United States (that the United States refused to forgive).

The economic collapse thus began before the U.S. stock market crash of 1929. To pay the war debts and satisfy domestic demand, Germany printed enough money to cause an incredible inflation in the early 1920s. In 1923 a loaf of bread cost wheelbarrows of money. U.S. financiers provided Europe with loans for a modest recovery in the late 1920s until the crash of 1929. As banks failed, industries closed, farm prices tumbled, and unemployment rose, Europeans and Americans sought simple solutions and government action. While the theory of Keynes that government spending should be employed to stimulate the economy in a depression was not published until 1936, many people and governments instinctively knew that a depression was no time to worry about balanced budgets.

The appeal to government action in the emergency took many forms. In the United States it resulted in the election of Franklin D. Roosevelt in 1932 and the creation of the New Deal. In the Soviet Union, the new Bolshevik government had already taken over direction of the economy and avoided a depression entirely. In Italy, Germany, and Japan, and in many of the new struggling states of eastern Europe, anti-democratic parties emerged that demanded a military buildup and conquest of foreigners and communists (usually expressing their demands in extremely nationalistic and religious terms). These were the fascists.

The word "fascism" was coined in Italy (as was "totalitarianism" for total control). The movement originated in Italy in the social turmoil of the postwar years (1919–1921). A 1922 march on Rome by the supporters of Benito Mussolini (1883–1945) led to his appointment as prime minister by the king. With emergency powers, he assured a fascist election victory and by 1926 had turned Italy into a single-party, dictatorial state.

It was Mussolini's model that appealed to Adolf Hitler (1889–1945). His Nazi party added a strain of anti-Semitism that was stronger in Germany than in Italy. Both parties had wide popular support, especially among members of the middle class who felt squeezed between the big corporations and the socialist labor unions. Hitler came to power, as Mussolini had, by stretching an electoral mandate beyond recognition. Like Mussolini, he initially commanded a plurality rather than a majority. The Nazi vote varied between 30 and 38 percent of the electorate in the party's early parliamentary victories of 1932. On 30 January 1933, Hitler became the chancellor of Germany. In February he used a fire in the parliament building as an excuse for an emergency decree that effectively ended the constitution of the Weimar Republic. The police state, with its elite SS units commanded by Heinrich Himmler (1900–1945), took over. Unions, opposition political parties, and newspapers were silenced, their leaders jailed. Measures against Jews intensified with the Nuremberg Laws in 1935, which deprived German Jews of citizenship and civil rights and

made intermarriage or sexual relations between Christians
and Jews illegal. Mob vandalism of Jewish shops and syna-
gogues was encouraged. With the war came concentration
camps, initially production factories to which Jews (and
some other groups: gypsies, socialists, and communists)
were sent as slave laborers. In 1942, these camps and additional ones were directed to the extermination of the entire
Jewish population of Europe. By the end of the war six million had perished.

Japanese fascism was modeled on Germany's but there
were important differences. Japanese society was more
homogeneous than German. There was no equivalent of
German anti-Semitism. Fascism in Japan was more the
product of a military seizure of power than a popular election. The Japanese parliament (Diet) was never won by the
fascists, but that did not matter. The military was subject
only to the emperor. According to the constitution, once
the military was engaged in war, it was relatively immune
to legislative objections.

The economic situation in Japan was also not as serious
as that in Germany. The Japanese economy boomed from
1905 to 1918. As in Germany, World War I was followed
by an economic slump and inflation; the Japanese situation
was exacerbated by an earthquake that destroyed Tokyo in
1923. After a slight revival, the depression came earlier and
more severely than that in the United States (a bank crisis
in 1927 was followed by a crop failure in 1931 that led to
famine). The difference was that the Japanese government
was able to stimulate the economy to end the depression by
1936. Economic recovery came too late, however. In the
depths of the depression, a series of military coup attempts
led to the appointment of military men rather than politicians as prime ministers. A military takeover of a puppet
regime in Manchuria in 1931, followed by full-scale war in
China after 1938, gave the military ministries full rein to
create a totalitarian state. Whereas in Italy and Germany
fascism led to war, in Japan war led to fascism. The nationalization of industry and the propagandizing of the population that enabled the military to form squads of suicide
(*kamikaze*) pilots came during the war, not before.

Though the Second World War is normally dated from
1939, it really began with the Japanese invasion of China
in 1931 and the ineffective condemnation by the League of

American troops, crossing the Elbe River in April 1945, meeting Russian soldiers who had come from the East. (The New York Public Library)

Nations. The impunity with which the Axis powers (Japan, Germany, and Italy) were able to conquer was underscored by the Italian invasion of Ethiopia in 1935, the German assistance to the Spanish fascists in the Spanish Civil War in 1936, and the German annexation of Austria in 1938 and Czechoslovakia in 1939. The League and Western governments objected, but did nothing. Even when Germany invaded Poland in 1939 (having secured a nonaggression pact with the Soviets), Britain and France declared war but did nothing.

It was the German lightning attack (*blitzkrieg*) of Western Europe that finally provoked a response, and that was almost too late. While French generals schooled in World War I dug trenches, the German general staff planned and carried out the first modern mechanized attack, using the internal-combustion engine. German tanks and planes raced across Belgium, Holland, and France in the spring of 1940 as if there were no speed limits. The aerial bombing of Dutch cities, the first of civilian populations, was a prelude to the Battle of Britain in the summer of 1940. British determination, the leadership of Churchill, the newly invented radar system, and the Royal Air Force gave Hitler his first setback: two German planes were shot down for every one the British lost. Hitler turned instead to plan secretly for an invasion of the Soviet Union the following summer, 1941. Expecting a quick victory, Hitler sent four million German troops into Russia on 22 June 1941, without warm clothing or antifreeze.

The Soviets were unprepared for the rapid German blitzkrieg. Instead of meeting it head on, they retreated, sacrificing scorched earth for time. Time and "General Winter" came to the Russian rescue in December, with German troops twenty miles outside of Moscow. December of 1941 was to prove a turning point in the war.

On the morning of 7 December 1941, Hawaiian time (December 8 on the other side of the international date line in Japan and China), Japanese planes attacked the U.S. Pacific fleet at Pearl Harbor, the British colonies of Hong Kong, Malaya, and Singapore, and the foreign concessions in Shanghai. The U.S. fleet was severely crippled. The United States, Britain, and China suddenly became allies, and (with the German declaration of war against the United States) were joined by unoccupied France and the Soviet Union as well. The Japanese army's advance in China and Malaya was extraordinarily rapid. Hong Kong fell by Christmas, "Fortress Singapore" by the end of January 1942. By May the Philippines had surrendered and Australia was under attack.

Another turning point occurred in 1942. The U.S. navy began a series of victories in the Pacific with the Battle of the Coral Sea off Australia in May 1942, and in November the Soviet Union started house-to-house fighting in the Battle of Stalingrad, inflicting a loss of a half-million Germans and beginning a counteroffensive that ended in Berlin. Allied victories continued in 1943 in North Africa, in the sea lanes of the North Atlantic, in Italy with the defeat of Mussolini, and in Burma against the Japanese. The Allied landing on Normandy, France, on D-Day—6 June 1944—made the liberation of Europe certain. Then it was a question only of whether Russian or American, British, and Canadian troops would get to Berlin first. It was roughly a draw in April 1945, and one that largely determined postwar spheres of influence. "Everyone impos-es his own system as far as his army can reach," Stalin said. The only major change was the U.S. withdrawal west of Berlin and the Soviet withdrawal from Austria. The agree-ment between Stalin, Churchill, and Roosevelt at Yalta in February 1945, which divided Eastern Europe into spheres of influence, was largely adhered to.

By early 1945, victory over Japan was also becoming inevitable. A single air raid on March 10 burned down half of Tokyo. Whether out of concern for the costs of an inva-sion or in an attempt to beat the Russians to the punch, Harry S. Truman (who had become president after Roosevelt's death) ordered the first use of an atomic bomb on the city of Hiroshima on 6 August 1945, and another on Nagasaki three days later. On August 15 the war was over.

❧ 10 ❧

Nationalism and Communism

Revolution and Independence

Nationalism and communism were two of the most powerful forces of the twentieth century. Many of the revolutions of the twentieth century were called nationalist or communist. Some revolutions changed from nationalist to communist or had elements of both from the beginning.

In general, nationalist revolutions were those in which an entire nation asserted itself. Usually the goal was to gain independence from a colonial power or powers. Sometimes nationalism was a response to actual political colonialism, sometimes to more subtle economic, social, or cultural influence. One could, for instance, speak of Canadian nationalism directed against the dominance of the United States over Canadian media without implying that Canada was an actual colony of the United States.

Communist revolutions often shared the nationalist goals of political independence, especially in colonies. But communist revolutions were also social revolutions, directed against some members of the nation as well as foreign colonial powers. Communist revolutions were directed against those members of the nation who were perceived to be part of the "ruling class" or in league with the colonial power.

Communist revolutions, thus, had a more definite domestic agenda than nationalist revolutions. They often became civil wars. They marked a more radical break

279

with the past economic and social system. They resulted in greater domestic turmoil, political violence, and authoritarian measures.

United States policy favored some nationalist revolutions and opposed all communist revolutions. With the end of communism today, it is unlikely that the United States will have to oppose communist revolutions any longer. But there will continue to be nationalist revolutions or movements, and there will likely be revolutions driven by other goals as well. Some of these other goals may be similar to the anti-American, anti-colonial, or egalitarian pronouncements of the communists. Some may be based on religious or cultural values, with or without nationalist elements. In any case, it will be useful for Americans to be able to distinguish between different movements that threaten to destabilize the world. And it is useful for citizens to understand how their government is accustomed to respond to revolutionary movements.

Would it be preferable to oppose (or support) all revolutions? How should we distinguish between beneficial and harmful changes throughout the world? Which of these revolutions are likely to become more frequent? Which should the United States support? Which should we oppose? These are key questions for all citizens of the twenty-first century.

THE CHINESE NATIONALIST REVOLUTION OF 1911

The Chinese nationalist revolution of 10 October 1911 ended not only the Qing (or Ching) empire but thousands of years of monarchy. It replaced the emperor with a republican (representative) government. The revolution occurred because the empire was already bankrupt. In that sense, the revolution did not require a leader. But with Sun Yat-sen (1866–1925) the Chinese revolution had a leader who tells us much about nationalist revolution. Like many nationalist leaders and many young Chinese at the turn of the century, Sun spent a good deal of his time outside of China. Educated in Honolulu and then Hong Kong, Sun was a professional revolutionary who raised funds among Chinese businessmen and cultivated contacts in secret societies from Singapore to San Francisco. He combined an enthusiasm for the popular nationalism of the Taipings with a deep fondness for Western science, secularism, and democracy. His "three people's principles" were "nationalism, democracy, and socialism." By nationalism he meant ridding China of the Manchu dynasty. By democracy he meant establishing a republican constitution with executive, legislative, and judicial branches and equal rights for all citizens. By socialism he meant the doctrine of the American socialist Henry George, which essentially called for a 100 percent tax on land sales in order to prevent real estate speculation. It was a program which reflected Sun's travels and experience in the West more than the immediate problems confronting China. One modern historian writes:

This astonishing program ignored all the basic problems facing the country: the agrarian question, peasant unrest, the threat from abroad, and the resistance put up by the traditional structures to all necessary change.[1]

Indeed, these problems that Sun did not address, especially the agrarian question of land distribution and the power of the landlords, eventually wrecked the republic. But in 1911 Sun was hailed for his optimism and prestige rather than his program. He was in Denver, Colorado, when he read the news of the October 10 Revolution and left immediately for China. He arrived to be sworn in as first President of the Republic of China on January 1, 1912.

The Republic did not last. In a few months Sun was forced to accept Yuan Shih-k'ai, candidate of the army and warlords, as president. Yuan opted for the old order rather than national or social revolution. When Yuan died in 1916, the warlords carved up China among them, and a series of student protests (called the May 4th movement after the first one on May 4, 1919) began a second revolution that called for new ideas, youthful leadership, national independence, individualism, and eventually communism.

Dr. Sun Yat-sen (1866–1925). Photo taken on March 28, 1910 in San Francisco by the INS, one year before his movement overthrew the Manchu dynasty and his presidency of the Republic of China. (New York Public Library)

THE COMMUNIST REVOLUTION IN RUSSIA

If Sun was an odd sort of "nationalist" to lead the Chinese nationalist revolution, V.I. Lenin was an equally odd Marxist to lead the Russian Revolution. Most Russian and European Marxists in the years before 1917 agreed that Russia was ripe for revolution. But even when it occurred, in March 1917 (February according to the old Russian calendar), they saw it as a "bourgeois" or middle-class revolution. In Marxist theory such a revolution was equivalent to the English revolution of the seventeenth century, the French revolution of 1789, and the continental revolutions of 1848. This was because Russian economic development in 1917 was only approaching earlier Western levels. Industrialization had barely gotten underway in the 1890s. Capitalism was at an infant stage of development. The middle class was still very small and the urban working class was a minor force. Thus, Marxists looked to the Russian revolution, like the early bourgeois revolutions of Europe, to abolish feudalism (already begun in 1861), depose the king (czar), establish parliamentary governments, and institute individual rights, free labor, and a wage system. In terms of the Marxist vision of historical stages, that was all one could expect or hope for.

Lenin was not satisfied with this view, however, and looked for reasons why the bourgeois revolution might be telescoped and the next stage of history, the socialist revolution, ushered in. First he suggested that the Russian experience might call for a special "dictatorship" of workers and peasants which would help the bourgeois revolution. After helping the bourgeoisie, this dictatorship would relinquish power to the capitalist class. But then Lenin began to ask what would happen if there were actual socialist revolutions in Europe at the time that this special "dictatorship of the proletariat and peasants" occurred. Perhaps it would not have to relinquish power after all. Perhaps it could move directly to the socialist revolution. Most European socialists saw Lenin's position as little more than wishful thinking. Some, like Rosa Luxemburg in Germany and Leon Trotsky (before 1917) in Russia, argued that Lenin's plan would more likely end in a permanent dictatorship. In fairness to Lenin, however, no socialists imagined that the socialist revolution could occur in only one nation; in fact, most believed that the advent of socialism would have to be international. Most European socialists also believed that England and Germany, Belgium and perhaps France were approaching the stage of full capitalist development that would make a socialist revolution possible. So the expectation of a general socialist revolution was dawning. While no one expected it to begin in Russia, Lenin—as a Russian—had to consider the implications of a Russian revolution. When it came, Lenin was as surprised as anyone.

The immediate background to the Russian revolution was the strain of World War I. It brought military defeat and social dislocation on an unprecedented scale. By 1915 a successful Russian advance into German Prussia had been reversed, and a German-Austrian offensive had overrun the most populous and most industrialized provinces of the Russian Empire. By February 1917 eight million soldiers were killed, wounded, or missing. Disaffected soldiers, striking workers, and women demanded bread to feed their families and an end to the war.

Czar Nicholas II (r. 1894–1917) was no more incompetent than many absolute rulers of empires. But the war created problems that magnified normal incompetence. The probability of ruin was converted to a certainty by the utter reliance of Nicholas on his wife, the Czarina, and by her devotion to the dissolute monk Gregory Rasputin. When the Czarina, at Rasputin's suggestion, urged the dismissal of the army commander, Nicholas complied and took over direct military command himself. Absent from the capital, power passed to the Czarina, and thus to Rasputin. The nobles, the liberal aristocracy, the members of the Duma, even the European ambassadors, realized that the Czar would have to abdicate if Russia was to continue the war.

The Czar abdicated in March of 1917. The immediate beneficiary was the provisional government, made up of the liberal aristocracy and initially headed by Prince Georgi Lvov. But the provisional government was unable to gain any popular support, even when headed by the socialist Alexander Kerensky (1881–1970). It never sank roots into the country because it refused to consider either of the two things the people wanted most—peace and land.

Into this vacuum stepped Vladimir Ilyich Ulyanov, who had taken the underground name Lenin. In April Lenin arrived in St. Petersburg. During his European exile, he had kept up an untiring correspondence with Russian revolutionaries. He was the acknowledged head of the Bolshevik party. Immediately, he recognized the frailty of the provisional government and organized for a second revolution.

During the summer of 1917 there were two possible sources of authority, the provisional government and the Soviets. The Soviets were councils (of workers in factories and soldiers in the army). Since an earlier "Bloody Sunday" uprising in 1905, these councils had been a radical alternative to the more middle-class Duma (parliament). "All Power to the Soviets" and "Land, Peace and Bread" were Lenin's slogans. As millions of soldiers "voted with their feet" to end the war, the provisional government found itself in the same defenseless position as the Czar a few months before. Hardly a shot was fired as the Bolsheviks took over the government buildings in November 1917. Actually, the Bolsheviks were able to take power by default. Instead of "seizing it," one historian has written, "the Bolsheviks were rather 'lifted' to power by a wave of popular indignation and resentment in the autumn of 1917." They filled a vacuum, the historian continued:

> A kind of gold-rush atmosphere prevailed. The peasants were seizing the lands of the large landowners, the soldiers were deserting their units or refusing to take orders from their commanders, the workers were assuming control over production in the factories, national minorities were setting up autonomous nations—everywhere a gigantic scramble was underway that central authority, weakened as it was, could not realistically aspire to control.[2]

The Bolsheviks kept power by ending the war and then eliminating internal opposition. Despite the opposition of Western allies and some Bolsheviks, Lenin accepted whatever peace the Germans demanded. The Treaty of Brest-Litovsk gave up a major part of European Russia but it ended the war. It did not, however, bring internal peace to the Bolsheviks. An assassination attempt that wounded Lenin and killed several aides provided the reason, or excuse, for the deployment of the Cheka secret police in a "red terror" against opponents of the regime.

The revolution was not consolidated until 1921. There was opposition on many fronts. There were nobles and monarchists who wanted the Czar returned. There were members and supporters of the provisional government who were dismissed when Lenin dissolved the Assembly in favor of the Soviets. There were 100,000 troops of Russia's former allies (including 7,000 Americans) hoping to reverse the revolution and get Russia back into the war. They were joined by Czarist officers who mobilized a "White" army against the new Soviet Red Army. Under the brilliant direction of Trotsky (1879–1940), the Red Army was victorious by 1921. The urgency of civil war and famine made all challenges to the Bolsheviks seems like threats to the revolution. When in 1921 the stronghold of loyal sailors at Kronstadt demanded greater autonomy, they too were brutally suppressed by Trotsky. Authority and order would no longer be challenged.

THE APPEAL OF THE RUSSIAN REVOLUTION

It is difficult for modern Americans to understand the widespread appeal the Russian Revolution had for the less fortunate peoples of the world after 1917. Americans frequently interpret Lenin's prediction of "worldwide socialist revolution" as a declaration of subversive intent and see the spread of communism as the result of deceit and conquest. (It is interesting that U.S. President Woodrow Wilson's goal at the same time to dominate the world with American products and principles is rarely seen as coercive or subversive.)

In fact, there were matters of principle and practice in the years following the Russian Revolution that attracted many of the peoples of Asia, Africa, and Latin America. Some of these, like the commitment to take the land from the landlords and give it to the peasants, were evident as early as the Civil War of 1918 to 1921 and contributed decisively to the victory of the Red Army. Others, like the Soviet declarations against Western imperialism and in favor of national autonomy, appealed to Asians and Africans at a time when the League of Nations was establishing a new colonial "mandate" system over former German colonies.

What appealed most to the political leaders of the colonies and former colonies of the West, however, was the economic development and social progress that the Soviet Union demonstrated in the decades after the revolution. Between 1921 and 1939 the Soviet share of world output increased from 1.5 percent to 10 percent. In the same period literacy increased from about 50 percent to about 90 percent of the Soviet population. Change was especially striking in Soviet Central Asia. Those who lived on the borders of the Soviet Union in Turkey, Iran, and India could draw their own conclusions. The Soviets did not have to foment revolution in the developing countries. In most cases they simply offered an example.

INTERNATIONAL REVOLUTION
VERSUS "SOCIALISM IN ONE COUNTRY"

In fact, Soviet policy shifted very soon after Lenin's death in 1924 from a policy of encouraging world revolutions to a policy often opposing them. The shift was a result of the rise of Stalin and the victory of his policy of "socialism in one country." Lenin and Trotsky believed that socialism could not survive if limited to the Soviet Union. That is why they insisted on the need for a world revolution. Lenin established the Communist International in 1919 to provide a "world party of revolution." While the prospects of revolution in Europe seemed bright in 1919, they dimmed by 1924 when Lenin died.

Just before his death, Lenin complained about the increasing importance of bureaucrats in the communist party. Their rise was due partly to the heavy loss of Bolsheviks (who were never many) in the Civil War. ("Communists in front" had been the slogan in hard battles, and the White Army generals always made a point of killing the Bolsheviks.) Thus, many of the most dedicated and capable leaders had been replaced by opportunists, former Czarist officers, and conservative bureaucrats. Stalin was in the last category. Stalin was temperamentally suited to increasing the hold of this "bourgeois and Tsarist hotch-potch" (as Lenin called the bureaucrats) on the party and on Soviet society. His conservative, self-protective instincts also inclined him to fear revolution as potentially unsettling. Given the decline of revolutionary sentiment in Europe, Stalin argued that the new Soviet task was to protect "socialism in one country." This became official Soviet policy by 1928. Under Stalin's heavy hand it frequently became an excuse for the revival of simple Russian nationalism and the betrayal of communist revolutionaries in the rest of the world. At times there was little difference between the anti-revolutionary policies of Stalin and those of many Western capitalist leaders.

COMMUNISM COMES TO CHINA

The Chinese nationalist revolution of 1911 did not bring China national independence. Nor did the Versailles Peace Conference, which rejected Chinese claims to Shantung Province, taken by Germany during World War I. When it became known during the Conference that the warlord in control of Shantung had agreed to sell the province to the Japanese, the students of Beijing became enraged. Wall posters expressed their furor: "Don't Forget our National Humiliation"; "Throw Out the Warlord Traitors"; "Boycott Foreign Goods." On May 4, 1919, a demonstration of thousands of students energized the entire nation. Students in other cities closed the universities. Foreign boycotts were organized by merchants. Workers and clerks went on strike, demanding that the government not sign the Versailles treaty. It did not. But the May 4th Movement accomplished much more. It sparked an intellectual revolution in which new magazines sprang up like flowers and old ideas were pulled up like weeds. In his *New Youth* magazine Chen Duxiu [Ch'en Tu-hsiu], a professor at Beijing National University, challenged the young "to fight Confucianism, the old tradition of virtue and rituals, the old ethics and the old politics . . . the old learning and the old literature." In a society which revered the old instinctively, these ideas, one student remembered, "came to us like a clap of thunder which awakened us in the midst of a restless dream."[3]

Chinese historians see the May 4 Movement of 1919 as a more important turning point in Chinese history than the Revolution of 1911. It ushered in a cultural revolution and it radicalized Chinese political thought. By 1921, Chen, assisted by an obscure young magazine editor named Mao Zedong [Mao Tse-Tung], and ten other men founded the Chinese Communist Party in Shanghai. Chinese thinkers moved increasingly to the left. By the time of World War II the most frequently translated foreign authors were Marx, Engels, and Lenin. The liberal Hu Shi [Hu Shih] complained that the "slaves" of Confucius and Zhu Xi [Chu Hsi], the twelfth century neo-Confucian, had been replaced by the slaves of Marx.

Mao Zedong was not a slave of Marx. The son of a well-to-do peasant in the countryside of Hunan Province, Mao did not have the advantages of those in his generation who attended the better schools. He was just as well off. Without the doctrinaire education of the Confucian or Western educated elite, Mao could combine theory and practice. "Marxism-Leninism has no beauty," he told his fellow communists much later. "It is simply very useful." He challenged "those who regard Marxism as a religious dogma":

> Your dogma is less useful than excrement. We see that dog excrement can fertilize the fields and man's can feed the dog. And dogmas? They can't fertilize the fields, nor can they feed a dog. Of what use are they?[4]

The founding of the Chinese Communist Party was part of a developing alliance between Sun Yat-sen's embattled Nationalist Party and the Soviet Union. Sun first sought the help of the United States, England, and France in his attempt to hold competing Chinese warlords in check and govern China. When they refused, he accepted assistance from the Soviet Union. Sun's aide Chiang Kai-shek (1887–1975) was sent to the Soviet Union to study and returned with Russian advisers. The Russians helped by opening the Whampoa Military Academy, headed by Chiang, which became the training ground for a Chinese army. They also aided the development of the Nationalist Guomindang (GMD) [Kuomintang] party organization. The Russians also delivered the Chinese Communist Party members to the GMD, requiring each of them to accept the direction and discipline of the GMD.

By 1926 the GMD was the most influential political force in China. But this was largely due to the popularity of the communists who had been very successful in attracting members, recruiting 1.2 million workers and 800,000 peasants during 1926. Chiang was torn between his need of communist organizing abilities and his dissatisfaction with their radical programs. He was more comfortable with the conservatives in the GMD, including many landlords, bankers, merchants, and army officers. With Stalin's help, the Comintern (Communist International) not only required communist obedience to the GMD, but also prohibited revolutionary activity. After a march in 1926–1927 into northern China, where Chiang gained the support of many of the old warlords, he decided to purge the GMD of the communists, labor unions, and proponents of land reform. On March 21, 1927, the workers of Shanghai declared a general strike. The next day they won control of the city. Chiang saw his chance. He ordered the workers and communists to disarm and allow the GMD army to retake the city. Reluctantly, they obeyed. Chiang seized the opportunity and on the morning of April 12, 1927, began a reign of terror that massacred tens of thousands of workers and peasants in Shanghai and the rest of China. The Chinese Communist Party never fully recovered in the cities. Building again, almost from scratch, it recognized a source of strength it had sometimes neglected—the peasants.

Six months before the purge of 1927, Mao Zedong had gone back to his native Hunan province and discovered the revolutionary potential of the peasants.

> During my recent visit to Hunan, [Mao wrote] I made a first hand investigation. . . . I saw and heard of many strange things of which I had been unaware. I believe the same is true of many other places, too. All talk directed against the peasant movement must be speedily set right. All the wrong measures taken by the revolutionary authorities concerning the peasant movement must be speedily changed. Only thus can the future of the revolution be benefited. For the present upsurge of the peasant movement is a colossal event. In a very short time, in China's central, southern and northern provinces, several hundred million peasants will rise like a mighty storm, like a hurricane, a force so swift and violent that no power, however great, will be able to hold it back. They will smash all the trammels that bind them and rush forward along the road to liberation. They will sweep all the imperialists, warlords, corrupt officials, local tyrants and evil gentry into their graves.[5]

Mao's Soviet Marxism had not fully prepared him for such a realization. Although the communists had recruited peasants before 1927, he was trained, like most Marxists, to look to the urban workers as the revolutionary force and dismiss the peasants as a backward, "reactionary" element. In Hunan Mao realized that the peasants were already in revolution and that Chinese revolutionaries had better find a place for them in their theory or get out of the way.

It was this realization and the organization of the Chinese peasantry that made

Mao Zedong during the Long March, 1934

the Chinese Communist Party unique. Even after the Russian Revolution, Soviet Marxists were distrustful of the peasantry. It had been an uneasy alliance of workers and peasants during the Civil War. An early attempt to turn the great landed estates into collective (common) farms met with widespread resistance from peasants who wanted their own private farms. When well-to-do farmers (*kulaks*) revolted and middle-class farmers slaughtered their animals rather than turn them over to a collective farm, Stalin repressed them brutally. Even today, sixty years later, Soviet agriculture is the weakest element in the Soviet economy.

Soviet and Chinese communist revolutions began with the promise of land reform and took over the large estates of the wealthy. In both instances the mass of peasants benefited. Both the Soviets and the Chinese then experimented with various forms of collectivized agriculture. In general, the peasants of both societies preferred private, family farms. The more important difference between Soviet and Chinese communism was the Soviet insistence on industrial growth. In effect, Russian agriculture subsidized the rapid pace of Soviet industrialization. Whether that industrialization was the product of Stalin's paranoia or a wise preparation against a hostile world, it was built on the backs and bodies of the peasantry.

The Chinese Communist Revolution remained more peasant-based, agrarian, and rural. "China's basic social conflict was rural," the historian Lucien Bianco has written.

> The two opposing sides were the peasant masses and the landed upper class. Alongside the dire poverty and exploitation suffered by immense numbers of peasants, all other problems seemed minor.[6]

The Chinese Communist Party regained its strength in the Chinese countryside after the "Long March" of 1934 in which a remnant escaped another annihilation attempt by Chiang Kai-shek, marching six thousand miles through the rugged terrain of western China. In the small frontier town of Yenan a new party and Red Army was created which was even more dedicated to mobilizing peasant support. The principles of the "Yenan Way" that Mao devised were intended to insure that the party, army, and peasantry were one. Leadership was to come from the bottom up. Bureaucracy was to be further reduced. Soldiers were to learn to live with the people, in the villages. Schools were established to spread literacy and public health, and to teach the concept of "serve the people."

Especially after the Japanese invasion, begun in 1931, the communists appeared to most Chinese as the national party as well as the party of the people. Chiang and the GMD squandered rich political, financial, and military support from the United States and European powers in attempting to defeat the communists rather than the occupying Japanese. During World War II Western support of the GMD blinded many outside observers to the success of the communists in winning peasants to their cause. It appeared to some Western observers that:

> Mao's chances of success were very slim. Clearly outclassed in numbers and material, he dominated only a small territory; he had no money, no resources, no allies. Worst of all, the master of Russian communism had abandoned him; they had recognized Chiang Kai-shek, his mortal enemy, as the leader of China, and yielded Manchuria to Nationalist sovereignty.[7]

The Western support and propaganda blitz for Chiang (in part of which he was photographed with Roosevelt, Churchill, and Stalin as one of the "Big Four") had little effect on Chinese peasants. Instead they were converted by the actions of the communists and the Red Army in village after village.

> What strange soldiers they were, who paid for what they bought, cleaned up the rooms they stayed in, mingled socially with villagers, and were not above lending a hand in the fields![8]

The conscripted soldiers of the GMD were often as brutal as, and frequently more corrupt than, the Japanese. When the Japanese invaded Honan in 1944, the peasants help them disarm the GMD. The American general Joseph Stilwell understood the tragedy of American support of the GMD better than anyone:

> Chiang Kai-shek is confronted with an idea, and that defeats him. He is bewildered by the spread of Communist influence. He can't see that the mass of Chinese people welcome the Reds as being the only visible hope of relief from crushing taxation, the abuses of the Army and [the terror of his] Gestapo. Under Chiang Kai-shek they now begin to see what they may expect. Greed, corruption, favoritism, more taxes, a ruined currency, terrible waste of life, callous disregard of all the rights of men.[9]

On the day the Japanese surrendered (August 14, 1945), the Soviet government signed a treaty of friendship with Chiang Kai-shek and the United States Government insisted that all Japanese troops surrender to the GMD rather than the Red Army. When Mao refused, President Truman gave the extraordinary command that the defeated Japanese troops "maintain order" until they could surrender properly to the GMD. The U.S. Marines helped the GMD recover control of major cities from the communists. But in the Civil War that followed, the Nationalists found themselves limited to their city garrisons, surrounded by a sea of guerrillas in the countryside. Finally, after four more years of war, Chiang Kai-shek fled to Taiwan and the Red Army marched into Beijing. On October 1, 1949, Mao proclaimed the liberation of China and the establishment of the People's Republic.

THE COMINTERN AND INDIA

If the Chinese communists were eventually successful despite Stalin's Communist International, the Indian communists were not. In India as in China, the decisions of the International, especially after the rise of Stalin, had more to do with Russian national interests than those of international labor. Not only did policy keep shifting, but it continually seemed to shift in the wrong direction. At the first communist international meeting in 1919 the Indians and other colonials were ignored. Lenin insisted that the European revolution was about to occur momentarily and that the demise of capitalism in Europe would mean the end of colonialism. The masses in the colonies had only to be patient. By the second meeting in 1920, it became clear that revolution was not imminent in Europe. Thus, a policy for the colonies was necessary.

India of course was different from China. It was a colony of the British empire as well as a society of vast social inequalities. The question for Indian communists was whether to join the essentially middle-class nationalists that formed the Indian National Congress party or to agitate for radical social change. The firebrand of the Indian left was Mahendra Nath Roy (1886–1954). Roy left India in 1915 to raise arms and funds for Indian independence, first in Germany and then in the United States. He was arrested in the United States after the American entry into the war in 1917 but he jumped bail, settled in Mexico, began an independent study of Marxism, and founded the Communist Party of Mexico in 1919. At the second Congress of the Communist International in Moscow in 1920 Roy differed with Lenin on the crucial issue of whether to fight or join national colonial elites like the Indian National Congress. Lenin said to join them. He thought that the colonial world lacked the ingredients for socialist revolution: capitalism was insufficiently developed and there was no revolutionary working class. Insofar as there was a mass revolution developing in India, Lenin thought, it was around Gandhi. Further, Lenin argued, the national independence of colonies like India would destroy European capitalism (and not incidentally lessen pressure on Soviet Russia). Roy said it was necessary to fight the middle-class Indian National

Congress because it would only substitute Indian exploiters for English ones. He argued that the Indian people were already revolutionary. He said that workers and peasants were looking for radical leadership, an independent communist party, not a middle-class party that would use their energy for its own advantage. Gandhi might be a political revolutionary, Roy agreed, but he was a social reactionary (that is, he would prevent needed social change).

The Second Congress took the unusual step of adopting both Lenin's and Roy's programs in 1920. But by 1921 Roy's efforts to organize an Indian communist army in Afghanistan had been dismantled by the Soviets as a bargaining chip for a Soviet trade treaty with Britain. Finally, at the Sixth Congress of the Comintern, in 1928 (after the policy of aligning with the nationalist forces in China had resulted in the slaughter of the communists), Roy's program of a separate communist party was accepted. But then it was too late. Between 1920 and 1928 Gandhi had captured the spirit of the Indian masses for the Indian National Congress Party and any sep-arate or opposing revolutionary movement was wasted effort. Roy himself pointed out that his ideas of 1920 were not appropriate in 1928. There was now, he said, a significant socialist group in the Indian National Congress. For that he was expelled from the Communist International in 1929, and he returned to India to strengthen the radical wing of the Congress.

WORLD WAR I AND GANDHI

The Indian National Congress was transformed from a rich man's debating society to a mass party for Indian independence by World War I and the leadership of Mohandas Karamchand Gandhi (1869–1948). During World War I, "village India saw Europe in its sordid wartime clothes," one historian has written, "and was not impressed with what it saw."[10] Over a million Indians enlisted in the war. Many fought and died in Europe. India itself was policed by only 15,000 British troops. Their reduced numbers increased their brutality. A German warship in the Bay of Bengal showed that British protection was not guaranteed. Indian Muslim loyalties were frayed by the British war on Muslim Turkey. To wartime casualties and victims of food shortages were added twelve million victims of an influenza epidemic. Finally, the Russian Revolution and Woodrow Wilson's espousal of national self-determination changed Indian expectations irrevocably. When the British reassessed their policy towards India after the War, "responsible self-government" (similar to that of Canada, white South Africa, and Australia), barely considered in 1914, was "the policy of His Majesty's Government." It was to be just a matter of time and proper preparation. For the British in India, and the official Rowlatt Committee, however, the postwar period was also a time to reassert discipline. Troubled by political protests during the war, the commission report called for harsh measures: for Indians, press freedoms were limited; trial without jury was allowed.

Gandhi returned to India in 1915, during the war, and was greeted as the Mahatma [Great Soul]. He had spent twenty years in South Africa, serving the

Indian community in Natal as a lawyer, developing and practicing his philosophy of non-violent resistance. Gandhi began to win a popular following among Indian peasants the same way.

> Always traveling third class, dressed as the poorest peasant—or holiest *sadhu*—the Mahatma drew crowds and attention at every platform stop, reaching India's masses as no politician before him had ever done, embracing poverty and suffering in his own person, experiencing daily the plight of the "lowest of the low" becoming their guru, not just another political leader. His was a potent charisma, for in India no other appeal had as much force as a religious one.[11]

When the Rowlatt Committee report was put into law, Gandhi professed moral outrage. It was a breach of trust, he said, for the English to deny India a free press and jury. The Indian soul had been shocked by this abuse. Thus, instead of the usual political meeting he called for a *hartal*, a traditional Indian religious "strike" when the soul was stopped. *Hartals* were held in a number of large cities. In some cases they were only one-day work strikes. In others the enthusiasm erupted into riots.

AMRITSAR AND AFTERMATH

In Amritsar in the northern Punjab where worker shortages were already severe and tensions ran high, the fear of riots led to the prohibition of public meetings. On Sunday, April 13, 1919, 10,000 peasants from neighboring villages came to "The Garden," a walled-in field, to celebrate a Hindu festival. Without warning, General R.E.H. Dyer ordered his troops to fire on the unarmed men, women, and children trapped in the enclosure. They fired 1650 rounds of ammunition in ten minutes, leaving 400 Indians dead and 1200 wounded. The massacre at Amritsar was compounded by an indifferent British response. Initial approval gave way, under pressure, to the dismissal of General Dyer who on his return to England was celebrated by British conservatives as the "Savior of the Punjab." A few Indians expressed their outrage to the viceroy directly: Rabindranath Tagore, winner of the Nobel Prize for Literature in 1913, resigned his British knighthood. Millions of other Indians followed Gandhi's revolutionary call for nonviolent resistance.

In the wake of the Amritsar massacre, Gandhi became the undisputed leader of the Congress and the Indian people. He was the first Indian leader to unite the masses with the upper classes and Muslims with Hindus. He won Muslim confidence by committing himself to the campaign to save the *kilafat* (caliphate) of Turkey from what appeared to be a British attempt to remove the leader of the Muslims, fragment the old Ottoman empire, and secularize the remaining parts. He won over bright young men like Subhas Chandra Bose (1897–1945) to work for the Congress rather than pursue a prestigious career in the Indian Civil Service. He won the heart of the young, brilliant, urbane, Oxford-educated Jawaharlal Nehru, son of Motilal Nehru, a founder of the Congress. He inspired the unarmed, exploited masses of Indians by declaring the only victory they could win—suffering—to be the most effective path to independence. "The purer the suffering, the greater the progress," he told them. Indian suffering would undermine the only weapon the English had—physical force—with moral authority. Gandhi promised the practical reality of a moral victory. In one year—by December 31, 1921—he told his followers India would achieve *svaraj* (self-rule). He defined *svaraj* in a way that was intended to make people think what they could do for themselves. *Svaraj* was having no need of the English. Indeed, it was overcoming the fear of the English, even the fear of suffering and death.

Whether or not Gandhi's vision was bound to breed disappointment, it did. The *kilafat* campaign began to unravel when a Muslim army heading to Turkey was turned back in Afghanistan and the returning soldiers found their homes taken over by Hindus. Then, when the Turkish government under Atatürk abolished the caliphate in 1924, Indian Muslims felt further betrayed and isolated. Finally, Muslim fears of being a persecuted minority in an Indian national state were inflamed when the Congress refused to guarantee a third of the seats to Muslims. Muhammad Ali Jinnah (1876–1949), the Muslim leader, left the Congress in disgust. Gandhi's 1921 campaign of noncooperation built during the year, but as the end of the year approached without independence, many became frustrated. Gandhi suggested the process of mass civil disobedience was like an earthquake. Suddenly, the government would be unable to function. "The police stations, the court houses, etc., all shall cease to be government property and shall be taken charge of by the people." In January of 1922 Gandhi was ready to begin another campaign when a mob at the small village of Chauri Chaura seized a police station and murdered twenty-two Indian constables. Gandhi called off the campaign. He said God had warned him that India was not yet ready for nonviolent resistance. He turned away from political agitation, choosing to spend his days (when not in jail) in spinning and weaving, teaching, and social work until, he said, the people gained the necessary self-control for *svaraj*. He did not return to the national political arena until 1929.

GANDHI, NEHRU, AND SOCIAL CHANGE

Who was right about Gandhi: Lenin or M.R. Roy? Certainly Lenin was right in calling Gandhi a genuine revolutionary, but perhaps Roy was also right when he said that Gandhi was a conservative when it came to social change. The developing left wing of the Congress party in the 1920s also found Gandhi's leadership wanting. Gandhi's decision to withdraw after the violence at Chauri Chaura had very little support in the Congress. Motilal Nehru and other moderates pleaded in letters from jail that Gandhi should continue the struggle. "To sound the order of retreat just when public enthusiasm was reaching the boiling point was nothing short of a national calamity," wrote Subhas Bose.[12]

What is the attitude of the cartoonist towards Gandhi? The original caption from May 25, 1942 read as follows: "Gandhi defends India: How many non-violent non-cooperators would appear?" (New York Public Library).

It would be a mistake to perceive Gandhi as opposed to social change. He unerringly chose the plight of the dispossessed as his own. Whether it was underpaid indigo-producing peasants who asked for his help or exploited textile workers at the plant of a friend and benefactor, Gandhi was there—to fast, to mediate, to support a strike or the organization of a union. His principal cause in the twenties was the most exploited sector of Indian society, the untouchables, whom he called "children of God." Almost alone, he called attention to the plight of untouchables, which he considered a blight on Hinduism, eventually securing the abolition of the status.

While it would be difficult to think of anyone who was more of an idealist than Gandhi (in the sense of having an "idealistic" view of human nature), it would also be a mistake to call him "impractical." He was a brilliant strategist. He had an incomparable knack for choosing just the right issue to arouse the popular imagination and confound the English. In the process, he could also confound the left wing of the Congress. The salt tax is a good example. It was the issue that brought Gandhi's return to national politics in 1929. "Rather than see the young radicals tilt against the government and probably plunge the country into violence," one historian has written, Gandhi "decided to keep the whole situation in control by leading a non-violent movement himself."[13] His decision to challenge the British salt tax was inspired. Salt was not expensive and the tax was hardly disputed, but every peasant paid a tax on salt because it was a government monopoly. Typically, Gandhi's campaign was devastating in its simplicity and its mass appeal. He simply announced that he would walk to the sea and take salt without paying the tax. The government tried to look the other way, but Gandhi's well-publicized, leisurely sixty-mile walk to the sea drew the attention of the world in 1930. The government had no choice. Thousands of people had to be arrested. Gandhi showed again how easy it was to choke the government on its own laws if only people were willing to break the law in a nonviolent way and go to jail. This was also a protest that involved women in larger numbers than ever before. Once a man or woman had consciously broken the law, gone to jail, or protested the arrest of the Mahatma, they never again had the same respect for British law.

Perhaps the most accurate judgment of Gandhi was not that of Lenin or Roy, but of the man who was the chosen successor of the Mahatma, the younger Nehru. Jawaharlal Nehru called himself a socialist, by which he meant (like so many in his day) to distinguish himself from the communists of the Soviet Union and men like Roy. Along with Subhar Bose, he founded a "Socialist Independence for India League" in 1928, which immediately demanded "complete independence" from the British Empire. In this way he and the younger radicals pitted themselves against Gandhi, the elder Nehru and the Congress policy of independence within the empire. Gandhi, always capable of winning a dissident, brought the young Nehru back into the Congress Party by offering him the presidency the following year. While the rich, handsome, self-sacrificing son of Motilal was destined, like a legendary hero of India, to serve his country, Gandhi selected him in 1929 for the Congress presidency and again, more importantly, at independence in 1947 to be India's first Prime Minister. They did not always see eye to eye. Nehru was often frustrated by Gandhi's vagueness, his reduction of everything to personal, religious and moral issues. He looked in vain for a program. He felt uneasy with Gandhi's preoccupation with the spinning wheel and his dismissal of industry. But Jawaharlal Nehru believed that Gandhi was more than a nationalist revolutionary. He suggested that Gandhi was more socialist than he knew.

> Gandhi, functioning in the nationalist plane, does not think in terms of the conflict of classes, and tries to compose their differences. But the action he has indulged in and taught the people has inevitably raised mass consciousness tremendously and made social issues vital. And his insistence on raising the masses at the cost, whatever necessary, of vested interests has given a strong orientation to the national movement in favor of the masses.[14]

NATIONALIST AND SOCIALIST REVOLUTION

The Indian revolution, Nehru aside, was a nationalist, not a socialist revolution. There was no social revolution in India, at least nothing like the wholesale restructuring that occurred in China. One wants to ask how that matters. Is India better off today because it avoided a communist revolution, or might one argue the reverse? Would a Mao have been better than a Gandhi? Of course that would have been impossible. Gandhi was as Indian as Mao was Chinese. But history is not inevitable. A more intelligent Soviet policy would have enhanced the appeal of Indian communists. A more intelligent United States policy might have aided Chiang Kai-shek. (One more intelligent still might have brought Mao to power earlier.) The question is what are the advantages and disadvantages of each type of revolution.

India today has a bustling middle class, some say over fifty million strong. Indians claim the "world's largest democracy." No one disputes the middle word. There is also in India an enormous gap between the very wealthy and the very poor. The streets of major cities are full of the homeless and squatters. Crippled children begging are a common sight. Sanitation facilities for the poor are nonexistent. There are flies everywhere.

By 1980, China had largely eliminated homelessness, begging, and flies. Everyone worked. Everyone shared the poverty of the country. While some lived well, no one had thousands of times the income of someone else. Since 1980, China has become more like India. It has opened up to the world market and allowed new inequalities: greater prosperity and deeper despair.

In capitalist societies, be they Chinese or Indian, Bombay or Hong Kong, people are free to starve or buy the block. Their choice is often not their own, but they can act as if it is. In communist societies people were protected from extreme poverty and social inequalities, including their own failure or success. In communist societies people were often more respectful, suspicious, secure, and cautious. In capitalist societies they were often more coarse, aggressive, experimental, and anxious. These were the choices that people made for themselves or imposed on others. When they were imposed on others in a national revolution, there was very little the outsider could do. More generally, like the Comintern and the U.S., the outsider often blundered, getting the least desired result.

FOR FURTHER READING

On Chinese twentieth-century history John King Fairbank's *The Great Chinese Revolution 1800–1985* is a rich, personal, and somewhat conservative interpretation. Other valuable studies are Lucien Bianco's *Origins of the Chinese Revolution 1915–1949*, and H. R. Isaacs' *The Tragedy of the Chinese Revolution*. For the best introduction to the life of Mao Zedong, see Jonathan D. Spence's *Mao Zedong*.

Among the better introductions to the Russian Revolution are Theodore H.

Von Laue's *Why Lenin? Why Stalin,* Christopher Hill's *Lenin and the Russian Revolution,* and Isaac Deutscher's *The Unfinished Revolution: Russia 1916–1967.* John Reed's *Ten Days that Shook the World* still captures much of the drama of the period (as does Warren Beatty's film *Reds*). On the importance of the Russian Revolution for the rest of the world see C.K. Wilbur's *The Soviet Model and Underdeveloped Countries.* Other useful titles include Leon Trotsky's *History of the Russian Revolution,* Victor Serge's *Year One of the Russian Revolution,* and Steve Wright's pamphlet, *Russia: The Making of the Revolution.* On the decline of the revolution see Alan Gibbons, *How the Russian Revolution Was Lost* and, for a comparative perspective, Robert Strayer's *The Communist Experiment: Comparing the Soviet Union and China.*

For a general introduction to Indian history see *A New History of India* by Stanley Wolpert. For differing interpretations of Gandhi see *Gandhi: Maker of Modern India?* edited by Martin Deming Lewis. Louis Fischer's brief biography, *Gandhi,* is still a good read. For recent biographies of Gandhi see Yogesh Chadha's *Gandhi: A Life* and David Arnold's *Gandhi: Profiles in Power.* Gandhi's *An Autobiography* is fascinating but ends in 1921. Sir Richard Attenborough's film *Gandhi* is highly recommended by all but the most extreme purists or political critics.

On the question of socialism in India the essays in B.R. Nanda's *Socialism in India* are useful. On nationalism, *Nationalism on the Indian Subcontinent* by Jim Masselos is an introductory text. Nehru's *The Discovery of India* is well worth reading.

NOTES

1. Jean Chesneaux, Marianne Bastid, Marie-Claire Bergere, *China from the Opium Wars to the 1911 Revolution,* trans. Anne Destenay (New York: Random House, 1976), p. 367.
2. Albert S. Lindemann, *A History of Socialism* (New Haven: Yale University Press, 1983), p. 203.
3. Both quotations cited in Harold Isaacs, *The Tragedy of the Chinese Revolution* (Stanford: Stanford University Press, 1951, 1961), pp. 53, 54.
4. Boyd Compton, ed., *Mao's China: Party Reform Documents, 1942–44* (Seattle: University of Washington Press, 1952), p. 22. Cited in Lucien Bianco, *Origins of the Chinese Revolution, 1915–1949* (Stanford: Stanford University Press, 1971), p. 79.
5. Mao Tse-Tung, *Report on an Investigation of the Peasant Movement in Hunan* (Peking: Foreign Language Press, 1967), p. 1.
6. *Ibid.,* p. 82.
7. Lionel Max Chassin, *The Communist Conquest of China* (Cambridge, Mass: Harvard University Press, 1965), p. 247.
8. Bianco, *op. cit.,* p. 158.
9. Theodore H. White, ed., *The Stilwell Papers* (New York: William Sloane Associates, 1948), pp. 315–322. Quoted in Franz Schurmann and Orville Schell,

eds., *Republican China* (New York: Vintage, 1971), p. 273.

10. Percival Spear, *A History of India*, vol. 2 (Harmondsworth: Penguin, 1965), p. 183.
11. Stanley Wolpert, *A New History of India* (New York: Oxford University Press, 1977), pp. 295–296.
12. Subha Bose, *The Indian Struggle* (London, 1935), p. 90.
13. Spear, *op. cit.*, p. 202.
14. Jawaharlal Nehru, *India's Freedom* (London, 1962), p. 68. Cited in P. C. Joshi, "Nehru and Socialism in India, 1919–1939," in *Socialism in India*, ed. B.R. Nanda (New York: Barnes & Noble, 1972), p. 129.

❊ 11 ❊

Individual
and
Society

Freedom
and Authority

Are people becoming robots in modern society? Do we have more freedom than our ancestors? Does modern technology make us more alike? Whatever happened to rugged individualism? Whatever happened to accepting authority?

This chapter will attempt to determine if we have become more, or less, individualistic, independent, or free in the last two hundred years. We will attempt to determine the direction of change for human self-identity and freedom and the forces that determine that change.

To make that assessment we will have to examine a large number of factors. To what extent does technology determine who we are? Does industrial technology free us to grow, or stamp us with the same mark? Do the robots liberate us, or imitate us? How important are our cultural ideas of freedom and liberty? Where do they come from? What do they mean? How do we account for authoritarian movements in the twentieth century? Are they throwbacks from an earlier age, or harbingers of things to come? Is mass society inherently more anonymous? Does anonymity breed eccentricity or conformity? How about standard of living? Are the people of poor countries as free as the people of rich countries? These are some of the factors we must consider. We begin with the factor that, more than any other, distinguishes modern society from all past societies: industrialization.

299

INDUSTRIALIZATION AND INDIVIDUALITY

The process of industrialization created opportunities for individuality that were unimagined in traditional society. The specialization of labor that industrialization depended upon multiplied the number of job options and the number of job experiences available.[1] By the nineteenth century, one did not have to choose merely between working in the church, working for the state, or pursuing a profession in law, science, or business. A vast host of opportunities presented themselves. Even the laborer, who was bound by the necessity of survival rather than the luxury of choice, would develop differently—individually—by the job he or she was forced to take. A list of occupations or trades that would have numbered in the dozens in the eighteenth century could be numbered in the hundreds in the nineteenth century, and in the thousands by the early twentieth century. Whether one chose by education, or merely by market demand, it was possible for the first time in human history to lead a life that was vastly different from that of one's neighbors and friends.

The proliferation of choices entered every aspect of life. It was necessary to ask not only what one was to do, but where one was to live, how one was to spend leisure time, what one was aiming for, how one was to bring up the children, and whom one was to marry.

Nineteenth- and early twentieth-century literature is full of signs of the new joys and agonies of individual choices and separate lives. While the popular "rags to riches" novels suggested alternative life goals for the working class, the middle-class novels, which had been unnecessary in an earlier, more communal age, opened one's eyes to the privacies of the lives of the boss, the butcher, the mayor, or neighbor in hundreds of pages of details.[2] Newspapers, like novels, had to detail events as well as purchasing possibilities in the advertisements that were unknown or unnecessary in a simpler age. At the intellectual apex of society, "romantic" novelists and poets sung of individual insight and feelings in an orgy of introspection and self-awareness.

The new age echoed the sentiments of Rousseau's *Confessions* (completed in 1770):

> I am undertaking a work which has no example, and whose execution will have no imitator. I mean to lay open to my fellow-mortals a man just as nature wrought him; and this man is myself.
>
> I alone. I know my heart, and am acquainted with mankind. I am not made like anyone I have seen; I dare believe I am not made like anyone existing. If I am not better, at least I am quite different. Whether Nature has done well or ill in breaking the mould she cast me in, can be determined only after having read me.[3]

The individualistic assumptions of the age of romanticism (from Rousseau to the middle of the nineteenth century) are those of Emerson's essay on "Self-Reliance":

"To believe your own thought, to believe that what is true for you in your private heart is true for all men—that is genius. . . . Trust thyself: every heart vibrates to that iron string. . . . Whoso would be a man, must be a nonconformist."[4]

Nineteenth-century romanticism invented a whole stock of images and ideas that have since become the core of Western individualism. The genius, the hero, the nonconformist, the artist, the intellectual, the pioneer, even the inventor, are inventions of nineteenth-century imagination. The importance of imagination, creativity, personality, self-expression, dreams, the unconscious, and self-conscious- ness has evolved since the nineteenth century in European and American culture. Modern literature, modern psychology, modern art, modern political ideals cannot be understood except as elaborations of this unique departure in world history. Modern men and women are the first to begin with a culture that values individ- ual expression and opportunity above conformity and authority.

CLASS AND INDIVIDUALITY IN THE NINETEENTH CENTURY

The personal visions of romantic philosophers and poets were expressed for all to read. But in the early nineteenth century few could read. What about the working classes and lower classes of industrial society? Did they also experience greater indi- viduality in the course of industrialization and the expansion of market society? Most of our knowledge of the lower classes comes from the records and the laws of their administrators. Perhaps, if we adjust for their critical eye, we see evidence of a greater freedom of individual expression among the governed as well.

In 1851 the interior ministry of Munich, Germany, issued the following assess- ment of popular morality:

> Increasing impiety, widespread laziness and pleasure-seeking, the lack of domesticity, the ever-growing overestimation of self, the newly rising indifference to the interest of the community when a question of per- sonal advantage is involved—all these are phenomena which, the more they emerge, the more emphatically they reveal that the basic pillars of the social order are deteriorating.[5]

Public administrators complained of popular "immorality" in dancing, drinking, sexuality, and even dress. "Is it still possible to tell the chambermaid from the lady, the valet from the royal councilor, the counting house clerk from the banker?" a Bavarian parliamentarian asked rhetorically. Even the farmer, he added, had adopt- ed the middle-class burger's coat "with its metal buttons."[6]

It is always difficult to tell how much of this is new, and how much is the tradi- tional complaint of the upper class, the administrator, or the older generation. But the complaints of nineteenth-century administrators are full of new words: self- esteem, emancipation, independence, libertine comportment, social ambition, impudence, isolation, wildness, and egoism. Further, the causes of such behavior were often found in the social changes that accompanied the capitalist industrialization of the period. "All sense of what is just and proper is being lost. . . . The dignity of the family bond, the discipline of the household, is disappearing. . . . The trend to a more independent lifestyle is predominant. . . . Such a variety of distractions are now offered . . . the bonds have loosened not only between master craftsman and journeyman, between employer and servant, but among the members of the smaller family circle as well."[7]

Although "dating" was a later, twentieth-century source of individual growth, the popularity of dances during the nineteenth century, and the declining influence of the family in matchmaking, seem to have increased individual social contact and romantic experimentation. Statistics from Germany show, for instance, a marked increase in the percentage of bridal pregnancies in the nineteenth century, suggesting both greater moral mobility and romantic choice—key signs of greater self-definition.

The passing of the traditional guild relationship of master and apprentice could also increase the leisure time and opportunity for self-expression. Outside of factories, and before the development of twentieth-century techniques of "scientific management," the worker could follow personal urges and inclinations denied by the earlier watchful master or the later time-conscious manager. An observer of a mid-nineteenth-century New York shipyard describes the morning's work:

> In our yard, at half-past eight a.m., Aunt Arlie McVane, a clever, kind-hearted, but awfully uncouth, rough sample of the "Ould Sod," would make her welcome appearance in the yard with her two great baskets, stowed and checked off with crullers, doughnuts, ginger-bread, turn-overs, pieces, and a variety of sweet cookies and cakes; and from the time Aunt Arlie's baskets came in sight until every man and boy, bosses and all, in the yard, had been supplied, always at one cent a piece for any article on the cargo, the pie, cake and cookie trade was a brisk one. Aunt Arlie would usually make the rounds of the yard and supply all hands in about an hour, bringing the forenoon up to half-past nine, and . giving us from ten to fifteen minutes "breathing spell" during lunch; no one ever hurried during "cake-time."
>
> After this was over, we would fall to again, until interrupted by Johnnie Gogean, the English candy-man, who came in always at half-past ten, with his great board, the size of a medium extension dining table, slung before him, covered with all sorts of "stick," and several of sticky candy, in one-cent lots. Bosses, boys, and men—all hands, everybody—invested one to three cents in Johnnie's sweet wares, and another ten to fifteen minutes is spent in consuming it. Johnny usually sailed out with a bare board until 11 o'clock at which time there was a general sailing out of the yard and into convenient grogshops after whiskey.[8]

One is struck, in passages like this, by both the opportunities for personal growth in the leisurely, convivial atmosphere of the early industrial working place and also by the similarity of individual actions. Working men were still not bound to the routines of the machine (at least outside of the factories), they were still able to gratify individual needs for fun and comradeship at work, but they all, "bosses, boys, and men—all hands," lay out their cent for Aunt Arlie, their couple of cents for Johnnie Gogean, and sail out to the grogshop.

The opportunities for individual expression in leisure activity have increased greatly since the middle of the nineteenth century, but so has the discipline of the working place. By the end of the nineteenth century workers were more often governed by the discipline of the machine than by the appearance of Aunt Arlie or the need for grog. "It is no longer simply that the individual workman makes use of one or more mechanical contrivances for effecting certain results," the American economist Thorstein Veblen pointed out in 1904. That used to be the case: machines added to the workman's ability to do his work. But the "particularly modern" character of machine work, Veblen adds, is that the discipline of machine production dominates the workman.

> He now does this work as a factor involved in a mechanical process whose movement controls his motions. . . . The process standardizes his supervision and guidance of the machine. Mechanically speaking, the machine is not his to do with it as his fancy may suggest.[9]

Instead of encouraging the expression of the worker's creativity (the way tools and simple machines did in the traditional working place), the modern factory of machines requires constant attention, mechanical thinking, and conformity.

> His place is to take thought of the machine and its work in terms given him by the process that is going forward. His thinking in the premises is reduced to standard units of gauge and grade. If he fails of the precise measure, by more or less, the exigencies of the process check the aberration and drive home the absolute need of conformity.
>
> There results a standardization of the workman's intellectual life in terms of mechanical process, which is more unmitigated and precise the more comprehensive and consummate the industrial process in which he plays a part. . . . The machine process is a severe and insistent disciplinarian in point of intelligence. It requires close and unremitting thought, but it is thought which runs in standard terms of quantitative precision. Broadly, other intelligence on the part of the workman is useless; or it is even worse than useless, for a habit of thinking in other than quantitative terms blurs the workman's quantitative apprehension of the facts with which he has to do.[10]

Whether the working classes of industrial society were more or less individualistic at the end of the nineteenth century than they were at the beginning, or middle, of the century would be difficult to say. What is clear is that the capitalist
industrial revolution initiated processes that both individualized human experiences and required new kinds of mechanical conformity. We will look first at the
positive side of this development—the liberal ideal of the late nineteenth century—and then return to some of the negative features of modern "managed society."

THE TRIUMPH OF LIBERALISM

Any exploration of individuality in the modern age must come to grips with the triumph of Western middle-class liberalism at the end of the nineteenth century. Like
the earlier Western ideals of romanticism, liberalism was a uniquely Western credo
of the age of industrialization. Like romanticism, it was a philosophy of the new,
educated middle class that put individual freedom in the forefront.

One speaks of the "triumph" of liberalism perhaps a bit optimistically. Liberalism
never became the majority philosophy in European and American society or elsewhere. But liberal ideals were enunciated with more care and power in the nineteenth century (more broadly, from 1776 to 1914) than before or since. The nineteenth century hosted the "triumph" that liberalism knew.

Its ideals were freedom of thought, freedom of expression, toleration, diversity,
general education and suffrage (voting), the capacity of reason, the power of ideas,
and the sanctity of the individual. We could trace its growth in the gradual extension of the suffrage, in the abolition of serfdom and slavery, in the development of
mass education, in the developing gospel of free trade, or even in the growth of
social welfare legislation, though liberalism always stopped short of socialism.

We prefer to look at one of the most famous documents of the movement and
the era, John Stuart Mill's essay *On Liberty*, which he wrote with his wife, Harriet
Taylor, between 1855 and 1858, and published in 1859 (the year Darwin published
the *Origin of Species*). "The object of this essay is to assert one very simple principle," Mill wrote.

> That principle is that the sole end for which mankind are warranted,
> individually or collectively, in interfering with the liberty of action of
> any of their number is self-protection. That the only purpose for which
> power can be rightfully exercised over any member of a civilized com-
> munity, against his will, is to prevent harm to others. His own good,
> either physical or moral, is not a sufficient warrant. He cannot right-
> fully be compelled to do or forbear because it will be better for him to
> do so, because it will make him happier, because, in the opinion of
> others, to do so would be wise or even right. These are good reasons for
> remonstrating with him, or reasoning with him, but not for compelling
> him.[11]

John Stuart Mill (1806–1873). (Radio Times Hulton Picture Library)

That statement shows both the liberation and limitation of middle-class, capitalist liberalism. It carries the class concept of liberty (in Hobbes and Locke) into the dawning age of universal suffrage and toleration. (Mill includes the working classes, but excludes children and "barbarians.") It brings to logical conclusion the recognition, implicit in Hobbes, that there are no absolute truths, but only power and human reason. And it magnifies the importance of the individual while further limiting the power of the state and the community. But it accepts a view of the individual as sacred in its separateness (the isolated free-choosing atom of market society) by its assumption that a line can be drawn between individual action and "harm to others." *On Liberty* is a testament to individual integrity and freedom because it no longer has to assume the community interest and mutual responsibility that market society was annihilating. The doctrine (to put it crudely) that one's freedom ends where another's nose begins is a useful guide to political legislation only in a society where people relate as strangers.

Mill's defense of freedom of thought and expression would (unfortunately) make little sense in a premarket community governed by traditional absolutes. It is based on assumptions that would not be accepted in traditional society: that the majority opinion might be wrong; that even when it is right it must be challenged or it will become dogma or prejudice; that making choices, even "wrong" ones, is essential to individual growth.

Market society created the necessary conditions for Mill's individualism, skepticism, rationality, and preference for process. It freed the individual to have his or her own opinions. Without eternal goals, it sanctified the creation and discussion (the market exchange) of ideas. Without community, it glorified individual freedom. But individuals without community might find themselves whispering in the wind with nothing to say.

That was never a problem for Mill. He was probably the best educated person of his time. But what was the meaning of his freedom from restraint for the uneducated and the lower classes? Mill gives a revealing set of examples when he discusses the possibility that free expression can lead to damaging actions:

> No one pretends that actions should be as free as opinion. On the contrary, even opinions lose their immunity when the circumstances in which they are expressed are such as to constitute [by] their expression a positive instigation to some mischievous act. An opinion that corn dealers are starvers of the poor, or that private property is robbery, ought to be unmolested when simply circulated through the press, but may justly incur punishment when delivered orally to an excited mob assembled before the house of a corn dealer, or when handed about among the same mob in the form of a placard.[12]

Why those two examples among so many possibilities? Clearly, it is on this side of the political-economic debate that Mill sees the way ideas become actions. The danger he feels to free expression comes not from upper-class ideas of war or racism or from middle-class ideas on hanging thieves, imprisoning debtors, or malicious profiteering in false advertising. The danger line for Mill between ideas and action is when the unruly mob acts according to socialist or anarchist ideas.

Ultimately, Mill is speaking for the freedom of his class, much like Hobbes and Locke. The difference is that his class is not the profit-seeking middle class, but the educated, intellectual middle class. He is speaking for freedom "intellectual, and through that to the moral nature of man."[13] That Mill defended freedom of the press in almost absolute terms is a milestone in the history of human freedom and individuality. That it did not occur to him that the poor and working classes of his time had no press or access to the media is a sign of the limitations of middle-class liberalism. The suggestion that he might have objected to the contents of a poor people's press may be a sign of the intentions of middle-class liberalism.

The failure of liberalism in the twentieth century had much to do with the new disillusionment with human reason and goodness in the wake of two world wars. It was also crippled by the numerous strategies of the twentieth century to manage and manipulate rather than educate and listen (as we will shortly see). But it also has much to do with the contradictions in liberalism itself. Mill (like Locke) was attempting to reconcile a particular kind of individual opportunity (albeit the very important opportunity for self-expression and freedom of thought) with the maintenance of a world of private property and the inequalities in power, education, and opportunities for expression that such a world implied. If John Stuart Mill was cautious about encouraging full freedom of individual expression for all classes on all issues, one can imagine the temerity, even the terror, of more self-interested souls.

MANAGED MASS SOCIETY:
TWENTIETH-CENTURY CORPORATISM

Any judgment about the state of individuality in the twentieth century must balance the historically unprecedented concern for "the self" in modern culture against the enormous number of ways in which the individual is manipulated and managed. An understanding of some of the methods of modern control might provide a context for understanding the various quests for self-identity.

The workshop is a good place to start. The symbol for most people, and the reality for many, of the controlled working environment is the assembly line. Henry Ford writes in his autobiography that "the idea in a general way came from the overhead trolley that the Chicago meat packers used in dressing beef." The first modern assembly line was actually a "disassembly line" developed in the slaughterhouses of Chicago and Cincinnati in the late nineteenth century. Ford first tried the idea in 1913 in the manufacture of generators. Instead of having each man assemble the 29 parts of a generator, he put 29 men on a moving assembly line, and each one fit a single part. By powering the line and raising it for each reach, he was able to produce four times the number of generators in the same man-hours. Later in the year, Ford introduced the assembly line for the production of the entire car. By 1914 the process produced cars in an eighth of the time required earlier.

The world would never be the same. Three hundred thousand Model T Fords were made that year. By 1924 the plant was producing almost 2 million. At $290 each, Ford had halved the price in ten years and put more than half of the world's cars on the road. Mass production had shown the way to mass consumption. The age of the private automobile brought opportunities for privacy, leisure, and personal mobility that must be accounted as one of the chief sources of individuality in the twentieth century. At the same time, Ford's success with the assembly line meant that the division of labor (which some called "the division of man") was to be a permanent feature of industrial society.

More than the assembly line was needed to turn the kind of workers that Aunt Arlie knew into the human machine parts that Thorstein Veblen foresaw. Even before Henry Ford began to engineer the modern workshop, another American engineer, Frederick Taylor, initiated a technique of managing labor which came to be known as industrial engineering. Analyzing each worker's job into a series of machinelike actions—bending, turning, pushing, and lifting—and timing each component of work with a stopwatch, Taylor distinguished the "essential" from "nonessential" actions of the job and designated the most efficient motion and time for each step. "What I demand of the worker," Taylor explained, "is not to produce any longer by his own initiative, but to execute punctiliously the orders given, down to their minutest details.[14]

Taylor expected that the benefits of his "scientific management" of work would accrue to the workers and owners alike, but his own account of the process at Bethlehem Steel in the 1890s shows how the lion's share of increased productivity went to company profits.

"Now, Schmidt, you are a first-class pig-iron handler and know your business well" [he told a strong but untrained worker]. "You have been handling at a rate of twelve and a half tons per day. I have given considerable study to handling pig iron, and feel sure that you could do a much larger day's work than you have been doing. Now don't you think that if you really tried you could handle forty-seven tons of pig iron per day instead of twelve and a half tons?"

[Skeptical but willing,] Schmidt started to work, and all day long, and at regular intervals, was told by the men who stood over him with a watch, "Now pick up a pig and walk. Now sit down and rest. Now walk—now rest," etc. He worked when he was told to work, and rested when he was told to rest, and at half past five in the afternoon had his forty-seven tons loaded on the car. And he practically never failed to work at this pace and do the task that was set him during the three years he was at Bethlehem; and throughout this time he averaged a little more than $1.85 per day . . . 60 percent higher wages than were paid to other men who were not working on the task work. One man after another was picked out and trained to handle pig iron at the rate of forty-seven tons per day until all of the pig iron was handled at this rate.[15]

In the early days of scientific management workers rankled at a 60 percent increase in pay for almost a 400 percent increase in work. They bristled at the arrogance of the stopwatch and clipboard men, fresh out of college, telling them how to shovel and lift. Often they went out on strike. But throughout the course of the twentieth century, so much intelligence and expertise was devoted to the multiplying disciplines of disciplining workers—sciences of management, industrial psychology, business administration—that workers often lost awareness of how they were being manipulated and mistook manipulation for corporate concern.

As early as 1924 Elton Mayo, one of the founders of "industrial psychology," discovered in his experiments with the workers at Western Electric's Hawthorne Works outside of Chicago that whenever he made changes in the working conditions of an experimental "control group" their productivity increased. Whether he increased or lowered the lighting, humidity, or temperature, or merely returned conditions to what they had been before, production increased. The "Hawthorne effect" that he discovered was that the workers responded favorably to being the objects of an experiment. The mere existence of the clipboard men—hovering, changing something, and watching—was enough to give the workers a feeling of management's concern. The lesson for management was not that the workers could take an active role in the running of the workplace, but that they could be manipulated like children who were eager for parental attention.

Much of twentieth-century education, science, and engineering went into the manipulation of the working place. Efforts at efficiency, productivity, and more

Charlie Chaplin in Modern Times

"rational" organization often had the effect of making grown men and women workers more mechanical in their behavior and more childlike in their thoughts and feelings. In a similar way, many of the new fields of knowledge of the twentieth century were devoted to the manipulation of the public and the consumer. Though it would be difficult to measure, it is quite probable that the amount of time and resources spent by the fledgling discipline of psychology (for instance) in the twentieth century on manipulation and management has been much greater than that spent on increasing individual autonomy. In the corporate world of the twentieth century there was usually more money available for studies, research, and training in fields that were geared to convincing rather than finding out. Academic departments, whole schools and research institutions, publishing companies, media resources (often with corporate support) were run in the interest of discovering ever new ways of molding public or consumer opinion—designing ever more subtle ways of what an earlier generation, less attuned to public relations, might have called lying.

The capacity of just two fields—public relations and advertising—to manipulate opinion, to influence individual choice while pretending to broaden the realm of individual choice, is enormous. A few examples from the career of just one practitioner of the new techniques in the 1930s, Edward Bernays, speaks volumes.

Bernays explains in his memoirs how he helped George Washington Hill of the American Tobacco Company induce women to smoke cigarettes in public. On the advice of a psychoanalyst who said that women view cigarettes as "torches of freedom," Bernays planned an Easter Parade of women smokers in New York City in 1929. He had his secretary send telegrams to 30 leading debutantes in the city that read:

> IN THE INTERESTS OF EQUALITY OF THE SEXES AND TO FIGHT ANOTHER SEX TABOO I AND OTHER YOUNG WOMEN WILL LIGHT ANOTHER TORCH OF FREEDOM BY SMOKING CIGARETTES WHILE STROLLING ON FIFTH AVENUE EASTER SUNDAY[16]

The event created a national stir. Pictures of the women were printed in newspapers throughout the country. Women responded from New York to San Francisco by smoking publicly. "Age-old customs," Bernays learned, "could be broken down by a dramatic appeal, disseminated by the network of media."[17]

But that was only a beginning for George Washington Hill's American Tobacco Company. Women were not smoking the company's Lucky Strikes because the green package with the red bull's eye clashed with the colors of their clothes. In the spring of 1934, Hill called Bernays into his office to ask what could be done. Bernays suggested changing the package to a more neutral color. Hill thundered disapproval: he hadn't spent millions of dollars advertising a package to change it. Bernays countered: then change the color of fashion to green. That was the kind of idea George Washington Hill liked. He authorized $25,000.

> That was the beginning of a fascinating six-month activity for me— to make green the fashionable color. . . .
>
> Some years before I had asked Alfred Reeves, of the American Automobile Manufacturers Association, how he had developed a market for American automobiles in England, where roads were narrow and curved.
>
> "I didn't try to sell automobiles," he answered, "I campaigned for wider and straighter roads. The sale of American cars followed."
>
> This was an application of the general principle which I later termed the engineering of consent. Like an architect, I drew up a comprehensive blueprint, a complete procedural outline, detailing objectives, the necessary research, strategy, themes and timing of the planned activities.[18]

And what activities! Psychological studies were made of associations with green. The director of the leading fashionable society ball was given the whole $25,000 budget from "a nameless sponsor" to make it a "green ball." A silk manufacturer was encouraged to "bet on green" and gave a luncheon for fashion editors with green menus, all-green food, a talk by a psychologist on green, and a lecture by the head of the Hunter College art department on "green in the work of great artists."

> I had wondered at the alacrity with which scientists, academicians and professional men participated in events of this kind. I learned they welcomed the opportunity to discuss their favorite subject and enjoyed the resultant publicity. In an age of communication their own effectiveness often depended on public visibility.[19]

As newspaper stories heralded a "green autumn" and a "green winter," a color fashion bureau was organized. "It alerted the fashion field to green's leadership" in clothing, accessories, and even interior decoration. Fifteen hundred letters were sent to interior decorators and home-furnishing buyers on "the dominance of green" to ensure that they would join the trend. The head of the Green Fashion Ball was persuaded to sail to France to secure the cooperation of the French fashion industry and the French government, which cooperated in recognition of the buying power of American women. An invitation committee for the Green Fashion Ball was formed that included some of the most important names in American society: Mrs. James Roosevelt, Mrs. Walter Chrysler, Mrs. Irving Berlin, and Mrs. Averell Harriman. The committee held a series of luncheons with representatives of the accessory trades to encourage them to make green accessories available for the green gowns from Paris.

As the campaign gained momentum, other manufacturers jumped on the bandwagon. One announced a new emerald nail polish. Another introduced green stockings. Green window displays began to appear in stores, first in Philadelphia, and finally by September in Altman's Fifth Avenue store in New York. Vogue and Harper's Bazaar featured the new green fashions on their covers. Finally in November, "the unsuspecting opposition" joined the campaign. "Camel cigarettes showed a girl wearing a green dress with red trimmings, the colors of the Lucky Strike package."[20]

Even the competition had recognized that Lucky Strikes were the height of fashion.

The "green revolution" of 1934 raises a number of interesting questions about the use of resources in corporate, commercial society. What were all of these people doing promoting "green" in the depths of America's economic depression? With fundamental economic issues to tackle, how did so many intelligent and influential people consume their time and energy in activity that was at best meaningless, and ultimately harmful to health? Is this the way that "the best and the brightest" of corporate society confront crisis? Are there no guidelines for more useful activity?

The Lucky Strike campaign raises even more gnawing questions, however, about the meaning and possibilities of individuality in a society dominated by commercial and corporate interests. Who, besides George Washington Hill and Edward

Bernays, knew what they were doing? What kind of freedom or compulsion motivated the manufacturers (of accessories, for instance) who hopped on the "green revolution" to their own profit? What kind of individuality was displayed by the intellectuals, journalists, and society people who joined the campaign? When artists and psychologists lectured that autumn on the importance of green, were they saying what they wanted to say? Were they expressing their own choices or individuality? If they were manipulated into thinking that the "issue of green" was important, how about all of the women who thought they had chosen to buy green dresses? When the whole context, the very alternatives, of consumer decision making are created by those who have something to sell, what kind of freedom of choice in fact exists?

THE TRIUMPH OF TOTALITARIANISM

In the Great Depression of the 1930s, corporate manipulation of individuality reached its height not in the United States, but in Nazi Germany. The Nazi concentration camps were in some ways only a further extension of the corporate quest for efficiency and profit maximization. When the directors of I. G. Farben (the German multi-national corporation that manufactured everything from Bayer aspirin to synthetic gasoline) chose Auschwitz as the site of its synthetic rubber plant, they did so on the promise of slave labor from the concentration camp that they could work to death and supervision by the SS soldiers.

> Nor was the policy hidden from the top echelons of I. G. Farben's managerial elite. They were very much involved in the operation and made frequent trips to Auschwitz to see how things were going. According to the affidavit of Dr. Raymond van den Straaten, a slave at Auschwitz, on one occasion, five of I. G. Farben's top directors made an inspection tour of I. G. Auschwitz. As one of the directors passed a slave scientist, Dr. Fritz Lohner-Beda, the director remarked, "The Jewish swine could work a little faster." Another I. G. Farben director responded, "If they don't work, let them perish in the gas chamber." Dr. Lohner-Beda was then pulled out of his group and kicked to death.[21]

Karl Marx's view that capitalism treated workers as things often turned out to be a perceptive metaphor of the managed societies of the twentieth century, but in Nazi Germany it was a literal fact. Major German corporations not only worked the slave laborers of the concentration camps to death, they also used their bodies as guinea pigs for quasi-medical experiments, profited from the manufacture of the gas used to kill them, and then turned their bodies into soap, their hairs into rugs, and their gold fillings into jewelry.

Through it all they behaved not like fanatics, but like thorough business executives. When Himmler informed others of the mass exterminations, "He spoke,"

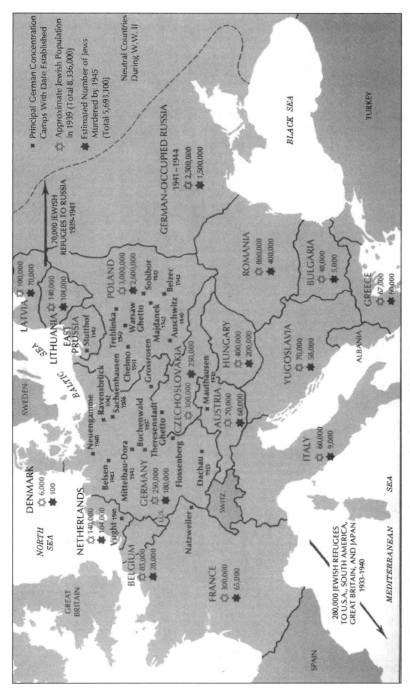

German Concentration Camps and Jews murdered in World War II.

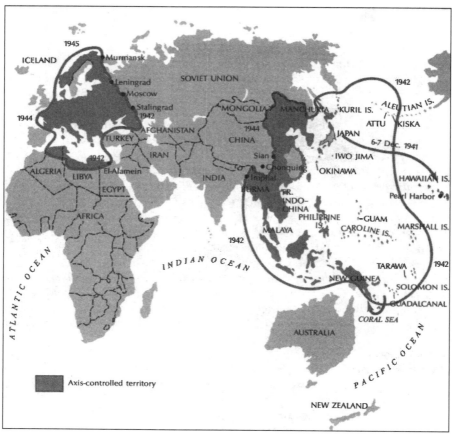

World War II: Greatest extent of Axis expansion

according to one observer, "with such icy coldness of the extermination of men, women and children, as a businessman speaks of his balance sheet. There was nothing emotional in his speech, nothing that suggested an inner involvement."[22] Similarly, Hitler's chief architect Albert Speer recalled: "My obsessional fixation on production and output statistics blurred all considerations and feelings of humanity."[23]

In some ways, the business attitudes of Himmler, Speer, and the executives of such corporations as I. G. Farben, Krupp, Audi, and Telefunken that used concentration camp labor are just further extensions of the corporate, commercial mentality that evolved elsewhere, especially in America, in the twentieth century. From the assembly line, industrial engineering, psychological and managerial techniques for increasing production or consumption, public relations and advertising, it is but

In a world that seemed to be falling apart, Hitler mobilized the German masses with a barrage of symbols and spectacles—banners, uniforms, parades, salutes, songs, and slogans —that offered certainty in exchange for personal identity. Without a "self," every German could become part of a new corporate whole.

a series of steps to the world of concentration camp factories, economic revival through militarization, and the propaganda techniques of Goebbels or the technocratic efficiency of Himmler and Speer. Once human values are subordinated to the mechanistic values of output strategies, cost minimization, and profit maximization, the concentration camp becomes little more than an efficient factory. It thus became possible for executives like I. G. Farben's Dr. Fritz Ter Meer to lunch with American counterparts at Standard Oil before the war, secure patent agreements that would prevent Standard Oil from manufacturing synthetic rubber even after the war started, witness the murder of Dr. Lohner-Beda, socialize at Auschwitz while as many as ten thousand inmates were being exterminated daily, and then plead after the war that "no harm had been done" by the Farben pharmaceutical experiments because the inmates "would have been killed anyway."[24]

Market society need not lead inevitably to Auschwitz, of course. In other societies it did not; the Nazi experience of Germany was unique. At the least, however, market society established a "service mentality" of secondary goals that could be used on behalf of any set of primary goals. Hitler's goals of racial extermination, militarization, totalitarian control, and world domination could be implemented as efficiently as any other set of goals. The profit-and-loss mentality could be most effective when it was essentially oblivious to or unconcerned with what was being measured. Indeed, in a militarized society where one was expected to follow orders without question, the corporate, technocratic system could work most effectively.

Hitler was able to use the large corporations because he guaranteed them large profits at a time when their very existence was challenged by German socialists and communists. Once German industrialists realized that Hitler's use of the word "socialist" in the National Socialist German Worker's Party was nothing more than a fraud to capture working-class votes, they contributed to the Nazis for their own corporate survival.

Germany's humiliation in World War I, the removal of the emperor, the loss of territory, the war reparation payments, and the admission of "war guilt" demanded by the Treaty of Versailles were sources of frustration that Hitler's nationalist rhetoric promised to counter. The economic breakdown, especially the disastrous inflation of the early 1920s and the continuing high numbers of unemployed—6 million in 1932—turned people to radical solutions. Hitler's anti-Semitism struck deep chords in German culture and offered the Jews as easy scapegoats—for the defeat in war and the economic catastrophe.

The appeal of Hitler, however, had more to do with irrational forces than rational calculation. He offered in his hypnotizing speeches and mass spectacles a rigorous certainty in traditional, absolutist values that had been all but destroyed by the successes as well as the disasters of capitalist society. The successes of German capitalism had destroyed the traditional securities of family, village, guild, and church, and created in its place the anonymous, vulnerable, isolated individual of modern society. In Erich Fromm's telling phrases, the individual in modern capitalist society was "free from" the various constraints of the medieval world—free from the obligations of serfdom, guild regulations, religious orthodoxy, and traditional authorities, and thus free from their protection and security. As an isolated competitor, employee, consumer, soldier, or taxpayer, he was only one of the mass audience. He had been divided for conquest, propagandized for sales, and never instructed or encouraged to develop the positive, potential side of his or her new individuality into "freedom to" be something. Thus, since the only freedom people knew was negative, they sought "an escape from freedom." The failure of capitalism was that the system had no advantage in encouraging individual growth. Rather, it profited more by the dependence of the individual as employee or consumer.

Individuals had to be educated to the point of proficiency in their jobs and advertising literacy, but more than that was superfluous, even detrimental. By the 1920s the failure of capitalism in Germany was more general. It not only failed to encourage individual growth; it failed to provide enough jobs, and the currency was practically worthless.

In *Escape from Freedom*, Erich Fromm attributed the rise of Nazism to Protestantism as well as capitalism. Protestantism, he argued, was a cultural reinforcement of the social disintegration of capitalist society. The classic Protestant posture of the individual alone, answerable only to God, was a religious equivalent of the capitalist isolation before competitors and the market. It too offered only negative "freedom from." The Protestant was free from the institutional structure, rituals, sacraments, and social salvation of the Catholic church. Here too, the result was that the individual did not learn to develop in the necessary give-and-take of an institutional structure.

Thus, according to Fromm, in the collapse of traditional securities and values in Germany in the 1920s and 1930s, the burden of a meaningless individuality was too much to bear. Hitler gave people a new community (the German nation and "master race"), enemies to unite against (Jews, socialists, and communists), and an overriding purpose (world dominion). All of the relativities of advanced market society were abolished by an act of will. All questions were answered. "Hitler is always right."

Hitler frankly recognized the appeal of absolute authority for the Germans who felt their isolation more painfully as their old society disintegrated around them. He wrote in *Mein Kampf*:

> The psyche of the great masses is not receptive to anything that is half-hearted and weak. [They] would rather bow to a strong man than dominate a weakling. . . . The masses love a commander more than a petitioner and feel inwardly more satisfied by a doctrine, tolerating no other beside itself, than by the granting of liberalistic freedom with which, as a rule, they can do little, and are prone to feel that they have been abandoned. They are equally unaware of their shameless spiritual terrorization and the hideous abuse of their human freedom.[25]

Hitler realized the value of the mass meeting, the parade, and the spectacle, in channeling these feelings of loss and loneliness (see his film *The Triumph of the Will*) toward a new hierarchical community.

> The mass meeting is also necessary for the reason that in it the individual, who at first, while becoming a supporter of a young movement, feels lonely and easily succumbs to the fear of being alone, for the first time gets the picture of a larger community, which in most people has a strengthening, encouraging effect. . . . When from his little workshop or big factory, in which he feels very small, he steps for the first time into a mass meeting and has thousands and thousands of people of the same opinions around him, . . . then he himself has succumbed to the magic influence of what we designate as "mass suggestion."[26]

American films, especially musicals like Busby Berkeley's "Dames" of 1934, satisfied some of the same longings—to obliterate the self in a larger identity—that the German masses felt. Berkeley's camera angles turned chorus girls into petals for workers who felt turned into machines. He gave unity beauty, and titillation too.

The Nazi state was only the most pernicious of totalitarian regimes that swept Europe in the second quarter of the twentieth century. Much of Hitler's ideology and practice (except for anti-Semitism) was actually borrowed from Mussolini's fascist Italy after 1922. Italian fascism had already developed (by 1930) the system of total (that is, totalitarian) state control through a hierarchy of corporations administered from the top down, and through the assault on democracy, reason, thought, liberty, and individuality that became pervasive in the fascisms of Germany and Eastern Europe.

Even Stalinist Russia ended the brief experiments with new forms of freedom, individual liberation, and popular participation initiated in the hopeful wake of the revolution in 1917. (In one such experiment, even the position of conductor of the symphony orchestra was dropped for being coercive.) But despite the secret police, the bureaucracy, the purges, and the terror, the worst features of Stalinism were always rationalized as emergency measures to preserve "socialism in one country," and thus create the conditions for an eventual "withering away of the state."

From the late 1930s until his death in 1953, the image of Joseph Stalin was never far from any Soviet citizen. This picture was taken at a resort on the Black Sea in 1950. (Sovfoto)

Although that was of small consolation to the victims of the regime, the doctrinaire commitment to eventual individual liberation and a democracy more complete than the "bourgeois democracy" of the propertied prevented some of the worst excesses of the fascist regimes. At least the Soviet example of modernization that was championed by various emerging nations meant an ultimate commitment to human rights, greater democracy, and individual freedom, whereas the exportation of fascism (from Spain to the Philippines) did not. Fascism made total individual subordination a matter of faith rather than temporary necessity. Its ideal was the complete suppression of individuality and the brutal extinction of individuals and minorities who were deemed outside of the "national will."

FOR FURTHER READING

There is virtually an infinite number of ways of approaching the question of individuality in the nineteenth and twentieth centuries. For the role of the romantic movement, one might turn to Isaiah Berlin's lectures in *The Roots of Romanticism*, Jacques Barzun's *Romanticism and the Modern Ego*, and Morse Peckham's *Beyond the Tragic Vision: The Quest for Identity in the Nineteenth Century*.

For individuality in popular culture there is a superb collection of essays in the multivolume *A History of Private Life*, edited by Philippe Aries and Georges Duby. For this chapter, volume 4, *From the Fires of Revolution to the Great War*, is particularly useful. In addition, there are E. G. West's *Education and the Industrial Revolution*, I. Pinchbeck and M. Hewitt's *Children in English Society*, R. W. Malcolmson's *Popular Recreations in English Society, 1700–1850*, Peter N. Stearn's *European Society in Upheaval*, as well as the works mentioned in the text.

For further study of J. S. Mill and liberalism, there are G. Himmelfarb's *On Liberty and Liberalism: The Case of J. S. Mill*, A. Ryan's *J. S. Mill*, and B. Mazlish's psychoanalytical *James and John Stuart Mill*, as well as J. S. Mill's *Autobiography* and *On Liberty*.

There are too many studies on modern economic and business history to name a few. I have quoted from M. Kranzberg and J. Gies's *By the Sweat of Thy Brow*, which is quite readable and introductory. Some of the more specialized monuments are E. P. Thompson's *The Making of the English Working Class* and Thorstein Veblen's *The Instinct of Workmanship and the State of Industrial Art*.

On Nazism, George L. Mosse's *The Fascist Revolution: Toward a General Theory of Fascism* is important, if a bit difficult. Richard Rubenstein's *The Cunning of History*, Raul Hilberg's *The Destruction of the European Jews*, and John Toland's readable *Adolf Hitler* are all recommended.

Other interesting approaches to the subject of individuality can be found in Richard Sennett's *The Fall of Public Man* and Christopher Lash's *The Culture of Narcissism*.

NOTES

1. Adam Smith recognized as early as the 1770s that factory production simplified the tasks of the worker. See his famous discussion of pin making in *The Wealth of Nations*, Book I, chapter 1.
2. Ian Watt's *The Rise of the Novel* makes this point in a rich discussion of particular novels.
3. Jean-Jacques Rousseau, *Confessions*, anonymous trans. of 1783 and 1790 revised by A. S. B. Glover (New York: Limited Editions Club, 1955), Pt. 1, Bk. 1, p. 3.
4. Ralph Waldo Emerson, "Self-Reliance," in Emerson, *Selected Prose and Poetry*, ed. Reginald L. Cook (New York: Holt, Rinehart and Winston, 1950), pp. 165, 166, and 168.
5. Quoted in Edward Shorter, "Towards a History of *La Vie Intime*: The Evidence of Cultural Criticism in Nineteenth-Century Bavaria," in *The Emergence of Leisure*, ed. Michael R. Marrus (New York: Harper Row, 1974), p. 43.
6. *Ibid.*, p. 52.
7. *Ibid.*, pp. 46–47.
8. Quoted in Melvin Kranzberg and Joseph Gies, *By the Sweat of Thy Brow: Work in the Western World* (New York: Putnam, 1975), pp. 126–127.

9. Thorstein Veblen, *The Portable Veblen*, ed. Max Lerner (New York: Viking Press, 1948), pp. 335–336.

10. *Ibid.*, pp. 336–337.

11. John Stuart Mill, *On Liberty*, ed. Currin V. Shields (Indianapolis: Bobbs Merrill, 1956), p. 13.

12. *Ibid.*, pp. 67–68.

13. *Ibid.*, p. 67.

14. Kranzberg and Gies, *By the Sweat of Thy Brow*, p. 155.

15. *Ibid.*, pp. 155–156.

16. Edward L. Bernays, *Biography of an Idea: Memoirs of Public Relations Counsel Edward L. Bernays* (New York: 1965), p. 387, excerpted in Warren Susman, ed., *Culture and Commitment 1929–1945* (New York: George Braziller, 1973), pp. 133–134.

17. *Ibid.*

18. Bernays, p. 390. Susman, pp. 136–137.

19. Bernays, p. 391. Susman, p. 138.

20. Bernays, p. 394. Susman, p. 140.

21. Paul Hilberg, *The Destruction of the European Jews* (New York: Quadrangle, 1967), p. 595.

22. Quoted in John Toland, *Adolf Hitler* (New York: Ballantine Books, 1976), p. 1052.

23. Albert Speer, *Inside the Third Reich*, trans. Richard and Clara Winston (New York: Macmillan, 1970), p. 375.

24. Richard L. Rubenstein, *The Cunning of History: The Holocaust and the American Future* (New York: Harper & Row, 1975), p. 60.

25. Adolf Hitler, *Mein Kampf*, trans. Ralph Manheim (Boston: Houghton Mifflin, 1943, 1971), p. 42.

26. *Ibid.*, pp. 478–479.

Chronological Table of
a Divided World
1914–1945

Europe	Americas	Africa and Islamic World	Asia
World War I 1914–1918	Ford auto assembly line 1914		Warlords divide China 1916–1928
Russian Revolution 1917	United States enters World War I 1917		
Treaty of Versailles 1919			Amritsar massacre in India 1919
League of Nations 1920–1946	Height of Mexican social revolution 1920–1940		May Fourth Movement in China 1919
Fascist revolution in Italy 1922		Egypt gains independence 1922	
		German colonies in Africa become mandates of League of Nations, Britain, France, and South Africa 1922	
Hyperinflation in Germany 1923		Kemal Atatürk, President of Turkish Republic 1923	
Dictatorship of Stalin 1924–1953	E. Mayo's Hawthorne experiments 1924	"Rif Republic" of Morocco declared, then defeated by Spanish 1924	
		Pahlavi dynasty in Iran 1925–1979	

a. = *after*   *r.* = *ruled*

Europe	Americas	Africa and Islamic World	Asia
	A. Sandino leads seven-year Nicaraguan opposition to the United States occupation 1926		
			Chiang Kai-shek massacres Communists 1927
Great Depression 1929–1939	Great Depression 1929–1939		
	Vargas in Brazil 1930–1945		Gandhi's salt walk to the sea 1930
	Roosevelt, President of the United States 1933–1945		Japan invades Manchuria 1931
Nazi revolution in Germany 1933	U.S. "New Deal," 1933–1939		
Nuremberg laws 1935	Cardenas, President of Mexico 1934–1940	Italian invasion of Ethiopia 1935	Mao's Long March 1934
			Triumph of militants in Japan 1936
			Sino-Japanese War 1937–1945
World War II 1939–1945	Cooling of Mexican revolution a. 1940	World War II fought in North Africa, and African troops at other fronts 1939–1945	
	United States in World War II 1941–1945		Japanese conquest of South Asia 1941–1942
East, West Europe split 1945			Atom bomb and defeat of Japan 1945

a. = after   r. = ruled

Nobuaki Kojima, Untitled, 1964. Construction of painted plaster and strips of red-and-white cloth coated with polyethylene resin, 67-7/8 x 35-1/2 x 19-3/8". Collection, The Museum of Modern Art, New York.

IV

The Nuclear World

1945–Present

Indian street lined with cinemas and gigantic billboards

Preview of the Period
1945–Present

The American nuclear explosions over Hiroshima and Nagasaki in 1945, which ended World War II, forged the world by fire into a single sphere. Ecologically, economically, and politically the world became "Spaceship Earth." This new reality took shape with the formation of the United Nations in 1945 and the subsequent proliferation of UN organizations; the creation of the World Bank, the International Monetary Fund, international law, the International Court of Justice, and other courts and tribunals; the appearance of numerous global non-governmental organizations; and the summit meetings of world leaders, and conferences on a wide range of global issues.

Europe and the Soviet Union. Europe and the Soviet Union experienced a remarkable recovery after 1945. The devastation of the Second World War was much greater than is normally realized. Especially in Germany, where most cities were leveled, and in the Soviet Union, where twenty million people were killed and 30 percent of industrial capacity was destroyed, Europe in 1945 lay in ruins. The revival of Europe is particularly striking in those countries that suffered most. In West Germany the gross national product exceeded its prewar level by 1955, although the country had only half of its former territory. In 1990, West and East Germany united, the combined country becoming the centerpiece of a European Union after 1992. The Soviet Union became by some measures (military, scientific, and certain heavy industrial indicators) the second most powerful country in the world by 1960. The Soviet Communist Party, backed by the Red Army, controlled governments throughout eastern Europe and wielded influence from East Asia to southern Africa. But Cold War military expenses and domestic suppression took its toll. A failed

Hiroshima in 1945 after the U.S. dropped the nuclear bomb.

and expensive war in Afghanistan and a nuclear disaster in the Ukraine made reform imperative. Gorbachev's attempt to make the party more responsive led ultimately to its downfall and the independence of the former satellite countries. By the 1990s, Russia and its former satellites were struggling to introduce market economies and democratic governments. For Britain, which emerged from the war the most intact, the postwar years brought a lesser role on the world stage. The loss of colonies (especially India in 1947) and the competition from renewed European industry in the Common Market (after 1957) and the European Union (after 1992) reduced Britain to one among others. Until the late 1960s the economies of France, Italy, and Germany showed considerable strength (double that of the United States). Since then, alternating periods of "stagflation" (stagnation and inflation) and unemployment have taken their toll. In 2002, ten years after the formation of the European Union, the countries of Europe molded their economies even closer together with the adoption of a common currency, the Euro. Since 1945, the pendulum of European politics swung from conservative governments immediately after the war, directed by strong leaders (Churchill, Adenauer, de Gaulle, and de Gasperi), to liberal, labor, and democratic socialist governments, especially in France, Spain, Portugal, Greece, and Sweden, and communist municipal governments in Italy. A consequence of the shift left was the creation of welfare states from the 1960s to 1980s, offering such benefits as free medical care, four-week vacations, and free college education. The pendulum then swung back to the right, haltingly in the 1980s, and more decisively at the beginning of the twenty-first century.

Asia. Asia emerged from Western colonialism after 1945 and developed independent nations and industrial economies by 2000. It is interesting to compare the realization of Chinese independence with Indian, and both with the emergence of Japan after its defeat in the Second World War. The Chinese communist victory in 1949 meant a social revolution; Indian independence in 1947 did not. The Chinese social revolution was directed primarily against the large landowners. Many urban capitalists remained untouched. It was also directed against the traditionally conservative classes of scholars, bureaucrats, and professionals. Three hundred thousand scholars were purged in 1957 after the opening of the "Hundred Flowers" campaign. Eighty-eight percent of Chinese farm families were organized into communes during the "Great Leap Forward" in 1958. Bad planning and poor harvests combined to produce a major disaster. Between 1959 and 1966, moderates and intellectuals regained power, installed Liu Shaoqi [Liu Shao-ch'i] over Mao Zedong, reduced the size of communes, and provided economic incentives called Three Freedoms and One Contract. Mao then initiated the "Great Proletarian Cultural Revolution" (1966–1969), in which young "Red Guards," chanting slogans from Mao's "Red Book," closed colleges, forced doctors and scholars into the countryside, and jailed and executed party enemies. Possibly four hundred thousand died in the upheaval. The pendulum swung back again when Zhou Enlai [Chou En-lai] opened China to the West in 1972, and especially after Mao's death in 1976 and the accession of Deng Xiaoping [Teng Hsiao-P'ing] (one of Mao's former enemies).

Since 1978 China has opened its economy to foreign

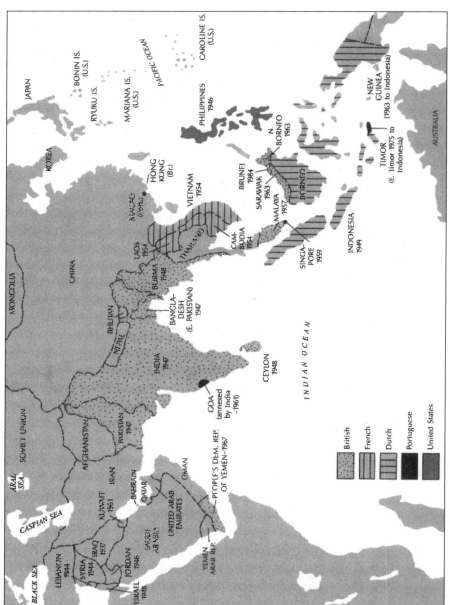

Independence in Asia. Dates of independence are indicated.

investment. Following the Japanese example of exporting to the world, China built entire cities as special tax-free export platforms, offering cheap Chinese labor to foreign capital. The communist party still monopolizes political power, but it includes business leaders in its membership. Gaps between the rich and poor, city and country, professional and peasant have widened, but a middle class (which didn't exist in 1978) now claims cars, vacations, and second homes. The return of Hong Kong to China in 1997 brought an end to Western colonialism in Asia and a first-world financial center to China. The unfinished agenda for Beijing is the independence of Taiwan, traditionally a part of China, but politically independent since 1949 when the defeated GMD (Guomindang) forces fled the mainland. Since then Taiwan has developed one of the strongest economies in Asia.

Indian society did not experience either the radical social revolution of China or the violent swings that followed. As a result, Indian society has greater extremes of wealth and poverty than does China. It also has more freedom of movement (up and down) and behavior (creative and corrupt). While India inherited a British parliamentary system and is often called the world's largest democracy, its succession of leaders from 1947 to 1989—Nehru (until 1964); his daughter, Indira Gandhi (prime minister 1966–1977 and 1980–1984); and her son Rajiv Gandhi (prime minister 1984–1989)—more closely resembled monarchy than democracy. After Rajiv Gandhi was assassinated in 1991, the Nehru/Gandhi legacy and the Congress Party which the family dominated was eclipsed by the BJP, a party with roots in the Hindu nationalist movement. Sectarian conflicts between Hindus and Muslims which had been suppressed by the secularism of the Congress Party have increased, as has conflict with Pakistan. The partition of British India and the creation of a separate Muslim Pakistan in 1947 led to the mass migration of twenty million people, Hindus and Muslims escaping from religious violence. Wars broke out between the two countries in 1947–1948, 1965, and 1971. In 1998 India and Pakistan announced nuclear tests, as tensions over disputed territory in Kashmir heated up.

The rise of Japan from the ashes of World War II is a story more like that of Germany than of India or China. No anticolonial revolution was necessary. In a sense there was a revolution, one carried out by the American occupation, largely General MacArthur and his staff. The constitution MacArthur imposed was more democratic than the U.S. Constitution, calling for sexual equality, collective bargaining, and radical land reform. Even more important was Article Nine, which renounced war forever, allowing Japanese industry to expand (without the military drain) at a faster rate than any in the world. The enormous productivity of Japan as an exporter of manufactured goods, especially electronics and automobiles, was a model to its neighbors, especially Taiwan and Korea, but also Singapore, Malaysia, and more recently China. Japanese success, however, led to a speculative bubble in which the prices of Japanese companies, real estate, and securities became grossly inflated. As a result the Japanese economy has contracted since 1990.

North Africa and the Middle East. North Africa and the Middle East since 1945 have shown the comparative impact of nationalism and internationalism in the modern world. This is a much more homogeneous region than Asia. The vast majority of its inhabitants are Muslim. Most speak Arabic. It was politically unified twice, by the Umayyad sultans in the ninth century and the Ottoman Empire beginning in the sixteenth. The Ottoman Empire shielded much of the area from Western colonialism, but not from the force of Westernization. As early as the eighteenth century, the success of Western military might and organization appealed to Ottoman officers and intellectuals. Thus, the first response to Westernization was secularization (Atatürk's Turkey, where state judges replaced clergy and piety was purely personal). Military officers elsewhere were similarly disposed to follow the Western example. Riza Shah Pahlavi, a former army commander, ruled in Iran from 1925 to 1941. His son continued his secular state building after the war (with one interruption, from 1951 to 1953, when the more liberal nationalist Mosaddeq came to power in a revolution but was overthrown with U.S. assistance). Muhammad Riza Shah Pahlavi governed with considerable U.S. aid, but with arrogant disregard for his opposition in the middle-class bazaars, among political radicals, and among the poor. The most organized force of opposition, however, turned out to be the opposition to secularization led by the Shi'ite clergy, especially the ayatollah Ruhollah Khomeini, who came to power in 1979. Since Khomeini's death in 1989, the Iranian clergy has permitted elections and reformed some of the more severe strictures of the Islamic regime. In Egypt, an army coup against King Farouk in 1952 paved the way for the republic and the progressive, secular presidency of Colonel Gamal Abdel Nasser (1918–1970). As in Iran, however, Muslim fundamentalism became more popular as secular, modernizing policies failed. In Egypt, strong rulers from the military outlawed Muslim fundamentalism and accepted U.S. aid and a military alliance. Political pluralism and opposition parties were discouraged, especially those that might capture the popular hunger for honest government and social justice. The creation of the state of Israel in 1948 did much to encourage Arab nationalism as a response to Jewish nationalism, not only among the Palestinians who were displaced, but also among the Jordanians, Syrians, and Egyptians, who suffered losses in the war of 1948–1949, again in the conflict over the Suez Canal in 1956, and especially in the Arab-Israeli Six-Day War of 1967 and Yom Kippur War of 1973. It is a tragic irony that the terrorism and rhetoric of anti-colonialism that was used by Zionist extremists like the "Stern Gang" and Irgun against British control of Palestine in 1947 have since become the explosive weapons of Palestinians against Israel and its U.S. and European supporters. Oil in the 1970s and early 1980s made Saudi Arabia, Kuwait, the United Arab Emirates, and Libya among the richest countries of the world, the first to gain that status without industrialization. None of the oil-rich used their instant wealth for long-term economic transformation. In another twenty years, it may seem as if they bubbled up like underground springs in the desert and then evaporated.

Sub-Saharan Africa. Sub-Saharan Africa since 1945 felt the burden of colonialism more than other regions. There were no independent states south of the Sahara in 1945 except for Liberia, Ethiopia and the colonial white-settler state of South Africa. Most of central Africa became independent in the early 1960s. In some cases, independence was achieved at great cost: Kenya, Zaire, Angola, Mozam-

bique, and Zimbabwe are examples. In others, it was attained relatively peacefully: such was the case in Ghana,
Nigeria, Cameroon, the Ivory Coast, and Senegal. But the
burden of colonialism remained after independence. State
boundaries had been created with no regard for natural
boundaries or differences in ethnicity or religion. While
the British and French provided some education, politics
was rarely part of it; often the first elections in African
colonies were those that brought independence.

Africa's economic development has been hampered by
some of the highest birth rates and urbanization rates in the
world, and by the scourge of AIDS. In the last twenty years,
20 million Africans, 83% of the global total, have died of
AIDS. Africans suffer more than others because the disease
originated in central Africa and because many of the
infected cannot afford the medications developed in the
West. The white domination of South Africa increased
after 1948 (while declining almost everywhere else). The
victory in that year of the Afrikaner-dominated Nationalist
party led to the imposition of official apartheid. The government insisted that black Africans were nationals of
"independent" tribal homelands and that they voluntarily
came to South African cities and mines for work. Near
these employment areas the government created "black
townships," resembling barracks, which despite strict control became the scene of protests in the 1960s and of a rapidly developing struggle for independence in the 1980s.
Isolated by the world community and hurt economically by
a global embargo, in 1990 the white government of South
Africa released Nelson Mandela, leader of the African
National Congress, from the isolated jail in which he had
been held for 25 years. In 1994 he was elected president of
South Africa.

The Americas. Latin America since 1945, as before, has
shown the difficulties of development after independence.
Since many of these states were pluralistic societies with
Europeans in the majority (a heavy majority in Costa Rica,
Argentina, Chile, and Uruguay), they offer instructive
comparisons with the United States, Canada, and Australia. The Spanish tradition of autocratic and bureaucratic
government continued after 1945. The conservative role of
the church and military is part of that tradition, although

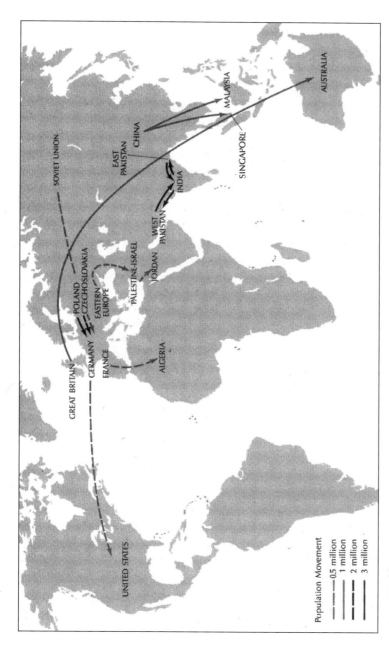

Major World Migrations, 1930–1955. This map shows the dramatic reduction in European migration to the Americas during the age of quotas in the United States. The quota system was particularly tragic for European Jews. We see the large number of refugees after the war from Eastern Europe to Germany as well as the migration of Eastern European Jews to Palestine/Israel, and the displacement of the Palestinians. By far the most significant migrations shown, however, accompanied the partition of India. Major migrations of Japanese to China and Koreans to Japanese-occupied territories are not shown, since most returned in this period.

the Peruvian military and the post-1960s church have also been a force for social change. Politics has meant taking a position on land reform and the plight of the urban unemployed in an area of the world where population increases and urbanization are (along with those of Africa) the highest.

Social change by revolution has been limited. The 1911 revolution in Mexico became "frozen" after World War 11, as did similar attempts in Bolivia to redistribute land to the peasants in the 1940s and 1950s. The most important attempts at social revolution on the left were the Cuban revolution in 1959, the Allende period in Chile (1970–1973), and the Nicaraguan revolution in 1979. The Cuban revolution of Fidel Castro toppled the government of Fulgencio Batista, a dictator supported by the U.S. government. Opponents of Castro, particularly in the United States, pointed to his close ties with Moscow and support of revolutionary movements elsewhere. Supporters pointed to his improvements in literacy, health care, and welfare for the Cuban peasantry. In 1961 the United States launched an invasion by Cuban exiles at the Bay of Pigs that failed immediately. In 1962 a shipping blockade of Soviet vessels by President Kennedy led to the dismantling of Soviet missiles in Cuba. An embargo on trade with Cuba has continued since.

Marxist socialism came to Chile as a result of the election of Salvador Allende as president in 1970. Opposed by the U.S. government, U.S. corporations, wealthy Chileans, and the Chilean military, he was deposed and killed in a military coup in 1973. The Sandinista revolution in Nicaragua in 1979 overthrew the dictatorship of the Somoza family, which the United States had installed in the 1930s and supported ever since. Supporters point out that in their first five years, the Sandinistas distributed more land (3.5 million acres) than had all other Central American countries combined in the previous twenty years. Opponents said most of the land became farm cooperatives rather than private property and that peasants became state workers. In the elections of the 1990s, the Sandinistas were defeated, with the help of the United States, but the country remained highly politicized and divided. Almost every home displayed the flag of the liberals or Sandinistas. Revolutions of the right, counterrevolutions, and military coups have

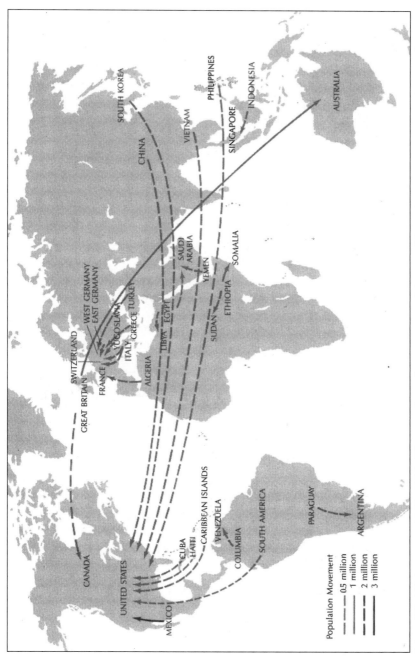

Major World Migrations, 1960–1985. This map shows the importance of Asian and Latin American migration to the United States, the postwar German magnet in Europe, and the pull of some of the oil-producing countries.

been more frequent in Latin America than elsewhere. Some of these, like Peronism in Argentina during World War II, combined an imitation of European fascism and an appeal to urban workers. The postwar regime of Stroessner in Paraguay and the Chilean counterrevolution of Pinochet after Allende made less pretense of popular support, requiring only the support of the wealthy and the military. Nevertheless, after 1990, Latin American military leaders returned to the barracks, reinvigorating democracy in most of the hemisphere.

The United States after 1945 became the dominant world power. The dollar became the world currency, replacing the British pound. U.S. international corporations manufactured the steel, automobiles, office equipment, airplanes, and consumer goods for most of the world. The dominance of U.S. corporations was especially strong in the underdeveloped world of Asia, Africa, and Latin America. If the United States grew richer at the expense of the underdeveloped world (and the gap between rich and poor nations increased), it also provided the political and economic stability for European prosperity. U.S. loans and investment were instrumental in the European economic recovery after the war. The United States, unlike Germany and Japan, did not demilitarize after the war, but instead provided an expanding "defense shield" for its economic allies. The Cold War with the Soviet Union from 1947 to 1989 was ideally suited to maintain U.S. dominance without the cost of combat. It broke down into actual "hot" war in Korea (1950–1953) and Vietnam (1964–1975). The Cold War also forced the Soviet Union to bankrupt its consumer sector in favor of the military and scientific.

The dominant position of the United States was challenged between 1960 and 1989 by the Soviet launching of the first satellite, Sputnik, in 1957; the political independence of the "nonaligned" nations; and the inability of the United States to control the newly independent African nations. U.S. will was sometimes blocked by Soviet veto and United Nations votes. In Vietnam, the U.S. suffered an embarrassing and extremely costly defeat (only to later win the peace). U.S. dominance, like that of Europe, depended on the monopoly of industrial production and easy access to raw materials from the underdeveloped world; it faced vigorous competition from newly industrialized countries, many of which the United States had helped create. Nevertheless, the U.S. worked towards the passage of free trade agreements (with Canada and Mexico) and similar "favored nation" agreements with numerous countries, including China, on the expectation that free trade would ensure American and global prosperity. U.S. governments generally placed less confidence in international organizations than markets. On issues of the global environment, empowering the International Criminal Court, and accepting the jurisdiction of the Court of International Justice, the United States was less forthright. Further, on evolving issues of human rights, such as health care, indigenous peoples, the death penalty, and number of prisoners, the United States lagged far behind other first-world countries, including its neighbor, Canada.

❧ 12 ❧

Industry and Capitalism

Markets and Governments

- In the last twenty years, the world's 500 largest corporations have increased sales sevenfold while their number of employees has remained flat.
- In a recent year, the world's 358 billionaires had a combined net worth of $760 billion, equal to the combined wealth of almost half (45 percent) of the rest of the earth's entire population of six billion people.
- The highest paid chief executive of a major American corporation in 1998 received 25,000 times the income of the average American worker. In 1958 the highest paid executive received "only" 125 times the pay of the average worker.[1]
- In 1820 the inhabitants of the richest country in the world enjoyed triple the income of the inhabitants of the poorest country in the world. Today the richest country's citizens average thirty times the income of the poorest country's citizens. One third of humanity lives on less than two dollars a day. Ninety-eight percent live on less than $25,000 a year.
- Global GDP (gross domestic product) was five times higher in 2000 than in 1950, a much greater increase than the doubling from 1900 to 1950.

Statements like these dramatize the contradictions in the modern world economy. How does it display such enormous productivity and inequality at the same

time? To understand this we must distinguish between two great historical processes that transformed life on the planet these last fifty years. They are industrial technology and market or capitalist economy. The industrial revolution is over two
hundred years old. The economic system we call capitalism is at least five hundred
years old. Both industry and capitalism have spread worldwide in the second half of
the twentieth century. But they are not the same. Industrialization is the creation
of modern technology, machinery, factories, and machine-made products. Capitalism involves the expanded use of money, credit, and stock ownership, for production, trade, and profit. Together industrialization and capitalism spawned the modern corporation and commercial production, but they did not always go hand in
hand.

Both the technological and the economic maps of the world economy have
changed drastically since World War II ended in 1945. Technology spread throughout the world since 1945. Some countries industrialized for the first time, some of
those already industrialized experienced a "second industrial revolution," and others borrowed or copied manufacturing capacity. Only rarely and briefly did industrial production decline, usually as a result of war or periodic recession.

The history of capitalism since 1945 has been more volatile. By the time of the
communist victory in China in 1949, almost a third of the world (from Eastern
Europe to the China Sea) stood outside the capitalist market economy. During the
years of the Cold War, another Third World of countries steered a middle course
between communism and capitalism. Not until 1989, when the Soviet Union collapsed, did capitalism enjoy an aura of inevitability. By the end of the twentieth
century, the Chinese Communist Party adopted market-based reforms and capitalism reigned supreme.

Ironically, the economies that attracted most attention as models of development between 1945 and 1990 were those of the Soviet Union and Japan. To understand why, we begin our story with these non-market economies. Together, they
show us how successfully planned economies could deliver, at least for a time.

STATE AND INDUSTRY: RUSSIA AND JAPAN

The initial stage of the industrial revolution, beginning in Britain in the second
half of the eighteenth century and spreading rapidly to the United States and to
Belgium, Holland, and parts of France, was certainly capitalist. No one could have
planned the first industrial revolution. But as people realized what industrialization
was, it became possible for countries like Germany, Norway, Sweden, and Denmark
to plan and direct more of the process, to marshal resources and capital more efficiently, to minimize the human cost and waste, or sometimes to monopolize the
benefits on behalf of the society or the state.

Between 1880 and 1945 the two largest industrial revolutions took place in
Russia and Japan. In Russia, especially after the Communist Revolution in 1917,
the state directed industrialization. In Japan, large capitalist corporations worked

closely with the state, maintained close cooperative relationships with each other, and instilled family-like loyalty in their workers with lifetime employment and "womb-to-tomb" health and welfare benefits.

Russia and Japan remained the most widely copied models for industrialization in the fifty years after World War II. Both countries emerged from widespread destruction during the war, the Soviet Union as a battered victor and Japan as vanquished pariah. Both had to construct entire cities, industries, even devastated regions from scratch. Both were far more successful at rebuilding their societies than anyone would have thought possible in 1945.

The Soviet Union lost 15 to 20 percent of its population and 20 to 25 percent of its capital assets during World War II. Its industrial production declined over 30 percent from 1940 to 1945. Yet, despite the end of U.S. wartime assistance and exclusion from world trade networks, Soviet economic growth increased 8 to 10 percent per year in the 1950s and 1960s. Soviet planners ignored consumer products and concentrated resources on heavy industry, research, and defense. This strategy paid off with the launching of the Soviet space satellite, Sputnik, in 1957. A light circling the nighttime sky told the world that the U.S.S.R. had beaten the United States to space. Even after the U.S. regained the lead with a landing on the moon in 1969, the Soviet scientific establishment, education system, and military remained global models.

Whether the Soviet economy prospered because of, or despite, centralized planning, from the 1950s to 1970s industrial production increased sevenfold. By the 1980s, however, the system was beginning to fall behind. A generation of workers who knew only sacrifice resented Soviet economic concentration on the military and heavy industry, especially as they became increasingly aware of the consumer economies of Western Europe and the United States. As U.S. President Ronald Reagan rocketed up the costs of military preparedness for both Americans and Russians in the 1980s, the Soviet economy buckled.

The economies of Eastern Europe rose and fell with that of the Soviet Union. The Soviets arrogantly treated Eastern European economies as their satellites. Nevertheless, under Soviet tutelage, many Eastern European societies completed a basic industrial revolution. Bulgaria, for example, increased manufacturing fivefold between 1950 and 1970. Like the Soviet economy, however, those of Eastern Europe declined after 1989 when they were forced to stand on their own before the global market.

In retrospect, these planned economies were not as successful as they appeared at the time. Planning was not democratic. Decisions were made at the top with little input or feedback from workers and citizens. Since all economic activity was to fall in step with the national plan, officials treated criticism as treason and punished independent thinkers with exile to work camps or death. At its best, planning required an enormous amount of information, accuracy, predictability, and compliance. It rewarded complacency and discouraged innovation. Even the propaganda of the Stalinist era praised the zeal of the dedicated Stakhanovite worker who always exceeded production quotas, while independent socialist intellectuals were sent to work mines in northern Siberia.

The Soviet system excelled in providing basic health care and a sound technical education to a wider percentage of the population than ever before, probably in any society in the world. The Soviet Union led the world in such measures as literacy, women doctors, trained engineers, low child mortality, and basic health care. But most of the women doctors were nurses, basic education was full of Marxist slogans and Soviet propaganda, professionals were poorly paid and subject to political tests, and corruption crippled the best intentions and noblest ideals. For a long time Soviet citizens accepted a trade-off: security, pride, and a rich cultural heritage in exchange for ever-watchful police and long lines for consumer staples.

But the 1980s brought pressures that the system could not bear. In response to the Soviet war in Afghanistan and an expanded U.S. military build up, Soviet military expenditures became more than the people were willing to accept. As Soviet industries began to compete on the world market, workers and managers realized that their products were inferior. At the same time an alternative appeared. Western film and television filled Soviet screens with supermarkets and shopping malls of consumer goods which were not even available at the end of the longest line or the most exclusive Dollars Only store in Moscow. "We pretend to work, and they pretend to pay us" was the joke of the last years. Eventually, in the wake of a debilitating war in Afghanistan, the Soviet people—soldiers and workers, but never citizens or consumers—refused to continue the pretense.

JAPAN INC.

Japan was the other industrialized nation to serve as a global model between 1945 and 1989. Like Russia, Japan had become industrialized between 1880 and 1940. Influenced by the example of the Soviet Union, Japan grew rapidly in the 1930s while much of the rest of the world fell into depression. And like the Soviet Union, Japan had to rebuild much of its industrial capacity after losing 25 percent of its wealth during the war. In addition to Hiroshima and Nagasaki, turned into a radioactive wasteland by the first, and so far only, use of nuclear weapons, and fire-bombed Tokyo, over sixty major urban centers had been heavily bombed by American planes.

It is simple to say that Japan chose capitalism for its rebuilding, while the Soviet Union chose communism. But Japanese capitalism had some features that looked more like Soviet communism than American or British capitalism. In Japan a close alliance of government officials, bankers, and private industrialists directed the economic revival. Japanese corporations were much larger than those that had led the industrialization of Britain or the United States. Japanese industrial firms, called *zaibatsu*, had huge concentrations of capital that invested in numerous industries and financial services, cooperating with each other to a degree that would have been illegal in the United States. The Japanese system relied heavily on controlling labor by guaranteeing lifetime employment and a vast socializing system that monopolized workers' time in return for treating them like members of a corporate family. Finally, Japanese industrialization concentrated on manufacturing products for export, which initially were not available to the average Japanese worker.

This Japanese system of capitalism also closely resembled the German system, which many Japanese studied and emulated at the end of the nineteenth century. Then in the 1930s and during World War II, this model of government economic management and labor cooperation grew deep roots under Japanese military government.

Japan Inc. succeeded after World War II by reviving wartime labor discipline and government control—thanks to the United States, the victorious occupying power which effectively governed Japan in the immediate postwar years. After a brief experiment with democratic reform, the U.S. Occupation Administration encouraged the Japanese to return to their prewar system of centralized industrial management. Increasingly preoccupied with the spread of communism, the United States worried more about aggressive labor unions and popular protest in Japan than about a return to wartime industrial management and consolidation.

Thus, what has been called the economic miracle of Japan Inc. after the war was actually a rebirth of a wartime system, sanctioned by the U.S. occupation. Familiar elements included lifetime employment and company-controlled labor unions in big firms, and governmental management of the economy by agencies like the Ministry of International Trade and Industry (MITI) and Economic Planning Agency. The Ministry of Finance and the Bank of Japan switched from war mobilization to planning the peacetime economy. Old companies like Toyota, Nissan, and Isuzu switched from army trucks to cars, Hitachi and Toshiba from military electronics to civilian appliances, and Nomura Securities sold stocks instead of war bonds.

Both the Japanese and Soviet economic booms between 1945 and 1989 relied on government economic planning and direction. Yet while the Soviet government exercised total control, the large *zaibatsu* also took part in running the Japanese economy. Japan was clearly more capitalistic, but to say that Japan was capitalist and the Soviet Union communist misses how much alike the two systems were.

Unlike Japan, however, the Soviet Union steered clear of foreign aid and global economics. Instead, it concentrated on building a strong national state. Soviets called it "socialism in one country." The U.S. government placed the Japanese on a path of growth through global engagement. One of the first acts of the American occupation force was to set the value of the Japanese yen at 360 to the dollar, a leap from 2.5 to the dollar before the war.[2] That meant that a Japanese-made doll that sold in the United States for a dollar before the war sold for less than a cent afterwards.

This was the beginning of a new model of economic development called a global export platform. The formula was for Japan to make money by exporting huge quantities of competitively priced products around the world. It began with items like inexpensive toys: "Made in Japan" became a mark of hastily assembled cheap material. In the 1950s and 1960s, Japanese factories exported imitations of U.S. and European consumer goods: radios, televisions, and household appliances. In the 1970s, the Japanese companies moved to larger, more expensive exports like automobiles, and graduated to quality production and technological innovation. As export income multiplied, Japanese corporations collected more dollars than they could wisely invest.

The decline of Japan Inc. after 1989 was financial, not technological. Throughout the 1990s and early years of the twenty-first century its industry invested heavily in technology and used far more robots and automated equipment than U.S. plants. Japanese companies invested more than their U.S. counterparts in research and development and won more patents for more new inventions. While the antiquated Soviet technology lay in shambles, Japanese factories were creating a twenty-first century standard for a new miracle age to come once the financial difficulties had been worked out.

Yet, the Japanese economy shrank between 1989 and the beginning of the next century. The Japanese stock market shriveled to a quarter of its 1989 value by 2002. Like the global Great Depression of the 1930s, the long depression in Japanese stock market values was a product of over-speculation in the previous decade. Prices paid for corporations and real estate soared into the stratosphere and created an inflationary bubble. Fed by the successes of Japanese exports, average Japanese citizens talked themselves into a buying mania for stock certificates and mutual funds in the 1980s. As often happens, the mania came on top of a market that was already inflated. In the Japanese case, a clubby culture of mutual back-scratching had already led corporations to buy each other's stock "permanently," without regard to its value. Banks entered bidding wars to loan the most money and bought the stock of their debtors at ever-inflated values.

By the end of the 1980s, Japanese banks were the largest in the world, a majority of the global top ten. In terms of real estate, the land around the imperial palace in Tokyo was said to be worth more than the entire state of California. Banks loaned money for home mortgages at such high rates that they tied up the finances of the borrowers' grandchildren. Paper billionaires sprinkled gold flakes on their sushi; and Japanese investors purchased the most expensive real estate and corporations in the world. In at least one case, a multibillion dollar deal almost fell through because the Japanese buyer insisted on paying a record-setting price that was more than the seller wanted.

Like previous financial bubbles, the speculative excesses of the 1980s left a mountain of debt on Japanese bank and corporate balance sheets. But the success of the Japanese model of economic growth through the cheap labor of a global export platform was not lost on Taiwan and Korea. These "Asian Tigers" followed the Japanese script to the letter: U.S. Cold War and military subsidies, heavy public investment in science, technology, and education combined with a disciplined work force; quality production of mass consumer goods, gradually moving up the ladder of cost and profitable return on investment. By 1997, as these Asian Tigers were on the brink of their own financial speculative crisis, Korea alone had five automobile companies, each able and eager to manufacture for a global market.

Despite their financial setbacks, Japan, Taiwan, and Korea enjoyed the most successful industrial growth the world had seen since the initial industrial revolution propelled Britain, Western Europe, and North America to global prominence over a hundred years before. But by tapping into a global market, these Asian industrial powerhouses were adding an enormous amount of productivity, at greatly reduced labor prices. If a single Korea could supply the world with all the cars it needed, what would happen if China, with a billion people, attempted to do the same?

CHINESE COMMUNISM:
ONE STEP FORWARD; ONE STEP BACKWARD

American mothers in the 1950s told their children: "Eat everything on your plate. There are people starving in China." In fact, the communist forces that took control of China in 1949 inherited a country that had been bled and starved for decades by Chinese warlords and occupying Japanese troops. In their first years of rule, the Chinese communists proved to be effective and honest administrators. They broke up the large agricultural estates of wealthy landlords and distributed the land to groups of peasants organized in communes.

Borrowing from the Soviet model, the Chinese communists passed a series of five-year plans which concentrated government investment in heavy industry. Under the first plan, for the period 1953–1957, national income grew almost 9 percent a year. Living standards improved as well. Life expectancy increased from a wartime low of 36 in 1950 to 57 by 1957, and the attendance of children in primary school doubled from 25 to 50 percent. Urban wages grew by a third, and the incomes of peasant farmers increased by a fifth.[3]

As these rising Chinese wages suggest, the Soviet model of industrialization benefited urban workers more than rural peasants. The party of the peasantry, the Chinese Communist Party, and its chairman, Mao Zedong, wanted to end this income gap, so in 1958, they introduced an economic policy centered on the Chinese peasantry. It was called the Great Leap Forward, and it turned out to be a tragic fall backward.

The Great Leap Forward was a 180-degree turn away from the first Stalinist five-year plan. Instead of concentrating capital in a few coastal cities and massive factories, Mao encouraged the creation and economic development of rural communes and agricultural cooperatives. He urged each of these communes to develop its own industry: small steel mills, power supplies, and machine tool plants.

The Great Leap Forward stumbled badly. Mao put his faith in revolutionary zeal rather than expertise, in the peasants rather than the intellectuals and bureaucrats. Fervent party officials responded to his call for a quantum leap in food production with hopes and promises. Quotas were inflated beyond reason or reality. Despite bad weather and a poor harvest, Mao chose to believe the inflated estimates of party yes-men. Their wishful thinking enabled Mao to take more grain than usual to feed city workers and meet scheduled debt payments to the Soviets. But workers could not be fed on false figures. Even when hunger and malnutrition became endemic in the countryside, Mao refused to believe that the Leap had failed. Redoubling his faith the next year, he redoubled the suffering. Millions died of starvation and malnutrition. The new agricultural communes turned out to be equally unprepared for industrialization. Barnyard steel furnaces were fed with needed pots and pans, and the resulting "steel" often proved unusable.

Throughout the 1960s, Mao continued to favor those who were "red" rather than "expert." He continued to struggle against opponents in the Communist Party whom he called "capitalist roaders." In the 1960s, Mao mobilized a generation of students against their teachers, children against their parents, and rural peasants against the city officials in the violent upheaval known as the Great Proletarian Cultural Revolution. By the time he died in 1976, there had been some successes as well as dramatic failures. Mao's communist government had reversed age-old inequalities between rich and poor, peasants and rulers, city and country. It had freed peasants and women from feudal and family ties so they could be workers and soldiers. But the costs had been heavy; China had still not industrialized, and scars left by Mao's experiments in constant revolution disfigured a generation.

CHINA SINCE MAO ZEDONG

In 1978, two years after the death of Chairman Mao, the Chinese Communist Party reversed course again. This time its watchwords were neither "red" nor "expert," but getting "rich," trying whatever "works," and retaining "power." While keeping a firm hold on the army, bureaucracy, and industrial policy, the Communist Party began to encourage private investment. First Chinese workers and investors, and then foreign investors, were allowed to buy stock in Chinese companies, even those owned by the state. Foreign corporations were allowed to set up factories in special export zones that included entire new cities near traditional shipping centers like the Pearl River Delta area of Hong Kong and Guangzhou (Canton) and the Yangtze River Delta area near Shanghai.

Millions of young workers were drawn to these new cities where they lived in dormitory housing, surrounded by barbed wire fences, and were paid about a twentieth of the wages in Europe and Japan. In 1978, Shenzhen, midway between Hong Kong and Guangzhou, was a sleepy fishing village of 25,000. By the year 2000, it contained over a million workers. In the same period, Chinese export earnings had increased fiftyfold. While much of the new wealth was funneled back to companies in Japan and Taiwan and worker incomes were only high by rural Chinese standards, there arose a new middle class of Chinese who could afford automobiles, personal travel, even second homes. The return of Hong Kong to Chinese jurisdiction in 1997 brought an additional first-world city, with its banks, merchant houses, capital resources, and entrepreneurs. By 2002 China replaced Mexico as capital's global favorite source of cheap labor, Japanese companies were using Chinese middle-class engineers and designers as they had previously used Chinese assembly workers, and Chinese companies were transferring production of some heavy goods like refrigerators to factories in the United States and Europe.

THE UNITED STATES AND WESTERN EUROPE

Russia, Japan, and China were playing catch-up in the decades after World War II. The economies that they were trying to catch up *to* were those of the United States and Western Europe, the countries that led the first industrial revolution and that benefited enormously from their near-monopoly in global trade in the years immediately after World War II. The years between 1946 and 1973 were particularly prosperous for the United States, which dominated the world economy.

It was an era of harmony between capital and labor. The interests of large corporations seemed to coincide with those of many Americans. Charles E. Wilson, secretary of defense in the Eisenhower administration, could assume that "what was good for the country was good for General Motors and vice-versa." U.S. corporations created tens of millions of well-paying jobs with health care benefits and pensions. A generation of American workers who could afford their own homes and two cars came to think of themselves as middle class.

The American post–World War II economy did not include everyone equally. The legal segregation of whites and blacks did not end until 1954, and the civil rights legislation that outlawed institutional discrimination did not pass Congress until the late 1960s. But the postwar economic boom drew blacks from the South to cities like Detroit, Chicago, and New York where there were jobs that might support a family and a home. Average African-American family income was half that of whites in 1947, but it climbed 131 percent from 1947 to 1973, a slightly higher rate than the white family increase of 105 percent.[4] The percentage of African-Americans in the middle class climbed from 5 percent in 1960 to 25 percent by the 1980s.

The wave of economic growth of the 1950s and 1960s created a shared sense of prosperity and achievement. Incomes were more equal than before or since. The richest executive received 125 times the income of the average worker, compared to 25,000 times today. In 1952, the tax rate for the wealthiest Americans was 92 percent of income. The 1950s was also a golden age of corporate citizenship. Companies operating in the United States paid 23 percent of all federal income taxes. By 1991 their contribution had declined to 9.2 percent.

THE WELFARE STATE

In Europe and America the fifties and sixties was the great age of the welfare state. Social welfare legislation—disability, sickness, and old age insurance—had originated in Germany in the 1880s, a period in which socialist parties were growing rapidly, especially among industrial workers. But it was the conservative Otto von Bismarck (German Chancellor 1862–1890) who pushed the government to guarantee social welfare, partly to undercut the appeal of German socialist parties. In the United States, the Great Depression of the 1930s posed such a threat to capitalism-as-usual that many conservatives supported President Franklin D. Roosevelt's introduction of the American version, Social Security.

After 1945, European socialist and labor parties extended social welfare beyond the social security and unemployment insurance. European governments added socialized medicine: free medical and hospital care to all citizens. Even at premier educational institutions, a college education was also free but required admissions tests. Most European governments invested extensively in public housing, public transportation, urban renewal, and the arts, including museums, concert halls, and symphony orchestras. European socialists also limited the prerogatives of corporations. A German policy of "co-determination" insured workers' representatives on corporate boards. German courts upheld the principle that people or corporations who owned property had certain responsibilities, making it illegal, for instance, to buy patents or copyrights in order to suppress them.

Scandinavian countries, led by Sweden, created a model of social welfare far more extensive than that of other European welfare states, with "cradle to the grave" benefits fully paid by the government through taxes. These included all medicines, doctors, and hospital expenses, all educational expenses through college, and subsidized housing, long vacations, parental leaves, and job relief and retraining opportunities.

The narrower United States model included modest old age, disability, and unemployment benefits. There was no socialized medicine. College education was more widely available in the United States than in Europe, though very few colleges were free. Some federal funds aided public housing, but public transportation, inner cities, and cultural resources were virtually ignored. Nevertheless, even the limited funding for social welfare in the United States was a testament to the unity of a nation: capitalists and workers, rich and poor, fortunate and not.

Two events after 1973 ended the heyday of Western prosperity and the welfare state. First, the countries, mainly in Western Europe and the United States, that most benefited from postwar prosperity suddenly had to share the world economy. New competitive capitalist industrialized states like Japan, Korea, and Taiwan vastly increased their global industrial capacity and put intense pressure on the older industrial powers. Second, the victory of capitalism over the Soviet Union after 1989 eliminated the need for conservative Western governments to provide social welfare to fight socialism. The competition of the newly industrialized countries of the Pacific Rim made the Western welfare state too expensive, and the Western defeat of communism made it unnecessary.

THE WEST AND THE REST

Some people argue that Europe and the United States prospered because they controlled the governments and economies of much of the rest of the world, at least since the 1880s. Western colonialism ended after World War II, but Western governments and corporations continued to exert a lot of influence on the newly independent countries of Africa and Asia. Most of Africa won political independence in the late 1950s and early 1960s. Yet the citizens of such former French colonies as Ivory Coast, Senegal, Mali, Cameroon, Gabon, and the Congo were expected to eat French bread and drive Renaults and Peugeots on Michelin tires, and they did, those who could afford to. Most Africans in newly independent countries worked on the same plantations or mines, performed menial jobs for the same white families, or their new African bosses. As in colonial days, African entrepreneurs existed, but most fit into a system that supplied raw materials and tropical foods inexpensively to the world market. The miners of gold and diamonds, like the farmers of peanuts or coffee, received very little for their labor. Profits went to the lavish lifestyles of owners, often Europeans, who lived comfortably in Africa or Europe, and to corporate headquarters in Paris, London, and New York. As a result, most agricultural and resource-producing economies did not grow with those of the West between 1946 and 1973.

THE OIL CARTEL AND SLICK

Raw materials are usually plentiful and cheap. Manufactures are expensive—that is where the money is made. Sometimes raw material producers were able to organize to curtail production and jack up the price. For generations the great diamond companies of South Africa, for instance, limited the supply of diamonds to support high prices, but their impact was limited.

By the 1970s, however, one raw material oiled the entire global economy, and it was highly concentrated in certain areas of the world. Some Middle Eastern governments gradually banded together and organized a cartel, a sort of union of oil-producing states. By the early 1970s, this cartel could practically prevent any single country from producing too much oil and drastically lowering prices.

In 1973 the oil cartel raised the price of oil, which had remained at roughly $10 a barrel since the 1950s, to $30 a barrel almost overnight and then in 1979–1981 to $50 a barrel. The increased cost filtered through the economy of Western industrial countries, raising the cost of transportation as well as the prices of all manufacturing processes that used oil and gas.

GLOBAL INDUSTRIAL COMPETITION

Still reeling from the new power of the oil cartel, U.S. manufacturers found the world of industrial producers had suddenly become more crowded. Smaller and more fuel-efficient Japanese cars, practically unknown on North American roads in 1970, gained increased popularity after 1973. U.S. automakers and unions exerted pressure in the United States against foreign imports. In response, Japanese companies started to hire American workers to produce cars in the United States. But the enormous excess productive capacity that Japanese automakers signaled did not begin to abate until auto companies began to merge, creating large multi-national corporations. At the same time, auto manufacturers in Korea and Taiwan followed the Japanese example, increasing the level of international competition.

While these new industrialized countries came on line, other countries flexed their economic muscles in different ways. Some, like India and Brazil, tried to build national industries by placing high tariffs on foreign imports. Some, like Indonesia, auctioned the rights to manufacture a projected national auto to the highest foreign bidder. China allowed foreign manufacturers to set up factories in China at the expense of high royalty payments and, unofficially, the chance for Chinese engineers to copy new technologies and patented secrets and set up Chinese companies. The intense international competition made workers accept lower wages, companies hunt for foreign workers, and businesspeople think less patriotically. "The United States does not have an automatic call on our resources," a senior executive of the Colgate Palmolive Company explained in 1991. "There is no mind-set that puts this country first."[5] "To be in business," said the head of a Canadian auto parts manufacturer that had shifted operations to Mexico, "your first mandate is to make money, and money has no heart, soul, conscience, [or] homeland."[6]

FREE MARKET FALLOUT
FROM THE DEFEAT OF COMMUNISM

Global competition after 1973 undermined the privileged position of European and American corporations and their workers. The welfare state took a bit longer to fall. Conservative critics since the 1930s targeted such measures as the progressive income tax (with higher tax rates for the wealthy than for the poor), mandated payroll deductions to fund worker's compensation, disability, and social security insurance, and some aspects of government regulation. In the difficult economic times after 1973, however, conservative interest groups successfully identified welfare in the public mind with poor relief (even though far more government assistance had always gone to the wealthy and to corporations). Well-funded interest groups played on middle-class and working-class anxieties about money in order to reduce the taxes of the wealthy. Their attack on "welfare cheats" was also racial coding, successfully exploiting the racial rift in the working class in hard times. This anti-welfare theme was combined with a general attack on the effectiveness and efficiency of government, which achieved widespread success with the elections of Margaret Thatcher as British prime minister in 1979 and of Ronald Reagan as president of the United States in 1980.

But conservative opponents found their greatest success with the defeat of the Soviet Union. When the Soviet Union cracked under the combined weight of Reagan's arms buildup and its own Vietnam in Afghanistan, vast new regions of the world opened to Western markets. First Poland, East Germany, and the former Soviet satellites, then Russia and the other former Soviet republics gave up communist central planning, sold national industries to private investors, and opened for business. A Wild West psychology of fast profit drove a new class of profiteers, often former government officials, disparaged by many as the Russian Mafia. Not only could the Sonys, McDonald's, Boeings, and Disneys of the world penetrate these newly created markets, but the Microsofts and Mitsubishis could also buy the talents of unemployed computer scientists and mathematicians for a song, benefiting from the considerable communist investment in education.

The end of communism meant much more than new markets, however. Since communism and socialism were equivalent in the minds of many, the end of communism meant the end of any reasonable alternative to capitalism. Any defense of government involvement in the economy seemed addlebrained. The way was clear for the public acceptance of supply and demand, markets, business models, and private profit as universal solutions for all problems.

U.S. corporations took advantage of their new prestige by discarding the social contract with labor that had formed the core of the welfare state. With the new free-market dogma to back them, corporations dropped pension, health care, and job guarantees. The U.S. government under Republican and Democratic administrations greatly reduced the taxes on the wealthy and social spending for the poor, including the abolition of federal welfare. Britain sold off national industries and drastically reduced funding for education and health. Even Sweden, after an economic downturn and conservative party victory, lowered taxes and drastically reduced welfare benefits. By the end of the 1990s, corporations and governments elsewhere in Europe and Japan learned to imitate the new system in order to remain competitive.

Markets were also supposed to solve international problems. Conservatives, who wanted to reduce government foreign aid, argued that poor countries would benefit more from increased foreign trade than from aid. American leaders of both political parties sought to extend free trade agreements with numerous countries: for example, the NAFTA (North American Free Trade Agreement) with Mexico and Canada and "favored nation" trade with China. For a while it worked. Between 1990 and 1997, private capital investment in developing economies far surpassed earlier transfers of foreign aid. But the enormous flows of private capital were erratic. Foreign investors chose flavor-of-the-month stock markets—Mexico one month, Malaysia the next—only to let them crash and become international pariahs when the mood soured. The interests of international financiers were rarely as constant as the interests of those who lived in the country.

After an Asian financial crisis in 1997, international investment fell drastically. By 2001, it had plummeted to half the 1997 level. Globalization of capital seemed less attractive to many who had previously supported it. Latin American growth slowed from a yearly average rate of 5.5 percent between 1950 and 1980 to 3.2 percent in the 1990s.[7] By 2002, according to the *New York Times*, "The vast majority of people living in Africa, Latin America, Central Asia, and the Middle East are no better off today than they were in 1989, when the fall of the Berlin Wall allowed capitalism to spread worldwide at a rapid rate."[8]

THE NEW CAPITALISM AND THE TELECOMMUNICATIONS REVOLUTION

What impact did the new, unrestrained capitalism of the 1990s have on industrial or technological development in the United States? The great success story of the 1990s was called the telecommunications revolution. But if this was a revolution, its elements were hardly new. The telephone was invented in 1876. Television came out of scientific laboratories in the 1930s, and into homes by the 1950s.

Nor was the computer revolution entirely capitalist. The predecessors of computers—code-breaking and radar—came from government contracts during World War I and World War II. The computer chip was a product of rocket research during World War II. Such elements as the computer mouse, the light pen, the video terminal, and the drawing tablet evolved under Pentagon contracts during the Cold War years. Artificial intelligence was heavily funded by the Defense Department, and the Atomic Energy Commission funded projects that led to the creation of database software. The Internet was developed by the Pentagon as a communications network that would survive a nuclear war. While corporations participated as the recipients of many of these contracts, it would be difficult to attribute any of these innovations to unbridled capitalism. "Every brilliant, important, farsighted Internet development came either from government agencies or universities," one entrepreneur concluded.[9] To the argument that these inventions would have come anyway, one historian of computers, Kenneth Flamm, recalled how U.S. military planners tried to convince businesses of the potential profits in computers but failed. As a consequence, the Defense Department had to finance their early development.[10] More than half of IBM's research and development budget in the 1950s and 1960s came from government contracts.

Private companies were effective in the 1980s and 1990s in building upon and commercializing these innovations in communications technology. Some became global powerhouses in barely twenty years: Microsoft, Intel, and the numerous makers of computer software, Internet browsers, and peripherals; Apple, Compaq, Dell, and the other computer makers; and a vast array of new companies created to do business on the World Wide Web. The entrepreneurial roots of some of these corporations have become part of the common folklore of modern capitalism. We hear of multibillion dollar computer makers who began in somebody's garage, nerds and mediocre students who quit school to realize a dream and became billionaires before they were forty. Between 1965 and 2000 the almost room-sized mainframe was transformed into the minicomputer that became the desktop PC and laptop computer. A child inherited the computing power of an entire corporation a generation earlier. Computer memory doubled every eighteen months. As in earlier stages of industrial capitalism (cotton textiles in the early nineteenth century, automobiles in the twentieth) the profits were enormous even as increasing competition, the proliferation of companies and manufacturing capacity, and technological innovation drove down the prices of the finished products. A single transistor, the basic ingredient of the computer chip, sold for $70 in 1965. By 1997 one could buy a million for less than a cent.[11] The period since 1980 has witnessed enormous entrepreneurial vitality, perhaps especially in the United States, where capitalism has been given freest rein. But one might wonder how much of this revolution would have occurred without tax-supported government programs.

Much of the wealth generated in the bull market from 1982 to 2000 bore no relation to industrial development. Private investors often chased short-term profits rather than technological innovation, especially those that required a long-term horizon. Vaulting stock prices attracted capital, energy, brains, and resources into further financial speculation rather than industrial production. Capitalism is an incredibly dynamic economic system. But it destroys as well as creates, its goal is making money rather than things, and it rewards wealth before need.

MARKETS AND TECHNOLOGY

We return to our opening question: How can markets provide the technological aids and comforts we desire? Assuming for the moment that our technology does not unduly strain our environment or ourselves (issues we will explore in succeeding chapters), is the free-market system the best way of attaining our technological goals?

Our brief survey suggests the answer is "yes" and "no." The case of Russia and Japan reminds us that non-market, government and corporate planning quite effectively created an industrial society and, in the case of Japan, a highly innovative technological system. Soviet planning was successful in heavy industry, especially its ability to industrialize quickly and in isolation. Nevertheless, many of the products of Soviet heavy industry were poorly made, compared to those of the capitalist countries. Post-Soviet steel mills have to be rebuilt from scratch. Russian aircraft are widely recognized as inferior to American. For many products of Russian heavy industry, the less said, the better. And yet, in certain areas—aerospace, at least—Soviet technology challenged that of the United States.

Did the planned economy doom Soviet technology? If we think so, we must explain the obvious success of planning in Japan, Korea, and Taiwan, or, for that matter, the United States military and governmental planning, from the control of the money supply by the Federal Reserve Bank to the federal budget. Clearly, a competitive market system that places risk and reward on the shoulders of individuals is likely to create incentives, perhaps even further innovation. But the periodic speculative booms of market systems remind us that financial speculation rewards money-making rather than technological innovation. Investors in Japan in the 1980s and the United States in the 1990s plowed money into greenbacks rather than blueprints; and the "best and brightest" were drawn to trading paper more than building things.

Even in the best of times, the spread of industrialization by global markets intensifies conflicts between enormous productive capacity and restricted consumption. Winner-take-all global markets attract enormous industrial capacity. Increasingly cheaper laborers and more automated factories produce unlimited quantities. But poorly paid worker and robots cannot purchase a fraction of what they produce.

Perhaps neither planning nor markets work as stand-alone solutions. All modern capitalist countries benefit from government involvement in the economy in myriad ways: Central banks, bankruptcy courts, patent bureaus, police patrols, contract law, and military contracts, to name but a few. And planning is not inherently despotic. Is democratic planning possible? Certainly Japanese planning was more democratic than Soviet. Would representative governments make more democratic decisions than the marketplace? Free markets and democratic governments deliver different models of what the people want. Government planners must recognize the peoples' needs as well as their wants, and in that distinction there is abundant room for abuse as well as foresight. Markets allow people to vote their wants at the marketplace, but by a system of one dollar, one vote—not one person, one vote.

Inevitably our future will require both democratic governments and enlightened markets. The extent to which we demand one or the other may depend on the degree to which we see ourselves as shareholders or citizens.

FOR FURTHER READING

Science and Technology in World History by James E. McClellan III and Harold Dorn is an excellent global history of technology. Arnold Pacey's *Technology in World Civilization* is the best overall introduction to the subject of technology over the last thousand years. Peter N. Stearns's *The Industrial Revolution in History* is a global comparative history. For approaches that make more of the distinction between capitalism and industrialization see Tom Kemp's *Industrialization in the Non-Western World* on particular countries and his *Historical Patterns of Industrialization* on topical issues.

On the debate over the importance of government and market capitalism in post-1945 industrialization there is a growing literature. Alice Amsden, *The Rise of "The Rest": Challenges to the West from Late-Industrializing Economies*, argues for the importance of the "developmental state" in successful cases. Similarly, Joseph E.

Stiglitz, a former chief economist of the World Bank, argues the limitations of free-market models and the importance of education and governmental regulation in *The Rebel Within*. The orthodox free-market argument is made by William Easterly, another World Bank economist, in *The Elusive Quest for Growth*.

Eric Hobsbawm's *The Age of Extremes: A History of the World, 1914–1991* sees 1950–1973 as a global "golden age" that belonged to the industrial capitalist countries. Patrick Carl O'Brien in "Intercontinental Trade and the Development of the Third World since the Industrial Revolution," *Journal of World History* 8:1 (spring 1997), shows that increases in world trade have vastly aided the economic development of poorer countries even though the gap between rich and poor economies has widened.

Two recent general economic histories make interesting reading on the subject of price movements. In *The Great Wave: Price Revolutions and the Rhythm of History*, David Hackett Fischer argues that much of history can be understood as the consequence of accelerating long-term price inflations (most recently after 1900), which are followed by collapse and eventual stability. By contrast, William Greider argues in *One World, Ready or Not: The Manic Logic of Global Capitalism* that the long-term effect of cutthroat competition in the global market is toward lower wages, profits, and prices (i.e., deflation).

Greider's book is part of an almost mainstream revival of neo-Marxist critiques of capitalism in the last few years. Among other interesting titles are Doug Henwood's *Wall Street: How It Works and for Whom*. For a thoughtful critique of market populism in American culture see Thomas Frank's *One Market Under God: Extreme Capitalism, Market Populism, and the End of Economic Democracy*. On very recent history see Robert Brenner's *The Boom and the Bubble*.

On the Soviet Union and Russia, J.P. Nettl's *The Soviet Achievement* is a classic account. Edward A. Hewett's *Reforming the Soviet Economy* looks at the strengths and weaknesses of the Soviet economy from the standpoint of the end of the Soviet era. For introductions to China, see John King Fairbank's *The Great Chinese Revolution 1800–1985* and Jonathan D. Spence's *In Search For Modern China*. For a comparison of Russia and China, see *Transforming Russia and China* by William G. Rosenberg and Marilyn B. Young. For a more recent comparison see Robert Strayer's *The Communist Experiment: Comparing the Soviet Union and China*.

On Japan, Patrick Smith's *Japan: A Reinterpretation* and John Dower's earlier essay "The Useful War" in his *Japan in War and Peace* argue for the wartime roots of postwar Japanese economic and social policy. By contrast, Thomas Carlyle Smith argues for the *Native Sources of Japanese Industrialization*. The standard introduction is Kunio Yoshihara, *Japanese Economic Development*.

The American Century by Donald W. White is an excellent history of the U.S. and Americans' sense of their importance in the world. On the history of oil and its global impact, there is no better place to start than *The Prize* by Daniel H. Yergin.

For a skeptical view of the computer or communications revolution see *Trapped in the Net: The Unanticipated Consequences of Computerization* by Gene I. Rochlin. Daniel Sichel's *The Computer Revolution: An Economic Perspective* questions the notion that computers have increased productivity. Kenneth Flamm's earlier historical overview, *Creating the Computer* details the U.S. government role. More recently, Charles H. Ferguson's *High Stakes, No Prisoners: A Winner's Tale of Greed and Glory in the Internet Wars* chronicles government creation and commercialization of the Internet. Michael Lewis's *The New New Thing: A Silicon Valley Story* details the initiatives of one important entrepreneur.

NOTES

1. The figures from Business Week Online, "Executive Pay, Up, Up, and Away" (April 19, 1999) are as follows: In 1958, the highest-paid executive was Arthur B. Homer, President, Bethlehem Steel, who received $511,249. Average worker pay was $3,904. In 1998 the highest-paid executive was Michael Eisner, CEO, Walt Disney, who received $575.6 million. Average worker pay was $22,976.

2. "We wanted the Japanese to be able to export," explained Tristan E. Beplat, an American financial affairs officer for the U.S. occupation forces. "We wanted them on our side politically, and figured that 90 percent of Japanese exports could sell at a 300 exchange rate, even though some were profitable at 200." Quoted by Kenneth N. Gilpin in "Tristan E. Beplat, 85, Banker Who Aided Japan After War," *New York Times*, December 3, 1997, obit.

3. John King Fairbank, *The Great Chinese Revolution 1800–1985* (New York: Harper & Row, 1987), p. 285.

4. In the next twenty years, 1973–93, African-American median family income (adjusted for inflation) actually declined 3 percent while that of whites rose 2 percent. See chart in *Left Business Observer* #69 (9 September 1995), p. 1.

5. *The New York Times*, 1991 (quoted in Robert Reich, *The Work of Nations* [New York: Alfred A. Knopf, 1991], p. 141).

6. Quoted in Suzanne Bilello, "Free Trade Pact Stirs Emotions," *New York Newsday* 7 August, 1992; cited in Henwood, *Wall Street: How It Works and for Whom* (London: Verso, 1997), p. 113.

7. Larry Rohter, "A Vicious Circle: Failures and Instability," *The New York Times*, April 13, 2002, p. A9.

8. Joseph Kahn, "Losing Faith: Globalization Proves Disappointing," *The New York Times*, March 21, 2002, p. A8.

9. Charles H. Ferguson, *High Stakes, No Prisoners: A Winner's Tale of Greed and Glory in the Internet Wars* (New York: Times Books, 1999).

10. Kenneth Flamm, *Creating the Computer* (Brookings Institute, 1988).

11. John Markoff, "Innovation to Double Chip Power May Cut Life Span of Computers," *The New York Times*, Sept. 17, 1997, p. 1.

Ecology and Resources

Economics and Technology

- Global warming from greenhouse gases (so called because they trap solar radiation like the glass roof of a greenhouse) has increased with mounting use of fossil fuels, making the earth warmer than it has been since the fourteenth century. The United States is responsible for a fourth of the world's emissions of greenhouse gases. Of the top five nations in carbon dioxide emissions, the United States is first with more than the combined total of the next four, China, Russia, Japan, and India.

- Melting glaciers are raising ocean water levels, threatening low-lying cities and settlements. Island nations like Tuvalu, home to 10,000 people in the South Pacific, could vanish within 50 years because of rising sea levels. In a hundred years, flood waters may displace 100 million coastal inhabitants. The United Nations estimates that global warming presently costs the world $300 billion a year.[1]

- The atmosphere's protective shield of ozone has been punctured above Antarctica, Chile, and Australia. The ozone shield over North America shrank 10 percent from 1960 to 1995. Increasing levels of ultraviolet radiation over the last twenty-five years already account for one to two million additional cases of skin cancer and ten to twenty thousand early deaths. The cause is the release of manufactured aerosol gases like freon into the atmosphere.

• As a result of above-ground nuclear testing between 1951 and 1963, 200 each by the United States and the Soviet Union, higher radiation levels are likely to cause the cancer deaths of 11,000 people in the United States alone.[2]

• The World Bank reports that three hundred million people today are suffering from a lack of water, a problem that will confront three billion people in another twenty-five years.

Is Nature on life support? Have we lost our balance? What can we do to bring back the green?

A GREEN DREAM

When Lewis Mumford wrote his classic *Technics and Civilization* in the 1930s he believed the world was entering a new age of ecological well-being based on electric power. Mumford believed that electricity would usher in a third age of modern technology. The first age was the Age of Water, Wind, and Wood. Mumford's example was the Europe and America of the seventeenth and eighteenth century, a world driven by water- and windmills, with abundant forests for wood buildings. It was a clean and natural world, Mumford said, evoking the image of Dutch tulips, silent sailing clipper ships, and clean skies. Each additional windmill and watermill added power without polluting the environment or diminishing the wind and water that remained. Wood would always be available as long as people continued to plant trees. Then, according to Mumford, the industrial revolution of the nineteenth century, an Age of Coal, Iron, and Oil, darkened the skies with soot, filled the rivers with sludge, and robbed the earth's treasury.

As sources of energy, fossil fuels like coal and oil failed on two counts. Fossil fuels represented millions of years of the sun's energy, stored in the earth. A human inheritance for all time, its extravagant use in a few generations was a selfish choice: wasteful and unsustainable. "Mankind behaved like a drunken heir on a spree,"[3] Mumford wrote.

But the greedy consumption of the earth's stored energy was compounded by a second failing of fossil fuels: the release of eons of the earth's carbon into the atmosphere, polluting the air and warming the planet. In the short term, the industrial revolution of coal and oil, iron and steel, steam and railroads, produced ugly and dirty cities. Charles Dickens called it Coketown: "It was a town of machinery and tall chimneys, out of which interminable serpents of smoke trailed themselves forever and ever, and never got uncoiled. . . ."[4] Mumford called it a civilization in mourning: "the black boots, the black stove-pipe hat, the black cooking pots and pans and stoves."[5] But cities and rivers could be cleaned. The long-term impact of coal and oil was more serious—warming climate, melting glaciers, and rising oceans.

Nevertheless, Mumford saw a new age dawning. Electricity was a clean burning and non-polluting source of energy. Not only did electric light bulbs burn without the smoke of gaslight, electricity could be generated, transmitted, and stored cleanly and efficiently. Electric generators could be based on watermills, windmills, solar power, even new forms of geothermal energy that came from different temperatures in the earth. An advantage of these sources was their size. They could be scattered about, serving local and regional needs, unlike coal and oil, which concentrated resources in a central location—the Mesabi range of Minnesota for coal, northern Alaska or the Gulf of Mexico for oil, for instance. The Age of Electricity could end the horrible historical detour of industrial "carboniferous capitalism," according to Mumford. It could return the earth to the ecological balance of the Age of Water, Wind, and Wood. Nature might be healed.

Mumford's crystal ball was evidently a bit cloudy. For most of the twentieth century, electric power was produced and distributed on the massive scale of the industrial revolution. Further, coal and other fossil fuels, not water or wind power, generated electricity. Only recently have the large electric utilities allowed small-scale generators to contribute to their larger grids. And only recently have wind and solar power generators been taken seriously as alternate sources of power. Mumford may have been right about the possibility, but he did not foresee what actually happened.

DAMMED IF YOU DO

Why did the Green Dream of the 1930s end in a rude awakening after the Second World War? Let us begin with the dream of clean hydroelectricity, or water-generated electric power. Mumford imagined a new age of water wheels (perhaps like recent aerodynamic windmills) producing electricity. Instead, most twentieth-century electric power was generated by huge centralized plants, often fueled by high-carbon, smoke-spewing coal or oil. But even when cleaner water power generated electricity, it was usually in the form of gigantic dams that became the rage in the 1930s and after. In the decade when Mumford contemplated a future of wind and water wheels, President Franklin D. Roosevelt ordered a different brave new world of electrification. The model was Hoover Dam, a huge ice cream cone of a structure on the Colorado River, that practically created farming and dense settlement in Nevada and southern California. "Pridefully, man acclaims his conquest of nature," FDR's Interior secretary, Harold Ickes, declared at the dedication of the dam in 1935. When it was completed, Hoover Dam was the largest source of electricity on the planet. It soon became a model for water management and electrification everywhere. As early as 1942 Hoover was dwarfed by the Grand Coulee Dam on the Columbia River in Washington State.

The United States was not alone in seeking giant sources of electrical power. V.I. Lenin, the architect of the Soviet Revolution, declared that socialism equals Soviets plus electricity. In the 1930s, the United States helped the Soviet Union build a large dam on the Dnepr River. Others quickly followed. Today, the world's highest dam is in Tajikistan, formerly one of the central Asian Soviet Republics. The dam with the greatest hydroelectric capacity is in Russia, followed by the

Jawaharlal Nehru (1889–1964), first president of India, and Muhammad Ali Jinnah (1876–1948), "founder of Pakistan" (on the right), before partition.

Itaipu on the Parana river between Brazil and Paraguay. Big dam projects appeal to governments of developing countries as a sign of progress and modernity. India's first president, Jawaharlal Nehru, described dams as the "temples of modern India." His proposal in the 1950s for a huge dam on the Narmada River is still a government priority despite increasing protests by environmentalists and the withdrawal of the World Bank from the project in 1993. Mao Zedong was unable to dam the Yangtze river in his lifetime, but it is possibly his only project that the current Chinese government is carrying out, despite the protests of some of the million people who will have to be relocated.

Globally, dams have become more popular than airports. The planet currently accommodates 40,000 large dams (over four stories high) and 800,000 smaller ones. In forming reservoirs these dams have shifted so much weight that geophysicists believe they have slightly altered the speed of the earth's rotation, the tilt of its axis, and the shape of its gravitational field.[6]

DAMNED IF YOU DON'T

The current debate over the Narmada River dams in India underscores the complexity of the issue. Even opponents of the dams point out that 80 percent of the rural population of India has no electricity. For many of the world's inhabitants, water is becoming a precious commodity. Dams can provide desperately needed water as well as electric power. Many world leaders share Joseph Stalin's belief that "water that gets to the sea is wasted water."

Indian peasants living in the planned flooded reservoir on the Narmada River protested the disruption of their lives. But the problem is much deeper—and shallower. Eventually dams cease to work. Dams trap silt and salt deposits in the reservoir of water that the dam creates. While the salt makes the water brackish and kills fish the silt raises the water level to the lip of the dam, making it useless except as an expensive waterfall. Long before that happens, however, the reduced water meanders downstream too slowly to deposit new soil and clean out the salts. Once swift and powerful rivers—the Colorado, the Nile, and the Yellow River of China—now only occasionally reach the sea. The formerly rich alluvial lands of these deltas, replenished by silt deposits carried in raging rivers, now are trapped by dams, leaving the delta to gradually erode, become brackish with salt water, and eventually disappear.

Yet the mystique of dams as the answer to modern needs remains unquestioned, even among those who know better. I recently met an Egyptian who was driving a taxi in New York because he was losing his farm on the Nile Delta to soil erosion. When I suggested that the problem was the Aswan Dam, he replied that he knew that, "but the country needs the power." In Brazil in 2001, in the midst of a drought, the huge Itaipu dam not only reduced the flow of water downstream, but the stagnant water of its large reservoir evaporated much more quickly than free-flowing water would have. But the solution of the Brazilian government was to build another dam, slated to be the world's third largest, in the Amazon basin.[7] Current Chinese leaders respond to the drying up of the Yellow River by building the dam on the Yangtze, despite scientific and political criticism from around the world. In addition, in order to bring power to the poor province of Yunnan in southwestern China, the Chinese government plans eight dams on the Mekong River, reducing the flow of water for sixty million people downstream in Southeast Asia who depend on the Mekong for their food and livelihood.[8]

If some people never learn, others knew all along. Lewis Mumford and other environmentalists were critical of FDR's dam strategy in the 1930s. Their skepticism has now become almost common sense and government policy. For instance, the United States is considering tearing down the dams on the Columbia River to revive the salmon runs of the pre-dam era. But technological wrong turns are not made purely out of ignorance. And there were many other technological wrong turns in the decades after Mumford's prediction that the world was turning green.

IRRIGATION, FERTILIZERS, AND PESTICIDES

Irrigation, or channeling water to farmland, was a common practice for thousands of years in areas that received little or irregular rainfall. Dams were constructed long before the age of electricity for this purpose. Irrigation canals solve and cause the same problems as dams. At best, they can provide water when necessary, but they always provide water without silt and they build up harmful salts instead.

Agriculture after the Second World War became newly reliant on irrigation. To solve the problem of inadequate silting and failing soil, modern irrigated farms took advantage of two technologies unavailable to the ancients—chemical fertilizers and pesticides—both invented for the army during the Second World War. Fertilizers derived from chemical explosive research and development. Pesticides grew out of research in biological weapons. After the war, chemical and biological research continued in private companies, mainly for peacetime use.

Large corporate farms, which were increasingly prominent in American agriculture, chose chemical fertilizers and pesticides because they offered a sense of control and predictability. Especially as corporate farmers focused on single crops planted continually over large farms, they required chemical aids for depleted soil and specialized pests. Between 1947 and 1960 the use of pesticides in the United States increased over five times.

Like drugs, fertilizers and pesticides were addictive; the more they were used, the more they were needed, because they allowed over-planting that depleted the soil of nutrients. Nitrogen fertilizers leached into ground water tables, reservoirs, and lakes. Some lakes were so fertilized they produced enough algae to consume all of the water's oxygen, killing the lake and its aquatic life. Pesticides killed not only the target insects, but others as well, including the natural predators of the target insects.

The widely heralded Green Revolution of the period underscores the intoxicating hopes of scientific agriculture. The combined talents of international government agencies like the World Bank, chemical companies, and government officials in developing countries turned to the problem of famine and insufficient food in developing countries like India and Mexico. They invented new seeds that grew faster with the aid of high doses of chemical fertilizers. The revolution began with the development in the 1950s of a Mexican wheat that depended on heavy doses of a particular fertilizer. It continued in the next decades with rice and corn planted in Asia. By some very important measures the revolution succeeded: It increased per capita grain production 40 percent between 1950 and 1984, averted famines in India and Pakistan, and earned one plant breeder a Nobel Peace Prize in 1970.

There were damaging side effects, however. The planning and expertise of global scientists and manufacturers replaced local knowledge and initiative. Peasant farmers who previously used a wide range of seed varieties were pressured to use just one—the new miracle seed which they had to purchase. As alternate seeds and crops were eliminated, so too was the complex environmental diversity in which they thrived. Single crops require targeted fertilizers and pesticides, and more of each every year in a spiraling cycle of mutual dependence. But as pests evolved to resist the pesticides, new miracle crops—and new pesticides—had to be developed.

The case of the "miracle rice" invented by the International Rice Research Institute (IRRI) is instructive.[9] In 1966 IRRI scientists combined a wild rice from Taiwan with standard rice to produce a plant that absorbed large amounts of fertilizer, grew quickly and abundantly, and could be harvested mechanically. This seed

(IRRI number 8) came to be known as "miracle rice." It was so popular, farmers in south and southeast Asia abandoned their old rice for IR8, which they planted widely. The new rice grew so fast that farmers could plant three crops a year. But its success posed problems. With no fallow period, the soil required more fertilizers to restore nutrients, and there was no interruption in the life cycle of the pests. Insects adapted to take advantage of vast fields of the single crop. In response, scientists modified the formula. But the insects adapted as well. Each new formula countered a new problem; one strain poisoned the fish in the rice paddies; another was susceptible to a new pest. Each new seed also required the farmers to buy more of the fertilizers and the special pesticides targeted to the particular pests that had evolved to attack the new plant.

As the IRRI solved each new problem, each new variety of rice seed was more productive than its predecessor and therefore more popular with farmers. But each new variety was also more refined, more isolated from its ancestors. The scientists were improving yield through constant specialization, one result of which was a reduction in genetic diversity. Fewer species of rice were planted, leaving entire regions vulnerable to a single pest. Similarly, each new variety of rice was itself less genetically diverse, as scientists bolstered the specific genetic attributes they sought. And as seeds became more adapted for particular qualities, so did the particular insects that fed on these plants adapt and thrive. It was as if the variety of plant and insect life was sucked into a volcano that spitted out one form of each.

The pace of seed change and insect adaptation picked up speed. By 1970 the Institute introduced IR20, which was resistant to a persistent problem disease but particularly susceptible to a new pest, a brown plant-hopper. IR26 could resist the plant hopper, but not the wind, which flattened the stalks before they could be harvested. Institute researchers found a record of a wind-resistant strain of rice in rural Taiwan. They were relieved to learn that the wind-resistant strain was the same plant that, combined with ordinary rice, had formed the first "miracle rice." The researchers went to Taiwan to retrieve the original genetic material. But everywhere they went, farmers had switched to IR26 and the original wild plant was nowhere to be found. No one had cared to plant a wild and outdated variety and so it had become extinct.

Science is never stumped by small problems, and so the researchers found another way to develop wind resistance for IR36. But in another four years, the brown plant-hoppers were back and hungry. A few years later, researchers were introducing IR72.

The Green Revolution provided an opportunity for chemical companies to develop and sell fertilizers and pesticides on a much larger scale than was possible in the United States and Europe. In fact, as pesticide use became unpopular or illegal in the developed world, the "undeveloped" agricultural regions of Asia appeared as huge potential markets. Further, such markets could be supplied locally with factories that took advantage of cheap labor, negligible worker protection, and lax or nonexistent environmental law.

BHOPAL

One such plant was established by the Union Carbide Company in Bhopal, India. On December 3, 1984, the Bhopal plant was the scene of one of the world's worst industrial accidents. More than 3,000 people were killed immediately and 200,000 injured when 40 tons of pesticide gases were accidentally released. Because the company refused to reveal the exact nature of the chemicals (on the grounds that it was a trade secret), many more people died, and the city of Bhopal became a toxic sink.

The Indian government tried to sue the company and its management in U.S. courts but was effectively rebuffed. Eventually Union Carbide agreed to settle for $470 million, a small fraction of the several billion dollars that would have likely been awarded in a U.S. court. Some years later, Union Carbide merged its finances, and submerged its name, with Dow Chemical (a company no longer associated in the public mind with the napalm of the Vietnam War).

American chemical companies were by no means the only threats to the environment of developing countries like India. In 1999 Greenpeace, the environmentalist organization, named four other sites in India as "Global Toxic Hotspots." One was the Hindustan Insecticides factory in the southern state of Kerala. Three others in the northern state of Gujarat were government effluent plants that had been supported by the World Bank.

Bhopal Union Carbide isocyanate gas disaster. (New York Public Library)

SILENT SPRING TO EARTH DAY

The reason why pesticide companies transferred their attention to foreign markets like India was that they had come under public pressure in the United States. Some pesticides, most notably DDT, had been banned from American markets in the wake of a remarkable burst of public concern about the environment. The 1950s was an age of environmental innocence. In the immediate years after World War II, Americans and Europeans looked only towards rebuilding from the devastation of war and achieving material prosperity. Many people spoke of progress as the conquest of nature. Others believed nature was an infinite resource to be exploited by human effort. In this context, few criticized the developing role of pesticides and fertilizers.

It took a biologist and popular writer by the name of Rachel Carson to alert the American public about the danger of pesticides. Carson had studied the effects of pesticides while she worked for the U.S. Government Fish and Wildlife Service. But it was her successful popular books on the marine life that gave her the freedom and independence to write a book that would challenge the corporate sponsors of pesticides and those in the government who approved their use. Carson showed how pesticides like DDT not only killed the targeted insects but were passed along in the food chains. In an evocative passage she described how DDT used on fruit trees was passed on to worms and then to birds, potentially causing a "silent spring." Carson's achievement was to force the public to see the interconnections of nature. She challenged the popular perception that chemical pesticides were miracles without consequence. "Elixirs of death," she called them, suggesting that they contaminated every step of the food chain, accounting eventually for the increase in human cancer deaths—a claim made more poignant by the knowledge that Carson herself had been diagnosed with cancer. She died shortly after *Silent Spring* was published.

Silent Spring, thirty-one weeks on the best seller list in 1963, inaugurated the modern environmental movement in the United States, and through its many translations in much of the rest of the world as well. In the United States, the book hit a raw nerve. Lake Erie had just been declared dead. The Cuyahoga River had burst into flame. Industrial cities like Pittsburgh and sun cities like Los Angeles were sealed in permanent shrouds; on some days children were cautioned not to breathe the outside air.

Pesticide manufacturers marshaled their forces in and out of government, but President Kennedy called for an investigation of Carson's findings. His Scientific Advisory Committee concluded that the issue was even more serious than Carson had indicated. In response, the U.S. government and dozens of states outlawed the use of DDT, and the Agriculture Department began to take a critical attitude toward the use of chemical pesticides generally.

People began to think differently about the environment. A popular magazine, *National Geographic*, which had once run articles with titles like "Synthetic Products: Chemists Make a New World" and "Coal: Prodigious Worker for Man" began to feature stories on "Nature's Dwindling Treasures" and "Our Ecological Crisis." In 1970, Senator Gaylord Nelson of Wisconsin, whose previous interest in environmental issues had been ignored by his Congressional colleagues, called for a national "Earth Day" which he modeled on the public teach-ins that had been used so successfully against the U.S. war in Vietnam. On April 22, 1970, some twenty million people (one tenth of the U.S. population) participated in environmental demonstrations in cities across the county. Within months, President Nixon established the Environmental Protection Agency. Legislation against pesticides (1972) and toxic substances (1974) followed. With clean-water and air legislation, recycling laws, measures to remove lead from gasoline and paints, and other pollution restrictions, environmental awareness entered the American mainstream.

TECHNOLOGICAL TEMPLATE

Dams, irrigation, fertilizers, and pesticides were interrelated and interdependent. Each made the other more acceptable, even necessary. And together they constituted a technological system, pattern, or template in which artificial, engineered, abstract solutions were preferred to natural ones.

In fact, an examination of other technologies of the post–World War II period might suggest that these choices were part of an even larger template—and that it was almost the opposite of what Lewis Mumford predicted in the 1930s.

Another popular environmentalist writer, Barry Commoner, described this technological complex as a technology of synthetic and throwaway products. In a book titled *The Closing Circle*, published in 1972, he showed how pesticides and fertilizers were part of a larger pattern that included animals raised in feed lots, large lead-burning car engines, detergents replacing soap, synthetic fabrics replacing natural wool and cotton, and a widespread use of chemicals in industry.

THE SYNTHETIC, THROWAWAY TECHNOLOGY

According to Commoner, the United States had shifted after the war to a technology of synthetic products and processes that required enormous expenditures of energy and the use of non-renewable resources in order to produce things that could be easily thrown away.

> In general, the growth of the United States economy since 1946 had a surprisingly small effect on the degree to which individual needs for basic economic goods have been met. That statistical fiction, the "average American," now consumes, each year, about as many calories, protein, and other foods (although somewhat less of vitamins); uses about the same amount of clothes and cleaners; occupies about the

same amount of newly constructed housing; requires about as much freight; and drinks about the same amount of beer (twenty-six gallons per capita!) as he did in 1946. However, his food is now grown on less land with much more fertilizer and pesticides than before; his clothes are more likely to be made of synthetic fibers than of cotton or wool; he launders with synthetic detergents rather than soap; he lives and works in buildings that depend more heavily on aluminum, concrete, and plastic than on steel and lumber; the goods he uses are increasingly shipped by truck rather than rail; he drinks beer out of non-returnable bottles or cans rather than out of returnable bottles or at the tavern bar. He is more likely to live and work in air-conditioned surroundings than before. He also drives about twice as far as he did in 1946, in a heavier car, on synthetic rather than natural rubber tires, using more gasoline per mile, containing more tetraethyl lead, fed into an engine of increased horsepower and compression ratio.[10]

In every one of these cases, Commoner went on to show, not only did Americans fail to live any better, but the ecological impact of the new technology was disastrous. Washing detergents, mass-marketed after the war instead of soap, had an environmental impact similar to the nitrates in fertilizer. Like the synthetic fertilizers, detergents required considerably more energy to create than their natural equivalent. And like the nitrates in synthetic fertilizers, the phosphates in detergents taxed the oxygen in water with algae growth to the point where lakes began to die.

Synthetic fabrics, which replaced organic materials (like cotton and wool) after the war, had a similar effect. Sheep and cotton plants grew from the natural energy of sunlight, rain, and soil nutrients. There was no pollution. Nylon requires six to ten chemical reactions up to 7000° F. (the melting point of lead), and high-temperature combustion fuel as well as the original raw material, oil or gas. Besides wasting irreplaceable resources, there are polluting waste fumes, and the final product cannot be broken down, except by fire (and more smoke). The same is true of plastics. Like other synthetic materials, plastics are made to last forever.

The greatest single source of urban environmental pollution, the automobile, told a similar story. Not only did the number of cars and miles driven increase about 200 percent in the twenty years after the war, but the amount of lead in the atmosphere (almost totally from automobile exhaust) increased 400 percent. The reason, then, for increased smog and leaded air was the kind of cars and the kind of gasoline that was increasingly produced since the 1940s. Between 1945 and 1968 Detroit built larger and heavier cars with more power, requiring more lead in the fuel to meet the ever-higher combustion ratios.

This is one technology that changed after Commoner's book was published—but only partially, and for a time. In response to the rise of gasoline prices and the Japanese marketing of smaller cars in the 1970s, Americans demanded smaller, more fuel efficient cars. In addition, environmentalists won a phaseout of leaded gasoline, and a graduated reduction of carbon emissions. But larger cars returned with cheaper gas, and automobile companies found a double bonus in sport-utility vehicles, or SUVs. Larger vehicles always returned higher profits than smaller vehicles, but SUVs were also classified as trucks, thus claiming exemption from auto emissions standards. As a consequence, the reductions in imported oil, gasoline use, and carbon emissions that occurred in the 1970s were reversed by the 1990s.

WHY THE WRONG TEMPLATE?

Why did an unforeseen switch in the technological template occur at mid-century? Why instead of a clean, natural technology did there occur such an ecologically damaging one? One could blame the science and the scientists. One recent environmental history, John McNeill's *Something New Under the Sun*, points out that one scientist invented both the lead-based fuel and freon gas for air conditioning. But scientists work in a social context, for business or industry or government.

One could blame consumers. Certainly people chose to buy SUVs in the '90s and after, despite their environmental impact. But consumers also make their choices in a context that includes information, peer values, alternatives, and costs. An individual might not consider the environmental impact of buying an SUV because no public information or advertising challenged the positive SUV advertising. A context in which environmentalists rather than SUV manufacturers shaped the debate might lead to different choices. Informed citizens might balance the advantages of private cars with the social costs of sprawl, congestion, pollution, roads, traffic deaths, highway police, and even military actions or preparedness to ensure adequate oil. If governments, like those in Europe, created or subsidized more railroads and public transportation and taxed gasoline to cover its environmental or health costs, the context would be different.

Both Mumford and Commoner believed that corporate profit played a far greater role in shaping the late-twentieth-century template than did scientific invention or consumer preference. In some cases, like chemical fertilizers replacing soil or air conditioning replacing trees and fans, the new technology could be sold while the old one could not. In most cases, however, the new technologies simply commanded higher profits than the old. This was true of synthetic fabrics vs. natural ones, detergents vs. soap chips, aluminum and concrete vs. steel and lumber, trucks vs. railroads, leaded vs. unleaded gas, large cars vs. small ones.

PRIVATE PROFITS AND SOCIAL COSTS

Private corporations, unlike governments, are not responsible for an entire technological template. Each corporation only makes decisions to make and market particular products. In doing so, they need only consider potential profit against costs. But a private corporation may not include all of the social costs that a government might face and have to pay for. In a famous analysis, Garrett Hardin argued that in the use of a common resource (like the medieval common pasture or the natural environment), there is inevitably a conflict between private gain and social cost. On the medieval commons, it was profitable for each villager to add an animal to graze since the profits were his but the costs were shared. But if everyone followed the logic of personal interest and added a cow to graze on the commons, the public resource would be depleted and there would not be enough grass for everyone. Some ecologically minded economists saw Hardin's "Tragedy of the Commons" as a lesson in the private exploitation of natural resources.

As long ago as 1950 the economist K. W. Kapp published a book called *The Social Costs of Private Enterprise*, in which he pointed out that the conventional thinking of business managers fails to account for the social costs of their productivity. Like the individual in the commons, each corporation considers only its private costs for material and labor when it computes its profits. Kapp argued that if these companies were forced to add the costs of environmental degradation to their balance sheets, many of them would be forced to discontinue production.

The private profit of U.S. corporations in switching from old to new technologies outweighed the considerable environmental costs. The entire profits went directly to the "innovating" companies, and the environmental costs were shared with all inhabitants of the planet, including future generations.

PRIVATE AND PUBLIC TECHNOLOGY

The distinction between private and public, market and government, may be a useful analytical exercise, but the post–World War II economy blurred the distinction. In fact, many of the new technologies that Commoner discussed were products of the war. Two others that he does not mention—asbestos and nuclear energy—show the interaction of private and public, corporate and governmental sponsorship. The first, asbestos, was another disastrous postwar technology: one prodded by government in its origins and protected by corporate-legal consensus in its demise. The other, nuclear technology, originated as one of the most elaborate government investments of the century. To the extent to which it has since been restrained, in its military and peaceful forms, such restraint has been due to both public opinion and the law.

Asbestos, made of fire-resistant mineral fibers, was considered a miracle insulator during World War II. The main producer for both government and private contracts was the Johns Manville Company of Manville, New Jersey. In the boom years of asbestos production, Manville basked in the gratitude of Polish immigrant workers from the depleted anthracite coal country of eastern Pennsylvania. But after twenty years of hard factory work in Manville, many became very sick and died. Their wracking cough and collapsing lungs, caused by inhaling the fish-hook fibers of the miracle insulation, acquired the name asbestosis. By the 1970s the death spread to wives and children who had not even worked in the plant. People recalled the "summer snow" that filtered over the town, the flecks of fiber on a sweater or jacket dusted off at home, and the company landfill for the school baseball diamond.

In an earlier day, it might have been possible to take steps: wet down the fibers at the plant, install filters, provide protective masks for the workers, inform them of the danger, provide frequent medical checks. But despite warnings from its own doctors and insurance company, Manville chose to deny responsibility, save money, and instruct physicians not to alarm the workers.

By the time the company took responsibility, it was too late. The world had learned that their schools and hospitals and courthouses and homes were lying in ambush; a new roof, a remodeled room, a crushed wall might release the fish-hook fibers into the lungs of students, patients, and trial lawyers as it already had the residents of Manville. So the company left town, choosing instead the clean mountain air of Denver. Under the threat of what appeared to be a never-ending series of claims, Johns Manville filed for a kind of sham bankruptcy, on the grounds that it could only pay claims if the courts capped its liabilities.

Far more ecologically damaging than asbestos was the creation of a nuclear power industry after World War II. While asbestos lay dormant for 20 years after exposure, radioactive wastes would be lethal for 2,000 years. The nuclear power industry was more government-directed than asbestos. Initially, in establishing the Atomic Energy Commission in 1946, the government determined to emphasize military uses and maintain a government monopoly on the technology.

Private companies entered nuclear energy production through government contracts. The first were awarded to Westinghouse and General Electric as part of the effort by the U.S. Navy to develop nuclear-powered submarines. An "Atoms for Peace" speech by Eisenhower in 1953 and the passage of an Atomic Energy Act the following year ushered in the era of commercial nuclear power production.

Safety was a primary concern of both government and private industry. Both feared the implications of a nuclear accident. Government feared a public outcry that would terminate the program. One strategy used to deal with this was that of regulation by the AEC and its successor, the Nuclear Regulatory Commission. Another was secrecy: keeping the public "confused" about the consequences of radioactive fallout, as Eisenhower urged the AEC in 1953.[11] For business the danger of disaster was bankruptcy. The solution was the Price-Anderson Act, passed by Congress in 1957, and renewed since, making the government responsible for damages beyond the minimum allowed by private insurance companies. This was the most important of extensive "social costs of private enterprise" in nuclear power that were absorbed by the taxpayer. Westinghouse and General Electric, their suppliers, and the utility companies would not have to go the way of Johns Manville.

Thus began a corporate-government alliance that worked as long as the government socialized the risks and provided effective oversight. In fact, members of the Atomic Energy Commission, like its first chairman, Dr. Edward Teller, were vigorous proponents of nuclear energy. Many passed through the revolving door between regulatory power and private employment. While Eisenhower warned against the undemocratic collusion of an emerging "military-industrial complex" in 1960, he did not seem to include the nuclear power industry in his concern. The 1960s and early 1970s were a golden age for the industry. General Electric and Westinghouse competed vigorously in providing power companies and public utilities with inexpensive, ready-to-operate "turnkey" plants. Ironically, the appeal of nuclear power grew in the context of the emerging environmental movement. New laws limiting carbon pollution increased the costs of converting and filtering old fossil-burning plants at the same time as the new nuclear plants became available.

In the 1970s it became increasingly clear to nuclear regulators at the AEC that many of the nuclear reactors were not as safe as imagined. But in order not to alarm the public and, by so doing, end the rush to nuclear power, the Atomic Energy Commission decided to minimize the problem. In response, activist members of the Union of Concerned Scientists challenged the agency's conduct and pressured the agency to suspend licenses and hold public hearings. In an environment of widespread public concern about the environment, in March 1979, the atomic energy plant at Three Mile Island in Pennsylvania suffered the much-feared core meltdown and radioactive gases spread beyond the plant, forcing the evacuation of nearby towns and a public panic. As the accident came only twelve days after the debut of *The China Syndrome*, a popular film about a chillingly similar nuclear accident, the public outcry was deafening. The American nuclear power industry went into an eclipse from which it is only now beginning to recover.

COMMUNISM, A SEA OF COTTON, AND CHERNOBYL

Big governments, which became the model after World War II, were generally no more effective at avoiding poor ecological choices than private corporations were. The pursuit of national power by political leaders and bureaucrats could be as insensitive to natural environment as was the profit motive. In fact, one of the most severe "natural" disasters of the postwar period occurred as a result of the planning and direction of a government officially immune to market forces, the communist government of the Soviet Union. In a period of thirty years, the Soviet government set out deliberately to divert rivers in an irrigation project that would destroy the Aral Sea, then the fourth largest lake in the world.

The Aral Sea, in what were the Kazakh and Uzbek Soviet Republics, was fed by two of the great rivers of Central Asia, which brought the snowmelt from the Western end of the Himalayas. In the 1950s, Soviet officials and scientists started to channel these rivers, the Syr Darya and Amu Darya, into irrigated fields to grow enough cotton to make the Soviet Union independent. That part was a success, though the poor quality of the cotton limited its appeal to countries in the Soviet sphere of influence. To Soviet officials and scientists, channeled rivers were more useful than an inland sea. One scientist put the case clearly:

> I belong to those scientists who consider that drying up of the Aral is
> far more advantageous than preserving it. First, in its zone, good fertile
> land will be obtained. . . . Cultivation [of cotton] will pay for the exist-
> ing Aral Sea, with all its fisheries, shipping, and other industries.
> Second . . . the disappearance of the Sea will not affect the region's
> landscapes.[12]

As ever more water was diverted to irrigation, and the Aral Sea began to dry up
and shrink, its salt content increased. Waters that had provided forty thousand tons
of fish a year in the 1950s provided nothing by the 1990s. Twenty of twenty-four
fish species became extinct. To add insult to injury, the canneries on what had been
the shore of the Aral Sea were kept operating with fish from the Baltic Sea, airlift-
ed across Russia to the Pacific coast, from where they were sent by Trans-Siberian
rail to Central Asia.

By 1990, the Aral Sea became a salt flat and a new ecological nightmare unfold-
ed. The sea had modified the temperatures of the surrounding area, cooling the
summer and warming the winter. Without the sea, a longer winter shortened the
growing season. The sea had also provided humidity and rain for the area. By contrast, the salt from the drying salt bed was lifted by winds and carried for hundreds
of miles. It coated the cotton plants, eventually killing them. It destroyed various
plant species and the animals dependent on them. By 1990 nearly half the mam-
mal species and three quarters of the bird species that had prospered in the 1960s
had disappeared. The deepening drought lowered water tables and turned them
saline. An uninhabitable great salt desert replaced the ecosystem that had been the
region of the Aral Sea.

The destruction of the Aral Sea was a painfully slow process, little noticed by
the outside world while it occurred. But the meltdown of the nuclear power plant
at Chernobyl in the Soviet Ukraine in 1986 riveted the world's attention to the
ecological failures of the Soviet communist regime and to the dangers of nuclear
power. It may not be too much of an exaggeration to say that it ended both. The
core meltdown at Chernobyl was more serious than that at Three Mile Island, and
because it happened in Europe, which continued to rely on nuclear energy for much
of its electricity needs, the impact was far greater. Clouds of radioactive materials
floated for ten days not only over the Ukraine but as far north as Finland and
Sweden and as far south as Greece and the Balkans. Thirty-one people were killed
in the accident, but hundreds of thousands of people in the Soviet Ukraine, and in
its northern neighbor Belarus, had to abandon their homes, many permanently.
The inhabitants of Chernobyl were exposed to radiation levels a hundred times
greater than was caused by the atomic bomb over Hiroshima. As the main cloud
drifted north, Belarus received most of the radiation. The incidence of childhood
thyroid cancer in Minsk, its capital, increased from five in the eight years before
1986 to over three hundred and climbing in the eight years following. But that was
only the beginning. Estimates for the eventual cancer toll range from 14,000 to

475,000.[13] A leading ecological historian summarizes the environmental impact this way:

> Some nuclear wastes and part of Chernobyl's fallout will be lethal for 24,000 years—easily the most lasting human insignia of the twentieth century and the longest lien on the future that any generation of humanity has yet imposed.[14]

The disaster at Chernobyl crystallized Ukrainian and Byelorussian resentment toward the Soviet Union, fanning independence movements which ultimately brought an end to the Soviet state. But Soviet duplicity and mismanagement in the crisis symbolized for many in Europe the betrayal of the nuclear promise. At Chernobyl (and Three Mile Island) the impossible happened. Because the ecological effects of uncontrolled nuclear energy were so momentous, people had to believe that certain things could not happen. Primary among such things was the core meltdown that had now occurred twice, first without the loss of life in the richest country in the world and now, with considerable human losses, in the largest. Almost in retaliation, the Soviet Union was reduced to its parts and nuclear energy was put on the defensive throughout the world. Even in its demise Chernobyl emphasized promises that could not be kept. The huge coffin of concrete that was to permanently enclose the destroyed reactor and its radioactive ingredients sprang leaks within years, making a mockery of the promises that nuclear waste could be safely buried for thousands of years.

NEW DIRECTIONS?

Whether the worst excesses of the post–World War II decades were products of greed or government, have they been reversed? Some certainly have. Especially in the United States and Europe, nuclear energy (though attempting a revival) no longer goes unquestioned; asbestos has been replaced; the Great Lakes are cleaner, and the air of Pittsburgh and Los Angeles is breathable; the non-returnable economy has turned into the recycling society; automobiles run on lead-free engines; laws and government agencies protect endangered species and fine polluters. On the other hand, nuclear power continues to supply over half of the electrical needs of France and some other European countries; the use of fossil fuels has increased, and our landfills and garbage dumps are filled with consumer products that become obsolete more quickly with each passing year.

How about the template of contemporary technology? Are we any closer to Lewis Mumford's dream of a sustainable technology? In favor of such a conclusion, we could point to two characteristic contemporary technologies: silicone and lasers. Silicone is the miracle material of the modern age. It is used in medicines, food processing, skin and hair products, antiperspirants, medical devices, and surgery. Its use in plastic surgery, especially breast implants, has achieved a certain notoriety, though it is also used in the repair of retinal detachment. But the use of silicone that makes it the emblematic material of the modern age—our wood or steel—is the silicone chip, that magic miniature powerhouse that runs our computers, cell phones, and even carburetors. Where would we be without the silicone chip?

More important is where it comes from. Silicone is no rare bat deposit or precious metal. It comes from sand, one of the most common ingredients on the planet. It is more available than wood, a virtually inexhaustible raw material. Unlike fossil fuels, sand will never be in short supply.

Lasers are also important in the modern technological template. Lasers are light waves used in communications technology. As with silicone, the highly concentrated, very short beams of light originate in something that is neither precious nor scarce. And just as silicone replaced scarce raw materials, light replaces electricity and copper wires. In the modern telecommunications industry, these light waves are sent through fiber-optic strands of glass—another product made from sand. We might even say that modern telecommunications project Mumford's ecological future beyond the costly production of electricity (by dams or any other means). An industry that once was electronic now relies on the routine transmission by lasers of light pulses which carry billions of bits of information (voice, video and data) through glass fibers.

At least two caveats are in order before we declare a new age of natural technology, however. First, we have not factored in the energy and environmental costs of changing sand into silicone or light into laser photons. The production of silicone from sand (or silica) requires temperatures of at least 500° Centigrade, and the inhalation of silica dust can cause silicosis. Cosmetic silicone gel implants have been the subject of a number of damage suits. Lasers are generated by a very high voltage of electricity. The word "laser" stands for "light amplification by stimulated emission of radiation." The release of radiation can pose human and environmental dangers.

Also the perplexing combination of promise and danger in the contemporary technological template can be seen in the development of biotechnology, especially the cloning of organisms. On one hand, cloning holds out a promise of infinite natural abundance. Stem cells, the basic building blocks of human cells, can be reproduced as limbs, organs, or tissue. On the other hand, the prospect of humans actually creating natural organisms evokes the specter of "unnatural" meddling, the "unhallowed art" of Frankenstein.

Despite the emerging template of telecommunications and biotechnology, many of the elements of the old technology, the industrial use of fossil fuels and limited natural resources, of pollution and energy hyperconsumption, still exist, even in North America and Europe. The automobile, the single greatest cause of environmental pollution, is still produced, in greater absolute and per-capita numbers, and is still the main mode of transportation. Chemicals, plastics, synthetics, throwaways (computers rather than bottles) still flood the economy and landfills. And if we turn our attention from the United States, in which 4 percent of the world's population control 44 percent of the world's resources, to the rest of the world, the spread of the old technology template becomes critical.

CAIRO SKY

"Clear as the sky above Cairo," they used to say in Egypt in the 1960s. Today they just cough. The air quality of Egypt's principal city, where 40 percent of Egyptians reside, has ten to a hundred times the number of particles considered safe. Cairo's air causes an estimated 10,000 to 25,000 deaths per year. The lead alone may reduce the average child's IQ by four to five points.

There are traditional causes of air pollution over Cairo: sandstorms off the Sahara, the burning of rice straw by farmers north of the city in the fall, and pottery factories and metal smelters near the city. But all these together did not detract from the legendary image of Cairo's clear skies.

Since the 1960s, Cairo has changed in the same way as Mexico City, Brazil's São Paulo, Bangkok, and Beijing. Progress, some call it. "Smog is good," one resident of Cairo (who might have lost some of the IQ points) wrote to an Internet bulletin board recently. Smog is good, he said, because it means that Cairo is industrialized and modern. Good or bad, certainly many Cairenes wanted the jobs and material things that accompanied the pollution. If the air of Cairo has become like that of Los Angeles in the sixties, it is because Cairo has become almost like Los Angeles in the 1960s. There are now 1.2 million cars and numerous factories. But the smog of Cairo is worse than 1960s Los Angeles. There are no freeways in Cairo. While this puts an upper limit on the number of cars (there are over ten million people in greater Cairo), it means that traffic is often stalled. In addition, leaded gasoline is still in use, and while there are laws limiting vehicle pollution, there is virtually no enforcement.

Cairo smog is a product of Egyptian poverty and the striving for the things that Americans and Europeans have. Public transportation is impoverished, most people cannot afford clean-burning engines, the government can't afford inspection, lead smelting factories cannot afford filters, and there is neither the tax base nor the civic integrity to provide adequate public services.

SUSTAINABLE GLOBAL INDUSTRIALIZATION?

Some of the worst aspects of the Western industrial template have been exported to areas of the world where their damage is often greater but unpunished. Industries like chemicals, pesticides, and tobacco, which have been under pressure by ecologically minded governments in Europe and North America, have found ready markets in Asia, Africa, and Latin America, where environmental policies are weaker. Consumers in countries like India face a global double standard:

"The double standard isn't simply a matter of ethics and markets, of international conventions and big business. As individuals, we see it staring us in the face every day from our medicine cabinets, from inside our refrigerators, at the hardware store," says Lezak Shallat of Consumers International. "You think you're doing the best for your family, only to discover that you are poisoning them with banned pesticides in lice shampoos or growth hormone in supplements in the milk," states Shallat. "What's more, nowhere is it stated on these products that other consumers, with more information at hand, have found them to be unfit for consumption. It's a classic situation of adding insult to injury—and then mixing in the profit.[15]

But how about the globalization of desirable industrialization? People in Cairo, in Beijing, in Lagos and Mexico City want indoor plumbing, refrigeration, efficient transportation, quality health care, as well as clean air and water. From an ecological standpoint, the Western template of the last fifty years may offer them little hope. To take one example, the private automobile would seem a disaster on a global scale. In addition to the its use of oil, a limited resource, and its responsibility for most of the ozone depleting carbon in the world, it requires a staggering amount of the world's resources in energy and materials. The process of just building a car generates as much air pollution as driving it for ten years, and leaves behind 29 tons of waste for each ton of car.[16] The United States has over 200 million vehicles for fewer than 300 million people. India has 8 million cars for more than a billion people; China has 13 million cars for 1.3 billion people. (Twenty years ago China had virtually no private automobiles.) If China alone were to equal the Japanese ratio of one car for every two persons, it would need an additional 600 million cars, more than doubling the current world total. It is difficult to imagine the ecological possibilities of a world of five to ten times the cars when the current auto production in the industrialized countries already uses more than half the world's rubber, much of its oil and raw materials, accounts for a widening hole in the ozone, and requires the paving of vast regions of land that could support crops. In the United States, roads and parking lots require 60,000 square miles, more than half of the 100,000 square miles that grow wheat.[17] Of course, paving cropland is part of the same template that requires miracle seeds, irrigation, pesticides, and chemical fertilizers.

From a political standpoint, however, it is difficult, if not hypocritical, for North Americans, Europeans, and Japanese to tell Chinese and Indians that they cannot have individual automobiles because there are now too many. The current moment, in which the average American uses 50 to 100 times as much energy as the average inhabitant of Bangladesh, is not a propitious time for the American to convince the Bangladeshi that he or she has to conserve energy.

In coming decades, it is likely that energy and environmental policies will increasingly be debated in these global terms. As developing countries demand their places at the table, international laws and courts of public opinion will have to consider the claims of the less fortunate for ecological justice. If the world is not going to face extreme shortages of water, food, energy, and materials, it will have to find a new technological template and the will to bring it into being.

FOR FURTHER READING

A number of recent titles provide valuable entry points to our subject. Michael Meyerfeld Bell's *An Invitation to Environmental Sociology* is an excellent introduction to some of the larger issues. Ramachandra Guha's *Environmentalism: A Global History* is the best introduction to the environmental movement. For a general history of the environment in the twentieth century, it would be difficult to do better than J.R. McNeill's *Something New Under the Sun.*

This chapter has focused on some of the classics of North American environmental history and environmentalism. Foremost among these is Lewis Mumford's *Technics and Civilization*, still a rich interpretive overview. Students are also encouraged to read Rachel Carson's *Silent Spring*, a masterpiece of persuasive writing. We have also followed the argument of Barry Commoner's *The Closing Circle*, still worth reading. William Kapp's *The Social Costs of Private Enterprise*, which we have also used, is dated but valuable. The Worldwatch Institute publishes untold volumes and reports on environmental issues; among the most useful are the annual *State of the World* volumes by Lester R. Brown et al. David Macauley's *Minding Nature: the Philosophers of Ecology* provides essays on some of these modern ecological thinkers including Mumford, Commoner, and Carson.

A number of very good environmental histories deal with different subjects than those covered in this chapter. *This Fissured Land: An Ecological History of India* by Madhav Gadgil and Ramachandra Guha offers a general ecological history as well as a study of Indian caste and forest use. Vaclav Smil's *China's Environmental Crisis: An Inquiry into the Limits of National Development* is a valuable overview of Chinese food and energy needs. The same author's *Energy in World History* is an interesting overview of energy history, with some striking graphs and drawings. Susanna Hecht and Alexander Cockburn's *The Fate of the Forest: Developers, Destroyers and Defenders of the Amazon* deals with the deforestation of the Amazon rain forest and with Chico Mendez. Martin V. Melosi's *Coping with Abundance: Energy and Environment in Industrial America* is a valuable introduction to American environmental history in the twentieth century. There are useful essays collected in Donald Worster's *The Ends of the Earth* and J. Donald Hughes's *The Face of the Earth: Environment and World History*. Martin O'Connor brings together essays on the question of sustainability in *Is Capitalism Sustainable? Political Economy and the Politics of Ecology*.

NOTES

1. Katharine Q. Seelye, "Global Warming May Bring New Variety of Class Action," *New York Times*, September 6, 2001, p. A14.

2. Study by the Centers for Disease Control and Prevention, reported in James Glanz, "Almost All in U.S. Have Been Exposed to Fallout, Study Finds," *New York Times*, March 1, 2002, p. A14. The estimate of 100 million affected by coastal flooding comes from William K. Steven, "Scientists Say Earth's Warming Could Set Off Wide Disruptions," *New York Times*, Sept. 18, 1995, p. A8.

3. Lewis Mumford, *Technics and Civilization* (New York: Harcourt, Brace, and World, 1934, 1963), p. 158.

4. Charles Dickens, *Hard Times*, chapter V.

5. Mumford, *op. cit.*, p. 163.

6. Jacques Leslie, "Running Dry: What happens when the world no longer has enough fresh water?" *Harper's Magazine*, July 2000, p. 44.

7. The dam on the Xingu River near Belo Monte would increase Brazilian hydro-electric capacity 15 percent. Opposed by Brazilian environmental groups, the dam would open the Amazon to large farming and mining interests and encourage local development. Larry Rohter, "Brazil Searches for More Energy," *New York Times*, October 21, 2001, p. A12.

8. "Chinese Dam May Threaten Food Source of Neighbors," *New York Times*, September 30, 2001, p. A13.

9. Michael Meyerfeld Bell, *An Invitation to Environmental Sociology* (Thousand Oaks, Calif.: Pine Forge Press, 1998), p. 128.

10. Barry Commoner, *The Closing Circle* (New York: Knopf, 1972), figures and quotation from pp. 143–154.

11. *New York Times*, 20 April 1979, p. 1.

12. Quoted in Norman Precoda, "Requiem for the Aral Sea," in *Ambio* 20:3–4 (1991), p. 111, cited in J.R. McNeill, *Something New Under the Sun* (New York: W.W. Norton, 2000), p. 164.

13. V. K, Savchenko, *The Ecology of the Chernobyl Disaster* (Paris: UNESCO, 1995), p. 2, cited in J.R. McNeill, *Something New Under the Sun* (New York: W.W. Norton, 2000), p. 313.

14. J. R. McNeill, *Something New Under the Sun* (New York: W.W. Norton, 2000), p. 313.

15. Dipankar De Sarkar, "New Markets for Bad Products," *The World Paper Online*, Aug. 1997.

16. J. R. McNeill, *Something New Under the Sun* (New York: W.W. Norton, 2000), p. 311.

17. Lester Brown, *Paving the Planet: Cars and Crops Competing for Land* (Alert 2001–1), World Watch: Earth Policy Institute, Feb. 14, 2001.

❧ 14 ❧

Identity and Global Culture

Nation and World

"Who am I?" a student recently asked. "My mother's from Asia; my father was born in Europe; and we live in the United States among people whose ancestors came from Africa but whose first language is Latin American Spanish."

Globalization has created confusions of identity not only in the United States but throughout the world. Ten years after the Japanese multinational Sony purchased Columbia Pictures and led many Americans to fear that Japan would dominate American culture, one leading Tokyo daily recently suggested that the language of Japan be switched to English. The paper noted that Japanese teenagers were already speaking a Japanglish that included such phrases as "chekaraccho" for "check it out, Joe," and "denyru" for "go to Denny's Restaurant." At the same time, the Japanese Health and Welfare Ministry banned the excessive use of English words in official documents, but Japanese newspapers noted that there would probably be little "foro-uppu" ("follow up").[1]

South Korean parents are sending their preschool children for surgery to snip the tissue under their tongues so that they can better pronounce the difficult "l" and "r" sounds that have long stigmatized Asians when speaking English. "Learning English is almost the national religion" in South Korea, according to one educator, but experts say that pronunciation is almost entirely cultural and only a few people are born with tongues so tight that they can be helped by these "frenectomies."[2]

Japanese and Korean are not likely to disappear, but it is estimated that *half* of the six thousand languages spoken in the world today will become extinct in the next generation. One of the last speakers of Livonian, the national language of the rulers of the Baltic Sea eight hundred years ago, eighty-year old Pauline Klavina, recites an old Livonian poem that will soon be meaningless:

> *My language is the tongue of the sea*
> *It sounds like a divine voice*
> *I shall never forget it*
> *As I cannot forget my mother*[3]

Cultures live not only through language, but also through objects. In October 1996, the government of Iran complained of an invasion of American sexuality by means of the widely popular Barbie doll. To fight back, Iran's Institute for the Intellectual Development of Children and Young Adults created the doll Sara and her brother Dara, both clothed in long black robes. Shopkeepers in Tehran, the capital, welcomed the homegrown dolls though they expected sales to be modest.[4]

The forces of global homogenization occur within cultures as well as among them. A generation or two ago, one did not have to travel far in the United States to savor unique regional cooking, recognize different accents, or feel a shift in the pace of life. Now national television has blended the sounds of local newscasts into the same Middle American English. National restaurant chains have buried local dishes and ingredients in the same gravy. Rush-hour traffic stalls us in front of shopping malls that could be anywhere.

To the extent that our identity depends on our particular time or place, on our nation, region, or culture, we are losing or have lost our roots. And what is true for Americans is even more true for other "netizens" of the world. "We're all Americans in cyberspace, no matter what our nationalities," Kenji Sato of Japan remarked.[5] How has this occurred? What does it mean? Will it continue?

NATIONAL IDENTITY IN EUROPE
AND THE UNITED STATES, 1950–1970

In the 1950s and 1960s European and American[6] cultures were different in ways that immediately struck anyone traveling back and forth. European automobiles seemed tiny compared to those made in the United States. Their small size, tight suspensions, and responsive steering suited narrow roads that ran through each town. A long article in *Life* magazine at the end of July 1958 pointed out how laughable it was to think that Americans would ever like such "bugs." The United States was creating a network of highways to accommodate the large, soft-riding gas guzzlers manufactured by Detroit. The New Jersey Turnpike opened in 1949; the federal Interstate Highway Act passed in 1956.

Europeans and Americans differed on other means of transportation as well. Trains linked almost every European city and town. Within European cities and towns, more people traveled by bicycle than by automobile. In 1962, the streets of a city like Amsterdam overflowed with bicycles; a full bicycle rack, not a parking lot, encircled the central train station.

Housing patterns differed accordingly. Europeans lived in villages, towns, and cities. Rivers and railroads connected one town with another. Until the beginning of the twentieth century this pattern still marked the United States. But after World War II the new American suburbs, impossible without automobiles, sprouted up in the United States and changed all that. Farms and fields made way for "developments" of mass-produced wooden frame houses. First came the economical two-bedroom Cape Cods of Levittown, Long Island, in 1947, and later the quintessentially American sprawling single-level "ranch" houses. These new homes were less solid than the typical stone or brick townhouses of Europe, but offered more space and better plumbing and electric wiring. The American norm became multiple bathrooms, "family rooms," driveways and garages.

Travelers between Europe and the United States in the 1950s and 1960s would also notice differences in food consumption. Middle-class Americans ate more meat and more food overall than their European counterparts. Europeans ate bigger lunches and later dinners than Americans, drank far more wine, and generally took more time to eat, more frequently making meals into social events.

As different as Europe was from America, so were the national and regional cultures different from each other. In the United States, New Englanders ate different foods from Texans. Grits, chicken-fried steak, and boysenberry syrup were unknown beyond their cultural centers: the South, Texas, and California. And the difference among European countries was that, according to Benjamin Barber,

> There was no "Europe" in Europe. In the world before McWorld, the Swedes drove, ate, and consumed Swedish; the English drove, ate and consumed English, . . . In France one ate non-pasteurized Brie [cheese] and drank vin de Province in cafes and brasseries that were archetypically French; one listened to Edith Piaf and Jacqueline Françoise on French national radio stations and drove 2CV Citroens and Renault sedans without ever leaving French roadways—two-lane, tree cordoned affairs that took you through half the villages in France on the way, say, from Paris to Marseilles.[7]

"McWorld" is Barber's term for what has happened since then. The national and regional cultures that survived into the 1960s have been blended increasingly into a single global culture, shaped by fast-food outlets like McDonald's, shopping malls, and satellite television.

It is easy to criticize this change, but we must remember that many people chose McWorld. Many Europeans found the world of fast foods and American suburbs attractive. Instead of living in medieval townhouses with medieval plumbing, they chose McMansions with large lots and swimming pools. In the 1960s, Beaune, France, became a living museum of the seventeenth century since residents found it profitable to sell out and move into the spacious homes in the nearby suburban development. Perhaps only historians mourned the loss of old ways and regretted the conversion of living history into homogeneous tourist towns and Disneylands.

SILVER SCREENS AS NATIONAL MIRRORS

In the delightful British film *Passport to Pimlico* (1949), the residents of Pimlico Street in London discover an ancient will from the Duke of Burgundy that indicates they are really "Burgundians" and therefore not bound by British law, including post-war rationing and trade restrictions. Proud of their new identity, they form a government, and an unfettered marketplace that prospers, thanks to its freedom. When the British Foreign Office decides to crack down on this foreign country within its borders by imposing trade sanctions, customs duties, and passport restrictions on the Burgundians of Pimlico, British citizens as a whole are appalled. The Burgundians have reminded them of the true qualities of British character: independence, grit, self-sufficiency, community feeling, and ability to "go it alone together." Reminded by these "foreigners" of what it is to be British, the people of London rise to their defense. In the end, a proper British compromise emerges and everyone becomes British again—only more so.

In addition to providing entertainment, numerous films in the post–World War II years reflected on national identity. Possibly sensing the gathering forces of globalization, Britons had to know they were British. In addition to a hunger for identity, the idea that nations had different cultures floated in the air in the 1950s and 1960s. It caught the aroma of espresso in Italian coffee houses, the wine in French bistros, and the pilsner in German beer gardens. Sociologists and anthropologists found a receptive audience for books on national character and national cultural traits.

Whether one looked at the way people drove or dined, significant differences abounded. Everything seemed to have national boundaries: literature, music, dance, painting, for instance. Russians were the best dancers, Germans the best composers, and French the best visual artists. French philosophers were existentialists, like Jean Paul Sartre, focusing on the meaning of existence. English philosophers were logical positivists, preoccupied with the meaning of sentences. There *was* something distinctly American about the abstract painting of the 1950s, the pop art of the 1960s, or the music of Aaron Copland or Leonard Bernstein or Broadway musicals. But national differences were easiest to observe in the cultural medium that enjoyed a fiftieth anniversary at mid-century—the movies.

The 1950s and 1960s witnessed vibrant national film industries in European countries as well as the United States. In many cases a few personalities dominated, especially directors. According to the French *auteur* theory of film popular at the time, directors were the main creators of a film. Powerful and prestigious directors like François Truffaut in France, Federico Fellini in Italy, and Ingmar Bergman in Sweden had the will and the means to express personal visions, often drawn from their own life experiences. Nevertheless, movies were public arts in conception, execution, and distribution, unlike novels or paintings which were the result of individual effort. In order to make a successful film, a director required the assistance of hundreds of actors and technicians, private and public financial backers, and the approval of critics and large audiences. For these reasons, we can interpret the films of these great directors as expressions of individual genius and as creations of a particular national culture. In fact they both shaped and reflected those cultures.

The films of François Truffaut practically defined what foreigners saw as a quintessentially French obsession with love. Young love, marital love, adulterous love, the relationship between love and sex, love and friendship, love and passion: all were central concerns of Truffaut and many other French filmmakers. Truffaut's *Jules and Jim* (1961) explored the connection between love and friendship through a classic love triangle, but one in which the young woman loved two men.

Italian films dealt with the more earthly aspects of love. Federico Fellini's *La Dolce Vita* (1959) and his *Eight and a Half* (1963) recalled sexual exploits more than

In this scene from Frederico Fellini's Eight and a Half, *Guido (played by Marcello Mastroianni), a film director suffering from writer's block, finds himself among his memories. The mixture of dream and reality, personal and public, past and present was characteristic of Fellini, and of late-twentieth-century culture.*

love, with more guilt than analysis, in a style rich in dream imagery and dripping with symbolism. By contrast, Truffaut's lighthearted characters were more straightforward in discussing their feelings, and apparently less troubled by guilt.

Ingmar Bergman's films came to represent Scandinavian seriousness. In early black and white films like *Wild Strawberries* (1957), one could feel the chill of a remote father or insensitive Protestant pastor like the winter wind over the icy Swedish landscape. Later bright color memoirs like *Fanny and Alexander* celebrated traditional holidays with food and dress that almost shouted "This is who we were, and who we are."

The United States drew filmmakers from all over the world in the decades after World War II. Yet the Hollywood style of strong storytelling, smooth, seamless, invisible camera movement, and the priority of action over character, shaped the work of immigrant directors from the great prewar wave that included Alfred Hitchcock from England and Ernst Lubitch from Germany to the post-war generation that included Milos Forman from Czechoslovakia and Russian emigrés like Andrei Konchalovsky.

FILM AND NATIONAL IDENTITY IN ASIA

The movies of Japan, China, and India revealed worlds of ritual and belief far removed from American and European sensibilities, and introduced different styles of filmmaking. The Japanese director Yasujiro Ozu rejected Hollywood's first rule of filmmaking—keeping the camera unobtrusive and the editing seamless. He radically changed the perspective by moving his camera around its subject and edited shots for aesthetic connections rather than advancing the story. Even the titles of his films in the fifties and sixties—*Late Spring, Early Summer, Late Autumn, Early Autumn*, and so on—suggest an imagery and rhythm very different from that of the West and often described as quintessentially Japanese. After the Communist victory in 1949, Chinese filmmakers borrowed techniques of Soviet directors such as close-ups of heroic common people and fast cutting from one shot to another. But the more polished 1960s films, like *The East Is Red*, took their inspiration from the stage traditions of Peking opera and the mass demonstrations of the Great Proletarian Cultural Revolution. By contrast, Hong Kong filmmakers invented the Kung Fu films.

India had many film industries in the 1950s and 60s, and still does, one for each of the regional languages spoken in the subcontinent. The largest is the Bombay film industry, sometimes called Bollywood. It specializes in films in Hindi, which was designated the national language of India after British colonialism ended. With their beautiful stars and fantasy song and dance sequences, these films were so popular that they probably helped spread the Hindi language throughout India and strengthen the country's national identity.

The searches for national and individual identity were joined in the very popular Indian film *The Guide* (1965), directed by Vijay Anand after a novel by R. K.

Choosing civil society over family in Kanoon (The Law)—the public prosecutor trembles as he accuses the judge, his future father-in-law, of being the murder.

Narayan. The handsome lead was Raju, an Indian tour guide who introduced Indians of all regions, castes, religions, social classes, and languages, as well as foreigners, to one of India's great tourist sites, the city of Udaipur with its beautiful mountains, lakes, and palaces. As a tour guide Raju is worldly and cosmopolitan, an ingratiating host and talented linguist. He easily answers questions in English, Hindi, Gujarati, Bengali, and Punjabi. But his success corrupts him and he is sent to jail, from which he emerges a broken man who has lost everything. Ashamed to return home, he wanders into a village where he is mistaken for a holy man, a role he decides to play for all it is worth. Step by step, Raju is transformed into the saint he only pretended to be.

Films that explored national identity did not usually travel well beyond the nation's borders. Yet the Bombay film industry of the 1950s crafted some films that addressed distinctly Indian concerns, but appealed to foreigners at the same time. The films *Awaara* (The Vagabond, 1951) and *Kanoon* (Law, 1960) explored the conflicting demands of citizenship and parental authority. In *Awaara*, the Vagabond is the son of a judge who is raised by a criminal because the judge has disowned him. Similarly, in *Kanoon*, a young lawyer must confront a judge, his own father, whom he believes to be a murderer. Of course India was not the only country which needed to justify the claims of civil law over blood ties and traditions of vengeance. These films also drew large audiences throughout South Asia and the

Middle East in other newly independent states that were struggling to create civil societies. *Awaara* was extremely popular in Iran, Iraq, Turkey, the Soviet Union, Syria, and Egypt.

India was not alone in attracting audiences from far beyond its borders after 1950. The entire Arab speaking world enjoyed Egyptian films. Indonesian films drew a large audience across southeast Asia, and Mexican films were shown in all of Latin America. National film industries also prospered in Brazil, Iran, Turkey, and the Philippines.[8]

HOLLYWORLD

If the 1950s and 1960s was an age in which films helped create national identities and audiences, the period since then has been marked by the power of international and global forces. Such forces were partly technological. Television, satellite discs, VCRs, CNN, cell phones, and the Internet, in addition to jet planes and mass tourism, blurred national differences. Improved sound dubbing techniques eliminated the need for subtitles, opening up international mass audiences for blockbuster films.

Hollywood was particularly well suited to take advantage of the new possibilities. The Hollywood-style action film was easily understandable across cultural boundaries. Audiences around the world were attracted to aspects of American culture that were increasingly visible. U.S. economic and political power also aided the global distribution of Hollywood films as a profitable export industry, especially after Ronald Reagan, a former head of the Screen Actor's Guild, became president in 1981 and gave former Hollywood associates a free hand in U.S. trade policy.

By 1991, nine out of the ten top-grossing films in Germany were American. All the top ten in England, Egypt, Argentina, and Brazil came from Hollywood. In Italy, five out of the top ten were Italian, five American. In Japan the top four were American, though the rest were Japanese. Some countries with strong restrictions on cultural imports staved off the American threat, most notably India, which in 1971 replaced the United States as the producer of most feature films. Other countries which were less able to ward off the pressure of U.S. trade negotiators, like Indonesia, lost their national audiences to Hollywood. Even previously vital film industries in England, Germany, and Italy almost disappeared.

The problem with a single "Hollyworld" was not just the loss of the best European and Asian directors to the United States; nor was it only the increasing similarity of films as French, Indian, and Indonesian directors copied Hollywood's successful formulas. In addition, Hollywood in the 1980s and 1990s gave prominence to a new American culture.

THE TRANSFORMATION OF AMERICAN CULTURE

The American culture that Hollyworld marketed worldwide in the last decades of the twentieth century had changed considerably from the one Americans knew in the 1950s and early '60s. It had become less communal, more competitive, less idealistic, more cynical, less concerned with common needs, decorum, and propriety and more preoccupied with sex, violence, and money. One recent social commentator has described the change as a shift from a traditional society that valued loyalty, team play and the mastery of a vocation to an "ornamental culture" driven by celebrity and image, "a society drained of context, saturated with a competitive individualism that has been robbed of craft or utility, and ruled by commercial values that revolve around who has the most, the best, the biggest, the fastest."[9]

U.S. media after the Second World War presented an ideal America that, with one major exception, encouraged a sense of common decency and communal responsibility. The theme of common sacrifice permeated films about the Second World War made immediately afterwards. Typically, recruits from different classes and ethnic backgrounds recognized their common humanity and patriotism in the course of some dangerous mission that required the submersion of individual egos for the good of the whole. President Eisenhower (1953–61), the general retired from the war serving out a well-deserved rest on the golf course as president, personified the calm complacency of the fifties. His successor, President Kennedy (1961–63), epitomized the idealism of American postwar culture in his creation of the Peace Corps and his inauguration appeal: "Ask not what your country can do for you, but what you can do for your country."

The major exception to American harmony was the racism and institutional discrimination that was the legacy of African-American slavery. A country of towns divided by railroad tracks into separate white and black neighborhoods, where only white faces appeared in airports, board rooms, and television shows, was hardly a golden age of harmony. But the recognition of that long-festering injustice led the United States through a struggle over civil rights that gradually brought equality in the eyes of the law, though not an end to racism. The assertion of the civil rights of blacks also became a model for other groups, including Native Americans, women, and homosexuals. Racism also obscured the other social tensions of the Cold War decades. Advocates of racial equality were often accused of having communist sympathies or being communist dupes. Tensions simmered not only between races, but among ethnic groups as well: between Italians and Irish in the Bronx, Jews and Poles in Pittsburgh, Anglos and Mexicans in Los Angeles. Nevertheless, the white face of American culture in the 1950s and early 1960s projected a willing smile, jutting jaw, and can-do confidence.

American culture wiped the smile from its face in the 1970s. The searing conflict in Vietnam, the countercultural or sexual revolution, the oil crisis, and the sense of an America in decline left a more serious and mature culture. In the 1980s, a new self-centered cheerleading culture declared (as one auto ad put it) that America was back. But by the time the United States could light the silver screens and liquid crystal displays of the world, U.S. culture had become less generous, more crude, and more aggressive than it had ever been.

HOLLYWORLD AND McWORLD

Foreign viewers, and many Americans, saw the change as increased attention to sex and violence. The long-running television crime show of the 1950s, *Dragnet*, rarely showed anyone killed. When death was portrayed on the screen it was noble or deserved, dramatic or balletic, but never messy. After 1965, the daily news footage of the Vietnam War brought dying into the living room. Film directors like Arthur Penn (*Bonnie and Clyde*, 1967) and Sam Peckinpah (*The Wild Bunch*, 1969) detailed the damage bullets could do. Sex also made its debut. The rules of 1950s television prohibited the depiction of a husband and wife in a bed. Even the word "bed" was taboo because it might offend viewer sensibilities. For American movie-goers of the period "adult" and "foreign" were almost code words for films with sexual content. With stars like Brigitte Bardot, French films titillated American art-theater audiences with their single obligatory shot of a woman's breast.

Most film cultures of the world took an even more restrained approach to depicting sexuality. The first Japanese screen kiss of a boy and girl occurred only in 1946, and that was by order of American censors in the postwar occupation administration who believed it to be part of democracy education.[10] Indian censors, who replaced the colonial British censors when India became independent in 1947, continued the British "no kissing policy" of their predecessors.

However, by 1980 the great Indian actress and film pioneer, Devika Rani, spoke for many film industries when she complained: "Movies today copy too much of the West. . . . In the last ten years too much sex has come into them—women wearing nylons and putting buttons in their bras."[11] Even before sexually explicit Western films could be easily copied or imported, shown on VCRs or viewed by satellite or cable, Asian filmmakers looked for a way to compete. In 1988 American and Japanese films regularly filled so many Korean theaters that Korean exhibitors urged their government to allow pornographic films to be shown in certain theaters for the first time ever. Authoritarian governments in Korea and Japan preferred sexual to political expression, but only to a point. Japanese censors blurred the explicit nude scenes of Nagisa Oshima's bold breakthrough *In the Realm of the Senses* (1975), causing many Japanese art lovers to travel to Paris to view the uncensored version.

The impact of Hollyworld concerned far more than sex and violence. In the 1980s and 1990s Hollywood showed the world an America obsessed with the possession of things. Luxurious homes, dazzling cars, lavish environments, and upper-class lifestyles formed the glittering film images of an increasingly commercial culture. Shopping malls evolved into the global town squares of the 1990s. Shopping reigned as American's chief leisure pursuit, second only to watching television; aside from the shopping channels, television became consumer prep., bought and paid for by advertisers and their commercial clients.

Television, a medium that was thought to have no commercial application when it was invented, adopted an educational and cultural role for itself in the decades after the Second World War. Fredric Jameson, a cultural critic, dated the change in American consciousness to the suspension of commercial television programming in the days after the assassination of President Kennedy in 1963. The range of cultural programming, of commercial-free public sharing, the deeply emotional impact of the society's collective mourning, Jameson argued, presented a utopian vision of what television could be but was not. For those who made money by selling advertising time or toothpaste the vision was a nightmare, and sufficient warning to make sure it never happened again.[12] First public television, with government and volunteer funding, broadcast educational and cultural programming, in effect releasing commercial networks from any responsibility for non-commercial service. Then by the end of the century, reduced government funding forced public television to accept a level of advertising as well. In short, the mission of television, the mall, Hollywood, global exporters, advertisers, American manufacturers, and often the U.S. Department of State became one: the selling of America and the creation of a world of happy customers.

SELLING THE AMERICAN DREAM

The selling of America began with the selling of selling. Aside from traveling salesman jokes, the most popular image of the salesman in the years after World War II was the pathetic Willy Loman in Arthur Miller's play, *Death of a Salesman* (1949). Americans in the 1950s and 1960s found businessmen vapid (*The Organization Man*) and colorless (*The Man in the Gray Flannel Suit*). Hollywood made more films about teachers and waiters. Time magazine selected only two businessmen as Man of the Year from its first cover in 1927 to 1990: Walter Chrysler in 1928 and the president of General Motors in 1955.

By contrast, the businessmen, or rather businesspeople in the lingo and reality of the 1990s, were bigger than rock stars. Three businesspeople graced *Time* magazine's People of the Year covers in just that decade. Films and television series portrayed young executives, lawyers, stockbrokers, secretaries, financiers, and other corporate employees, sometimes even at work. Masters in Business Administration became masters of the universe, outranked only by young blue-jeaned company founders who dropped out of school to became millionaires before they could shave. Advertising, marketing, and public relations—criticized in books like Vance Packard's *The Hidden Persuaders* in the 1950s as dishonest and manipulative—took central place in university enrollments and faculty prestige.

Typically, a university president of the 1950s, a philosopher of ethics who could smell self-serving hyperbole at fifty paces, was satisfied with one part-time assistant to handle all his press and public relations. By the 1980s a university public relations staff much smaller than a hundred would be unthinkable. By the 1990s, academic research and judgment was a saleable commodity. The great news-gathering operations of television networks had largely given themselves over to entertainment, and politics was directed by financial contributors, lobbyists, pollsters, and spin doctors. Image had won out over substance.

In the 1950s and 1960s, many artists perceived commerce as inauthentic. Pop artist Andy Warhol's silkscreens of Campbell soup cans created a sensation in the art world of the 1950s because they challenged the traditional distinction between art and advertising. But as corporate logos of the 1980s and 1990s branded civic centers and sports arenas, and flashed their messages in ever new media, professional associations of advertisers and corporate sponsors broke down the walls that distinguished commerce from the rest of life. Advertisers gave themselves artistic awards. Schools sold their students' attention or thirst to corporate sponsors. Even the human body became an appropriate place to display advertising: A young Australian who shaved his bare head for advertisers complained only that it wasn't any larger.[13]

SELLING AND CITIZENSHIP

Are people who see themselves primarily as consumers, or whose main frames of reference are commercial, less thoughtful, less independent thinkers and citizens? Benjamin Barber says they are: "More and more people throughout the world are becoming consumers of McWorld rather than citizens. Spending more time in front of a TV screen or at a mall or in a movie theater . . . much more time than they spend in school, church, the library, a community service center, a political back room, a volunteer house or a playing field. Yet only these latter environments elicit active and engaged public behavior and ask us to define ourselves as autonomous members of civic communities . . . "

In this view, the global market forces of the last decades have transformed cinema from a weekly hour or two of escape into a new agenda for human nature. Combined with television, global advertising agencies, international marketing, and public opinion molders, the new McWorld threatens the future of democracy, according to Barber. "On the level of the individual, capitalism seeks consumers susceptible to the shaping of their needs and the manipulation of their wants while democracy needs citizens autonomous in their thoughts and independent in their deliberative judgments."[14]

IDENTITY AND COMMERCE

We are becoming more alike because we are all becoming customers, consumers of the greatest new thing. Produced and distributed better, internationally and globally on a mass scale, these things in turn create common life experiences. Cell phones, hamburgers, music videos, packaged cereals need neither passports nor translators. Our separate national fashions and languages have not been eliminated as much as they have been made redundant.

In the summer of 2000, a sheep farmer in southern France, Jose Bove, became something of a French national hero for vandalizing a McDonald's under construction. While Bove, the leader of a French farm union, declared himself against "McDomination" and the "imperialism" of American eating habits, especially U.S-exported hormone-fed beef and the American habit of "le snacking", he did not object to international trade. He sold half his sheep milk to local producers of a world-renowned French export: Roquefort cheese. The United States had just imposed a crippling 100 percent tariff on Roquefort in retaliation for a European ban on American hormone-treated beef. In French court, McDonald's pleaded its national French credentials; its 750 French outlets used ingredients that were 80 percent French and 100 percent European. In fact, the French McDonald's menu was actually "international" or "multicultural." Besides Le Grand Mac with beer, it offered daily specials loosely based on street food from throughout the world: the McIndia, the McSahara, and the McCanada.

By the beginning of the twenty-first century, commerce shaped identity more than language or nation. Even nationalist diehards found it difficult to fight the forces of commercial globalization. After the collapse of the Soviet Union, dormant strains of Russian nationalism resurfaced. Nationalist Russian leaders urged their countrymen to renounce Western alliances, Western democracy, and Western market solutions to the problems of the Russian economy. For most Russians, the memory of Stalinist tyranny was too recent to induce nostalgia, but the Russian Czars were exhumed for a reassessment.

In 1999, one great Russian director who did not emigrate to Hollywood, Nikita Mikhakov, created a film tribute to the anti-Western Czar Alexander III, *Barber of Siberia*. Mikhakov also played the Czar in the film and briefly used the resulting popular association with the Czar to run for president of Russia. Personally, professionally, and politically, he symbolized the nationalist Russian goal of reviving Russian power and prestige, of a Russia that could do it alone. Yet Mikhalov worked in a world in which the professional and financial rewards of filmmaking emanated from Hollywood. In order to qualify *Barber of Siberia* for an American Academy Award for "Best Picture" rather than the less lucrative "Best Foreign Film" prize, Mikhalov made most of his film (70 percent of the dialogue spoken by his Russian nationalists) in English.

By the beginning of the twenty-first century, however, Hollyworld was no longer located in California, or solely American. European and Asian film studios were copying the Hollywood formula of sex, action, and violence. Sony of Japan still owned Columbia Pictures, and the French conglomerate Vivendi had bought Universal Studios as well as a number of other American media properties. The largest media conglomerates in the world included two German publishers, Bertelsmann and Von Holtzbrinck, who controlled over sixty percent of the U.S. book market, and an English publisher who had bought much of the rest. Was this the beginning of a new millennium of international cooperation and global citizenship? Or was it a brave new world in which separate cultures, languages, and national identities were all fusing into the common identity of customers?

ALTERNATIVES TO McDOMINATION

While the spread of international commercial culture was the dominant trend at the beginning of the twenty-first century, there were both old and new alternatives to "McDomination." The old response to cultural conquest was to fight to hold on to traditional values. To counter modern Hollyworld sexuality and McWorld commercialism, many people at the end of the twentieth and beginning of the twenty-first century embraced religious fundamentalism. Barber called this response *jihad*, using the Muslim term for struggle against the irreligious or infidel, a term associated with organizations like the Muslim Brotherhood, which originated in Egypt in 1928. The founder of the Society of Muslim Brothers, Hassan al-Banna, called for *jihad* against foreign and Egyptian capitalists. He believed they exploited Egyptian laborers and corrupted traditional culture with "wine, women, and sin." For Banna, the renewal of Egypt had to begin with the reform of Islam since even its great religious university "graduated religious literates, not . . . . spiritual guides."[15] Suppressed in the mid-1950s, the Society went underground in Egypt and spread throughout the Muslim world, alternately tolerated and outlawed.

Muslim Brotherhoods urged their national governments to establish Islamic law, the *shari'a*, for all Muslim citizens, leaving minorities of other religions to govern themselves. Some Christians in a predominantly Muslim country like Jordan worried about how such a system would work, dreading the prospect of sexually segregated public beaches and a ban on liquor sales. Nevertheless, the Muslim Brotherhood attracted a broader range of voters in Jordan than the other political parties, each of which appealed to particular tribal and ethnic groups.

In Egypt, where members of the Brotherhood were in jail or exile, moderate Muslims organized a Central Party in Egypt in the late 1990s, trying to create a secular society following Islamic principles of charity, social justice, honest government, and communal responsibility. Characteristic of the movement, one leader, A.M. Elmessiri, a leading scholar and public intellectual, was a former Marxist who had become a devout Muslim without losing his love of English literature and Woody Allen films, or his penchant for critical analysis of Western culture. Muslim resistance to global culture embraced a wide range of views, from those who wanted to recreate the world of seventh-century Arabia to those who merely sought their own culture's route to modernity.

Muslims were hardly the only group to turn to traditional religious values in resisting cultural globalization. Orthodox Jews in Israel sought many of the same things as the Muslim Brotherhood: separation of the sexes in public places; government enforcement of religious law; and legal restrictions on sexuality in advertising, immodest dress, and commerce on the Sabbath. Even in the United States, various Christian fundamentalists opposed population planning, sexuality in film and television, and pornography on the Internet, whether it originated at home or abroad.

New alternatives to McDomination also emerged in recent years. For those who embraced twenty-first century technology, the enormous range of options, even commercial ones, could bolster, rather than limit, personal identity. Hollyworld could not monopolize every theater screen in the world. The five or six global media conglomerates not only had to compete with each other, but also with a myriad of independent producers of books, magazines, films, or cultural events. If the major television networks broadcast the same news stories in eerie simultaneity, cable and satellite television offered commercial, public, and independent news and programming from all over the world. If every neighborhood multiplex offered the same six films and the local video store carried all of a hundred titles, a single catalog or Internet supplier might provide thousands of films from India alone. With the resources available on the Internet, the range of information, images, sound, and opinion dwarfs what anyone could have imagined fifty years ago.

Even as consumers, Internet shopping frees the individual from monopoly markets. Sites that compare hundreds of competing retailers in an instant reduce the global corporation to the same playing field as a garage sale. A collective of peasants in the mountains of Peru uses a website to sell handmade sweaters throughout the world. A student with a desktop computer assembles the leading insurance companies in the country to bid on her auto insurance policy. When everything can be reduced to price, and all prices made instantly knowable, brand loyalty disappears. When it has to be a first edition Hemingway, an '88 Buick with fuschia upholstery, or a hotel in Lisbon with a tub instead of a shower, we are still in charge.

We may have lost the sharp differences between national cultural styles that existed in the 1950s, but we can access information from any part of the world, even from other languages with translation technology. We can live electronically in different cultures, see ourselves as others see us, and draw from all that the world experiences.

The tools of modern culture also enable people to celebrate their traditions as they bring them to a global audience. With her film *Monsoon Wedding*, director Mira Nair invites the world to India to see the bridegroom's family arrive in Delhi from Houston. As her characters connect with cell phones, fast foods, and stories of unexpected identities, we realize that no one is all Indian or all American anymore. And yet, the film shows how a traditional ritual or dance can still heal a universal longing in the Indian characters while at the same time it enlightens and moves an audience who arrived at the theater as foreigners so that they leave feeling like family.

Zacharias Kunuk's alternative to Hollyworld is making films about his people, the Inuit (formerly referred to as Eskimo). He made his first feature, *The Fast Runner (Atanarjuat)*, in his Inuktitut language, with Inuit actors, to teach young Inuit men the skills he believes many have lost. One scene, for instance, shows how to cut ice and make an igloo in a storm. But the film is also a love story based on an ancient Inuit myth, the screen enactment of which brought tears to the eyes of Inuit people in northern Canada and Nunuvut (carved from Canada's Northwest Territory in 1999). A third audience, at film festivals in Canada and France where it won awards, was moved by the director's ability to bring complex personalities out of mythic characters and by the stunning visual quality of the film. The critic for the *New York Times* was struck by the "dozen shades of white from the bluish glow of the winter ice to the warm creaminess of coats made of polar bear fur" created with aid of a "widescreen digital camera."[16]

For Kunuk, as he puts on some more dog skins for a snowmobile seal hunt with rifle and camera, there is no conflict between traditional life and modern global culture. "If it were up to me, I would go back to the law of the Inuit, the law of nature. I would live like that while checking e-mail in the morning, calling halfway around the world to do business, watching wars in my living room on television. It is possible to do both in this day."[17]

If there is a contradiction between McDomination and the lives of artists like Mira Nair and Zacharias Kunuk, it is a contradiction between the many and the few. Most people in the world take their cues from McWorld, unaware that they are acting in a play they haven't chosen. Few people direct their own dreams. But this difference between the many and the few is not entirely the age-old difference of inherited social class, the rich and the poor. It is possible today for people like Zacharias Kunuk to create lives for themselves that are very different from those they were scripted to play. Modern technology and education create the possibility for everyone to write their own scripts. The contradiction is between what our technology enables and what our society produces, between what we can learn and what we are told.

FOR FURTHER READING

On American suburbanization, see Kenneth T. Jackson's *Crabgrass Frontier*, James Howard Kuntsler's *The Geography of Nowhere*, Robert Fishman's *Bourgeois Utopias: The Rise and Fall of Suburbia*, and Donna Gaine's *Teenage Wasteland* for various critical perspectives. For a recent favorable reassessment of suburbia, see *Picture Windows: How the Suburbs Happened* by Rosalyn Baxandall and Elizabeth Ewen. The journalist David Halberstam's *The Fifties* is a highly engaging biography-based history of the decade in the United States.

I have described some of the arguments of Benjamin R. Barber, *Jihad vs. McWorld*, a work well worth reading in its entirety. Thomas L. Friedman's *The Lexus and the Olive Tree* is another popular and more positive treatment of cultural change and commercial globalization. One of the better recent collections of essays on the subject is Roger Rosenblatt, ed., *Consuming Desires: Consumption, Culture, and the Pursuit of Happiness*. Another is Fredric Jameson and Masao Miyoshi, eds., *The Cultures of Globalization*. Edward Said's *Culture and Imperialism* is also an interesting critique of the global dominance of American culture.

For a general introduction to film in a global context, see Robert Sklar's *Film: An International History of the Medium*. On Indian film I have found Sumita S. Chakravarty's *Indian Popular Cinema 1947–1987* excellent. On Asian film, see John A. Lent, *The Asian Film Industry*. For a wide survey of filmmaking, *Third World Film Making and the West* by Roy Ames is most useful. For the relationship between film and modernity, see the essays in *Cinema and the Invention of Modern Life*, edited by Leo Charney and Vanessa R. Schwartz. On the commercialization of modern culture in America, see *Culture Jam: The Uncooling of America* by Kalle Lasn and *Nobrow: The Culture of Marketing, the Marketing of Culture* by John Seabrook. Among other interesting interpretations of modern American culture are Susan Faludi's *Stiffed* and Robert D. Putnam's *Bowling Alone*.

I have found it useful to explore some of the tensions between identity and modern global culture through the medium of film, but other cultural expressions could serve as well. Among them, some students might be interested in studying sport in an international context. Arjun Appadurai's essays in his *Modernity at Large: Cultural Dimensions of Globalization* include one on cricket after the British left India. Essays on soccer in various cultures appear in *Football Culture: Local Conflicts, Global Visions*, edited by Gerry Finn and Richard Giulianotti.

NOTES

1. Nicholas D. Kristof, "Stateside Lingo Gives Japan Its Own Valley Girls," *New York Times*, 19 October 1997, p. A3.
2. Barbara Demick, "The World: Some in S. Korea Opt for a Trim When English Trips the Tongue; Asia: Parents are turning to specialty preschool and even surgery to give their children a linguistic advantage," *The Los Angeles Times*, March 31, 2002.
3. Michael Specter, "Baltic's Onetime Rulers Have Shrunk to a Handful," *New York Times*, 4 December 1997.
4. Afshin Valinejad, Associated Press, "Barbie May Soon Meet Her Match: Iran Creates Line of Dolls to Counter Western Icon, *Boston Globe*, 25 October 1996, p. A2.
5. Kenji Sato, "Borderless," in "How the World Sees Us: A Special Issue," *New York Times Magazine*, 8 June 1997, p. 64.
6. In this chapter when referring to the culture of the United States I frequently use the common phrase "American culture" rather than the more correct but awkward and less understood "U.S. culture" or "North American culture."
7. Benjamin R. Barber, *Jihad vs. McWorld* (New York: Ballantine Books, 1996), p. 52.
8. India produced 763 films in 1983, Hong Kong 200 by the 1950s, Iran peaked at 90 in 1970, Mexico at 120 in 1970, Philippines at 250 in 1971, Turkey reached 300 in 1972. "By 1955 the countries producing 50 or more films a year includ-

ed Burma, Pakistan, and South Korea, and both Pakistan and South Korea had at least doubled this level of output by 1970. The countries producing 50 films a year were joined in the 1970s by Thailand, Indonesia, and Bangladesh." Roy Ames, *Third World Film Making and the West* (Berkeley: University of California Press, 1987), pp. 63–64. Ames also points out that U.S. and Japanese films declined as a percentage of world output 1950–1975, during which time world production increased from three to four thousand, over half coming from Asia.

9. Susan Faludi, *Stiffed: The Betrayal of the American Man* (New York: William Morrow, 1999), as reviewed by Michiko Kakutani, "What Has Happened to Men? An Author Tries to Answer," *New York Times*, 28 September 1999, p. E1.

10. Alan Riding, "East of Suez," a review of Ian Buruma, *The Missionary and the Libertine* (New York: Random House, 2000), in *New York Times Book Review*, 24 September 2000, sect. 7, p. 6.

11. John A. Lent, *The Asian Film Industry* (Austin: University of Texas Press, 1990), p. 4.

12. Fredric Jameson, *Postmodernism, or The Cultural Logic of Late Capitalism* (Durham: Duke University Press, 1991), p. 355.

13. Kalle Lasn, *Culture Jam: The Uncooling of America* (William Morrow/Eagle Books), 1999.

14. Barber, *Jihad vs. McWorld*, p. 97, p. 15.

15. Quoted in Richard P. Mitchell, *The Society of the Muslim Brothers* (New York: Oxford University Press, 1969), p. 223, p. 213.

16. A.O. Scott, "A Far Off Inuit World, in a Dozen Shades of White," *New York Times*, March 30, 2002, p. B9.

17. Clifford Krauss, "The Saturday Profile: Returning Tundra's Rhythm to the Inuit, in Film," *New York Times*, March 30, 2002, p. A4.

Chronological Table of the Nuclear World

1945–Present

Europe	Americas	Africa and Islamic World	Asia
	United Nations 1945		
Woman suffrage: France, Italy 1945–1946	Spread of synthetics in U.S. economy a. 1945		
	Cold War with Russia begins a. 1946		Philippine independence 1946
U.S. Marshall Plan 1947		Nationalist party wins South Africa and mandates apartheid 1948	British leave India and Pakistan 1947
NATO 1949		Founding of Israel and first Arab-Israeli War 1948	Communist victory in China 1949
W. German recovery a. 1949			Indonesian independence 1949
Death of Stalin 1953	Korean War 1950–1953	Nasser takes control of Egypt 1954	
	Cuban "communism" a. 1959	Independence of most sub-Saharan African states 1960–1975	Chinese-Russian split a. 1960
	U.S. war in Vietnam 1964–1975		Chinese Cultural Revolution 1966–1969
Worker, student protests 1968		Drought and famine in African Sahel 1968–1974	Vietnamese Tet offensive 1968

a. = *after*

Europe	Americas	Middle East and Africa	Asia
Common Market includes Britain 1973	Chile's Democratic Marxism 1970–1973		
Socialist, communist party gains in W. Europe 1974–1976	U.S. "Golden Age" economy and Welfare State 1945–1973		Death of Mao 1976
Margaret Thatcher, Prime Minister 1979–1990	U.S. war in Vietnam 1964–1975	Shah of Iran deposed 1979	China opens to West 1978
	Civil war in Nicaragua and El Salvador 1979	Black majority rule in Zimbabwe 1980	China opens to global markets 1979
	Oil crisis, economic contraction, and inflation 1973–1982	Iran-Iraq war 1980–1988	
		Deepening struggle in South Africa 1985–present	Global rise of Japanese economy 1980–1990
	Reagan presidency 1981–1989	Nelson Mandela released from prison after 28 years 1990	
Fall of Berlin Wall 1989	Falkland Islands War 1982	Mandela elected President of South Africa 1994	
Fall of communism in the Soviet Union 1985–1991	End of military regimes followed by liberalization in Latin America 1990s	Rwanda massacre of Tutsis by Hutu majority 1994	
Breakup of Yugoslavia and war in Bosnia 1991–1995		Al-Jazeera, cable television from Qatar, founded 1996; opens Arab media world.	
	U.S. bull market 1982–2000	Joseph Mobutu, dictator of Zaire (Congo), defeated, exiled, and died 1997	Hong Kong handover to China 1997
		28.5 million of the 40 million people with AIDS/HIV live in sub-Saharan Africa	Long Japanese recession 1990–2002
The Euro replaces currencies of 12 countries of European Union 2002	Terrorist attack on U.S. opens war on global terrorism 2002	Several peace plans between 1993 and 2002 fail to solve the Palestinian-Israeli conflict 2002	India and Pakistan test nuclear weapons, threaten war 2002

❧ Index ❧

401

CREDITS

Illustrations provided courtesy of the collection of Markus Wiener unless otherwise credited. Maps and charts redesigned from the 1989 edition. For credits, please consult this earlier edition.

Text credits listed in the footnotes. For additional information, please check the 1989 edition, pp. 427–428.